Index to the 1800 Massachusetts Federal Census
for the County of
Plymouth

Rebecca M. Sullivan
Deborah Lee Larsson

Index to the 1800 Massachusetts Federal Census
for the County of
Plymouth

October 2014

ISBN: 978-1502775726

FOREWARD:

This is the fifth volume of several containing the heads of household that were enumerated in the 1800 United States Federal Census in Massachusetts. Our fifth volume is comprised of those towns in Plymouth County. In order to make it easy for the researcher, towns are alphabetized, followed by an alphabetical index of Plymouth county.

We have made every attempt at correctly transcribing each town. However, many of these documents are torn, covered with ink, tape marks, rips and poor handwriting. Spelling errors have been left as they were originally written. Any names & enumerations illegible are denoted with an asterisk.

This book should be used as a guide and research aid. When possible the actual image should be obtained for proper verification and citation. Visit the National Archives website to find out more on how to obtain census images. www.archives.gov/research/census.

In order to get all of the information on one page to make for easy reading we had to reduce the size of the font.

Drop us a line, we'd love to hear what you're researching: rsulli1219@aol.com

Becky & Deb
October 2014

Check out our other books:

Index to the 1800 Massachusetts Federal Census for the Counties of Barnstable, Dukes & Nantucket, Volume 1

Index to the 1800 Massachusetts Federal Census for the County of Worcester, Volume 2

Index to the 1800 Massachusetts Federal Census for the County of Essex, Volume 3

Index to the 1800 Massachusetts Federal Census for the Counties of Norfolk & Suffolk, Volume 4

INDEX

Plymouth County Stats

Microfilm Reel Number: M32-16

Town:	Page Numbers:	Enumerated By:
Abington	33-42	Unknown
Bridgewater	47-68	Unknown
Carver	5-12	Unknown
Duxbury	91-104	William White
Halifax	13-18	Unknown
Hanover	123-132	Unknown
Kingston	27-30	Unknown
Marshfield	93-104	Unknown
Middleborough	69-90	Unknown
Pembroke	31-44	Unknown
Plimton	19-26	Unknown
Plymouth	1-26	Nathan Hayward
Rochester	105-118	Unknown
Scituate	119-136	Unknown
Wareham	109-113	Unknown

TOWN	PG#	LN#	LAST NAME	FIRST NAME	FREE WHITE MALES					FREE WHITE FEMALES					TOTAL ALL OTHER	TOTAL SLAVES	TOTALS	DISTRICT/ TOWNSHIP	NOTES
					under 10	10 to 16	16 to 26	26 to 45	45 and over	under 10	10 to 16	16 to 26	26 to 45	45 and over					
Abington	33	1	Reed	Tho			1		1			1	1	1			5		
Abington	33	2	Reed	Isaac	1	1		1		2			2				7		
Abington	33	3	Reed	Daniel		1		1	1			1	1				5		
Abington	33	4	Reed	James					1	1			1	2			5		
Abington	33	5	Reed	Stephen	1				1					2			4		
Abington	33	6	Richmond	Andrew	1			1		3			1				6		
Abington	33	7	Reed	Paul	1			1					1	2			5		
Abington	33	8	Reed	Jacob Jun	1			1			2	2	1				7		
Abington	33	9	Ramsdel	Edmond					2					2			4		
Abington	33	10	Ripley	Willm		1	1	1		3	1		2	1	1		11		
Abington	33	11	Shaw	Silas	2		1	1		1		1					6		
Abington	33	12	Stetson	Whitcom	2		1					1					4		
Abington	33	13	Shaw	Daniel			2		1			1	1	1			6		
Abington	33	14	Sprague	Willm		1	1		1		1			1			5		
Abington	33	15	Shaw	Ezra		1			1			2		1			5		
Abington	33	16	Shaw	Calvin	1		3		1	1	2		1	4			13		
Abington	33	17	Stetson	Jacob	1		1			1		1					4		
Abington	33	18	Smith	James	2			1		1			1	1			6		
Abington	33	19	Stoddard	Nathan					1	2		1					4		
Abington	33	20	Stetson	Ephraim		1			1	2			1				5		
Abington	33	21	Stetson	Peleg					2	1		1					4		
Abington	33	22	Smith	Zenus	2		2	1		2		1	1				9		
Abington	33	23	Smith	Jacob		1	1		1	1	2			1			7		
Abington	33	24	Shaw	Joseph		1	1		1			1	1	1			6		
Abington	33	25	Smith	Nehemiah	3				1	1	2			1			8		
Abington	33	26	Stetson	Oliver	3	1				1			1				6		
Abington	33	27	Shaw	Elijah		1	1		1	1	1			1			6		
Abington	33	28	Shaw	Ebenezer			1		1	2			1				5		
Abington	33	29	Stetson	Levi	1	1	1		1	1	1	1		2			9		
Abington	33	30	Shaw	Brackley	1	2		1	1	2	1	1	1	1			11		
Abington	33	31	Seamon	Thomas					1	1		1		2			5		
Abington	33	32	Shaw	Levi				1					1				2		
Abington	33	33	Shaw	Jacob	1			1		1			1				4		
Abington	33	34	Shaw	Asa	1			1		1	1		1				5		
Abington	33	35	Shaw	Brackley Jun		1	1			2		2					6		
Abington	33	36	Shaw	Abram Jun	1			1		3			1				6		
Abington	33	37	Shaw	Abram		1			1		3			1			6		
Abington	33	38	Tirril	John					1					1			2		
Abington	33	39	Tirril	Isaac	1	1	2	1	1	1	2	1		1			11		
Abington	33	40	Torrey	Josiah					1	2	3	1	1		1		9		
Abington	33	41	Townsend	Eunice		2	2			1	1			1			7		
Abington	33	42	Thayer	Saml		1	1	1		3	1		1				8		
Abington	33	43	Torrey	David		1	2	2	1			1		1			8		
Abington	33	44	Tirrel	Thos	1			1	1	3	2			1			8		
Abington	33	45	Townsend	Ezekiel					1		1	1	1				4		
Abington	33	46	Tolman	John			1		1					1			3		
Abington	33	47	Townsend	Ezekiel Junr		1		1					1				3		
Abington	33	48	Torrey	Willm	3			1					1				5		
Abington	33	49	Thaxter	Gridley	1	2		1		4		1	1				10		
Abington	33	50	Thomson	Joseph	1			1		2		1					5		
Abington	33	51	Tirril	Nathl			1		1	1		1					3		
Abington	33	52	Tirril	Lemuel	1		1		1			3		1			7		
Abington	35	1	Nash	Peter			2		1			1					4		
Abington	35	2	Noles	Saml	1				1	1		2		1	1		7		
Abington	35	3	Nash	Matthew		1	1		1			1		1			5		
Abington	35	4	Nash	Luke	2	1	1	1	1	3	2	1	1				13		
Abington	35	5	Nash	Daniel	1			1	1	2		2		2			9		
Abington	35	6	Noyes	Eliab	1		2		1			1		2			7		
Abington	35	7	Noyes	Benjm	3			1					1				5		
Abington	35	8	Noyes	Ephraim	3	1	1	1			1	1	1				9		
Abington	35	9	Noyes	Ichabod			1							2			3		
Abington	35	10	Noyes	Daniel	1			1	1	1		1		1			6		
Abington	35	11	Orcut	Elijah		1	1		1	1	1			1			6		
Abington	35	12	Porter	John				1	1			1		1			4		
Abington	35	13	Porter	Seth		1	1		1				1	1			5		
Abington	35	14	Porter	John M. Jun			2	1		2			1				6		
Abington	35	15	Pool	Benjm	1	1		1		2	1		1				7		
Abington	35	16	Pool	Aseph			1					1					2		
Abington	35	17	Pool	Joshua	1			1						1			3		
Abington	35	18	Pool	Jacob	1		1		1	1	1	1		2			8		
Abington	35	19	Pool	James	1	3		1					1				6		
Abington	35	20	Puffer	John	2			1		1				1			5		
Abington	35	21	Pratt	Philip Junr	1		1					1					3		
Abington	35	22	Pratt	Noah	3			1				1	1				6		
Abington	35	23	Pratt	Nathl			1			1				1			3		
Abington	35	24	Pool	Micah	2	1	2	1			1	2	1	1			11		
Abington	35	25	Pratt	Jane			1				1		1				3		
Abington	35	26	Pool	Joseph			2		1			1	2	2			8		
Abington	35	27	Pratt	Philip Junr	1			1		3	3		1	1			10		
Abington	35	28	Pool	Joseph Junr					1					2			3		
Abington	35	29	Porter	Willm			1		1					1			3		
Abington	35	30	Pain	Zebulon		1	2		1	1			1	1			7		
Abington	35	31	Pain	Zebulon Junr	5	2	2	1		1	2		1				14		
Abington	35	32	Pratt	Thos	1				1			1		1			4		
Abington	35	33	Penniman	Bethuel		1	1		1		1			1			5		
Abington	35	34	Parkman	Daniel					1		1	1	1	1			5		
Abington	35	35	Reed	Bela			1	1		1		1		1			5		
Abington	35	36	Reed	James	4	1		2	1	1	1	1	1	1			13		
Abington	35	37	Ramsdel	Noah	2			1		2			1	1			7		
Abington	35	38	Reed	John	2		1	1		1		1	2	1			9		

TOWN	PG#	LN#	LAST NAME	FIRST NAME	M under 10	M 10 to 16	M 16 to 26	M 26 to 45	M 45 and over	F under 10	F 10 to 16	F 16 to 26	F 26 to 45	F 45 and over	TOTAL ALL OTHER	TOTAL SLAVES	TOTALS	DISTRICT/TOWNSHIP	NOTES
Abington	35	39	Reed	Obediah		1			1					1			3		
Abington	35	40	Reed	Joel	2			1		2			1				6		
Abington	35	41	Reed	Obediah Jun	3	1		1		1			1				7		
Abington	35	42	Reed	Bezer			1					1		1			3		
Abington	35	43	Remington	Thos				1						1			2		
Abington	35	44	Remington	Thos Jun			1					1					2		
Abington	35	45	Reed	Micah		2		1		1	1			1			6		
Abington	35	46	Reed	Daniel Jun	2	3	1	1		2			1				10		
Abington	35	47	Reed	Saml	3					3	1	1	1				10		
Abington	35	48	Reed	Thos Junr	1	3		1		2		1	1				9		
Abington	37	1	Harris	Oliver	1	1		1		3			1				7		
Abington	37	2	Harris	Susanah		1					1			1			3		
Abington	37	3	Harris	John	2	1		1		3			1				8		
Abington	37	4	Harris	Abial	2	1			1	1	1	2	1				9		
Abington	37	5	Hill	Jonathan	1				1	1	1			1			5		
Abington	37	6	Hunt	Thos Junr	1			1		1		1	1				5		
Abington	37	7	Hunt	Ephraim		1	3					1	1	1			7		
Abington	37	8	Hill	Joseph		2		1			1	2		1			7		
Abington	37	9	Howe	Nathl 2d	1			1	1		2		2				7		
Abington	37	10	Hearsey	David		2		1				1	1	1			6		
Abington	37	11	Holbrook	Willm	1	3	1	1		1			1	1			9		
Abington	37	12	Hobart	Noah	2	1	1						1	1			6		
Abington	37	13	Hearsey	Isaac	1		1	1					1	1			5		
Abington	37	14	Hearsey	Thos	3			1		1			1				6		
Abington	37	15	Hearsey	Daniel	1			1		3			1				6		
Abington	37	16	Hearsey	Joseph				1						1			2		
Abington	37	17	Hobart	Aaron Jr		2			1	3	1		1				8		
Abington	37	18	Hobart	Aaron		1	1		1	1	1	2		1	1		9		
Abington	37	19	Humble	Majn	1		1	1		1	1	1		1			7		
Abington	37	20	Hobart	Elijah	1			1	1	4	2	1	1				11		
Abington	37	21	Hearsey	Jane								1	1	1			3		
Abington	37	22	Hunt	Thos	2	2	2		1			1	1				9		
Abington	37	23	Houpe	Deborough								2					2		
Abington	37	24	Jenkins	David		2	2		1	3		1	1	1			11		
Abington	37	25	Jenkins	Malichi	1			1		1		1	1				5		
Abington	37	26	Jenkins	Isaiah Jun	1			1		3			1				6		
Abington	37	27	Jenkins	Isaiah		2	1		1	2	1	1		1			9		
Abington	37	28	Jenkins	Merit		2						1					3		
Abington	37	29	Jenkins	Joseph	3			1		3			1	1			9		
Abington	37	30	Jacobs	Joseph	1	1	1		1	1	1		1				7		
Abington	37	31	King	John	1		2	1				2	1	1			8		
Abington	37	32	Keen	Ebenezer				1						1			2		
Abington	37	33	Lazel	Luther		1		1					1	1			4		
Abington	37	34	Lincoln	Joseph				1		2	2	2	1	1			9		
Abington	37	35	Lane	Charles	3			1	1	1			1	1			8		
Abington	37	36	Lane	Daniel Jun		2	3		1	3		1	1	1			12		
Abington	37	37	Lane	Andrew			1					1					2		
Abington	37	38	Lovel	Obediah			1		1		1			1			4		
Abington	37	39	Lovel	Caleb	1			1		2	3	1					8		
Abington	37	40	Noyes	Matthew	1	1		1			1	1		1			6		
Abington	37	41	Nash	Jonathan				1					1				2		
Abington	37	42	Nash	Nathl			1			4		1					6		
Abington	37	43	Nash	James	1	2		1		2			1				7		
Abington	37	44	Nash	John		1		1					1				3		
Abington	37	45	Nash	Lydia		1							1				2		
Abington	37	46	Nash	Asa	1			1		1			1				4		
Abington	37	47	Norton	Benjm	1			1					1				3		
Abington	37	48	Norton	Saml	1		1	1		3	2	1	1				11		
Abington	39	1	Dyer	Christopher	1	1		1		3	1		1				8		
Abington	39	2	Dunham	Cornelus		2	1		1	1		1		2			8		
Abington	39	3	Dyer	Bela	1	1	1	1		2	1	2	1	1			11		
Abington	39	4	Dyer	Jacob			1		1					1			3		
Abington	39	5	Dyer	Jacob Jun			1					1					2		
Abington	39	6	Dyer	James		1	1				1	1		1			6		
Abington	39	7	Dunbar	Stephen			1	1						3			5		
Abington	39	8	Dammond	Joseph				1					1				2		
Abington	39	9	Elkins	Robert	2	3		1		1			1				8		
Abington	39	10	French	Barnabas	1			1		3	2		1	1			9		
Abington	39	11	Faxon	Elisha	1		1	1		1		1	1				6		
Abington	39	12	Ford	Jacob			3	1			1	3		1			9		
Abington	39	13	Ford	Jonathan			1					1					2		
Abington	39	14	Ford	Lydia			1			1				1			3		
Abington	39	15	Ford	David	1			1		2			1				5		
Abington	39	16	Ford	Noah	1		1	1		2	1		1				7		
Abington	39	17	Fulerton	John	1		1	1				1	2	1			7		
Abington	39	18	Farer	Benja				1						1			2		
Abington	39	19	Gurney	John	1	2			1	2	1	3		1			11		
Abington	39	20	Gurney	Asa			1	1		1		1	1				5		
Abington	39	21	Gurney	Jeremiah	1			1		1			1				4		
Abington	39	22	Gurney	P. Joseph	2			1			1		1	1			6		
Abington	40	1	Gurney	Noah Junr	3			1		2			1				7		
Abington	40	2	Gurney	Daniel	1			1		1			1				4		
Abington	40	3	Gurney	Nathan			1		1					1			3		
Abington	40	4	Gurney	Joseph Junr		1		1		1	1		1				5		
Abington	40	5	Gurney	Thos Jrn	1	1		1		3			1				7		
Abington	40	6	Gurney	Joseph				1					1				2		
Abington	40	7	Gurney	Zachary			1			2		1					4		
Abington	40	8	Gurney	Gideon			1						1				2		
Abington	40	9	Gurney	Saml	1		1	1	1	2			1	1			8		
Abington	40	10	Gurney	Noah				1			1		1				3		

TOWN	PG#	LN#	HEADS OF HOUSEHOLD LAST NAME	FIRST NAME	FREE WHITE MALES under 10	10 to 16	16 to 26	26 to 45	45 and over	FREE WHITE FEMALES under 10	10 to 16	16 to 26	26 to 45	45 and over	TOTAL ALL OTHER	TOTAL SLAVES	TOTALS	DISTRICT/ TOWNSHIP	NOTES
Abington	40	11	Gurney	Jacob		1	1	1		2	1	2		1			9		
Abington	40	12	Gloyd	David	2		2	2		2			1				9		
Abington	40	13	Green	Rachel										1			1		
Abington	40	14	Gardner	Caleb	3				1	3			1				8		
Abington	40	15	Gloyd	Cloe								2					2		
Abington	40	16	Gardner	Benjm				1				1	1				3		
Abington	40	17	Gurney	Nathan Jr			2	2		2			1		1		8		
Abington	40	18	Gardner	Noah	1			1		5			1				8		
Abington	40	19	Hearsey	Obediah	1	2		1		1	1	1			1		8		
Abington	40	20	Hearsey	Luther	1		1			2		1					5		
Abington	40	21	Harden	Seth		1		1				1	1				4		
Abington	40	22	Harden	Jacob	1		1	1			1	2	1				7		
Abington	40	23	Hearsey	Seth	1		1	1		2			1				6		
Abington	40	24	Her*t	Ebenz K.		1	1		1	1	2	2	1				9		
Abington	41	1	Vining	Asa	2			1					1				4		
Abington	41	2	Vining	Richard	2			1		2		1	1				7		
Abington	41	3	Vining	David	1			1				1					3		
Abington	41	4	Vining	Elisha					1	1		1	1	1			5		
Abington	41	5	Vining	Ebid	2	1		1		1	1	4	1				11		
Abington	41	6	Vining	Benjm		1	1	1		1		2					6		
Abington	41	7	Whitman	Ephraim		1	3	1	1	1	2	1	1	1			12		
Abington	41	8	Whitmash	Levi	2	1		1		1			1	1			7		
Abington	41	9	Wales	Willm	1	2	1	1		3	1		1	1			11		
Abington	41	10	Willett	Anna								1		1			2		
Abington	41	11	Willet	John			1			1			1				3		
Abington	41	12	Wilks	John		1	1	1		2	1	1	2	2			11		
Abington	41	13	Whiting	Thos			2		1	1		1	1				6		
Abington	41	14	Whiting	Barzilla		1	1	1	1	2		1	1				8		
Abington	41	15	Whiting	Jotham	1				1	1	1	1	1	1			7		
Abington	41	16	White	John	3	3		2		1	1	1	1				13		
Abington	41	17	White	Micah	2	1		1		1	1		1				7		
Abington	41	18	Bailey	Jack											6		6		
Abington	41	19	Darte	Anthony											3		3		
Abington	41	20	Goold	B*i											5		5		
Abington	41	21	Thomson	Joseph											9		9		
Abington	41	22		Charles											6		6		Last name left blank
Abington	42	1	Adams	*			1					1					2		
Abington	42	2	Alden	Saml		1	1	1	1	1	1		1				7		
Abington	42	3	Arnold	H. Thos.	3		1		1				1				6		
Abington	42	4	Bates	Eleazer		1			2					2			5		
Abington	42	5	Bates	Josiah			1			1		1	1				4		
Abington	42	6	Bates	James		1		1				1		1			4		
Abington	42	7	Bowker	Liberty	1		1			1		1					4		
Abington	42	8	Blanchard	Jesse	1		1					1		1			4		
Abington	42	9	Blanchard	Dean			1	1		2		1					5		
Abington	42	10	Blanchard	Eli	1		1					1					3		
Abington	42	11	Blanchard	Adam			2		1	3				1			7		
Abington	42	12	Blanchard	Thos Jrn	3	1		1		1		1					7		
Abington	42	13	Beals	Zelotus	2			1				1					4		
Abington	42	14	Bennet	Hannah								1	1				2		
Abington	42	15	Burrel	Benony	2		1		1	3	1	1					9		
Abington	42	16	Burrel	Isaac			2		1	1	1			1			6		
Abington	42	17	Beals	Benjm			2		1				2	1			6		
Abington	42	18	Brown	Woodbridge	2	1		1			2		1				7		
Abington	42	19	Brown	Saml		1	1	1	1	2		1	1	2			10		
Abington	42	20	Briggs	Richard	4	2			1		1		1	1			10		
Abington	42	21	Brown	Daniel	1		2	1		1		1	1				7		
Abington	42	22	Bates	Joseph					1					2			3		
Abington	42	23	Bicknell	Luke	1	2	2		2	1	1	1		2			12		
Abington	42	24	Bicknell	Nathl 2d	1		1					1					3		
Abington	42	25	Bicknell	Jacob			4		1	1	1	1		1			9		
Abington	42	26	Burrel	John	1	1	1	1			1	1	1				7		
Abington	42	27	Bates	Eleazer 2d		1	3					1	1				6		
Abington	42	28	Bennet	George	2			1		1		1	1	1			7		
Abington	42	29	Bennet	E. Nathl		1				3	1		1				7		
Abington	42	30	Bennet	John	1			1		3			1				6		
Abington	42	31	Beals	Melzer	1			1				1					4		
Abington	42	32	Beals	Noah	1	1	2		1	2	1	1					9		
Abington	42	33	Blanchard	Adam Jr	2			1		2		1		1			7		
Abington	42	34	Churchill	David	1		1					1					3		
Abington	42	35	Churchill	Levi		1	1			1							3		
Abington	42	36	Cobb	Edward			1			1		1					3		
Abington	42	37	Cushing	Ezra Junr			1				1						2		
Abington	42	38	Cobb	John	2	2	1	1		2			2				10		
Abington	42	39	Clark	Jonathan	1		1		1	1	2			1			7		
Abington	42	40	Cushing	Ezra	1	1	1		1			1		1			6		
Abington	42	41	Cushing	Brackley	2		1										3		
Abington	42	42	Cushing	Zattue	1			1		3		1		1			7		
Abington	42	43	Curtis	Joshua	4			1		1		1	1				8		
Abington	42	44	Curtis	Rufus			4	1					1	1			7		
Abington	42	45	Chamberlin	John	1	1	3		1	1	3	1	1				12		
Abington	42	46	Colson	John		1			1					1			3		
Abington	42	47	Cook	Levi	3	2	1	1		1	1	1	1				11		
Abington	42	48	Chubuck	James	3	2			1	1	1		1	1			10		
Abington	42	49	Chubuck	Jeremiah	1		1	1		1		1					5		

TOWN	PG#	LN#	LAST NAME	FIRST NAME	FREE WHITE MALES under 10	10 to 16	16 to 26	26 to 45	45 and over	FREE WHITE FEMALES under 10	10 to 16	16 to 26	26 to 45	45 and over	TOTAL ALL OTHER	TOTAL SLAVES	TOTALS	DISTRICT/ TOWNSHIP	NOTES
Bridgewater	47	1	Alger	James			1		1			2		2			6		
Bridgewater	47	2	Alger	Abiezer		1	1	2		2		2	1				9		
Bridgewater	47	3	Alger	Joseph	3		1			3	1		1				9		
Bridgewater	47	4	Alger	Edmund		2	2	1				2		1			8		
Bridgewater	47	5	Alger	Ebenezer	2		1			2			1	1	1		8		
Bridgewater	47	6	Alger	Nathan	2		1			1			1	1			6		
Bridgewater	47	7	Alger	Huldah	3								1	1			5		
Bridgewater	47	8	Ames	Abiel	2		1			1		1	2	1			8		
Bridgewater	47	9	Ames	John		3	1	1	2	1	1	2		1			12		
Bridgewater	47	10	Ames	John Junr			1			1		1					3		
Bridgewater	47	11	Ames	Joshua		2		1		2			1	2			8		
Bridgewater	47	12	Ames	Jonathan	3	2		1		1	1		1				9		
Bridgewater	47	13	Ames	Thomas					1		1		1	1			4		
Bridgewater	47	14	Ames	Nathaniel					1					1			2		
Bridgewater	47	15	Ames	Abiah				1				1		1			3		
Bridgewater	47	16	Ames	James	2			1			1		1	1			6		
Bridgewater	47	17	Angier	John			1					2					3		
Bridgewater	47	18	Ash	Henry					1					1			2		
Bridgewater	47	19	Bartlett	Samuel					1				1	1			3		
Bridgewater	47	20	Bartlett	David	1		1			1		1					4		
Bridgewater	47	21	Brett	Daniel	1	1		1		1			1				5		
Bridgewater	47	22	Leach	Ichabod		2		1			1		1				5		
Bridgewater	47	23	Leach	Bezer	1			2		2			1				6		
Bridgewater	47	24	Leach	Thomas	1	1		1		1		1	1				6		
Bridgewater	47	25	Leach	Abraham	1	1	1			1		1		1			7		
Bridgewater	47	26	Leach	Bethiah								3	1	1			5		
Bridgewater	47	27	Leach	Mehitabel	1	1	1			3	2		1				9		
Bridgewater	47	28	Pratt	Jonah	1		1			1			1				4		
Bridgewater	47	29	Shaw	Asahel	1	3		1		1	2		1				9		
Bridgewater	47	30	Sears	Abner					1				1	2			4		
Bridgewater	47	31	Tisdell	Abraham					1			1	1	1			4		
Bridgewater	47	32	Waldon	Benjamin			1			1		1					3		
Bridgewater	47	33	Weston	Seth	1		1			1			1				4		
Bridgewater	47	34	Wilber	George		1		1				1		1			4		
Bridgewater	47	35	Wilber	Gideon	1	1	2	2			1	1	1				9		
Bridgewater	47	36	Wilber	Baruch		1	1					1					3		
Bridgewater	47	37	Wilber	Isaac	1		1		1	2	3		1				9		
Bridgewater	47	38	Wilber	Lemuel	1		1		1			1		1			5		
Bridgewater	47	39	Wilber	Lemuel Junr	1			1				1					3		
Bridgewater	47	40	Wood	Simeon	2	1	2		1		1	2		1			10		
Bridgewater	47	41	Hooper	Luther		1			1	1	1	2	1				7		
Bridgewater	47	42	Hooper	Nathaniel					1					1			2		
Bridgewater	47	43	Hooper	David			2		1	2	1		1				7		
Bridgewater	47	44	Hooper	Apollos			1	1					1				3		
Bridgewater	47	45	Biganeer	John Frederic					1						2		3		
Bridgewater	49	1	Dunbar	Barnabas	4	2	2	1	1	4	2	1	1	1			19		
Bridgewater	49	2	Dunbar	Silas	2	1			1					1			5		
Bridgewater	49	3	Dale	Silence					1				1	1			3		
Bridgewater	49	4	Edson	Samuel					1					1			2		
Bridgewater	49	5	Edson	Samuel Jun		2		1				2		1			6		
Bridgewater	49	6	Edson	Noah	4	2		1			1		1				9		
Bridgewater	49	7	Edson	Liberas	2	1		1		1		1	1				7		
Bridgewater	49	8	Edson	Rebecca									2				2		
Bridgewater	49	9	Edson	Mary		1				1				1			3		
Bridgewater	49	10	Ford	Prince	2	1		2		1			2	1			9		
Bridgewater	49	11	Fobes	Timothy			1	1				1		1			4		
Bridgewater	49	12	Fobes	William			1			1	1	1		1			5		
Bridgewater	49	13	Fillebrown	James	2	2		1		2		1	1				9		
Bridgewater	49	14	Gurney	David	3			1		2		1	1				8		
Bridgewater	49	15	Hayward	Jonathan		1	2	1			1	1		1			7		
Bridgewater	49	16	Hayward	Edward	2		1	1				1	2				7		
Bridgewater	49	17	Hayward	Thomas	1		1	1		2	1		1	1			8		
Bridgewater	49	18	Hayward	John			1	1				1	2				6		
Bridgewater	49	19	Hayward	Daniel	1	1		1			1	2	1				7		
Bridgewater	49	20	Evan	Thomas											10		10		
Bridgewater	49	21	Jotham	Luther											5		5		
Bridgewater	49	22	Jotham	Calvin											4		4		
Bridgewater	49	23	Tarbut	Tobey											3		3		
Bridgewater	49	24	Tarbut	Jacob											5		5		
Bridgewater	49	25	Bennet	James											2		2		
Bridgewater	49	26	Fuller	Isaiah											2		2		
Bridgewater	49	27	Jonah	Thomas											4		4		
Bridgewater	49	28	Alden	Solomon				1					1				2		
Bridgewater	49	29	Alden	Noah				1		2			1				4		
Bridgewater	49	30	Alden	Amasa		1						1					2		
Bridgewater	49	31	Alden	Alexander	1		1	1		1			1				5		
Bridgewater	49	32	Alden	Asahel	1	1		1		1			1				5		
Bridgewater	49	33	Aldridge	Daniel		1		2	1	2		1	2				9		
Bridgewater	49	34	Aldridge	James		1									1		2		

TOWN	PG#	LN#	LAST NAME	FIRST NAME	FREE WHITE MALES under 10	10 to 16	16 to 26	26 to 45	45 and over	FREE WHITE FEMALES under 10	10 to 16	16 to 26	26 to 45	45 and over	TOTAL ALL OTHER	TOTAL SLAVES	TOTALS	DISTRICT/ TOWNSHIP	NOTES
Bridgewater	49	35	Crane	Jonathan	1			1	1			1		1			6		
Bridgewater	49	36	Conant	Martin	1		1			2		1					5		
Bridgewater	49	37	Dunbar	Samuel			1			3			1				5		
Bridgewater	49	38	Dunbar	Jesse				1				2	1				4		
Bridgewater	49	39	Dunbar	Eliab	2		1			1			1				5		
Bridgewater	49	40	Deane	Abiel	2	1		1		2	2			1			9		
Bridgewater	49	41	Edson	Lucy			1	1		2	1	1					6		
Bridgewater	49	42	Ellis	Ebenezer	2	1	2		1	1	1			1			9		
Bridgewater	50	1	Fobes	Solomon	2		1			1				1			6		
Bridgewater	50	2	Fobes	Joshua				1		1				1			3		
Bridgewater	50	3	Fobes	Robert		1	2		1	1				1			6		
Bridgewater	50	4	Fobes	Daniel	1		1		1		1	1		1			6		
Bridgewater	50	5	Fobes	Avery		1		1						1			3		
Bridgewater	50	6	Greene	Robert	1	2		1						1			5		
Bridgewater	50	7	Hayward	Amos			1	1					2				4		
Bridgewater	50	8	Hayward	Walter	1			1					1				3		
Bridgewater	50	9	Hayward	Robert		2	1	1				1	1	1			7		
Bridgewater	50	10	Keith	Seth	2	2	1	1		3		1	1				11		
Bridgewater	50	11	Keith	Jeremiah		1		1		1	1	1		1			6		
Bridgewater	50	12	Keith	Daniel				1						1			2		
Bridgewater	50	13	Keith	Daniel Junr				1		1				1			3		
Bridgewater	50	14	Keith	William		2		1		2		1		1			7		
Bridgewater	50	15	Keith	Salmon	1	2	2	1		1		1	1				10		
Bridgewater	50	16	Keith	Amos		1		1		1	1			2			6		
Bridgewater	50	17	Keith	Solomon	1	2	1	1		1			1				7		
Bridgewater	50	18	Keith	Samuel			4	1	1				2	1			9		
Bridgewater	50	19	Keith	Edward	1			1		2		1	1				6		
Bridgewater	50	20	Leach	Joseph			1			1			1	1			4		
Bridgewater	50	21	Leach	Luke	2		1			2	2		1				8		
Bridgewater	50	22	Leach	Ebenezer	1		1						1				3		
Bridgewater	50	23	Leach	Jedediah	1		2		1			1		1			6		
Bridgewater	50	24	Leach	Bernice			1			1		1					3		
Bridgewater	50	25	Burr	John	2			1		1			1				5		
Bridgewater	50	26	Burr	Calvin	1	1		1		1		1					5		
Bridgewater	50	27	Burr	Elijah	3		1	1		2		1	1				9		
Bridgewater	50	28	Blakeley	William				1						1			2		
Bridgewater	50	29	Bolton	Philip				1		1			1				3		
Bridgewater	50	30	Colwell	Ebenezer	1	1	1	1				1		2			7		
Bridgewater	50	31	Copeland	Jonathan				1					2	1			4		
Bridgewater	50	32	Copeland	Jonathan Jun	3	1	1	1		1	1		1				9		
Bridgewater	50	33	Copeland	Joseph		1		1				2	1	1			6		
Bridgewater	50	34	Copeland	Ebenezer	1	1		1						1			4		
Bridgewater	50	35	Copeland	Ebenezer Jun			1			1							2		
Bridgewater	50	36	Copeland	Asa	3		1	1				1	1				7		
Bridgewater	50	37	Copeland	Caleb	3		1	1		3	1		1				10		
Bridgewater	50	38	Copeland	Salmon	1	1		1						1			4		
Bridgewater	50	39	Copeland	Anselm				1		1			1				3		
Bridgewater	50	40	Cook	John					1	1				1			3		
Bridgewater	50	41	Crane	John	1			1		3			1	1			7		
Bridgewater	50	42	Churchill	Eleazer	1			1		3	1		1				7		
Bridgewater	50	43	Dunbar	Simeon	1	2	1		1			1		1			7		
Bridgewater	51	1	Howard	Simeon	1			1		1				1			4		
Bridgewater	51	2	Howard	Nathan				1	1				1	1			4		
Bridgewater	51	3	Howard	Nathan Junr		2		1		1	1	2		1			8		
Bridgewater	51	4	Howard	Nathan 3d	1			1					1				3		
Bridgewater	51	5	Howard	Jonathan 3d	1			1					1				3		
Bridgewater	51	6	Howard	Jonathan 2d	2		2			2	1	1					8		
Bridgewater	51	7	Howard	Jesse					1					1	1		3		
Bridgewater	51	8	Howard	Jesse Junr		1							1				2		
Bridgewater	51	9	Howard	Lloyd		1				2			1				4		
Bridgewater	51	10	Howard	Seth	1	3		1		2			2				9		
Bridgewater	51	11	Howard	George		1		1						1			3		
Bridgewater	51	12	Howard	Nehemiah	2			1	2			1					6		
Bridgewater	51	13	Howard	James				1						1			2		
Bridgewater	51	14	Howard	James Junr	3	1	2	1		2	1	2	1				13		
Bridgewater	51	15	Howard	George Junr	1	2	1		1	1	2	1	1				10		
Bridgewater	51	16	Howard	Thaddeus		1		1		2	1		1				6		
Bridgewater	51	17	Howard	Alfred				1					1				2		
Bridgewater	51	18	Howard	Abiel				1		1			1				3		
Bridgewater	51	19	Inglee	James				1				1		1			3		
Bridgewater	51	20	Johnson	Thomas			2		2			1		1	1		7		
Bridgewater	51	21	Johnson	James		1	3			1		1					6		
Bridgewater	51	22	Johnson	Isaiah				1						1			2		
Bridgewater	51	23	Snell	Zebedee		1	1		2			1	2	1			8		
Bridgewater	51	24	Snell	Oliver	2			1		1			1				5		
Bridgewater	51	25	Snell	Zechariah	3			1				1		1			6		
Bridgewater	51	26	Snell	Nathaniel		1			2			2		1			6		
Bridgewater	51	27	Snell	Issachar	1	1			1			2	1	1			7		
Bridgewater	51	28	Snow	Jonathan	1	2		1		2		1	1				9		

			HEADS OF HOUSEHOLD		FREE WHITE MALES					FREE WHITE FEMALES					TOTAL ALL OTHER	TOTAL SLAVES	TOTALS	DISTRICT/ TOWNSHIP	NOTES
TOWN	PG#	LN#	LAST NAME	FIRST NAME	under 10	10 to 16	16 to 26	26 to 45	45 and over	under 10	10 to 16	16 to 26	26 to 45	45 and over					
Bridgewater	51	29	Snow	Silas		2	1					1	1	1			6		
Bridgewater	51	30	Snell	Isaachar Junr			1						1				2		
Bridgewater	51	31	Sturtevant	Ephraim			1			1	1		1				4		
Bridgewater	51	32	Southworth	Lemuel				1		1		1		1			4		
Bridgewater	51	33	Stock	John				1			1		1				3		
Bridgewater	51	34	Snell	Alvin	1		1					1					3		
Bridgewater	51	35	Southworth	Mary									2				2		
Bridgewater	51	36	Silvester	Seth	3			1		1			1				6		
Bridgewater	51	37	Turner	Samuel	1	1		1		2			1				6		
Bridgewater	51	38	Thompson	Thomas		1		1					2	1			5		
Bridgewater	51	39	Thompson	Thomas Junr	1			1		1	1		1				5		
Bridgewater	51	40	Thompson	James			1			1	1	1					4		
Bridgewater	51	41	Tirrel	Lemuel	2			1		3	1		1				8		
Bridgewater	51	42	Thayer	Seth	4	2		1			1		1				9		
Bridgewater	51	43	Thayer	Hannah									2				2		
Bridgewater	51	44	Thayer	Enos		1			1				1				3		
Bridgewater	52	1	Tilson	Holmes	1			1		1			1	1			5		
Bridgewater	52	2	Tibou	Amasa	3	1	1	1		2	3		1				12		
Bridgewater	52	3	Tilden	John	1		1		1	1			1				5		
Bridgewater	52	4	Thayer	Jeremiah	2	3		1				1	1				8		
Bridgewater	52	5	Thayer	Enoch				1		1			1	1			4		
Bridgewater	52	6	Thompson	Jacob	1			1		2		1					5		
Bridgewater	52	7	Tilson	Elisha	1			1					1	1			4		
Bridgewater	52	8	Wales	Thomas	1	1				1		1	1	1			6		
Bridgewater	52	9	Warren	Ebenezer	4	1		1		1	1	2		1			11		
Bridgewater	52	10	Warren	Nathan	3			1		2	2		1				9		
Bridgewater	52	11	Whitten	Joseph			2	1		1		1		1			6		
Bridgewater	52	12	Wales	John	1			1		3	1		1				7		
Bridgewater	52	13	Willis	Ephraim	2	3	1	1		1		1	1				10		
Bridgewater	52	14	Willis	John	1		1	1		3	1	1		3			11		
Bridgewater	52	15	Whiting	Philip	1	2		1					1				5		
Bridgewater	52	16	Manly	Lewis	4			1					1				6		
Bridgewater	52	17	Macomber	Thomas		1	1		1		1	1	1				6		
Bridgewater	52	18	Manly	Nathaniel		1			1	4	2	2		1			11		
Bridgewater	52	19	Manly	Daniel				1		1		1		1			4		
Bridgewater	52	20	Manly	Daniel Junr	3	1	1		1	1		1	1				9		
Bridgewater	52	21	Marshall	Hayward	2			1		1			1				5		
Bridgewater	52	22	Noyes	John	1	1	1		1	1	1			2			8		
Bridgewater	52	23	Noyes	Simeon			1			4	1						6		
Bridgewater	52	24	Hayward	Charles	3			1					1				5		
Bridgewater	52	25	Hayward	Cornelius	1			1						2			4		
Bridgewater	52	26	Hayward	Elijah 2d		1		1						3			5		
Bridgewater	52	27	Hayward	Elijah 3d	1	1		1		3			1				7		
Bridgewater	52	28	Hayward	Luther		2		1				1	2	1			7		
Bridgewater	52	29	Hayward	Solomon 2d				1		1	2		1				5		
Bridgewater	52	30	Hayward	Ezra				1					1				2		
Bridgewater	52	31	Hartwell	Daniel	1	2		1		3	1	2	1				11		
Bridgewater	52	32	Hartwell	Isaac	2		2	1		1			1				7		
Bridgewater	52	33	Harvey	David					1				1	1			3		
Bridgewater	52	34	Harvey	Nathan	2	1		1		2			1				7		
Bridgewater	52	35	Harvey	Oliver	2			1					1				4		
Bridgewater	52	36	House	Abel				1					1				2		
Bridgewater	52	37	Holmes	John			1			1		1					3		
Bridgewater	52	38	Howard	Edward	1	1		1	1	1			1	1	1		8		
Bridgewater	52	39	Howard	Daniel	1		1	2	1	2	2	4		1			14		
Bridgewater	52	40	Howard	Eliakim		1	3		1	1		2	1	2			11		
Bridgewater	52	41	Howard	Jonathan		1	2		1		1			2			7		
Bridgewater	52	42	Howard	Jonathan 2d		1	3		1			2	2	1			10		
Bridgewater	52	43	Howard	Gamaliel	1							2		1			5		
Bridgewater	52	44	Howard	Martin	2		1	1	1			1	1				7		
Bridgewater	53	1	Newberry	Lemuel	1		1		1				1				4		
Bridgewater	53	2	Orcutt	Ephraim	3	1			1			2	1	3			11		
Bridgewater	53	3	Orcutt	Nathan	1	2						1		1			6		
Bridgewater	53	4	Perkins	Richard				1					2	1			4		
Bridgewater	53	5	Perkins	William			1					1					2		
Bridgewater	53	6	Perkins	Nathaniel		1	1		1		1	3		1			8		
Bridgewater	53	7	Perkins	Nathaniel Junr	1		2			2			1				6		
Bridgewater	53	8	Packard	Jonathan			1		2		1			2	1		7		
Bridgewater	53	9	Packard	Elijah	3	1		1		2			1				8		
Bridgewater	53	10	Packard	Simeon	1			1		1		1	1				5		
Bridgewater	53	11	Ripley	Daniel	2			1		2	1	1	1				8		
Bridgewater	53	12	Ripley	Solomon			1	1		1			1	1			5		
Bridgewater	53	13	Ripley	Marlbry	2	1		1		1		1	1				7		
Bridgewater	53	14	Reed	John	2		2	1		1		1		1	1		9		
Bridgewater	53	15	Reed	Timothy	1			1					1				3		
Bridgewater	53	16	Reed	Ezekiel	1			1		2			1				5		
Bridgewater	53	17	Richard	Josiah		2	1		1		1		1	1			7		
Bridgewater	53	18	Richard	John				1				1	1	1			4		
Bridgewater	53	19	Richard	Seth	2	1						1					6		

12

			HEADS OF HOUSEHOLD		FREE WHITE MALES					FREE WHITE FEMALES					TOTAL ALL OTHER	TOTAL SLAVES	TOTALS	DISTRICT/ TOWNSHIP	NOTES
TOWN	PG#	LN#	LAST NAME	FIRST NAME	under 10	10 to 16	16 to 26	26 to 45	45 and over	under 10	10 to 16	16 to 26	26 to 45	45 and over					
Bridgewater	53	20	Richmond	Isaac	1	1	1	1		2			1				7		
Bridgewater	53	21	Ray	Jeremiah	2				1				1				4		
Bridgewater	53	22	Porter	Isaac	4			1		2	1		1				9		
Bridgewater	53	23	Packard	Abiah Junr				1		3			1				5		
Bridgewater	53	24	Packard	Howard		1		1		1			1				4		
Bridgewater	53	25	Packard	Thomas				1						1			2		
Bridgewater	53	26	Packard	Elijah	2			1		2			1				6		
Bridgewater	53	27	Packard	Cyrus	1	1		1		2		1					6		
Bridgewater	53	28	Packard	Lemuel	2	2	1		1				1	1			8		
Bridgewater	53	29	Packard	Parmenas	3	1	2	1		1	1			1			10		
Bridgewater	53	30	Packard	Daniel	1		1			2		2					6		
Bridgewater	53	31	Packard	Jonas	2	1			1	1	3	1		1			10		
Bridgewater	53	32	Packard	Nathan			1			1				1			3		
Bridgewater	53	33	Packard	Benjamin				1						1			2		
Bridgewater	53	34	Packard	Adin		1	1		1	1	1	1		1			8		
Bridgewater	53	35	Packard	Ransom	1			1				1					3		
Bridgewater	53	36	Perkins	Mark		1		1		4				1			7		
Bridgewater	53	37	Packard	Content		1	1			2		1		2			7		
Bridgewater	53	38	Perkins	Jonathan				1				1		1			3		
Bridgewater	53	39	Pratt	Thomas	2			1		3	2		1				9		
Bridgewater	53	40	Pettingill	Daniel	1			1	1	2			1	1			7		
Bridgewater	53	41	Pettingill	Akerman			2							1			3		
Bridgewater	53	42	Pettingill	Hugh	2	2		1		3		1	1				10		
Bridgewater	53	43	Pratt	Enoch	2	1		1		1			1				6		
Bridgewater	54	1	Packard	Jonathan 2d	3			1		1				1			6		
Bridgewater	54	2	Packard	Oliver				1				1					2		
Bridgewater	54	3	Phinney	Pelitiah				1						1			2		
Bridgewater	54	4	Packard	Zion	2			1		1		1	1	1			7		
Bridgewater	54	5	Phillips	Isaac	1			1		1			1				4		
Bridgewater	54	6	Phillips	Abiel	2			1		2	1		1				7		
Bridgewater	54	7	Phillips	Lewis	1			1		2			1				5		
Bridgewater	54	8	Reynolds	Jonas	1		1	1				2					5		
Bridgewater	54	9	Reynolds	Elizabeth							1			2			3		
Bridgewater	54	10	Reynolds	Joseph	1	1			1	1	1	1		1			7		
Bridgewater	54	11	Reynolds	Joseph Junr		1	1			2			1				5		
Bridgewater	54	12	Rickard	Jacob				1					1	1			3		
Bridgewater	54	13	Reynolds	Polly	1		1			2			1				5		
Bridgewater	54	14	Southworth	Perez	2	3			1	4	2		1				13		
Bridgewater	54	15	Sturtevant	Silas			1	1					1	1			4		
Bridgewater	54	16	Silvester	Joseph			1					1	1				4		
Bridgewater	54	17	Silvester	Joseph Junr	1	1		1		2	2		1				8		
Bridgewater	54	18	Snell	Shepherd	1			1		1			1				4		
Bridgewater	54	19	Shaw	William	1			1					1	1			4		
Bridgewater	54	20	Shaw	William Junr	1	2		1			1	2					7		
Bridgewater	54	21	Snell	Joseph	1	2			1	3	1			1			9		
Bridgewater	54	22	Shaw	Micah	2		1	1		2	1		1				8		
Bridgewater	54	23	Snow	Seth			1	1		2			1				5		
Bridgewater	54	24	Johnson	Isaac	3				1	1		1	1	1			8		
Bridgewater	54	25	Johnson	Bethiah		3	1			1		2	1				8		
Bridgewater	54	26	Kingman	Jonathan			1		1					1			3		
Bridgewater	54	27	Kingman	Joseph	1			1		1	1			1			5		
Bridgewater	54	28	Kingman	Jonathan Junr	2	1		1		1	1		1				7		
Bridgewater	54	29	Kingman	Caleb					1					1	1		3		
Bridgewater	54	30	Kingman	Abiah										1			1		
Bridgewater	54	31	Keith	Simeon		1	2		1	2	2			1			9		
Bridgewater	54	32	Knapp	Phebe						2	1	2		1			6		
Bridgewater	54	33	Lothrop	Lemuel			1			1			1				3		
Bridgewater	54	34	Lothrop	Mark		1	3		1	1	1		1				8		
Bridgewater	54	35	Lothrop	Zephaniah	2	1	1		1	1			2	1			9		
Bridgewater	54	36	Lothrop	Seth		2			1	1				1			5		
Bridgewater	54	37	Lothrop	Josiah				1						1			2		
Bridgewater	54	38	Lothrop	Josiah Junr		1		1		2	1			1			6		
Bridgewater	54	39	Lothrop	David			1			1	1		1	1			6		
Bridgewater	54	40	Lothrop	Jonathan			1	1							1		3		
Bridgewater	54	41	Lothrop	Daniel				1						1			2		
Bridgewater	54	42	Lucas	Lazares			1	1	1	2			1				6		
Bridgewater	54	43	Lincoln	Oliver			2		1			1		1			5		
Bridgewater	54	44	Macomber	Jacob				1		1		2		1			5		
Bridgewater	54	45	Mehurin	Jonathan	2			1		1		1	1				6		
Bridgewater	55	1	White	Micah				1						1			2		
Bridgewater	55	2	Willis	Zebulon	1			1		2			1	1			6		
Bridgewater	55	3	Williams	George					2		1		2	1			6		
Bridgewater	55	4	Williams	George Junr	1	1	1			1	1	2					7		
Bridgewater	55	5	Williams	Perez	2	1		1		2			1	1			8		
Bridgewater	55	6	Winslow	Jonah			1			1			1				3		
Bridgewater	55	7	Willis	Isaac					1					1			2		
Bridgewater	55	8	Willis	Isaac Junr	1	1		1		3	1		1				8		
Bridgewater	55	9	Withington	Ebenezer						1			2				4		
Bridgewater	55	10	Willis	John		2	1	1	1			1		2			9		
Bridgewater	55	11	Willis	Jonah	2		1	1		2		1					7		

TOWN	PG#	LN#	LAST NAME	FIRST NAME	FREE WHITE MALES					FREE WHITE FEMALES					TOTAL ALL OTHER	TOTAL SLAVES	TOTALS	DISTRICT/ TOWNSHIP	NOTES
					under 10	10 to 16	16 to 26	26 to 45	45 and over	under 10	10 to 16	16 to 26	26 to 45	45 and over					
Bridgewater	55	12	Willis	Jedediah	2		2		1		2	2		1			10		
Bridgewater	55	13	Green	Robert											2		2		
Bridgewater	55	14	Pierce	Peter											5		5		
Bridgewater	55	15	Jackson	John											6		6		
Bridgewater	55	16	Mingo	Cloe											5		5		
Bridgewater	55	17	Codner	Samuel											9		9		
Bridgewater	55	18	Travellar	Henry											3		3		
Bridgewater	55	19	Lewis	Peter											3		3		
Bridgewater	55	20	Jackson	Ephraim		1		1	1	1	2		1	1			8		
Bridgewater	55	21	Keith	Levi			1		1		1	1		1			5		
Bridgewater	55	22	Keith	Benjamin 2d	3	1			1		1			1	1		8		
Bridgewater	55	23	Keith	Jonathan	1	1	1	1	1	3	3	1	1				13		
Bridgewater	55	24	Keith	Levi 3d	1			1				1					3		
Bridgewater	55	25	Kingman	Matthew		1	1		1		1		1	1			6		
Bridgewater	55	26	Kingman	Abel	2	1		1		2		1	1				8		
Bridgewater	55	27	Kingman	Henry				1					1				2		
Bridgewater	55	28	Keith	Shepherd				1		4			1				6		
Bridgewater	55	29	Keith	Nathan	1	1		1			1	1	1				6		
Bridgewater	55	30	Kingman	Seth	4	1		1		1		1	1	1			10		
Bridgewater	55	31	Keith	Ambrose	1			1					1				3		
Bridgewater	55	32	Knolton	Thomas	2	1	1	1		1	1		1				8		
Bridgewater	55	33	Lincoln	Nehemiah	2	1	1		1	1	1	1		1			10		
Bridgewater	55	34	Leach	Nathan	1	1	2		1	2			1				8		
Bridgewater	55	35	Orcutt	Nathaniel		1		1		1			1				4		
Bridgewater	55	36	Orcutt	Leonard			1		1	1			1		1		4		
Bridgewater	55	37	Porter	John				1				1	2				4		
Bridgewater	55	38	Packard	William				1					1				2		
Bridgewater	55	39	Perkins	Jesse	1		1		1		1		1	1			6		
Bridgewater	55	40	Perkins	Zadoc	2		1						1				4		
Bridgewater	56	1	Packard	Jonah	1	1		1		1	1		1	1			7		
Bridgewater	56	2	Packard	Ames	1	1		1		1		1		1			6		
Bridgewater	56	3	Packard	Levi	2			1		1	1		1				6		
Bridgewater	56	4	Packard	Silas	2		1	2			1	1	1				8		
Bridgewater	56	5	Perkins	Jonathan Junr		1		1					1				3		
Bridgewater	56	6	Packard	Ebenezer				1					1				2		
Bridgewater	56	7	Packard	Robert	2			1		3	1	1					8		
Bridgewater	56	8	Packard	Lot				1		3			1				5		
Bridgewater	56	9	Packard	Eliphalet	3	1	1	1				1	2				9		
Bridgewater	56	10	Packard	Noah	2			1		3	1		1				8		
Bridgewater	56	11	Packard	Joseph	2			1		2			1				6		
Bridgewater	56	12	Phillips	Ebenezer			1						1				2		
Bridgewater	56	13	Packard	Abiah			1				1		1				3		
Bridgewater	56	14	Perkins	Luke	1	1	2		1				1				6		
Bridgewater	56	15	Packard	Kezia	2	1				1			1				5		
Bridgewater	56	16	Packard	Thomas Junr	3	1	1	1				1	2				9		
Bridgewater	56	17	Perkins	Jonah	2		1	1	1		1	1					7		
Bridgewater	56	18	Perkins	Shepard	1	1		1					1				4		
Bridgewater	56	19	Perkins	Abigail								1	1				2		
Bridgewater	56	20	Packard	Simeon				1					1				2		
Bridgewater	56	21	Packard	Isaiah	3			1		1	1	1	1				8		
Bridgewater	56	22	Packard	Zenas	2			1		2	1		1				7		
Bridgewater	56	23	Porter	James		1		1	1	1	1						5		
Bridgewater	56	24	Rathbun	Volentine W	1			1		1			1				4		
Bridgewater	56	25	Snell	Jonah				1				1					2		
Bridgewater	56	26	Snell	Elijah		1		1		1	1	1			1		6		
Bridgewater	56	27	Snell	Elijah Jun	2	1		1				1					5		
Bridgewater	56	28	Snell	Ephraim	1	1		1		2	3		1				9		
Bridgewater	56	29	Snell	Nathan			1		1	2	2	1		1			8		
Bridgewater	56	30	Snell	Nathan Junr	1	1						1					3		
Bridgewater	56	31	Snell	Caleb		1		1	1			1	2				6		
Bridgewater	56	32	Snow	Daniel		1	1		1		2	1	1				7		
Bridgewater	56	33	Snow	John	2	2		1		2		1	1				9		
Bridgewater	56	34	Sampson	Micah		2	1		1	1		2	1				8		
Bridgewater	56	35	Sampson	Stephen	1		1			1			1				4		
Bridgewater	56	36	Thayer	Abijah	1			1			1		1				4		
Bridgewater	56	37	Thayer	Leavitt	1	1	3	1				2	1				9		
Bridgewater	56	38	Thayer	Richard	1	1		1		1	2		1				8		
Bridgewater	56	39	Thayer	Abijah 2d			2						1		1		4		
Bridgewater	56	40	Tibou	William	4	2		1					1				8		
Bridgewater	56	41	Turner	Samuel	1			1		2		1	1				6		
Bridgewater	56	42	Thomson	Daniel				1					1				2		
Bridgewater	56	43	Thresher	Seth	2			1					1				4		
Bridgewater	56	44	Trask	William				1		1			1		1		4		
Bridgewater	57	1	Bacon	John				1		3			1				5		
Bridgewater	57	2	Bassett	Joseph				1			2		1				4		
Bridgewater	57	3	Bassett	Joseph 2d	2	2	3	1		1	1		1				11		
Bridgewater	57	4	Bassett	Joseph 3d	2			1		1			1				5		
Bridgewater	57	5	Bassett	Caleb	1	3		1		3		1	1				10		
Bridgewater	57	6	Benson	Jonathan		1	1		1	1	1		1				6		
Bridgewater	57	7	Benson	Ebenezer	1	1		1					1				4		
Bridgewater	57	8	Benson	David	1	1		1		4	1	3	1				12		
Bridgewater	57	9	Benson	Jonah	1	1		1		2	1	1	2	1			10		
Bridgewater	57	10	Blossom	Barnabas				1		3	1	1	1	1			8		
Bridgewater	57	11	Barrows	Joseph	1		1			2			1				5		
Bridgewater	57	12	Bolton	David	1			1		1			1				4		
Bridgewater	57	13	Bolton	John	1	1		1		3			1				7		
Bridgewater	57	14	Carver	Eleazer				1		1	3		1		1		7		
Bridgewater	57	15	Cary	Eleazer		2		1			1	1	1				6		
Bridgewater	57	16	Cary	Eliphalet		1		1					2				4		

14

TOWN	PG#	LN#	HEADS OF HOUSEHOLD		FREE WHITE MALES					FREE WHITE FEMALES					TOTAL ALL OTHER	TOTAL SLAVES	TOTALS	DISTRICT/ TOWNSHIP	NOTES
			LAST NAME	FIRST NAME	under 10	10 to 16	16 to 26	26 to 45	45 and over	under 10	10 to 16	16 to 26	26 to 45	45 and over					
Bridgewater	57	17	Crooker	Zenas	1		2	1		3			1	1			9		
Bridgewater	57	18	Clarke	Benjamin	3			1				1		1			6		
Bridgewater	57	19	Conant	Peter	1	1	2		1		1	1	1				8		
Bridgewater	57	20	Conant	Elias		1	1	1						1			4		
Bridgewater	57	21	Conant	Phineas	1	1		1		1	1		1				6		
Bridgewater	57	22	Conant	John				1						1			2		
Bridgewater	57	23	Edson	David		2		1		4		1	1	1			10		
Bridgewater	57	24	Edson	Ebenezer				1						1			2		
Bridgewater	57	25	Edson	Martha									1	1			2		
Bridgewater	57	26	French	William			1		1		1	1		1			5		
Bridgewater	57	27	Field	Richard			1		1	2	2	2	1				9		
Bridgewater	57	28	Field	William	2			1		1			1				5		
Bridgewater	57	29	Field	Jabez					2		1		1	1			5		
Bridgewater	57	30	Field	Barzillai	1			2		1		1					6		
Bridgewater	57	31	French	Levi	1			1					1				3		
Bridgewater	57	32	French	Dependence	2			1		1			1	1			6		
Bridgewater	57	33	Ford	Mark			1	1		1				1			5		
Bridgewater	57	34	Flinn	Thomas				1		1				1			3		
Bridgewater	57	35	Field	Daniel	1	1		1			1						4		
Bridgewater	57	36	Fuller	Jacob			1				1	1					3		
Bridgewater	57	37	Gurney	Mehitabel	2						1		1				4		
Bridgewater	57	38	Groves	Ephraim	1				1				1	1			4		
Bridgewater	57	39	Gurney	Zechariah					1					1			2		
Bridgewater	57	40	Gurney	Zechariah Junr	3	2		1		2	2		1				11		
Bridgewater	57	41	Gage	Thomas	1	1		1				1	1				5		
Bridgewater	57	42	Howard	Daniel 2d	1	2	1	1	1	1		2	1				10		
Bridgewater	57	43	Howard	Gideon	1	1		1		3		1	1				8		
Bridgewater	58	1	Howard	John	1	1		1		1	1		1				6		
Bridgewater	58	2	Howard	Alfred	2			1		2			1	2			8		
Bridgewater	58	3	Howard	Mary									4				4		
Bridgewater	58	4	Howard	Oliver	1	1	1	1		4	2	1	1				12		
Bridgewater	58	5	Howard	Barnabas			1		1			1		1			4		
Bridgewater	58	6	Howard	Ichabod	1	1			1	2	1		1				7		
Bridgewater	58	7	Howard	Robert		1			1				1	1			4		
Bridgewater	58	8	Howard	Robert Junr	1			1		2	1		1				6		
Bridgewater	58	9	Howard	Caleb	1	2		1		4	2	1	1				12		
Bridgewater	58	10	Howard	Jonas	1	1		1		2	2		1				8		
Bridgewater	58	11	Howard	Silence								2	1				3		
Bridgewater	58	12	Howard	Joshua	2		1						1				4		
Bridgewater	58	13	Hayward	Waldo	2	1	1	1					1				7		
Bridgewater	58	14	Hayward	Joseph		1	1		1		1	1		1			6		
Bridgewater	58	15	Hayward	Asaph	1		1	1		3		1	1				8		
Bridgewater	58	16	Hunt	John		1			1	1			1				4		
Bridgewater	58	17	Hunt	Mathew	1		2		1	2			1				7		
Bridgewater	58	18	Hobart	Nathaniel Junr	1	1		1		1	2		1				7		
Bridgewater	58	19	Horton	Isaac		1				1	1		1				4		
Bridgewater	58	20	Humphrey	James	2			1		2		1					6		
Bridgewater	58	21	Jameson	William		1	1	1			1	1		1			6		
Bridgewater	58	22	Jones	Asa	2		1	1		1			2				7		
Bridgewater	58	23	Alden	Oliver		1			1			1		1			4		
Bridgewater	58	24	Alden	Joseph	1	1	3	1		1	2			1			10		
Bridgewater	58	25	Alden	Caleb	2			1		3		1	1				8		
Bridgewater	58	26	Alden	Eleazer				1						2			3		
Bridgewater	58	27	Alden	Eleazer Junr	1		2					1	1				6		
Bridgewater	58	28	Alden	Joshua		1			1		1			1			4		
Bridgewater	58	29	Alden	Seth		1	2							1			4		
Bridgewater	58	30	Alden	Solomon Junr	1	1	1	1		1	1		2				8		
Bridgewater	58	31	Allen	Oliver	2	1		1		1			1				6		
Bridgewater	58	32	Allen	Benjamin	2			1					1				4		
Bridgewater	58	33	Alger	James 2d	2		1		1	1	2	1		1			9		
Bridgewater	58	34	Alger	James 3d	2			1		1			2				6		
Bridgewater	58	35	Ames	Joseph	1	1	1		1	1	1	2		1			9		
Bridgewater	58	36	Ames	Solomon	1			1	1			2		1	2		8		
Bridgewater	58	37	Ames	Simeon		1			1			1		2			5		
Bridgewater	58	38	Ames	Alexander	2			1		3			1				7		
Bridgewater	58	39	Ames	Solomon Junr	2			1					1				4		
Bridgewater	58	40	Ames	Bezer	3			1		2			1				7		
Bridgewater	58	41	Andrews	Silas				1					1	1			3		
Bridgewater	58	42	Ames	Seth	1			1					1				3		
Bridgewater	58	43	Andrews	Gideon	2			1		1			1				5		
Bridgewater	59	1	Eddy	Azor		1		1					1				3		
Bridgewater	59	2	Fobes	Jason		1	1		1	1	1			1			6		
Bridgewater	59	3	Fobes	Ezra		2			1	3	1	3	1				12		
Bridgewater	59	4	Fobes	Alpheus	3	1	2	1		1	1		1	2			12		
Bridgewater	59	5	Fobes	Ephraim					1					1			2		
Bridgewater	59	6	Fobes	Ephraim Junr			1	1						2			4		
Bridgewater	59	7	Fobes	Caleb			1			1		1					3		
Bridgewater	59	8	Fearing	Noah				1		1	2	1					5		
Bridgewater	59	9	French	Asa	1			1		1			1				4		
Bridgewater	59	10	Hayward	Beza	1				1					3			5		
Bridgewater	59	11	Hayward	Hezekiah		1	1		1	1				1			5		
Bridgewater	59	12	Hayward	Elijah	2	2			1				2				7		
Bridgewater	59	13	Hayward	Ziba			1	1	1		1	1		1			6		
Bridgewater	59	14	Hayward	Edward		1	1	1					1				4		
Bridgewater	59	15	Hayward	Timothy	1			1		3		2					7		
Bridgewater	59	16	Hayward	Benjamin					1			1		1			3		
Bridgewater	59	17	Hayward	Azariah	1		1		1			2		1			6		
Bridgewater	59	18	Hayward	Solomon	3	4			1	2			2				12		
Bridgewater	59	19	Hayward	Azariah Junr		1		1		2	2						7		
Bridgewater	59	20	Hayward	Eliab		1		1	1				2	1			6		

TOWN	PG#	LN#	LAST NAME	FIRST NAME	FREE WHITE MALES					FREE WHITE FEMALES					TOTAL ALL OTHER	TOTAL SLAVES	TOTALS	DISTRICT/ TOWNSHIP	NOTES
					under 10	10 to 16	16 to 26	26 to 45	45 and over	under 10	10 to 16	16 to 26	26 to 45	45 and over					
Bridgewater	59	21	Hayward	Thomas	2			1		2			1				6		
Bridgewater	59	22	Bryant	Job S	1			1		2			1				5		
Bridgewater	59	23	Bryant	Calvin	1			1		3			1				6		
Bridgewater	59	24	Brattles	Asa				1		3			1				5		
Bridgewater	59	25	Brett	Abigail			1						1	1			3		
Bridgewater	59	26	Brett	Susanna			1						1	1			3		
Bridgewater	59	27	Badger	William					1	1	1	1		1			5		
Bridgewater	59	28	Cary	Jonathan				1					2				3		
Bridgewater	59	29	Cary	Moses			2	1		2	1		1				7		
Bridgewater	59	30	Cary	Jonathan Junr	3	1		1		4	2		1				12		
Bridgewater	59	31	Cary	James				1					1				2		
Bridgewater	59	32	Cary	Simeon				1						1	1		3		
Bridgewater	59	33	Cary	Howard	2	2	1	1		1	1		1				9		
Bridgewater	59	34	Croswell	Benjamin				1					1				2		
Bridgewater	59	35	Curtis	Theophilus	3			1		2			1				7		
Bridgewater	59	36	Curtis	Barnabas		2	1	1		1		2	2	2			11		
Bridgewater	59	37	Cole	Ephraim	2	2		1			1		1				7		
Bridgewater	59	38	Cheeseman	Samuel			1		1	2		1		1			6		
Bridgewater	59	39	Cheeseman	Noah			1					1					2		
Bridgewater	59	40	Cary	Daniel	1	1		1		1			3	1			8		
Bridgewater	59	41	Crafts	Thomas	1	1		1		2	1		1				7		
Bridgewater	59	42	Crafts	John	1			1						1			3		
Bridgewater	60	1	Churchill	Ephraim	1			1					1	1			4		
Bridgewater	60	2	Churchill	Ephraim Junr			1					1	1				3		
Bridgewater	60	3	Churchill	James			1			1			1				3		
Bridgewater	60	4	Carr	Thomas				1					1	1			3		
Bridgewater	60	5	Carr	Daniel				1					1	2			4		
Bridgewater	60	6	Carr	Daniel Junr			1			1			1				3		
Bridgewater	60	7	Dill	James	3			1		2			1				7		
Bridgewater	60	8	Dyke	Samuel			1	1					1	1			4		
Bridgewater	60	9	Dyke	Samuel Junr	1	2		1				3	2				9		
Bridgewater	60	10	Dailey	Lewis	1	1		1		2	2		1	1			9		
Bridgewater	60	11	Dickerman	Manaseh	2	1		1		4		2					10		
Bridgewater	60	12	Dickerman	Samuel			1			1		1					3		
Bridgewater	60	13	Dunbar	Jacob				1						1			2		
Bridgewater	60	14	Dunbar	Jacob Junr			1			1	1		1				4		
Bridgewater	60	15	Dunbar	Ebenezer	2	2		1		1			1				7		
Bridgewater	60	16	Dunbar	Lemuel	2			1		1			1				5		
Bridgewater	60	17	Eames	Josiah		1		1					1				3		
Bridgewater	60	18	Eames	Elisha		1		1		1				1			4		
Bridgewater	60	19	Edson	Ichabod		1		1				1		1			4		
Bridgewater	60	20	Edson	William	1	1		1		3			1				7		
Bridgewater	60	21	Edson	Seth	2	1		1		3	1		1		1		10		
Bridgewater	60	22	Edson	James				1						1			2		
Bridgewater	60	23	Edson	Josiah		1		1		2	1	3	1				9		
Bridgewater	60	24	Conant	John Junr		1		1		1	1		1				5		
Bridgewater	60	25	Conant	Ezra	1	2	1	1					1	2			8		
Bridgewater	60	26	Conant	Zenas				1			1	1		1			4		
Bridgewater	60	27	Conant	Silvanus		1		1		2			1	1			6		
Bridgewater	60	28	Conant	Nathaniel				1				2		1			4		
Bridgewater	60	29	Conant	Andrew	1			1					1				3		
Bridgewater	60	30	Cowin	Joseph		1		1		1	4	1	1				9		
Bridgewater	60	31	Crane	Samuel				1									1		
Bridgewater	60	32	Cushman	Thomas	2			1			1			2			6		
Bridgewater	60	33	Carver	John		1		1				2		1			5		
Bridgewater	60	34	Cushman	William				1						1			2		
Bridgewater	60	35	Copeland	Daniel	1		1				1	2	1	1			8		
Bridgewater	60	36	Conant	Joanna										2			2		
Bridgewater	60	37	Dunbar	Peter	2	2		1	1		1		1				8		
Bridgewater	60	38	Dunbar	Elias		5						1					6		
Bridgewater	60	39	Darling	Benjamin	1			1	1				1	1			5		
Bridgewater	60	40	Dyer	Jason		1	1					1	2	2			7		
Bridgewater	60	41	Doggett	Mark	3		1					1	1				6		
Bridgewater	60	42	Dyer	John		1	1			1	1		1		1		7		
Bridgewater	60	43	Edson	Benjamin	3			1				1	1				6		
Bridgewater	60	44	Edson	Cyrus		1				2		1					4		
Bridgewater	61	1	Kinsley	Nymphas				1						2			3		
Bridgewater	61	2	Keith	Howe	3	1							1				6		
Bridgewater	61	3	Keith	Isaac			1			2			1				4		
Bridgewater	61	4	Keith	Benjamin				1					1				2		
Bridgewater	61	5	Keith	Benjamin Junr	2	1	1	1		2		1	1				9		
Bridgewater	61	6	Keith	Marshal	2		1					1					4		
Bridgewater	61	7	Keith	Robert		1		1					1				3		
Bridgewater	61	8	Keith	Jonathan	2	1		1		1	1		1				7		
Bridgewater	61	9	Keith	Hartwell	4	1		1				2	1				9		
Bridgewater	61	10	Keyes	Walter				1		2			1				4		
Bridgewater	61	11	Latham	Chilton				1						1			2		
Bridgewater	61	12	Lazell	Isaac			1	2		3	3	1	1		4		15		
Bridgewater	61	13	Lazell	Nathan	1	1	1	2		3	4	1	1	1			15		
Bridgewater	61	14	Lathrop	Jacob	1	1	1	1		3			1	1			9		
Bridgewater	61	15	Leach	Apollos	1		2	1		1			1				6		
Bridgewater	61	16	Leach	Nehemiah				1		2				1			4		
Bridgewater	61	17	Leach	Hassadiah		2					1	1		1			5		
Bridgewater	61	18	Leach	Levi		2				1		1					4		
Bridgewater	61	19	Leach	Libeus	2			1		3			1				7		
Bridgewater	61	20	Leach	Benjamin		1		1		3			1				6		
Bridgewater	61	21	Leonard	Samuel	1	2	2	1			1	2		1			10		
Bridgewater	61	22	Washburn	Solomon	3	1	1							1			7		
Bridgewater	61	23	Washburn	Jacob	1			1		2			1				5		
Bridgewater	61	24	Washburn	Zenas	1		1					1			1		4		

16

TOWN	PG#	LN#	LAST NAME	FIRST NAME	FREE WHITE MALES					FREE WHITE FEMALES					TOTAL ALL OTHER	TOTAL SLAVES	TOTALS	DISTRICT/TOWNSHIP	NOTES
					under 10	10 to 16	16 to 26	26 to 45	45 and over	under 10	10 to 16	16 to 26	26 to 45	45 and over					
Bridgewater	61	25	Whitmarsh	Jacob					1					1			2		
Bridgewater	61	26	Whitmarsh	Lot	1	2	2	1		2			2				10		
Bridgewater	61	27	Whitmarsh	Hannah									1	1			2		
Bridgewater	61	28	Whitten	Marlborough	3				1	1			1				6		
Bridgewater	61	29	Wade	James					1	1			1	1			4		
Bridgewater	61	30	Wade	Robert	1				1	1	2	2	2				9		
Bridgewater	61	31	Wade	Betty								1		1			2		
Bridgewater	61	32	Wade	Molly	2					1			1				4		
Bridgewater	61	33	Wales	Samuel				1		3			1				5		
Bridgewater	61	34	White	Lucy			1			1	2	1		1			6		
Bridgewater	61	35	White	Benjamin			1					1					2		
Bridgewater	61	36	Young	Robert	1	1	2		1	1				1			7		
Bridgewater	61	37	Young	Thomas	3	1		1		2			2	1			10		
Bridgewater	61	38	Barrel	William			1		1				1	1			4		
Bridgewater	61	39	Brown	Nathaniel		1			1	1				1			4		
Bridgewater	61	40	Bowker	Nelson	1		1			1		1					4		
Bridgewater	61	41	Churchill	Cornelius			1					1					2		
Bridgewater	61	42	Richards	Prince											4		4		
Bridgewater	61	43	Jess	Lucy											6		6		
Bridgewater	61	44	Crooker	Pero											2		2		
Bridgewater	61	45	Clap	Caesar											2		2		
Bridgewater	62	1	Alden	Joseph 2d				1		2			1				4		
Bridgewater	62	2	Melen	Samuel Junr				1					1				2		
Bridgewater	62	3	Alden	Sarah	2	1				1			1				5		
Bridgewater	62	4	Ames	Timothy	1				1	2	1			1			6		
Bridgewater	62	5	Ames	Noah			2		1		1			1			5		
Bridgewater	62	6	Ames	Daniel		1	2	1	1				2	1			8		
Bridgewater	62	7	Ames	Job	1	2	1		1		1			1			7		
Bridgewater	62	8	Alger	Daniel	1				1	2		1	1				6		
Bridgewater	62	9	Brett	Samuel					1				1	1			3		
Bridgewater	62	10	Brett	Samuel Jun		1	1		1	1	1	2	1				8		
Bridgewater	62	11	Brett	William		3		1		2		1	1				8		
Bridgewater	62	12	Brett	Isaac		2		1		1			1				5		
Bridgewater	62	13	Brett	Joseph	1			1				1					3		
Bridgewater	62	14	Beals	Jeremiah		1	1		1	2			1				7		
Bridgewater	62	15	Brattles	Samuel	3			1		1	2		1	1			9		
Bridgewater	62	16	Beals	Japhet	1	1			1				1	1			5		
Bridgewater	62	17	Beals	Isaac	1		4			1	1	1					8		
Bridgewater	62	18	Brett	Amasa	2			1		1	1		1				6		
Bridgewater	62	19	Brett	Calvin	2	1		1		2			1				7		
Bridgewater	62	20	Bryant	Philip	1		1	1	1	1		1					8		
Bridgewater	62	21	Bryant	Job	1		2		1		1			1			6		
Bridgewater	62	22	Bryant	Nathaniel	1			1		4			1				7		
Bridgewater	62	23	Hayward	Joseph					1					1			2		
Bridgewater	62	24	Hayward	Independence	2		1					1	1		1		6		
Bridgewater	62	25	Hall	Silvanus	2	2		1		2			1				8		
Bridgewater	62	26	Harden	John				1					1	1	2		5		
Bridgewater	62	27	Harden	John Junr	3			1		1			1	3			9		
Bridgewater	62	28	Harden	Nathan				1					1				2		
Bridgewater	62	29	Harden	Samuel	2		1	1		1		1	1				7		
Bridgewater	62	30	Harlow	Isaac		2	2	1					2				8		
Bridgewater	62	31	Harlow	Isaac 2d	1			1			1	1	1				5		
Bridgewater	62	32	Harvey	Betty			1							1			2		
Bridgewater	62	33	Harvey	Mehitabel	1					2			1				4		
Bridgewater	62	34	Harvey	Bezer	2		1			1			1				5		
Bridgewater	62	35	Holmes	Ellis			1		1	2		1		1			6		
Bridgewater	62	36	Holmes	Cornelius	3	1	2		1				1	1			10		
Bridgewater	62	37	Hooper	Hezekiah					1				1						
Bridgewater	62	38	Hooper	Winslow	1		1	2		2			1				7		
Bridgewater	62	39	Hooper	Joseph	1	1		1		2			1				6		
Bridgewater	62	40	Hooper	William	2	1		1					1				5		
Bridgewater	62	41	Hooper	James	1				1		1	1	1	1	1		7		
Bridgewater	62	42	Hill	David			1	1						2			4		
Bridgewater	62	43	Horton	Barnabas	1	1		1		1	1		1	1			7		
Bridgewater	62	44	Howard	Jonathan 3d	1		1			1			1				4		
Bridgewater	63	1	Perkins	Ebenezer	3			1		1			1				6		
Bridgewater	63	2	Perkins	James	1		1	1	1				2	3			9		
Bridgewater	63	3	Perkins	Rufus			3			1	1	1					6		
Bridgewater	63	4	Perkins	Abraham				1						1			2		
Bridgewater	63	5	Pierce	Jacob	2		1						1				4		
Bridgewater	63	6	Price	Benjamin	1				2			1		2			6		
Bridgewater	63	7	Pope	Benjamin	1	1	1						1				4		
Bridgewater	63	8	Pratt	Nathaniel	1	2			1	1	1	1		1			8		
Bridgewater	63	9	Pratt	Simeon	3		1	1			1		1				7		
Bridgewater	63	10	Pratt	Silvanus	1			1				2		1			5		
Bridgewater	63	11	Pratt	Asa				1				1					2		
Bridgewater	63	12	Pratt	Cornelius	3	1			1		1		1				7		
Bridgewater	63	13	Richards	James			1			1			1	1			4		
Bridgewater	63	14	Robinson	Dyer	3	1		1			1		1				7		
Bridgewater	63	15	Richards	Seth				1						1			2		
Bridgewater	63	16	Richards	Salmon	3	2		1				1	1				8		
Bridgewater	63	17	Ryder	Samuel			2						2				4		
Bridgewater	63	18	Sanger	Zedekiah	2	5	4	1	1	3		1	2				19		
Bridgewater	63	19	Shaw	Samuel	2			1				1		1	1		6		
Bridgewater	63	20	Snell	Benjamin		1			1	3		1	1				7		
Bridgewater	63	21	Snell	William		1			1	2		2	1	1			8		
Bridgewater	63	22	Storre	Elijah		1	1		1		1	1		1			6		
Bridgewater	63	23	Stetson	John		2		1		2							6		
Bridgewater	63	24	Pratt	Nathaniel					1			1		1			3		
Bridgewater	63	25	Porter	John	1			1		1			1				4		

17

TOWN	PG#	LN#	LAST NAME	FIRST NAME	under 10	10 to 16	16 to 26	26 to 45	45 and over	under 10	10 to 16	16 to 26	26 to 45	45 and over	TOTAL ALL OTHER	TOTAL SLAVES	TOTALS	DISTRICT/ TOWNSHIP	NOTES
			HEADS OF HOUSEHOLD		FREE WHITE MALES					FREE WHITE FEMALES									
Bridgewater	63	26	Pincin	William		1		1		1	1		1	1			6		
Bridgewater	63	27	Pincin	Benjamin				1		1	1		1	1			5		
Bridgewater	63	28	Pincin	Benjamin Junr	1		1			1		1					4		
Bridgewater	63	29	Pool	William	2		1			1			1				5		
Bridgewater	63	30	Parris	Benjamin	2				1	1			1	1			6		
Bridgewater	63	31	Perkins	Priscilla									1	1			2		
Bridgewater	63	32	Pool	Asa	2		1			1			1				5		
Bridgewater	63	33	Robinson	Benjamin	1	1	1		2	3		2	1	1			12		
Bridgewater	63	34	Robinson	William		2			1	3	1	1	1				9		
Bridgewater	63	35	Richards	Benjamin		2		1		1			1	2			7		
Bridgewater	63	36	Russel	Nathaniel	1		1	1					2	2			7		
Bridgewater	63	37	Russel	Abigail										1			1		
Bridgewater	63	38	Rogers	Samuel	3		1	1		1			1				7		
Bridgewater	63	39	Ramsdell	Joseph		1		1		3			1	2			8		
Bridgewater	63	40	Reed	Jonathan	3			1		2	1		1				8		
Bridgewater	63	41	Reed	Deborah		1	3				1			1			6		
Bridgewater	63	42	Shaw	Zechariah		1	1	1				1		2			6		
Bridgewater	63	43	Stetson	Ruth	1		1			2	2	2	1				9		
Bridgewater	63	44	Stetson	Abisha		1	1	1		2			1				6		
Bridgewater	63	45	Smith	Joseph				1			1			1			3		
Bridgewater	63	46	Smith	Joseph Junr		1				1		1					3		
Bridgewater	63	47	Smith	Henry T.	3			1		2			1				7		
Bridgewater	64	1	Snell	Pilycarpus		1		1		1	1		1				5		
Bridgewater	64	2	Snell	Stephen	2		1						1				4		
Bridgewater	64	3	Sever	Christopher	1	1		1		1			1				5		
Bridgewater	64	4	Thayer	John	1			1		3			1				6		
Bridgewater	64	5	Thomas	James				1					1				2		
Bridgewater	64	6	Thomas	Winslow	1			1		1		1	1				5		
Bridgewater	64	7	Torrey	Thomas			1	1						2			4		
Bridgewater	64	8	Torrey	Philip	2			1					1				4		
Bridgewater	64	9	Tirrel	John				1					1				2		
Bridgewater	64	10	Tirrel	John Junr			1			2		1					4		
Bridgewater	64	11	Vinton	William			2							1			3		
Bridgewater	64	12	Whitman	John	2	3	1		1	1		1		1			10		
Bridgewater	64	13	Whitman	Simeon	1			1						1			3		
Bridgewater	64	14	Whitman	Peter			1	1				1	3	1			7		
Bridgewater	64	15	Whitman	Benjamin				1		1		1	1				4		
Bridgewater	64	16	Whitman	Ezra	1			1		1		1	2	1			8		
Bridgewater	64	17	Whitman	Nicholas				1		1				1			3		
Bridgewater	64	18	Whitman	Eleazer		1	2	1				2	2	1			9		
Bridgewater	64	19	Whitman	Joseph	2	2		1					1				6		
Bridgewater	64	20	Whitman	Seth A.		1		1		1			1				4		
Bridgewater	64	21	Whitman	Nathan	2	1		1				1		1			6		
Bridgewater	64	22	Whitman	Benjamin Junr	1			1					1				3		
Bridgewater	64	23	Whitman	Isaac	1			1		2			1				5		
Bridgewater	64	24	Washburn	Levi	1	1	1		1	2	1	3	1				11		
Bridgewater	64	25	Washburn	Eleazer	1	2	2		1		1		1	1			9		
Bridgewater	64	26	Leonard	Silvanus	3			1		1	1		2	1			9		
Bridgewater	64	27	Leonard	Solomon				1			1		1				3		
Bridgewater	64	28	Leonard	Jonathan			1	1					1	1	1		4		
Bridgewater	64	29	Leonard	Nehemiah	1		1	1		2		1		1			7		
Bridgewater	64	30	Leonard	Jonas		2	1	2					1	1			7		
Bridgewater	64	31	Leonard	Barney	1			1					1	1			4		
Bridgewater	64	32	Leonard	David	2		2	1			2	1		1			10		
Bridgewater	64	33	Lewis	Eleazer		1			1					1			3		
Bridgewater	64	34	Mitchell	Edward Junr			2	1						2			5		
Bridgewater	64	35	Mitchell	Edward 3d			2	1		3			1	1			8		
Bridgewater	64	36	Mitchell	Theodore		1	1			1			2				5		
Bridgewater	64	37	Mitchell	William	1			1		2			2	1			7		
Bridgewater	64	38	Mitchell	Nathan	1			1		1	1	1	1		2		8		
Bridgewater	64	39	Mitchell	Daniel	1		1	1				1	1	1	1		7		
Bridgewater	64	40	Mitchell	Cary				1						1			2		
Bridgewater	64	41	Mitchell	John	1	1	1		1		2		1				7		
Bridgewater	64	42	Mehurin	Josiah				1		1	1	1	2		1		6		
Bridgewater	64	43	Mehurin	Josiah Junr	1			1					1				3		
Bridgewater	64	44	Morse	Ephraim	1			1	1				3	1			7		
Bridgewater	64	45	Orcutt	Deborah										1			1		
Bridgewater	64	46	Perkins	Jacob			2						1	1			4		
Bridgewater	64	47	Perkins	Enoch	3	1		1		2			1	1			9		
Bridgewater	65	1	Washburn	Salmon			1			1			1				3		
Bridgewater	65	2	Waite	James				1						1			2		
Bridgewater	65	3	Waite	James Junr	3	4	1					1	1	1			11		
Bridgewater	65	4	Whitman	Zechariah		1		1					2	1			5		
Bridgewater	65	5	Whitman	Noah		2	1		2	1			2	1			9		
Bridgewater	65	6	Willis	Benjamin		1		1	1					1			4		
Bridgewater	65	7	Willis	Joab			2	1				1	1	1			6		
Bridgewater	65	8	Willis	Daniel	3			1	1	1	3		1				9		
Bridgewater	65	9	Wetherell	Prince				1					1	2			4		
Bridgewater	65	10	Howe	Azor	2	1		1		4				1			9		
Bridgewater	65	11	Leonard	Jacob	2	1		1					1	1			6		
Bridgewater	65	12	Jones	John			1			2			1	1			5		
Bridgewater	65	13	Ashport	Cuff											5		5		
Bridgewater	65	14	Augustus	Casar											2		2		
Bridgewater	65	15	Pierce	America											7		7		
Bridgewater	65	16	Quawko	James											5		5		
Bridgewater	65	17	Kingman	David				1				1	1				3		
Bridgewater	65	18	Kingman	Ezra		1	1	1		2	2	1					8		
Bridgewater	65	19	Kingman	Barza	1			1		4				1	1		8		
Bridgewater	65	20	Keith	James				1			1		1	1			4		
Bridgewater	65	21	Keith	James Junr	3	2			1	1		1	2		1		11		

TOWN	PG#	LN#	LAST NAME	FIRST NAME	FREE WHITE MALES under 10	10 to 16	16 to 26	26 to 45	45 and over	FREE WHITE FEMALES under 10	10 to 16	16 to 26	26 to 45	45 and over	TOTAL ALL OTHER	TOTAL SLAVES	TOTALS	DISTRICT/ TOWNSHIP	NOTES
Bridgewater	65	22	Keith	Isaac	1	3		1		2			1				8		
Bridgewater	65	23	Keith	Holman	1	1		1		3	1		1				8		
Bridgewater	65	24	Keith	William	3	1		1			1	1					7		
Bridgewater	65	25	Keith	David			1		1	1		1		1			5		
Bridgewater	65	26	Keith	Levi	1	1		1	1				1				5		
Bridgewater	65	27	Keith	Zenas	2	1		1		1	1		1				7		
Bridgewater	65	28	Keith	Calvin	3		1					1					5		
Bridgewater	65	29	Keith	Eleazer		2	1		1		1			1			6		
Bridgewater	65	30	Keith	Eleazer Junr			1			1		1					3		
Bridgewater	65	31	Keith	John		2	1		1				1				5		
Bridgewater	65	32	Keith	John Junr			1					1					2		
Bridgewater	65	33	Keith	Thankful		2						1		1			4		
Bridgewater	65	34	Kinsley	Daniel	1	1		1			2		1				6		
Bridgewater	65	35	Kinsley	Rodulphus	1			1		2			1				5		
Bridgewater	65	36	Lazell	Silvanus			1		1	2	2		1		1		8		
Bridgewater	65	37	Lazell	John				1				1	1				3		
Bridgewater	65	38	Lazell	John Junr	2			1	1	1		1					6		
Bridgewater	65	39	Lazell	Byrum	1			1	1	2		1					6		
Bridgewater	65	40	Latham	Woodward		2		1				1		1			5		
Bridgewater	66	1	Latham	Seth				1					2				3		
Bridgewater	66	2	Lowden	Nathaniel				1				1		1			3		
Bridgewater	66	3	Mitchell	Cushing		3		1				1		1			6		
Bridgewater	66	4	Mitchell	Bradford		1	2		2	1		1					7		
Bridgewater	66	5	Mitchell	Nahum	1		1	1		1		2			1		7		
Bridgewater	66	6	Mitchell	Jacob				1					1				2		
Bridgewater	66	7	Mitchell	Seth				2				1	1				4		
Bridgewater	66	8	Mitchell	Seth Junr	3			1		1		1					6		
Bridgewater	66	9	Mitchell	Zenas	1			1				1					3		
Bridgewater	66	10	Marshall	Allen		1		1				1	1				4		
Bridgewater	66	11	Munro	Henry			1					1					2		
Bridgewater	66	12	Noyes	Ebenezer				1				1	1				3		
Bridgewater	66	13	Otis	Josiah	1	1	2		1		1	1		2			9		
Bridgewater	66	14	Orr	Hugh	2	1		1		3	1		2				10		
Bridgewater	66	15	Orr	Hector	1			1		2		1			1		6		
Bridgewater	66	16	Orr	Mary								1	1	1			3		
Bridgewater	66	17	Osborne	Thomas	1	2		1		3	1		1				9		
Bridgewater	66	18	Pratt	David		2		1		1			1				5		
Bridgewater	66	19	Pratt	Joshua	1	1		1		1	2		1				7		
Bridgewater	66	20	Pratt	Oliver	1		1			1			1				4		
Bridgewater	66	21	Phillips	Mark				1			2		1				4		
Bridgewater	66	22	Phillips	Mark Junr	2	1		1		2		1	1				8		
Bridgewater	66	23	Phillips	Thomas	1		1			1	1		1				5		
Bridgewater	66	24	Phillips	John	1			2		2			1				6		
Bridgewater	66	25	Phillips	Turner		2		1		1			1				5		
Bridgewater	66	26	Sprague	Ephraim		1	2	1		1	2						8		
Bridgewater	66	27	Swift	Isaac		1		1									2		
Bridgewater	66	28	Swift	Jireh	2	2	1	1		1		1	1	1			10		
Bridgewater	66	29	Swift	William				1				1	1				3		
Bridgewater	66	30	Swift	Isaac Junr			1	1		1		1					4		
Bridgewater	66	31	Starr	James		1		1		1			1				4		
Bridgewater	66	32	Starr	James Junr			1			1	1						3		
Bridgewater	66	33	Tucker	Benjamin	1	1											2		
Bridgewater	66	34	Tucker	Jedidah							1		1				2		
Bridgewater	66	35	Tolman	Daniel	1	2		1		2	1		1				8		
Bridgewater	66	36	Washburn	Daniel		1			1			2	1				5		
Bridgewater	66	37	Washburn	Oliver	3	1	1	1		1		1	1				9		
Bridgewater	66	38	Washburn	Calvin			2		1			1		1			5		
Bridgewater	66	39	Washburn	Thomas				1				1	2				4		
Bridgewater	66	40	Washburn	Benjamin				1				1	1				3		
Bridgewater	66	41	Washburn	Joshua	3	1		1			1		1				7		
Bridgewater	66	42	Washburn	Jeremiah		1		1				1	1				4		
Bridgewater	66	43	Washburn	Desire			1					1	1				3		
Bridgewater	66	44	Washburn	Rebecca								1	1				2		
Bridgewater	66	45	Washburn	Lois									1				1		
Bridgewater	67	1	Brown	John		1	1		1				1	1			5		
Bridgewater	67	2	Brown	Isaac	2	1		1		1			1				6		
Bridgewater	67	3	Brown	Charles	1			1		1		1					4		
Bridgewater	67	4	Briggs	George		1			1					2			4		
Bridgewater	67	5	Bisbee	John	4	1	1		1	2	1	1	1	1			13		
Bridgewater	67	6	Bonney	William	2			1		1			2				6		
Bridgewater	67	7	Brett	Uriah				1		2			1				4		
Bridgewater	67	8	Byram	Josiah				1		1	1	1		1			5		
Bridgewater	67	9	Byram	David	2			1		2			1				6		
Bridgewater	67	10	Byram	Matilda						1	1		1				3		
Bridgewater	67	11	Allen	Mary									1	1			2		
Bridgewater	67	12	Bolton	Betty								1	1				2		
Bridgewater	67	13	Bolton	Joseph				1		2			1				4		
Bridgewater	67	14	Cary	Ephraim	1		2		1		1			1			6		
Bridgewater	67	15	Chamberlin	Benjamin				1				1	2	1			5		
Bridgewater	67	16	Cary	Mary										3			3		
Bridgewater	67	17	Chamberlin	Lewis	1			1					1				3		
Bridgewater	67	18	Chamberlin	Nathaniel					1				1				2		
Bridgewater	67	19	Chamberlin	Joseph	1	1		1			1		1				5		
Bridgewater	67	20	Chamberlin	Thomas		1		1		3	1		1				7		
Bridgewater	67	21	Chamberlin	Isaac	3			1		2			2	2			10		
Bridgewater	67	22	Curtis	Simeon	2		2	1		3	1		1				10		
Bridgewater	67	23	Crandell	Ezra			1			1		1					3		
Bridgewater	67	24	Clift	Adna Winslow			1			2	2		1				6		
Bridgewater	67	25	Clift	Nathaniel		1				1		1					3		
Bridgewater	67	26	Dawes	Nathan			1		1	1		1	1				5		

TOWN	PG#	LN#	LAST NAME	FIRST NAME	FREE WHITE MALES					FREE WHITE FEMALES					TOTAL ALL OTHER	TOTAL SLAVES	TOTALS	DISTRICT/ TOWNSHIP	NOTES
					under 10	10 to 16	16 to 26	26 to 45	45 and over	under 10	10 to 16	16 to 26	26 to 45	45 and over					
Bridgewater	67	27	Edson	Joel	2	2	1	1	1				3	1			11		
Bridgewater	67	28	Fullarton	Asa		2	1	1						1			5		
Bridgewater	67	29	Faxon	Samuel	1	1		1		1	2		1	1			8		
Bridgewater	67	30	French	David	1		2			1		1					5		
Bridgewater	67	31	French	Silas		1		1			1		1				4		
Bridgewater	67	32	French	Daniel	1			1		1			1				4		
Bridgewater	67	33	Foster	Samuel	1			1	1	2			1				6		
Bridgewater	67	34	Gannett	Simeon		1	1		1	1	2	1	1	1			9		
Bridgewater	67	35	Gannett	Joseph	2	1		2		2	1		1				9		
Bridgewater	67	36	Gurney	Seth	3	1		1		1	1		1	1			9		
Bridgewater	67	37	Gardner	John	1			1		1	1		1				5		
Bridgewater	67	38	Harris	Benjamin				1						1			2		
Bridgewater	67	39	Harris	Arthur	1	1		1		1	1	1		1			7		
Bridgewater	67	40	Harris	William	1		1			2			1				5		
Bridgewater	67	41	Harris	John	1		1			1			1				4		
Bridgewater	67	42	Hayward	Sarah	1					1	1	1	1				4		
Bridgewater	67	43	Hatch	John		1		1	1				1	1			5		
Bridgewater	67	44	Hatch	Luther	2	1		1		2			1				7		
Bridgewater	67	45	Hayward	Oliver	1		1	1		1			3				7		
Bridgewater	67	46	Hill	Jacob	1	2		1	1	1		1					9		
Bridgewater	68	1	Hill	Josiah Junr				1		1	1		1				4		
Bridgewater	68	2	Hide	Ephraim		3	1			2	1		1				8		
Bridgewater	68	3	Hooper	John				1					1	1			3		
Bridgewater	68	4	Harden	Phebe		1					2		1				4		
Bridgewater	68	5	Harden	John 2d	2	1	1		1	2			1				8		
Bridgewater	68	6	Harden	Relief						1			1				2		
Bridgewater	68	7	Hearsey	William				1					1				2		
Bridgewater	68	8	Hearsey	Solomon		1	1		1	1			1				5		
Bridgewater	68	9	Hearsey	Stephen	2	1			1	5		1	1				11		
Bridgewater	68	10	Hearsey	Joseph		1							1				2		
Bridgewater	68	11	Hathaway	Ebenezer	1	1		1		4			1				8		
Bridgewater	68	12	Hobart	Seth	1	2		1		2	1	1	1				9		
Bridgewater	68	13	Howard	Jennet									1				1		
Bridgewater	68	14	Howard	Caleb		1		1			2		1				5		
Bridgewater	68	15	Hudson	Nathan		1		1					1				3		
Bridgewater	68	16	Hudson	John		2	1	1		1	1	1	1				8		
Bridgewater	68	17	Hudson	William				1					1				2		
Bridgewater	68	18	Hearsey	William Junr	1		1	1		1	2		1				7		
Bridgewater	68	19	Johnson	Josiah				1					1				2		
Bridgewater	68	20	Johnson	Nathan	2		1			1	1		1				6		
Bridgewater	68	21	Josselyn	Joseph	4	4		1		1			1				11		
Bridgewater	68	22	Josselyn	Mary									1				1		
Bridgewater	68	23	Angier	Samuel		1		1				1	1		2		6		
Bridgewater	68	24	Alden	Nathan				1		1			1				3		
Bridgewater	68	25	Alden	Nathan Junr	1	1	1	1		1		2	1				8		
Bridgewater	68	26	Alden	Jonathan		1	1	1		1			1				5		
Bridgewater	68	27	Alden	Isaac	2			1				1	1				5		
Bridgewater	68	28	Alden	Isaac Junr			1			2			1				4		
Bridgewater	68	29	Alden	Ezra	1		1					1					3		
Bridgewater	68	30	Allen	Simeon	1	1	1		1				2				6		
Bridgewater	68	31	Allen	Asahel			1	1			1	1	1				5		
Bridgewater	68	32	Allen	David	2		2	1	1	1	1	1	1				10		
Bridgewater	68	33	Allen	Isaac		2		1		1		1	1				6		
Bridgewater	68	34	Allen	Joseph		1	1	1		1		1					5		
Bridgewater	68	35	Allen	Barza			1			1		2					4		
Bridgewater	68	36	Allen	Matthew			1			4	2		1	1			9		
Bridgewater	68	37	Allen	Pratt	2		1			1			1				5		
Bridgewater	68	38	Barrel	James		1		1		2	1	1	1				7		
Bridgewater	68	39	Barrel	Joshua	1	2	1		1		1		1				7		
Bridgewater	68	40	Beals	Jonathan				1					1				2		
Bridgewater	68	41	Bates	Christopher	2	2		1		2			1				8		
Bridgewater	68	42	Bearce	Job	1		2		1	2	1	1		1			9		

TOWN	PG#	LN#	LAST NAME	FIRST NAME	FWM under 10	FWM 10 to 16	FWM 16 to 26	FWM 26 to 45	FWM 45 and over	FWF under 10	FWF 10 to 16	FWF 16 to 26	FWF 26 to 45	FWF 45 and over	TOTAL ALL OTHER	TOTAL SLAVES	TOTALS	DISTRICT/ TOWNSHIP	NOTES
Carver	5	1	Berry	John	1			1		1			1				4		
Carver	5	2	Washburn	William			1		1				1	1			4		
Carver	5	3	Attwood	John	1			1		3			1				6		
Carver	5	4	Attwood	William			2		1			1		1			5		
Carver	5	5	Shaw	Silvanus	2	2		1		2	1		1				9		
Carver	5	6	Thomas	Eli	1	1		1		2	1		1				7		
Carver	5	7	Hart	Swansey											5		5		
Carver	7	1	Ranhorne	Rebecca									1	1			2		
Carver	7	2	Sturtevants	William			2	1					3				6		
Carver	7	3	Cobb	Nehemiah	1	1	1		1			2	1	1			8		
Carver	7	4	Vaughan	Nathaniel	1			1		1	1		1				5		
Carver	7	5	Faunce	Daniel			2		1			2		1			6		
Carver	7	6	Cole	Job	1	1		1		2	2	1	1				9		
Carver	7	7	Cobb	Timothy		1	2		1			1		1			6		
Carver	7	8	Cobb	William				1	1				1	1			4		
Carver	7	9	Savery	Thomas			1		1		1	1		1			5		
Carver	7	10	Bisbee	Asaph	2	2		1		1	1		1				8		
Carver	7	11	Fuller	Isechar		1			1	2	2			1			7		
Carver	7	12	Howland	John Revd					1								1		
Carver	7	13	Howland	Calvin	1			1				2		1			5		
Carver	7	14	Barrows	James	1			1		1			1				4		
Carver	7	15	Burden	Gashum			1		1	1			1				3		
Carver	7	16	Cole	Sarah								1		2			3		
Carver	7	17	Cobb	Joseph		1			1	1				1			4		
Carver	7	18	Shaw	Levi				1					1				2		
Carver	7	19	Shaw	Benjamin	2	1		1		1	1	1	1	1			9		
Carver	7	20	Perkins	Gideon	2	1		1		1	2		1				8		
Carver	7	21	Lucas	Isaac L.	1	2		1		1	2		1				8		
Carver	7	22	Perkins	Luke	1			1			1		1				4		
Carver	7	23	Perkins	Samson			1					1					2		
Carver	8	1	Shurtleff	Francis		1		1			1		1				4		
Carver	8	2	Barrows	Carver			2	1					1				4		
Carver	8	3	Griffith	Ephraim	1			1		1			1				4		
Carver	8	4	Griffith	Obia	1		1			2		1					5		
Carver	8	5	Howes	Jacob	4			1					1				6		
Carver	8	6	Dolen	Thomas				1	1	2				1			5		
Carver	8	7	Dunham	Israel		1	1		1	1				1			5		
Carver	8	8	Sherman	Rufus		1	3		1			2	1				8		
Carver	8	9	Chase	Consider			1		1					1			3		
Carver	8	10	Chase	Levi	4	1		1		1			1				8		
Carver	8	11	Sherman	Nathaniel		1	2		1	1	1		1				7		
Carver	8	12	Shaw	James	2	1		1		2	1		1				8		
Carver	8	13	Shaw	Jonathan	2	1	1		1	2		2		1			10		
Carver	8	14	Churchill	Jabez	1		1	1		3	1		1				8		
Carver	8	15	Shurtleff	Barnabas		1	1		1		1	1		1			6		
Carver	8	16	Shaw	Joseph	1	1	4		1	2	2			1			12		
Carver	8	17	Attwood	John			1		2					1			4		
Carver	8	18	Ellis	Joseph			2	1	1			2		1			7		
Carver	8	19	Attwood	Samuel		2	1		1	3		2		1			10		
Carver	8	20	Attwood	Nathaniel	1	1		1	1	2	1		1	1			9		
Carver	8	21	Attwood	Joshua	4		1						1				6		
Carver	8	22	Attwood	Joseph	2		2		1	2	1		1				9		
Carver	8	23	Shurtleff	David	2	1	2		1	1	1	3		1			12		
Carver	9	1	Lucas	John			1	1	1			1	1	1			6		
Carver	9	2	Lucas	Beza	3			1					2	1			6		
Carver	9	3	Lucas	Abijah	3	1			1	2	1		1				9		
Carver	9	4	Robbins	Joseph	2			1			2	1					6		
Carver	9	5	Ward	Benjamin	1	1	1		1	1		1		1			7		
Carver	9	6	Holmes	Simeon					1					3			4		
Carver	9	7	Barrows	Andrew	2	2		1			1	2	1				9		
Carver	9	8	Ward	Drusilla	1						2		2	1			6		
Carver	9	9	Shaw	John Jr	2		1		1	2		2		1			9		
Carver	9	10	Shaw	John					1				1		1		3		
Carver	9	11	Attwood	Francis			1			1		1					3		
Carver	9	12	Hammond	Rowland			2		1		1	2					6		
Carver	9	13	Shurtleff	Benjamin	3	1	3		1	2	1			1			12		
Carver	9	14	Shurtleff	William				1					1				2		
Carver	9	15	Shurtleff	Ebenezer	1			1				1	1				5		
Carver	9	16	Shurtleff	Gideon	4	1		1		3	2		1				12		
Carver	9	17	Vaughan	John	3		2		1			2	1	1			10		
Carver	9	18	Vaughan	Samuel		1	3		1			2		1			8		
Carver	9	19	Pratt	Ephraim	3	1	1	1		1	1		1				9		
Carver	9	20	Vale	Jacob	2				1	1			1				5		
Carver	9	21	Lucas	Samuel	3	1	2		1			1	1	1			10		
Carver	9	22	Morton	Job		1			1	3	1		1	1			8		
Carver	9	23	Dolen	Ebenezer	2			1		3			1				7		
Carver	9	24	Dolen	Edward	1			1		1			1				4		
Carver	10	1	Pratt	Noah					1					1			2		
Carver	10	2	Pratt	Isaiah	1			1		2			1				5		

TOWN	PG#	LN#	LAST NAME	FIRST NAME	FREE WHITE MALES					FREE WHITE FEMALES					TOTAL ALL OTHER	TOTAL SLAVES	TOTALS	DISTRICT/ TOWNSHIP	NOTES
					under 10	10 to 16	16 to 26	26 to 45	45 and over	under 10	10 to 16	16 to 26	26 to 45	45 and over					
Carver	10	3	Pratt	Hannah		1				2			1				4		
Carver	10	4	Randsome	Benjamin	1			1		1	1	1	2	1			8		
Carver	10	5	Cole	Lemuel		1		1		2	1		1				6		
Carver	10	6	Cole	Lemuel	3	1			1		1		1				7		
Carver	10	7	Sherman	John	2	2		1			1		1				7		
Carver	10	8	Crocker	Heman	3	1			1	1	2			1			9		
Carver	10	9	Crocker	Mercy	2								1				3		
Carver	10	10	Bisbee	Jonah	1	1			1		1			1			5		
Carver	10	11	Randsome	David					1				2				3		
Carver	10	12	Randsome	Joseph		1	1	1			1	1	1				3		
Carver	10	13	Stephens	Edward				1		1							2		
Carver	10	14	Barrows	Joshua	1			1		1			1				4		
Carver	10	15	Lucas	Joanna			1							1			2		
Carver	10	16	Lucas	Barnabas	2	2		1		2			1				8		
Carver	10	17	Lucas	Nehemiah	2			1		1			1				5		
Carver	10	18	Cole	Betsey		1	1				1			1			4		
Carver	10	19	Cobb	Isaac	1	1		1	1	2	1		1				8		
Carver	10	20	Rider	Giles			1			1			1				3		
Carver	10	21	Vaughan	James		1		1		2			1				6		
Carver	10	22	Tilsn	Isaiah			1		1	1				1			4		
Carver	10	23	Cobb	Barnabas	2			1		3		1	1				8		
Carver	10	24	Cobb	Benjamin	2	2	1	1		1	1	1					9		
Carver	11	1	Stetson	Jonathan	1			1		1			1				4		
Carver	11	2	Perry	Jonathan	1			1		3	1		1				7		
Carver	11	3	Samson	Joseph	1			1		1			1				4		
Carver	11	4	Tilson	Jonathan	1			1		1			1				4		
Carver	11	5	Perry	Judah	2			1		1			1				5		
Carver	11	6	Wright	Moses	1	1		1		3			1				7		
Carver	11	7	Barrows	James	3			1		3			1				8		
Carver	11	8	Wrightington	Thomas	1	2	2		1	1				1			8		
Carver	11	9	Bumpus	Edward	1	1		1					1				4		
Carver	11	10	Bumpus	John	1			1					1				3		
Carver	11	11	Bumpus	Benjamin	2			1		1			1				5		
Carver	11	12	Bumpus	Daniel	3			1		2	1		1				8		
Carver	11	13	Bumpus	Thankful	1					1		1					3		
Carver	11	14	Harvey	Frederick	2			1		2			1				6		
Carver	11	15	King	Amaziah			2		1	2	2			1			8		
Carver	11	16	Dunham	Ebenezer	2			1		1	1		1				6		
Carver	11	17	Morton	Elisha			1	1						1			3		
Carver	11	18	Shaw	David				1						1			2		
Carver	11	19	Wright	Caleb	2			1		1			1				5		
Carver	11	20	Shaw	Crispus			1		1	1				1			4		
Carver	11	21	White	Benjamin		1			1					1			3		
Carver	12	1	Murdock	William	3			1					1	1			6		
Carver	12	2	Murdock	Elisha		1		1		4	1		1				8		
Carver	12	3	Standish	Nathaniel	1		1	1		3	2		1				9		
Carver	12	4	Gready	Martin			1						1				2		
Carver	12	5	Shurtleff	Lothrop			1			2		1					4		
Carver	12	6	Barrows	Peleg	3	1	2		1	1			1	1			10		
Carver	12	7	Shaw	Elder	1			1					1				3		
Carver	12	8	Morrisey	John	1			1					1				3		
Carver	12	9	Murdock	John	2		2	1		1	1	1	1	1			10		
Carver	12	10	McFarling	Huit	2		1	1		2			1				7		
Carver	12	11	Savery	Peleg	2	1		1	1	3			1				9		
Carver	12	12	Attwood	Caleb	1	1			1	2	2	2	1				10		
Carver	12	13	Munham	John				1		2	1		1				5		
Carver	12	14	Drew	Nicholas	1		1						1				3		
Carver	12	15	Lucas	Anselm			1			3			1				5		
Carver	12	16	Robbins	Eleazer	1		1			2	1	1		1			8		
Carver	12	17	Lucas	Ephraim	1			1		4			1				7		
Carver	12	18	Dunham	John		1		1					1				3		
Carver	12	19	Dunham	Caleb			1			2	1						4		
Carver	12	20	Dunham	Mary		2		1		3			1	1			8		
Carver	12	21	Cole	Joshua	1			1					1				3		
Carver	12	22	Wood	David	1	1		1	1	1	1	1					7		
Carver	12	23	Apling	John	1	1	1	1			1		1				6		
Carver	12	24	Lucas	Joseph		1		1			2		1				5		

TOWN	PG#	LN#	HEADS OF HOUSEHOLD		FREE WHITE MALES					FREE WHITE FEMALES					TOTAL ALL OTHER	TOTAL SLAVES	TOTALS	DISTRICT/ TOWNSHIP	NOTES
			LAST NAME	FIRST NAME	under 10	10 to 16	16 to 26	26 to 45	45 and over	under 10	10 to 16	16 to 26	26 to 45	45 and over					
Duxbury	91	1	Winslow	*				1	1			1	2	1			6		Tape Mark
Duxbury	91	2	Hall	*	1				1	1	1		1	1			6		Tape Mark
Duxbury	91	3	Kent	William		1	2		1	1	1	1		1			8		
Duxbury	91	4	Lewis	Luther			2					1		1			4		
Duxbury	91	5	Baker	Celia								1	1	1			3		
Duxbury	91	6	Eames	Benjamin	3	1	1		1	1	1	1		1			10		
Duxbury	91	7	Baker	Samuel			1						1				2		
Duxbury	91	8	White	Daniel	3	2			1	2	1		1				10		
Duxbury	91	9	Rogers	Peleg			1			2			1				4		
Duxbury	91	10	Lewis	Calvin	1	1		1		1	1		1				6		
Duxbury	91	11	Keen	Simeon	1		1						1				3		
Duxbury	91	12	Day	John			1			1			1				3		
Duxbury	91	13	Phillips	Elisha Esq			1	1			1		1	1			5		
Duxbury	91	14	Harte	Benjamin	1			1					1				3		
Duxbury	91	15	Hall	Adam			1	1					3	1			6		
Duxbury	91	16	Shearman	Ignatius		1		1	1	1		1	1	1			7		
Duxbury	91	17	Phillips	Daniel	3	1		2				1	1				8		
Duxbury	91	18	Shearman	Elizabeth		1				1	1	1		1			5		
Duxbury	91	19	Shearman	Lucy									1				1		
Duxbury	91	20	White	Elizabeth			1	1			1	2	2				7		
Duxbury	91	21	Hall	Luke	3		1						1				5		
Duxbury	91	22	Kea*	*			1				1			1			3		Tape Mark
Duxbury	91	23	Eames	Wm															Tape Mark
Duxbury	91	24	Dingley	J*			1						1				2		
Duxbury	91	25	Dingley	John	2		1			1			1				5		
Duxbury	91	26	Wetherly	Charles			1			2			1				4		
Duxbury	91	27	Dingley	Abner	1			1				1	1				4		
Duxbury	91	28	Dingley	Abner Jun	2		1	1		1	2		1				8		
Duxbury	91	29	Keith	George	2	2		1		4			1				10		
Duxbury	91	30	Peterson	Lydia									2		5		7		
Duxbury	93	1	Weston	Joseph	2	2	2		1	2	1	1	1				12		
Duxbury	93	2	Weston	Peleg			1						1				2		
Duxbury	93	3	Hathaway	Rufus Doct	1			1		2		1					5		
Duxbury	93	4	Simons	Cyrus				1					1				2		
Duxbury	93	5	Simons	Wm				1					1				2		
Duxbury	93	6	Simons	Wm Jun		1	1						1				3		
Duxbury	93	7	Simons	Seth	2	1	1			1			1				6		
Duxbury	93	8	Chandler	Abel	2			1		2	1	2		1			9		
Duxbury	93	9	Hatch	Zephemiah	1		1			1			1				4		
Duxbury	93	10	Weston	Asa	2	1	2		1			1	1				8		
Duxbury	93	11	Weston	Jacob	1	2		1		1	1		1	1			8		
Duxbury	93	12	Southworth	James			1	2	1		1	2		1			8		
Duxbury	93	13	Alden	Amharst		1		1		1			1	1			5		
Duxbury	93	14	Delano	Cornelius		3		1					1				5		
Duxbury	93	15	Delano	Lydia									3	2			5		
Duxbury	93	16	Kent	Ichabod			1	1				3		1			6		
Duxbury	93	17	Chandler	Henery	2			1					1				4		
Duxbury	93	18	Frazer	Samuel	2		2	1		2	1		1				9		
Duxbury	93	19	Samson	Nathan				1					4				5		
Duxbury	93	20	Thomas	Winslow	4			1		2	1		1				9		
Duxbury	93	21	Delano	Jepther	1			1		1	1	1	1	1			7		
Duxbury	93	22	Winslow	Edward															Enumeration left blank
Duxbury	94	1	Konder	William	1			1		5			1				8		
Duxbury	94	2	Drew	Reuben	2		1	1		1			1				6		
Duxbury	94	3	Drew	Syls	1				1		3	1	1				7		
Duxbury	94	4	Drew	Charles	2			1		2	1		1				7		
Duxbury	94	5	Soule	Simeon	1	1	2		1	1	2		1				9		
Duxbury	94	6	Peterson	Reuben	2	2	1		1	2	1	1		1			11		
Duxbury	94	7	Cushman	George	1	1		1		4	1		1				9		
Duxbury	94	8	Joyce	Asa	3			1		1			1				6		
Duxbury	94	9	Weston	Azra	2		6	1					1	1			11		
Duxbury	94	10	Weston	Azra Jun	2			1		1	1		1				6		
Duxbury	94	11	Drew	Joseph			1	1			1	1	1				5		
Duxbury	94	12	Chandler	Aron	1			1		1			1				4		
Duxbury	94	13	Putnam	Jonathan	1	1	1	1	1		1	3		1			10		
Duxbury	94	14	Brewster	Joshua	2	1		1		2			1				7		
Duxbury	94	15	Chandler	Thomas Jun			1			1		1					3		
Duxbury	94	16	Burges	Ruth									1	1			2		
Duxbury	94	17	Brewster	Joseph	2	1	1		1	2		2		1			10		
Duxbury	94	18	Alden	Abigail							2	2		1			5		
Duxbury	94	19	Taylor	John			1			1			1				3		
Duxbury	94	20	Hemet	Asa	1		1					1					3		
Duxbury	94	21	Winslow	Edward				1						2			3		
Duxbury	94	22	Simons	Charles			1			1				1			3		
Duxbury	94	23	Alden	Wrestling				1		1			3	5			10		
Duxbury	94	24	Alden	Josiah	2	1		1		2	1		1				8		
Duxbury	94	25	Alden	Lydia									2	2			4		
Duxbury	95	1	Holmes	Nathl			1			2			1				4		
Duxbury	95	2	Wadworth	Wait	2		1		1	1	2		1				8		
Duxbury	95	3	Samson	Elijah		1	1	1		2	1		1				7		
Duxbury	95	4	Sprague	Seth	2	1	2		1	4	1	3	2	1			17		
Duxbury	95	5	Weston	Michel				1		1		1	2				5		
Duxbury	95	6	Glass	Suraiah	1	2	1		1	1		1	2	1			10		
Duxbury	95	7	Glass	Nathl	1			1					1				3		
Duxbury	95	8	Bradford	Daniel			1			1			1				3		
Duxbury	95	9	Delano	Samuel			1	1	1			2		1			6		
Duxbury	95	10	Freeman	Enoch			2		1			2		1			6		
Duxbury	95	11	Waterman	Eliphalet	1			1				1					4		
Duxbury	95	12	Winsor	Joseph	1	2	2		1			1		1	1		10		
Duxbury	95	13	Winsor	John	1	2			1	2			2	1			9		

23

TOWN	PG#	LN#	LAST NAME	FIRST NAME	FREE WHITE MALES					FREE WHITE FEMALES					TOTAL ALL OTHER	TOTAL SLAVES	TOTALS	DISTRICT/TOWNSHIP	NOTES
					under 10	10 to 16	16 to 26	26 to 45	45 and over	under 10	10 to 16	16 to 26	26 to 45	45 and over					
Duxbury	95	14	Delano	Samuel Jun	2		1	1		2		1	1				8		
Duxbury	95	15	Bates	Seth	2			1		2			1				6		
Duxbury	95	16	Loreing	George			2							1			3		
Duxbury	95	17	Brown	Lydia										1			1		
Duxbury	95	18	Allyn	John Rvd	2			1		1	1		1				6		
Duxbury	95	19	Bradford	Gamaliel Esq			1	1	1	1			2	2			8		
Duxbury	95	20	Freeman	Wm	2		2	1		1			1				7		
Duxbury	95	21	Hunt	Thomas Jun	2	1	1	1	1	2	1	1	1				11		
Duxbury	95	22	Macfarlin	Sarah									1				1		
Duxbury	95	23	Alden	Judah Esquire	1	2			2	2	1	2	1				11		
Duxbury	96	1	Soule	Nathl	1			1		2			1				5		
Duxbury	96	2	Burges	Jacob	3	1	1		1	1		1	1				9		
Duxbury	96	3	Glass	James	1		2		1	1			1				6		
Duxbury	96	4	Samson	Thomas	2		1	1		2	1		1				8		
Duxbury	96	5	Soule	Josiah		2	1	1	1	3			1				9		
Duxbury	96	6	Patengal	Daniel	2	1	1										4		
Duxbury	96	7	Barton	John	2	1	1	1					1				6		
Duxbury	96	8	Partridge	Calvin	1		2	1	1	2		1	1				9		
Duxbury	96	9	Simons	Noah		1	1	1			1			1			5		
Duxbury	96	10	Delano	Malachi				1					1				2		
Duxbury	96	11	Peterson	Thadeus			2		1		2	1		1			7		
Duxbury	96	12	Delano	Judah				1						2			3		
Duxbury	96	13	Perkins	Calvin	1		1			1			1				4		
Duxbury	96	14	Delano	Asa	1			1		1			1				4		
Duxbury	96	15	Delano	Phillip	1		1	1		2	1		1				7		
Duxbury	96	16	Winsor	Wm		1	1	1		2	1	1	1				8		
Duxbury	96	17	Chandler	Aron	1			1		1			1				4		
Duxbury	96	18	Thomas	Charles	3			1					1				5		
Duxbury	96	19	Winsor	Jerusha		1		1		2		1					5		
Duxbury	96	20	Winsor	Edward Junr	1		2	1		1			1				6		
Duxbury	97	1	Walker	Samuel	2	1		1		2			1				7		
Duxbury	97	2	Soule	Ezekiel		2	3		1	1				1			8		
Duxbury	97	3	Soule	Wm	3	2		1		1		1					8		
Duxbury	97	4	Wadsworth	Joseph	1	2			1	1	2	1		1			9		
Duxbury	97	5	Drew	Isaac	4	1	2		2	3	2			1			15		
Duxbury	97	6	Southworth	Edward	1	2	2		1			1		1			8		
Duxbury	97	7	Southworth	Edward Jun	1		1	1		1		1					5		
Duxbury	97	8	Southworth	James Jun	1		1	1		1	1	1					6		
Duxbury	97	9	Thomas	Josiah		1				1		1					3		
Duxbury	97	10	Wadsworth	Eden	2			1			2		1				6		
Duxbury	97	11	Wadsworth	Joseph Jun	1			1					1				3		
Duxbury	97	12	Soule	Mercy				1						1			2		
Duxbury	97	13	Weston	Zebdiel		1	1	1						1			4		
Duxbury	97	14	Baker	Dotty	4			1					1				6		
Duxbury	97	15	Bradford	Zadoch	1	1		1		1		2					6		
Duxbury	97	16	Partridge	George Esquire				1			1	1	1				4		
Duxbury	97	17	Brown	Amos		1		1		2	1		1				6		
Duxbury	97	18	Prior	Joseph	2			1					1				4		
Duxbury	97	19	Holmes	Bartlett	2		1	2					1				6		
Duxbury	97	20	Bosworth	Benjm	2		2	1		2		1	1				9		
Duxbury	97	21	Churchel	Stephen	1		2	1					1				5		
Duxbury	97	22	Churchel	Peleg	2	1		1		2			1				7		
Duxbury	97	23	Bent	Lot	1		3		1	1		2	1	1			10		
Duxbury	97	24	Holmes	Nathl	2			1					1				4		
Duxbury	98	1	Winsor	Samuel	2	1	3		1	1		1		1			10		
Duxbury	98	2	Howard	Jesse	2			1		1			1				5		
Duxbury	98	3	Samson	Job	1	1		1		1	1		1				6		
Duxbury	98	4	Winsor	James	3			1		2		1	1				8		
Duxbury	98	5	Cushing	Joshua Jun	1		1	1		3		1	1				8		
Duxbury	98	6	Wadsworth	Zenoth	1			1		1			1				4		
Duxbury	98	7	Joyce	Lucy						2			1				3		
Duxbury	98	8	Cushing	Joshua					1					1			2		
Duxbury	98	9	Hunt	Judah		1		1		1		2	1	1			7		
Duxbury	98	10	Yendal	Samuel		1		1		4			1				7		
Duxbury	98	11	Sprague	Uriah		1			1		1	3		2			8		
Duxbury	98	12	Wadsworth	Ahira Jun				1				1					2		
Duxbury	98	13	Coomer	Wm	1	1		1			1		1				5		
Duxbury	98	14	Glass	Ezekiel	2			1	1				1				5		
Duxbury	98	15	Samson	Elijah Jun	2			1		1	1		1				6		
Duxbury	98	16	Samson	Studley	1	2		1		1	1		1				7		
Duxbury	98	17	Samson	Abner				1					1				2		
Duxbury	98	18	Samson	Bartlett				1		1			1				3		
Duxbury	98	19	Smith	Benjm	2	1	1		1	2	2	2	1				12		
Duxbury	98	20	Samson	Isaac	1			1		2			1				5		
Duxbury	98	21	Brewster	Cyrus	1			1					1				3		
Duxbury	98	22	Delano	Nathl	1	2			1	1			1	1			7		
Duxbury	98	23	Wadsworth	Robert				1		1		1	1				4		
Duxbury	98	24	Delano	Luther				1						1			2		
Duxbury	99	1	Bradford	Samuel	1	1		1	1		1	1					7		
Duxbury	99	2	Bradford	Seth		1		1	1			2	1				6		
Duxbury	99	3	Chandler	Bisbe	1	1			1	2	2		1				8		
Duxbury	99	4	Darling	Samuel	3	1		1		3		1					9		
Duxbury	99	5	Freman	Edmond		1	1	1	1			2		1			7		
Duxbury	99	6	Samson	Andrew		1		1		1			1				4		
Duxbury	99	7	Bradford	Seth Jun				1		2		1					4		
Duxbury	99	8	Chandler	Samuel		1			2	3	1	3		1			11		
Duxbury	99	9	Winson	Nathl		1	2		1	1	3	1		1			10		
Duxbury	99	10	Samson	Constant	1							1	1				3		
Duxbury	99	11	Delano	Isaac	1	1		1		3	2	1					9		
Duxbury	99	12	Soule	Abigal		2	1	1				1		2			7		

TOWN	PG#	LN#	LAST NAME	FIRST NAME	FREE WHITE MALES under 10	10 to 16	16 to 26	26 to 45	45 and over	FREE WHITE FEMALES under 10	10 to 16	16 to 26	26 to 45	45 and over	TOTAL ALL OTHER	TOTAL SLAVES	TOTALS	DISTRICT/ TOWNSHIP	NOTES
Duxbury	99	13	Wadsworth	Dura	2	2		1		3			1				9		
Duxbury	99	14	Wadsworth	Ira	1	1		1			1		1				5		
Duxbury	99	15	Loreing	Jotham		1						1	1	1	1		5		
Duxbury	99	16	Prior	Joseph			2	1	1		1	1	1	1			8		
Duxbury	99	17	Thomas	Peleg	1	1		1					1	1			5		
Duxbury	99	18	Thomas	Josiah		1				1			1				3		
Duxbury	99	19	Peterson	Joshua	2	2		1				1	1				7		
Duxbury	99	20	Barstow	Joseph	4	2		1		1			1				9		
Duxbury	99	21	Chandler	Ezekiel		1		1						1			3		
Duxbury	100	1	Cushman	Joshua		1		1						1			3		
Duxbury	100	2	Cushman	Ezra	1			1					1				3		
Duxbury	100	3	Prior	Benjm		1		1			1			1			4		
Duxbury	100	4	Prior	Jabez	1			1		1			1				4		
Duxbury	100	5	Prior	Mathew	1			1			1						3		
Duxbury	100	6	Prior	Eliphaz				1					1				2		
Duxbury	100	7	Prior	Sylvanus	2			1		2			1				6		
Duxbury	100	8	Loreing	Freeman	2	1	1	1		2			1				8		
Duxbury	100	9	Hall	Daniel	1	1		1					1				4		
Duxbury	100	10	Wadsworth	Senaca		2		1	1	1	2	1					8		
Duxbury	100	11	Hall	Joshua	2		1	1		1			1				6		
Duxbury	100	12	Hall	Lot			1			1			1				3		
Duxbury	100	13	Freeman	Benjm		1	3		1			2		1			8		
Duxbury	100	14	Samson	John			2		1	2		2	3	1			11		
Duxbury	100	15	Southworth	Nathl	1	1	1	1	1	1	1						8		
Duxbury	100	16	Samson	Sylvanus	1			1		2	1		2				7		
Duxbury	100	17	Hodges	Nathl Jr	2	1		1			1		1				6		
Duxbury	100	18	Delano	Sylv				1		1			1	1			4		
Duxbury	100	19	Hayward	Ester			2							1			3		
Duxbury	100	20	Watson	John			1			3			1				5		
Duxbury	100	21	Faunce	Susanna		1	1						1	1			4		
Duxbury	101	1	Glover	James	2			1					1				4		
Duxbury	101	2	Louden	Micah Jun	1			1					1				3		
Duxbury	101	3	Loudon	Micah				1			2	1	1				5		
Duxbury	101	4	Loudon	Sylvanus			1			4		1					6		
Duxbury	101	5	Carver	Zadoch	3			1					1				5		
Duxbury	101	6	Delano	John		1	2	1	1		1	2		1			9		
Duxbury	101	7	Partridge	Lucresia										1			1		
Duxbury	101	8	Addington	Cloe									1	1			2		
Duxbury	101	9	Samson	Miles			1	1						1			3		
Duxbury	101	10	Samson	Colson	3	2	1	1	1	1	1		1				11		
Duxbury	101	11	Phillips	Thomas		1		1		2	2		1				7		
Duxbury	101	12	Samson	Noah			1	1						2			4		
Duxbury	101	13	Foord	Joseph	1		1			1		1					4		
Duxbury	101	14	Samson	Ichobud	3	1		1					1				6		
Duxbury	101	15	Samson	Wm	3			2		1	3		1				10		
Duxbury	101	16	Samson	Anthony				1					1				2		
Duxbury	101	17	Chandler	Ira	3			1		1			1				6		
Duxbury	101	18	Chandler	Asa Jun	2			1		2		1		2			8		
Duxbury	101	19	MaCathla	Daniel	1	1	1		1	2	2		1				9		
Duxbury	101	20	Rusel	Stephen	2			1		2	1		1	1			8		
Duxbury	101	21	Ripley	Daniel	2			1		2		1	1				7		
Duxbury	101	22	Chandler	Phillip			2		1			1	1	1			6		
Duxbury	101	23	Chandler	Daniel			1					1					2		
Duxbury	101	24	Chandler	Asa		1	1		1			1		1			5		
Duxbury	102	1	Chandler	Peleg	1			1		3			1				6		
Duxbury	102	2	Weston	Abigal										3			3		
Duxbury	102	3	Delano	Zenus	1	1		1		2		1					6		
Duxbury	102	4	Brewster	Joshua	1	1		1		2	2		1				8		
Duxbury	102	5	White	Joseph	3		1	1		1			1	1			8		
Duxbury	102	6	Chandler	Stephen			1			2			1				4		
Duxbury	102	7	Chandler	Thomas				1					1	1			3		
Duxbury	102	8	Peterson	Nehemiah			2	1				1	1	1			6		
Duxbury	102	9	Gulver	Peleg		1	1		1	2	1	1	1				8		
Duxbury	102	10	Chandler	Wadsworth	1			1					1	1			4		
Duxbury	102	11	Soule	Joseph	1			1					1				3		
Duxbury	102	12	Frost	Isaac	1			1		1			1				4		
Duxbury	102	13	Chandler	Seva				1		1	2	2		1			7		
Duxbury	102	14	Phillips	Benjm	1			1					1	1			4		
Duxbury	102	15	Chandler	Howard	4			1			1		1				7		
Duxbury	102	16	Rusell	Lucy								2		1			3		
Duxbury	102	17	Clark	Elias	1			1		2				1			5		
Duxbury	102	18	Brewster	Nathan			1	1						1			3		
Duxbury	102	19	Loreing	Samuel	1	1			2	1	1	1	1	2			10		
Duxbury	102	20	Bradford	Lewis	1	2	1	1		1			1				7		
Duxbury	102	21	Ran	William	4			1			1		1				7		
Duxbury	102	22	Loreing	Levi					1			1		1			3		
Duxbury	102	23	Loreing	Perez		1	2		1			1	1	1			7		
Duxbury	103	1	Oldham	John	1	2			1	2		1	2				9		
Duxbury	103	2	Weston	Levi	2			1	1	1	4		1	2			12		
Duxbury	103	3	Simons	Jesse	1			1			1		1				4		
Duxbury	103	4	Simons	Nathl		1		1		5	1	1	1				10		
Duxbury	103	5	White	Tobias				1			1	1	1				5		
Duxbury	103	6	Simons	Levi	1			1						1			3		
Duxbury	103	7	Simons	Lydia										1			1		
Duxbury	103	8	Arnold	Edward		1	1		1				1	1			5		
Duxbury	103	9	Arnold	Wm				1						1			2		
Duxbury	103	10	Arnold	Dako			1			1			1				3		
Duxbury	103	11	Samson	Bradford	2		1	1					1				5		
Duxbury	103	12	Sprague	Huldah	1								1				2		
Duxbury	103	13	Fish	Adam	2	1	2		1	2	1	1	1				11		

TOWN	PG#	LN#	LAST NAME	FIRST NAME	FREE WHITE MALES					FREE WHITE FEMALES					TOTAL ALL OTHER	TOTAL SLAVES	TOTALS	DISTRICT/ TOWNSHIP	NOTES
					under 10	10 to 16	16 to 26	26 to 45	45 and over	under 10	10 to 16	16 to 26	26 to 45	45 and over					
Duxbury	103	14	Baker	Elijah	1	2	1		1		1	1		1			8		
Duxbury	103	15	Weston	Chandler	1			1		2			1	1			6		
Duxbury	103	16	Smith	Hannah										1			1		
Duxbury	103	17	Harlow	Gedion		1	1		2			1		2			7		
Duxbury	103	18	Baker	Thomas		1			1					1			3		
Duxbury	103	19	Hewet	Joseph				1		2			1				4		
Duxbury	103	20	Hatch	Josiah	2	1	1		1	2	1	1					9		
Duxbury	103	21	Peterson	Jebez	1			1				1					3		
Duxbury	103	22	Weston	Ichobud		1			1			1		1			4		
Duxbury	103	23	Eames	Isaac	2			1					1				4		
Duxbury	103	24	Randal	Thomas	2	1		1		2			1				7		
Duxbury	103	25	Keen	Lot		1	1		1	1				1			5		
Duxbury	103	26	Forde	Joshua	2	2		1		2			1				8		
Duxbury	103	27	Keen	Isaac		1		1				3		1			6		
Duxbury	103	28	Magoon	Joshua	2	1		1		2	1	1	1				9		
Duxbury	103	29	Curtis	Wm			1			3			1				5		
Duxbury	104	1	Baker	John		1			1	1				1			4		
Duxbury	104	2	Simons	Jesse		1	1	1			1		1	1			6		
Duxbury	104	3	Peterson	Thomas				1						1			2		
Duxbury	104	4	Peterson	William	1			1				1					3		
Duxbury	104	5	Peterson	Elijah			4		1			1		1			7		
Duxbury	104	6	Peterson	Luther	2		1		1	3			1				8		
Duxbury	104	7	Peterson	Judah		1	1					1					3		
Duxbury	104	8	Simons	Consider			1	1					2	1			5		
Duxbury	104	9	Wells	Robert	1	1			1	2				1			6		
Duxbury	104	10	Soule	Nathl		1			1	1				1			4		
Duxbury	104	11	Hanks	John	1				1				1	2			5		
Duxbury	104	12	Peirce	Joseph		1	1		1				1	1			5		
Duxbury	104	13	Samson	Mary										2			2		
Duxbury	104	14	Delano	Ichobud	1			1		6	2		1				11		
Duxbury	104	15	Howland	Perez	2	1			1					2			6		
Duxbury	104	16	Delano	Charles			1			3			1				5		
Duxbury	104	17	Waterman	Ephraim				1			1	3	1				6		
Duxbury	104	18	Samson	Nathl				1		3		2	1				7		
Duxbury	104	19	Weston	James	2			1						1			4		
Duxbury	104	20	Chandler	Anna										3			3		
Duxbury	104	21	Delano	Rheuben	1		1			2			1	1			6		
Duxbury	104	22	Goodwin	Job	1			1					1	1			4		
Duxbury	104	23	Freeman	Joseph	1	1	1	1				1	2	1			8		
Duxbury	104	24	Loreing	William		1	1		1		1	1		1			6		
Duxbury	104	25	Loreing	Wm Jun	1			1		1		1					4		
Duxbury	104	26	Barstow	James				1						1			2		

TOWN	PG#	LN#	HEADS OF HOUSEHOLD		FREE WHITE MALES					FREE WHITE FEMALES					TOTAL ALL OTHER	TOTAL SLAVES	TOTALS	DISTRICT/ TOWNSHIP	NOTES
			LAST NAME	FIRST NAME	under 10	10 to 16	16 to 26	26 to 45	45 and over	under 10	10 to 16	16 to 26	26 to 45	45 and over					
Halifax	13	1	Thomson	Zebediah			1	1					1				3		
Halifax	13	2	Thomson	Moses	1			1		1	1		1				5		
Halifax	13	3	Thomson	Thomas				1				1		2			4		
Halifax	13	4	Woods	Francis	1			1		1			1				4		
Halifax	13	5	Thomson	Ebenezer				1						2			3		
Halifax	13	6	Dunbar	Jane			3				1			2			6		
Halifax	13	7	Thomson	Ezekiel	2			1		1	1		1				6		
Halifax	13	8	Thomson	Eliab	1			1		2			1				5		
Halifax	13	9	Thomson	Jacob	1	1		1	1	3			1	1			9		
Halifax	13	10	Thomson	Ebenezer		1		1						2			4		
Halifax	13	11	Thomson	Nathaniel	3			1		2	2		1				9		
Halifax	13	12	Thomson	Levi				1			1		1				3		
Halifax	13	13	Thomson	Ezra	2	1	1	1		3		1	1				10		
Halifax	13	14	Woods	Joshua				1		3	1		1				6		
Halifax	13	15	Samson	Abiha	1	1	1	1				1	1				6		
Halifax	13	16	Woods	Ebenezer			1			2			1				4		
Halifax	13	17	Soule	Benjamin			2	1				1		1			5		
Halifax	13	18	Fuller	Samuel	2	1		1		2	1		1				8		
Halifax	13	19	Pratt	Consider		2	1	1		2			1				8		
Halifax	13	20	Bosworth	Waterman				1		4	1		1				7		
Halifax	13	21	Gray	Samuel				1			1			1			3		
Halifax	13	22	Thomson	Ebenezer		1		1					1				3		
Halifax	15	1	Lyon	Obediah	2	1	1	1			1	2		1			9		
Halifax	15	2	Tilson	Ephraim	2	1		1		2		2	1				9		
Halifax	15	3	Whitting	Abraham				1				1	2				4		
Halifax	15	4	Tinkham	Ephraim				1					1				2		
Halifax	15	5	Forrest	Asaph	1		1	1		2		1		2			8		
Halifax	15	6	Cushing	Benjamin	1		1				2		1				5		
Halifax	15	7	Tilson	John	2			1		3	1		1	1			9		
Halifax	15	8	Hefferds	John	1	1		1		2	1		1				7		
Halifax	15	9	Dunham	William				1						1			2		
Halifax	15	10	Goodwin	William	1	1		1					1				4		
Halifax	15	11	Causell	Sherebral		2		1		2	2		2				9		
Halifax	15	12	Holmes	Oliver		1	1	1		1	1	1		1			7		
Halifax	15	13	Bourne	Newcomb	2			1		1			1				5		
Halifax	15	14	Paris	Daniel	2			1		2			1				6		
Halifax	15	15	Bosworth	John	3			1					1				5		
Halifax	15	16	Bosworth	David	2	1		1		3			1				8		
Halifax	15	17	Thomson	Reuben	4			1		1			1	1			8		
Halifax	15	18	Drew	Thomas	1	1	1		1			2		2			8		
Halifax	15	19	Crooker	James	2				1	1			1				5		
Halifax	15	20	Bosworth	John			2		1					1			4		
Halifax	15	21	Bosworth	Hannah	2	1					2		1				6		
Halifax	15	22	Bosworth	Asaph	2			1		2			1				6		
Halifax	16	1	Bosworth	Richard	4	1	2		1	1	2	1		2			14		
Halifax	16	2	Bosworth	Salah	2	1	1	1		1	1		1	2			10		
Halifax	16	3	Waterman	Moses	2			1		1		1	1				6		
Halifax	16	4	Sturtevant	Zaba			1					1		2			4		
Halifax	16	5	Waterman	William					1					1			2		
Halifax	16	6	Inglee	Moses			1		1		1	1	1				5		
Halifax	16	7	Porter	Jonathan				1		4	1		1				7		
Halifax	16	8	Woods	William				1					1				2		
Halifax	16	9	Soule	Jacob				1				1					2		
Halifax	16	10	Thomson	Nathan			1						1				2		
Halifax	16	11	Thomson	Zacheus			1			3			1				5		
Halifax	16	12	Thomson	Isaac		2						2					4		
Halifax	16	13	Munroe	Bennel	1			1		1			1				4		
Halifax	16	14	Thomson	Adam		2	2	1					1	1			7		
Halifax	16	15	Thomson	Ichabod			1	1			1	1		2			6		
Halifax	16	16	Wood	Timothy		2		2	1	2	1		2	1			11		
Halifax	16	17	Tinkham	Joseph	1			1					2	1			5		
Halifax	16	18	Wood	Judah	3	1		1					1				6		
Halifax	16	19	Fuller	Ephraim			2	1				3					6		
Halifax	16	20	Bosworth	James	2		1	1		1	1		1	1			8		
Halifax	16	21	Thomson	Amasa				1						1			2		
Halifax	16	22	Sturtevant	Simion	3			1					1				5		
Halifax	16	23	Thomson	Asa		3		1				1	1				6		
Halifax	16	24	Thomson	Nehemiah	1			1		1			1				4		
Halifax	17	1	Sturtevant	Amasa				1		1			2	1			5		
Halifax	17	2	Sturtevant	Simion	1		1	1			1			1			5		
Halifax	17	3	Silvester	Sally	1		2						1	1			5		
Halifax	17	4	Hall	Jabez			1	1				1		1			4		
Halifax	17	5	Sturtevant	Stafford			2	1		2	2			1			8		
Halifax	17	6	Holmes	Solomon				1				2		1			4		
Halifax	17	7	Holmes	Nathaniel	4			1					1				6		
Halifax	17	8	Fuller	Thomas		1	3	1		1	1	1					8		
Halifax	17	9	Bosworth	Ichabod			1		1	1				1			4		
Halifax	17	10	Bearce	Andrew				1						1			2		
Halifax	17	11	Munroe	William	1			1		2		1					6		

TOWN	PG#	LN#	LAST NAME	FIRST NAME	FREE WHITE MALES					FREE WHITE FEMALES					TOTAL ALL OTHER	TOTAL SLAVES	TOTALS	DISTRICT/ TOWNSHIP	NOTES
					under 10	10 to 16	16 to 26	26 to 45	45 and over	under 10	10 to 16	16 to 26	26 to 45	45 and over					
Halifax	17	12	Briggs	John				1				1		1			3		
Halifax	17	13	Briggs	Seth			1			1		1					3		
Halifax	17	14	Chandler	Simeon			1			1		1					3		
Halifax	17	15	Palmer	Joshua	4	2		1		1			1				9		
Halifax	17	16	Waterman	Elisha		2	3	1			1	2		1			10		
Halifax	17	17	Sturtevant	Dependent		2	1	1			2	2		1			9		
Halifax	17	18	Waterman	Eleazer				1				2		1			4		
Halifax	17	19	Clarke	Alice	2					1			1				4		
Halifax	17	20	Waterman	Jabez		1	2	1				1		1			6		
Halifax	17	21	Sturtevant	Paul			1			2			1				4		
Halifax	17	22	Sturtevant	Barzillai	3		2	1		1			1				8		
Halifax	18	1	Soule	Jabez		1	2	1		1	1			1			7		
Halifax	18	2	Tilson	Joseph			1			3	1		1				6		
Halifax	18	3	Sturtevant	Winslow	1		1			2			1				5		
Halifax	18	4	Briggs	Abigail				1						2			3		
Halifax	18	5	Waterman	Isaac	1		1	1		3		1	1				8		
Halifax	18	6	Briggs	Rebecca	1							1	1	1			4		
Halifax	18	7	Drew	Job		2		1		1			1	1			6		
Halifax	18	8	Faxon	elisha	2			1		1		2	2	2			10		
Halifax	18	9	Sears	Holmes	2	1		1					1				5		
Halifax	18	10	Sears	Edward				1					1	1			3		
Halifax	18	11	Tilson	Ephraim				1				2	1	1			5		
Halifax	18	12	Waterman	John		1		1	1	2	1	1		1			8		
Halifax	18	13	Thomson	Jonah		1		1									2		
Halifax	18	14	Morton	Nathaniel	2	1		1		1			1				6		
Halifax	18	15	Pool	John	3	1	2		1	1	1	1		1			11		
Halifax	18	16	Leach	John			1	1		2							4		
Halifax	18	17	White	Joel	1	2		1		2		3		1			10		
Halifax	18	18	Bourne	Ebenezer				1		3	2			1			7		
Halifax	18	19	Thomson	Joseph			1			1			1	1			4		
Halifax	18	20	Carter	Benjamin M.				1				1		1			3		
Halifax	18	21	Thomson	Abel	1			1		1		1					4		
Halifax	18	22	Leach	Silvanus				1			1	1		1			4		
Halifax	18	23	Leach	Thomson				1	1	1			1				4		

TOWN	PG#	LN#	LAST NAME	FIRST NAME	FREE WHITE MALES					FREE WHITE FEMALES					TOTAL ALL OTHER	TOTAL SLAVES	TOTALS	DISTRICT/ TOWNSHIP	NOTES
					under 10	10 to 16	16 to 26	26 to 45	45 and over	under 10	10 to 16	16 to 26	26 to 45	45 and over					
Hanover	123	1	Carthell	Theoph				1	1	1				1			3		
Hanover	123	2	Gross	Peakes	1			1					1				3		
Hanover	123	3	Barrell	Elisha			1		1				2	2			6		
Hanover	123	4	Clapp	Michael	1			1		3			1				6		
Hanover	123	5	Jacobs	David	1	1		1			1	1		1			6		
Hanover	123	6	Jacobs	Perez			1			3	1		1				6		
Hanover	123	7	Jacobs	Nathaniel		2	1	1						1			5		
Hanover	123	8	Young	Job	4			1		1	1		1				8		
Hanover	123	9	Carter	Seth	3			1		2			1				7		
Hanover	125	1	Estes	Benjamin		1	1			1		1					4		
Hanover	125	2	Munroe	Shubael	2			1		2			1	1			7		
Hanover	125	3	Ramsdell	Mary										1			1		
Hanover	125	4	Josliyn	Christiana	1					1			1				3		
Hanover	125	5	Mallin	John Revd	1			1					1	1			4		
Hanover	125	6	Silvester	Joel	3			1		1			1				6		
Hanover	125	7	Bates	Seth		1		1		1	2		1	1			7		
Hanover	125	8	Bates	Joseph N.	2	1		1		2			1				7		
Hanover	125	9	White	Cornelius		1		1						1			3		
Hanover	125	10	Munroe	Mary									1	2			3		
Hanover	125	11	Robbins	Timothy		1	1		1			4		2			9		
Hanover	125	12	Stetson	Seth			1		1			1		1	1		5		
Hanover	125	13	Bates	Paul	2			1					1	1			5		
Hanover	125	14	Peterson	Mary									1	3			4		
Hanover	125	15	Stetson	Saml		2	1		1			1	1				6		
Hanover	125	16	Bates	Joshua	1			1					1				3		
Hanover	125	17	Bates	Enos				1									1		
Hanover	125	18	Dwelley	Aaron	1			1				1					3		
Hanover	125	19	Stirling	Ruth										1			1		
Hanover	125	20	Woodworth	John			1							1			2		
Hanover	125	21	Chamberlin	Josiah	1			1		1	2		1				6		
Hanover	125	22	Stetson	Nathaniel	3			1					1				5		
Hanover	125	23	Studley	Gideon		1	1		1			2	2	1			8		
Hanover	125	24	Bass	Benjamin	1	1	1		1	1	1	2	2				10		
Hanover	125	25	Prince	Melvin Negro											4		4		
Hanover	125	26	Dwelley	Melzar	2			1		1			1				5		
Hanover	126	1	Clark	Nathaniel			1	1						1	1		4		
Hanover	126	2	Silvester	Michael		1		1					1	1			4		
Hanover	126	3	Silvester	Edmund		1		1					1				3		
Hanover	126	4	Silvester	Robert				1			2	1	1				5		
Hanover	126	5	Randall	Elijah	1	1		1		1				1			5		
Hanover	126	6	Randall	Lott	1		1	1				2		1			6		
Hanover	126	7	Perry	Isaac				1				1		2			4		
Hanover	126	8	Pratt	Jonathan	2			1			1	1	1	1			7		
Hanover	126	9	Winslow	Oliver	1			1					1				3		
Hanover	126	10	Church	Timothy	2			1			1	1					5		
Hanover	126	11	Curtis	Simon	2	2			1	2			1				8		
Hanover	126	12	Curtis	Lemuel		1	1	1	1				2	1			7		
Hanover	126	13	Curtis	Malzar Esq	1	1	2		1			2		1			8		
Hanover	126	14	Curtis	Barker				1						1			2		
Hanover	126	15	Studley	Jabez			1		1			1	1				4		
Hanover	126	16	Wright	Lydia										1			1		
Hanover	126	17	Loper	Joseph	1			1	1				1	1			5		
Hanover	126	18	House	David				1					1	1			3		
Hanover	126	19	Briggs	Ezra			2	1					1	1			5		
Hanover	126	20	Curtis	Calvin		1		1		1							3		
Hanover	126	21	Curtis	Elienm		1		1			1		1				4		
Hanover	126	22	Curtis	Prince				1					2				3		
Hanover	126	23	Sprague	Priscilla									1	1			2		
Hanover	126	24	Simmons	Elisha	3	1	1	1		1			1				8		
Hanover	126	25	Simmons	Joshua				1					1	1			3		
Hanover	127	1	Whiting	Abel		1		1		1		1					4		
Hanover	127	2	Whiting	Thomas		1		1		1	1		1				5		
Hanover	127	3	Whiting	William		1		1		1			1	1			5		
Hanover	127	4	Whiting	Ozias			1			1	1						3		
Hanover	127	5	Whiting	Lydia							1	1	3				5		
Hanover	127	6	Whiting	Caleb	2	1		1		2	1		1				8		
Hanover	127	7	Whiting	Asa	2			1		1			1				5		
Hanover	127	8	Mann	Joshua	2	1		1		1			1				6		
Hanover	127	9	Dorman	Eills		1	1	1	1		1	1		1			7		
Hanover	127	10	Dorman	Ezra	2	1			1	2		1	1				8		
Hanover	127	11	Mann	Benjamin			1		1	1		2		1			6		
Hanover	127	12	Mann	Benja Junr	1				1			1		1			4		
Hanover	127	13	Mann	Levi	2	1		1		3			1				8		
Hanover	127	14	Mann	Charles			1			1		1	1				4		
Hanover	127	15	Curtis	Job				2						1			3		
Hanover	127	16	Curtis	Jesse		1		1						1			3		
Hanover	127	17	Curtis	Phebe									1				1		
Hanover	127	18	Hatch	Thomas	1		1		1				1	1			5		
Hanover	127	19	Gardner	Seth	1								1				3		

TOWN	PG#	LN#	LAST NAME	FIRST NAME	FWM under 10	FWM 10–16	FWM 16–26	FWM 26–45	FWM 45 & over	FWF under 10	FWF 10–16	FWF 16–26	FWF 26–45	FWF 45 & over	TOTAL ALL OTHER	TOTAL SLAVES	TOTALS	DISTRICT/ TOWNSHIP	NOTES
Hanover	127	20	Brooks	Joseph		1		1				3	1	2			8		
Hanover	127	21	Brooks	Samuel				1				1		1			3		
Hanover	127	22	Gray	Sarah										2			2		
Hanover	127	23	Briggs	Ezra	2			1	1	2			1				7		
Hanover	127	24	Turner	Isaac	1		1	1				1	1				5		
Hanover	127	25	Curtis	Amos				1					2	1			4		
Hanover	128	1	Mann	Joseph			1	1						1			3		
Hanover	128	2	Turner	Leah									1	1			2		
Hanover	128	3	Curtis	Anna		2	1			1		1	1	2			8		
Hanover	128	4	Bailey	Calvin	2		1	1		1			1				6		
Hanover	128	5	Bailey	John				2					1				3		
Hanover	128	6	Freeman	Asher Negro											4		4		
Hanover	128	7	Gray	James	2		1			2	1		1				7		
Hanover	128	8	Hatch	John	1		1	1				1	1	1			6		
Hanover	128	9	Curtis	John			1	1		1		1					4		
Hanover	128	10	Turner	Marlbry				1					1				2		
Hanover	128	11	Dwelley	Joshua	1		1			2		1					5		
Hanover	128	12	Randall	Stephen				1					1				2		
Hanover	128	13	Dwelley	Lemuel	1			2				1	1				6		
Hanover	128	14	Stetson	John			2	1					1	1			5		
Hanover	128	15	Bailey	Charles	2	1		1		2		1	1				8		
Hanover	128	16	Stockbridge	William	1	1	1	1		1	2		2				9		
Hanover	128	17	Perrey	Israel		1	2	1			1	1		1			7		
Hanover	128	18	Hobart	Mary		1						1		1			3		
Hanover	128	19	Nickerson	Joseph Negro											3		3		
Hanover	128	20	Rose	Timothy				1					1				2		
Hanover	128	21	Rose	Seth	1		1					1					3		
Hanover	128	22	Chatman	John	3			1		1			1				6		
Hanover	128	23	Stetson	Turner	1		1	1		2		1	1				7		
Hanover	128	24	Estes	Zilpah				1				1	1		1		4		
Hanover	128	25	Estes	Robert				1				1	1		1		4		
Hanover	129	1	Smith	Albert Esq	3	1		1		1	1		1				8		
Hanover	129	2	Bass	Benjamin Junr	2			1		1			1				5		
Hanover	129	3	Silvester	Jacob				1					1				2		
Hanover	129	4	Bates	Joseph				1					1				2		
Hanover	129	5	Macomber	Thomas			1						1				2		
Hanover	129	6	Silvester	Elijah	1		1			1			1				4		
Hanover	129	7	Dorman	Leah							1		1				2		
Hanover	129	8	Rose	Timothy Junr			1			2			1				4		
Hanover	129	9	Smith	Josiah		1	1			4			1				7		
Hanover	129	10	Salmon	Robert	2	3		1		2			2				10		
Hanover	129	11	Bates	Doughty	1	1	1			2			1				6		
Hanover	129	12	Bates	Gamaliel	3	1	1	1		1	1	2	1	1			12		
Hanover	129	13	Bates	Clement	2	1		1		1	1		1				7		
Hanover	129	14	Perry	Samuel B.	4	1		1		2	1		1				10		
Hanover	129	15	Bates	Thomas	2		1					1					4		
Hanover	129	16	Bates	Benjamin				1		1							3		
Hanover	129	17	White	Benjamin	1		2			2			1				7		
Hanover	129	18	Tubbs	Joseph			1			1		1					3		
Hanover	129	19	Tilden	Job Junr		1		1		3	1	1	1				8		
Hanover	129	20	Tilden	Job				3					1				4		
Hanover	129	21	Torrey	Meriam								1	1				2		
Hanover	129	22	Estes	Joseph			1			1		1					3		
Hanover	129	23	Wing	Batchelor		1	3	1	1		2		1				9		
Hanover	129	24	Wing	Hannah									3				3		
Hanover	129	25	Estes	Zaccheus	5	2		1	1				1				10		
Hanover	130	1	Estes	Mary	1	1	1			2			1				6		
Hanover	130	2	Wing	Isaiah				1					1				2		
Hanover	130	3	Stetson	Benja Junr			1					1					3		
Hanover	130	4	Barstow	Daniel		1		1	2		1	3	1	1			11		
Hanover	130	5	Long	Stephen Negro											6		6		
Hanover	130	6	Bailey	George		3	1	1			1	1		1			8		
Hanover	130	7	Bailey	Stephen	1	1	1	1		1	1		3	1			10		
Hanover	130	8	Turner	Amos		1	2	1			2		3				9		
Hanover	130	9	Winslow	Thomas		1	1			1		1					4		
Hanover	130	10	Clark	Mary									1				1		
Hanover	130	11	Gross	Zilpha									2				2		
Hanover	130	12	Hatch	Orpha			1	1				2	1				5		
Hanover	130	13	Ellis	Mordecai	1	1	2	1	1	1			1	1			9		
Hanover	130	14	Ramsdell	Joseph			1	1				1	1	1			5		
Hanover	130	15	Perrey	Adam	1	2	1	1		2			1				8		
Hanover	130	16	Ellis	Clark	1	1	1	1				1	1				6		
Hanover	130	17	Ellis	Mordecai Junr	2			1		2	1	3	1				10		
Hanover	130	18	Stetson	Nathl				1									1		
Hanover	130	19	Hill	Abner				1									1		
Hanover	130	20	Studley	Elihab	2		2	1		1	1	1	1				9		
Hanover	130	21	Studley	Japheth	2	2		1		1	1	1		1			9		
Hanover	130	22	Whitcomb	Saml	3			1					1				5		
Hanover	130	23	Bailey	John Junr		1	3			1	2				1		10		

TOWN	PG#	LN#	HEADS OF HOUSEHOLD		FREE WHITE MALES					FREE WHITE FEMALES					TOTAL ALL OTHER	TOTAL SLAVES	TOTALS	DISTRICT/ TOWNSHIP	NOTES
			LAST NAME	FIRST NAME	under 10	10 to 16	16 to 26	26 to 45	45 and over	under 10	10 to 16	16 to 26	26 to 45	45 and over					
Hanover	130	24	Whitney	James	1				1	1	1		1				5		
Hanover	130	25	Whiting	Thomas Junr	1		1	1		1	1	1					6		
Hanover	132	1	Whitman	Benjamin Esq	1	2		2		3	1		1				10		
Hanover	132	2	Curtis	Elisha		1			1		1			1			4		
Hanover	132	3	Curtis	Elisha Junr	1			1			1			1			4		
Hanover	132	4	Cushing	Ruth	1		1			1			2	1			6		
Hanover	132	5	Curtis	Reuben Junr	1			1				1					3		
Hanover	132	6	Stockbridge	David	1	2	3	1	1	2		1	2		1		14		
Hanover	132	7	Clark	Hannah			2							1			3		
Hanover	132	8	Clark	Belcher	3		2		1		2		1				9		
Hanover	132	9	Eells	Ruth		1	4	1						2			8		
Hanover	132	10	Wales	Atherton		1			1			1		1			4		
Hanover	132	11	Josleyn	Jonathan	2			1		2			1				6		
Hanover	132	12	Morton	Silas	2			1		2			1				6		
Hanover	132	13	Crooker	Tilden			2		1	2	2		1				8		
Hanover	132	14	Kingman	David				1		3	2		2				8		
Hanover	132	15	Eells	William	1				1	1	1		1				5		
Hanover	132	16	Barstow	John B.	4			1		2	2	1	1				11		
Hanover	132	17	Standish	Hannah									1	2			3		
Hanover	132	18	Josleyn	Olive								1		1			2		
Hanover	132	19	Josleyn	Seth	1			1		1			1				4		
Hanover	132	20	Curtis	Reuben			2							1			3		
Hanover	132	21	Stetson	Martha		1					1	2		1			5		
Hanover	132	22	Josleyn	Isaac	2	1	2		1		1	1		1			9		
Hanover	132	23	Rogers	Caleb				1			1			1			3		
Hanover	132	24	Stetson	Benjamin				1				1		1			3		
Hanover	132	25	Stetson	Edward	1		1					1					3		

TOWN	PG#	LN#	LAST NAME	FIRST NAME	FREE WHITE MALES under 10	10 to 16	16 to 26	26 to 45	45 and over	FREE WHITE FEMALES under 10	10 to 16	16 to 26	26 to 45	45 and over	TOTAL ALL OTHER	TOTAL SLAVES	TOTALS	DISTRICT/ TOWNSHIP	NOTES
Kingston	27	1	Sturtevant	Elijah					1	1	1	1	1	1			6		
Kingston	27	2	Gray	John		1		1			1		1	1			5		
Kingston	27	3	Fuller	Zepheniah	1	1		1					1				4		
Kingston	27	4	Lavery	Thomas	1			1		3			1				6		
Kingston	27	5	Winsor	Peter		1		1		1			1				4		
Kingston	27	6	Hacher	Betsey	1						1			1			3		
Kingston	27	7	Fuller	James			1			1		1					3		
Kingston	27	8	Fuller	John			1	1			1		1				4		
Kingston	27	9	Brewster	Eliha			2						1				4		
Kingston	27	10	Fuller	Josiah		1		1					1				3		
Kingston	27	11	Hartwell	Nathan	2			1		1			1				5		
Kingston	27	12	Dillano	Joshua			1	1			1	2		1			6		
Kingston	27	13	Cooper	Thomas				1					1				2		
Kingston	27	14	Dunham	Silas	1	2		1		3	3		1				11		
Kingston	27	15	Riley	Hezekiah	2	2				1		1		1			7		
Kingston	27	16	Cooper	Nathaniel	1	1		1		3	1		1				8		
Kingston	27	17	Mitchell	Benjamin			2	1					1				4		
Kingston	27	18	Cobb	Seth				1		1			1				3		
Kingston	27	19	Doten	Jacob				1			1		1				3		
Kingston	27	20	Brewster	Rebecca	1								1				2		
Kingston	27	21	Cobb	John			1	2	1	1	1	1	1				8		
Kingston	27	22	Cobb	Ebenezer				1					1				2		
Kingston	27	23	Brewster	Isaac		1		1				1	1				4		
Kingston	27	24	Brewster	Pelham		1				1		1					3		
Kingston	27	25	Thomas	John	3			1		1		1	2				8		
Kingston	27	26	Holmes	Ephraim		1		1					1				3		
Kingston	27	27	Holmes	Nathaniel		1	1					1					3		
Kingston	27	28	Holmes	Tilden	1			1		2		1					5		
Kingston	27	29	Holmes	Joshua		1		1					2				4		
Kingston	27	30	Holmes	Jedediah	2	2	3	1				1	1				10		
Kingston	27	31	Holmes	Abner	1	1	1	1		1	2	2		1			10		
Kingston	27	32	Holmes	Joseph				1				3	1				5		
Kingston	27	33	Holmes	Thomas	2			1		1			1				5		
Kingston	27	34	Holmes	Melatiah		1		1				3		1			7		
Kingston	27	35	Holmes	Jedediah	1	1	1			2			1				6		
Kingston	27	36	Holmes	Jonathan		1		1				3	1	1			7		
Kingston	27	37	Holmes	Silvester		1		1		2		1	1				6		
Kingston	27	38	Holmes	Jonathan		1			2			1	1				5		
Kingston	27	39	Hollis	Samuel	1			1		2		2		1	2		9		
Kingston	27	40	Holmes	Charles		1		1		1	1		1				5		
Kingston	27	41	Half	Elisha	2	2	1	1		1	1	2	1				11		
Kingston	27	42	Johnson	John		2		1		3	1	1	1				9		
Kingston	27	43	Johnson	Richard	1		1			2			1				5		
Kingston	27	44	Lucas	Nathan		1		1		1	1	1		1			6		
Kingston	27	45	McGlocklin	Robert			1	1				2	1	1			6		
Kingston	27	46	McGlocklin	John			1							1			2		
Kingston	27	47	McGlocklin	Elisha	2			1		2			1				6		
Kingston	27	48	Mitchell	John	1		2			1			1				5		
Kingston	27	49	Prince	Kimball				1					1				2		
Kingston	27	50	Prince	John	3			1		3		1	1				9		
Kingston	27	51	Samson	Samuel				1					1				2		
Kingston	28	1	Paris	Martin	2			1					1				4		
Kingston	28	2	Ring	Franis	1	1		2	1	1	2	2	1				11		
Kingston	28	3	Samson	Jeremiah	1	2	2	1		2	1	1	1				11		
Kingston	28	4	Samson	Oliver	1			1			2		1				5		
Kingston	28	5	Simmons	Noah		2	3	1	1				1				8		
Kingston	28	6	Thomas	Isaiah	1	2	1	1			2	2	1				10		
Kingston	28	7	Washburn	Ebenezer		1		1				1	2	1			6		
Kingston	28	8	West	Jonah		1		1					1				3		
Kingston	28	9	Washburn	Judah		1		1				1	1	1	1		6		
Kingston	28	10	Washburn	Bildao	2	1		1	1	3	1	1	1				11		
Kingston	28	11	Washburn	John	2			1		1	1		1				6		
Kingston	28	12	Washburn	Simeon	1			1					1		1		4		
Kingston	28	13	Washburn	Ezekiel				1					1	1	1		3		
Kingston	28	14	Waterman	Benjamin	1			1		1	1		1				5		
Kingston	28	15	Washburn	Elkanah	1			1		1	3		1				7		
Kingston	28	16	Tupper	Peleg	2			1		2	1		1				7		
Kingston	28	17	Faunce	Eleazer			2		1	1	1		1				6		
Kingston	28	18	Washburn	Jehial		1		1					1				3		
Kingston	28	19	Ring	Elizabeth	1	1						2	1				5		
Kingston	28	20	Eaton	Benjamin			1						1				2		
Kingston	28	21	Thomson	Timothy	1		1						1				3		
Kingston	28	22	Faunce	Tilden			1						1				2		
Kingston	28	23	Foster	Nathaniel	1		1					1					3		
Kingston	28	24	Russell	George			1			1			2				4		
Kingston	28	25	Holmes	Heman	2		1						1				4		
Kingston	28	26	Holmes	Pelham	1			1				1					3		
Kingston	29	1	Brewster	Wrestling Jr		1		1					2				4		
Kingston	29	2	Stetson	Samuel	2	1	3		1	3	2	1	1				14		

32

TOWN	PG#	LN#	LAST NAME	FIRST NAME	FREE WHITE MALES under 10	10 to 16	16 to 26	26 to 45	45 and over	FREE WHITE FEMALES under 10	10 to 16	16 to 26	26 to 45	45 and over	TOTAL ALL OTHER	TOTAL SLAVES	TOTALS	DISTRICT/ TOWNSHIP	NOTES
Kingston	29	3	Samson	Crocker	1	1			1	2		1	1				7		
Kingston	29	4	Samson	Desire		1					1	2	1				5		
Kingston	29	5	Samson	Priscilla		1				1		1	1				4		
Kingston	29	6	Brewster	Fear						2		1	3				6		
Kingston	29	7	Perkins	Daniel			1			1		1					3		
Kingston	29	8	Willis	Zepheniah	1		1	1		2		1	1		1		8		
Kingston	29	9	Cobb	Stephen	2		1			1		1					5		
Kingston	29	10	Drew	Judah	1					1		1	1				4		
Kingston	29	11	Cook	John	2		1			1		1					6		
Kingston	29	12	Morton	Ezra			1			1		1					3		
Kingston	29	13	Holmes	Anselm		2					1						3		
Kingston	29	14	Adams	Joseph		2		1			1		1				5		
Kingston	29	15	Bartlett	Peleg			1	1		1		1	1				5		
Kingston	29	16	Washburn	Rufus	2		1	1				1	1				6		
Kingston	29	17	Washburn	Silva	2					1			1				4		
Kingston	29	18	Cushman	James	3		2	1		1	2		1				10		
Kingston	29	19	Washburn	Phillip	2			1					1	1			5		
Kingston	29	20	Washburn	Seth			1			3			1				5		
Kingston	29	21	Drew	Seth		1	1	1			1	1	1				6		
Kingston	29	22	Bradford	David		1		1				1	1				4		
Kingston	29	23	Foster	Charles	1			1					1	1			4		
Kingston	29	24	Bradford	Elisha				1					1		2		4		
Kingston	29	25	Brewster	Thomas			1	1		1		1	1	1			6		
Kingston	29	26	Adams	John		1	1						1				4		
Kingston	29	27	Bearce	John			1	1					4				7		
Kingston	29	28	Bradford	Levi	1	2		1		1	1		1				7		
Kingston	29	29	Samson	Croade				1		2			1				4		
Kingston	29	30	Basset	Zeleach					2					1			3		
Kingston	29	31	Adams	Franis		1			2	2	2			1			8		
Kingston	29	32	Russell	Melzer	1			1		1			1				4		
Kingston	29	33	Holmes	Ephraim			1	1						1			3		
Kingston	29	34	Holmes	Nathaniel	1			1						1			3		
Kingston	29	35	Chandler	Mary		1	1				1	1		1			5		
Kingston	29	36	Ripley	Calvin		1	4	1		3	1	1	1				12		
Kingston	29	37	Waterman	Jonah			1	1				1	1				4		
Kingston	29	38	Adams	John				1					1				2		
Kingston	29	39	Adams	Melzer		2	3	1				1	1				8		
Kingston	29	40	Adams	Rufus	1		1						1				3		
Kingston	29	41	Adams	Ebenezer		1	3	1			2	1	1				9		
Kingston	29	42	Bartlett	John		2		1		1		2	1				7		
Kingston	29	43	Bartlett	Joseph		1				1		1					3		
Kingston	29	44	Bartlett	Rana		1	1					1	1	1			5		
Kingston	29	45	Bradford	James		2	2	1				1	1				7		
Kingston	29	46	Bradford	John			1	1	1			1	2				6		
Kingston	29	47	Bradford	Silvanus	3			1			2	1	1				8		
Kingston	29	48	Bradford	Stetson		1	2	1					2	2			8		
Kingston	29	49	Bryant	Peleg	2			1		2		1	2				8		
Kingston	29	50	Bradford	Ellis	2			1		2		1	1	2			8		
Kingston	29	51	Cushing	Seth	1			1		2		1					5		
Kingston	29	52	Cook	Mary				1				1	3	1			6		
Kingston	29	53	Cook	Elkanah		2		1		1		1					5		
Kingston	30	1	Cook	Amos	1	1	1		1	2	2	1		2			11		
Kingston	30	2	Cook	Robert		1	3	1	1			1		1			8		
Kingston	30	3	Cushman	Ebenezer		2	2	1			1	2	1				9		
Kingston	30	4	Cushing	Elijah		2	2	1				1	1				7		
Kingston	30	5	Negro	Cuff											6		6		
Kingston	30	6	Cook	Josiah		1	1	1		1	1	2	1	1			9		
Kingston	30	7	Drew	Samuel		1		1			1			1			4		
Kingston	30	8	Dawes	Ebenezer		1		1		2	2	3		1			10		
Kingston	30	9	Everson	Ebenezer		1	1	1		2	1	1	1	1			9		
Kingston	30	10	Eaton	Job				1						1			2		
Kingston	30	11	Eaton	Lot					2		1		1	1			5		
Kingston	30	12	Everson	Joseph		1	1			2			1	1			6		
Kingston	30	13	Everson	Samuel			1						1				2		
Kingston	30	14	Everson	Seth	1			1		2	1	2	1	2			10		
Kingston	30	15	Faunce	John	1			1	2		1	1	2	3			11		
Kingston	30	16	Faunce	Lydia		1						1	1				3		
Kingston	30	17	Faunce	Benjamin	1		1			1			1				4		
Kingston	30	18	Fish	Jacob	2	2	2	1		1	1			2			11		
Kingston	30	19	Fish	Nathaniel	2	1		1				3	1				8		
Kingston	30	20	Foster	Elizabeth		1								1			2		
Kingston	30	21	Negro	Quash											3		3		
Kingston	30	22	Fuller	Consider	1		1			3		1					6		
Kingston	30	23	Fuller	Jabez		1		1		2	2	1	1				8		
Kingston	30	24	Faunce	Elijah	1	2		1		1			1	1			7		
Kingston	30	25	Holmes	Robert		1	1	1				2		1			6		
Kingston	30	26	Thomas	Hannah			1						1	1			3		
Kingston	30	27	Bradford	Israel		1			1	3	1	1					7		
Kingston	30	28	Davis	Martha	1	2	1			2			1				7		

TOWN	PG#	LN#	LAST NAME	FIRST NAME	FREE WHITE MALES					FREE WHITE FEMALES					TOTAL ALL OTHER	TOTAL SLAVES	TOTALS	DISTRICT/ TOWNSHIP	NOTES
					under 10	10 to 16	16 to 26	26 to 45	45 and over	under 10	10 to 16	16 to 26	26 to 45	45 and over					
Kingston	30	29	Drew	Nehemiah					1		1	1	1				4		
Kingston	30	30	Wadsworth	Cephas		1			1			1		1			4		
Kingston	30	31	Sever	James	2		1	1			1		2				7		
Kingston	30	32	Inglee	Lemuel			1			1		2					4		
Kingston	30	33	Inglee	Moses	2		1	1		2		1	1				8		
Kingston	30	34	Cook	Silvanus		1			1			2	1	2			7		
Kingston	30	35	Stetson	Elisha	1			1	1	1			1	1			6		
Kingston	30	36	Sever	John	5		1	1		1		2	1				11		
Kingston	30	37	Sever	William		2		1		1		1		2			7		
Kingston	30	38	Drew	William	1			1		1	1	1	1				6		
Kingston	30	39	Washburn	Elisha		2		1		2		1	1				7		
Kingston	30	40	Davis	Timothy	1			1				1					3		
Kingston	30	41	Everson	Silvanus			2		1	2	1			1			7		
Kingston	30	42	Beal	David	1	2	1		1	2	1	3	1				12		
Kingston	30	43	Drew	Abijah	2	2			1	4		2	1				12		
Kingston	30	44	Drew	James		1			1			1		1			4		
Kingston	30	45	Drew	Zenas		1		1	1			3	1	1			8		
Kingston	30	46	Drew	Dorothy	1	1				1		2	1				6		
Kingston	30	47	Drew	Cornelius		2	1		1	1		1					6		
Kingston	30	48	Drew	Stephen			1	1		4		1	1				8		
Kingston	30	49	Samson	Joseph	1				2	1	1	1					6		
Kingston	30	50	Brewster	Wrestling					1					2			3		

TOWN	PG#	LN#	HEADS OF HOUSEHOLD		FREE WHITE MALES					FREE WHITE FEMALES					TOTAL ALL OTHER	TOTAL SLAVES	TOTALS	DISTRICT/ TOWNSHIP	NOTES
			LAST NAME	FIRST NAME	under 10	10 to 16	16 to 26	26 to 45	45 and over	under 10	10 to 16	16 to 26	26 to 45	45 and over					
Marshfield	93	1	Dingley	*	1			1		2			1				5		Tape Mark
Marshfield	93	2	Carver	Joshua	1		1	2				1		1			6		
Marshfield	93	3	White	Luther		1		1					1	1			4		
Marshfield	93	4	White	Benjamin				1			1			1			3		
Marshfield	93	5	Walker	Levi			1			3	1		1				6		
Marshfield	93	6	Baker	Joshua			1					1	1				3		
Marshfield	93	7	Howland	Jarusha									1	2			3		
Marshfield	93	8	Bourn	Rouse	2		1			2			1				6		
Marshfield	93	9	Samson	Sarah	1						1	1					3		
Marshfield	93	10	Weston	William	1	1		1			1			1			5		
Marshfield	93	11	Weston	Eleaner	1						1		1				3		
Marshfield	93	12	Baker	Charles Jun			1			1			1				3		
Marshfield	93	13	Fish	Thomas		1		1					2	2			6		
Marshfield	93	14	Eames	Rebeckah	1								1				2		
Marshfield	93	15	Hewet	Joseph	1		1	1				2	1	1			7		
Marshfield	93	16	Thomas	Judah		1	1	1	1	1	1		1	1			8		
Marshfield	93	17	Taylor	Jethro	1		2	1				1	1	1			7		
Marshfield	93	18	Baker	Charles		1	1	1				1		1			5		
Marshfield	93	19	Simons	Benjamin		1	2	2	1	1		2	1	1			11		
Marshfield	93	20	Thomas	Peleg		1		1		1		1		1			5		
Marshfield	94	1	Howland	Arthur	1			1				1	1				4		
Marshfield	94	2	Walker	Benjamin	3		1		1	2	1	1	1				10		
Marshfield	94	3	Walker	Betty										2			2		
Marshfield	94	4	Thomas	Zenus				1				3		1			5		
Marshfield	94	5	Thomas	Isaac			1			3			1				5		
Marshfield	94	6	Williamson	Timothy	1			1				2		1			5		
Marshfield	94	7	Williamson	Timothy Jr	1		1			1		1		1			5		
Marshfield	94	8	Keith	George				2				2					4		
Marshfield	94	9	Thomas	Nathaniel				1						1			2		
Marshfield	94	10	Thomas	Luther		1		1		1			2				5		
Marshfield	94	11	Shaw	William Revd	1			1		2	1		1	1			7		
Marshfield	94	12	Thomas	John	1		1	1		2	2		1				8		
Marshfield	94	13	Wright	Daniel		1		1			1	1		1			5		
Marshfield	94	14	Kent	Nathaniel			1	1		3	1		2	1			9		
Marshfield	94	15	Thomas	Charles			1			1		1					3		
Marshfield	94	16	Kent	Peleg		1		1					1	1			4		
Marshfield	94	17	Peterson	Samuel		1	1	1		1		1	1				6		
Marshfield	94	18	Bourn	Thomas			1			2			1				4		
Marshfield	94	19	Winslow	Snow			1							1			2		
Marshfield	94	20	Dingley	Jebez		1		1			1			1			4		
Marshfield	95	1	Baker	John				1						1			2		
Marshfield	95	2	Baker	Scolly	1	1		1		2			1				6		
Marshfield	95	3	Sprague	James				1						1			2		
Marshfield	95	4	Sprague	Luther	2			1					1				4		
Marshfield	95	5	Sprague	Melzer	1			1		2			1				5		
Marshfield	95	6	Foorde	Seth				1						1			2		
Marshfield	95	7	Foorde	Waterman		1		1						1			3		
Marshfield	95	8	Foorde	Lemuel			1	1					2	1			5		
Marshfield	95	9	Foorde	Malboro	2			1					1				4		
Marshfield	95	10	Lapham	Joseph		1		1			1	1		1			5		
Marshfield	95	11	Lapham	Jabez			1			1		1					3		
Marshfield	95	12	Foorde	Aruanah			2						2	1			5		
Marshfield	95	13	Hatch	Prince	2	1		1		1	1	1	1				8		
Marshfield	95	14	Wright	Jabez	1	1	1	1		1			1				6		
Marshfield	95	15	Lewis	Bela	1	1		1		2	1		1				7		
Marshfield	95	16	Stevens	William				1			3			1			5		
Marshfield	95	17	Stevens	Nathaniel	2			1			1						4		
Marshfield	95	18	Stevens	John	2			1		2			1				6		
Marshfield	95	19	Lowe	Wm	1	1	2		1	1		2	1	1			10		
Marshfield	96	1	Lowe	Thomas	1			1		1			1				4		
Marshfield	96	2	Williamson	Abner				1		1			1				3		
Marshfield	96	3	Lowe	Jeremiah	1			1	1		1			1			5		
Marshfield	96	4	Thomas	Abijah				1			1			2			4		
Marshfield	96	5	Foorde	Elisha Jun	3			1		2	2		1				9		
Marshfield	96	6	Foorde	Samuel	1		1	1					1	1			5		
Marshfield	96	7	Hunt	Joseph		1		2		1			1				5		
Marshfield	96	8	Walker	Daniel	2	1		1			2		1				7		
Marshfield	96	9	Walker	Asa		1		1		2			1				5		
Marshfield	96	10	Baker	William				1						1			2		
Marshfield	96	11	Baker	William Jun	2			1		1			1				5		
Marshfield	96	12	Thomas	William				1		2			2				5		
Marshfield	96	13	Lapham	Jesse			2		1			1		1			5		
Marshfield	96	14	Forde	Elisha	1	1		1						2			5		
Marshfield	96	15	Foorde	John	2			1		2			1				6		
Marshfield	96	16	Samson	Chandler			2	1		2			1				6		
Marshfield	96	17	Walker	Joel				1					1				2		
Marshfield	97	1	Little	Ephraim			1	1						1			3		
Marshfield	97	2	Little	John		1	1	1	1			2		1			7		
Marshfield	97	3	Hatch	Noah		1	1	1	1			1		1			6		
Marshfield	97	4	Tilden	Mary		1							1	2			4		
Marshfield	97	5	Oakman	Amos	2			1		1	1		1	1			7		
Marshfield	97	6	Truant	Samuel		1		1				1	1	1			5		
Marshfield	97	7	Truant	John			1	1						1			3		
Marshfield	97	8	Macumber	William		1		1		1			1	1			5		
Marshfield	97	9	Macumber	Wm Jun	3			1		2			1				7		
Marshfield	97	10	Tilden	Joseph	2	2	2		1	2			1	3			13		
Marshfield	97	11	Silvester	Hatch		1		1		1	1		1	1			6		
Marshfield	97	12	Tilden	Joshua			1	1	1		1						4		
Marshfield	97	13	Leonard	Elijah Revd	1							1	1				4		
Marshfield	97	14	Ewel	Jedediah	1			1				1	1	2			6		

TOWN	PG#	LN#	LAST NAME	FIRST NAME	M under 10	M 10 to 16	M 16 to 26	M 26 to 45	M 45 and over	F under 10	F 10 to 16	F 16 to 26	F 26 to 45	F 45 and over	TOTAL ALL OTHER	TOTAL SLAVES	TOTALS	DISTRICT/TOWNSHIP	NOTES
Marshfield	97	15	Ewel	Seth				1				1		1			3		
Marshfield	97	16	Rogers	Thomas Jun				1				1	2	1			5		
Marshfield	97	17	Rogers	Simeon			1	1						1			3		
Marshfield	97	18	Vinal	Lucy	1							1	1	2			5		
Marshfield	97	19	Ewel	Joseph	1	1		1		1	1		1				6		
Marshfield	97	20	Hall	Danforth	2			1				1	1				5		
Marshfield	97	21	Ewel	Christopher	1		1			1			1				4		
Marshfield	97	22	Little	George Esq	2		1	1		2	2	1	1				10		
Marshfield	98	1	Lewis	Daniel		1		1					1	2			5		
Marshfield	98	2	Joyce	John		1		1		1			2	1			6		
Marshfield	98	3	Baker	Bradbery			1						2	1			4		
Marshfield	98	4	Baker	Henry			1						1				2		
Marshfield	98	5	Sprague	James Jun	1		2	1					1				5		
Marshfield	98	6	Holmes	Abraham	1			1		2			1				5		
Marshfield	98	7	Toleman	Benjamin			2	1	1				1	1			6		
Marshfield	98	8	Simons	Thomas				1				1					2		
Marshfield	98	9	Dingley	Jacob	2			1		2			1				6		
Marshfield	98	10	Winslow	Thomas		1		1		1				1			4		
Marshfield	98	11	Keen	Benjm	1			2		1			1				5		
Marshfield	98	12	Rogers	Timothy		1		1					1				3		
Marshfield	98	13	Hall	Samuel		1	1	1		1			1				5		
Marshfield	98	14	Little	Thomas				1						1			2		
Marshfield	98	15	Little	Thomas Jun	2			1		2	1		1				7		
Marshfield	98	16	Thomas	Asa	1			1						1	1		4		
Marshfield	98	17	Little	Luther		1		1		2		1	1				6		
Marshfield	98	18	Little	Penelope								1	1				2		
Marshfield	98	19	Little	Jedediah	1			1		2			1				5		
Marshfield	99	1	Rogers	Thomas		1		1					2	1			5		
Marshfield	99	2	Rogers	Israel				1					1	1			3		
Marshfield	99	3	Rogers	Aurunah	2			1		1	1		1				6		
Marshfield	99	4	Rogers	Benjm	1	1	1						1				4		
Marshfield	99	5	Rogers	Zackeus				1						1			2		
Marshfield	99	6	Rogers	Zackeus Jun	2	1		1		1			1				6		
Marshfield	99	7	Silvester	Joseph				1						1			2		
Marshfield	99	8	Ewel	Job		2	2	1		2	2			1			10		
Marshfield	99	9	Ewel	James	2			1		3			1				7		
Marshfield	99	10	Clift	Bethia				1					1	1			3		
Marshfield	99	11	Shearman	Joseph	1		1	1		1			1	1			6		
Marshfield	99	12	Shearman	Ichabod	2			1		2	1		1				7		
Marshfield	99	13	Shearman	Aron	1		1						1				3		
Marshfield	99	14	Shearman	Abiel	3			1		2	2		1				9		
Marshfield	99	15	Hyland	John				1						1			2		
Marshfield	99	16	Shearman	Ebenezer		2	1	1		2		3		1			10		
Marshfield	99	17	Joyce	Thomas		1		1				1	1	1			5		
Marshfield	99	18	Joyce	Nathl				1						1			2		
Marshfield	99	19	Joyce	Samuel	2			1		2			1				6		
Marshfield	99	20	Joyce	David	3			1		2			1				7		
Marshfield	99	21	Joyce	Jonathan				1				1	1	1			4		
Marshfield	100	1	Rogers	Nathl Jun				1				2	2	1			6		
Marshfield	100	2	Silvester	Amasa	2			1		3			1				7		
Marshfield	100	3	Clift	Joseph				1						1			2		
Marshfield	100	4	Clift	Wills			1			1	1	1		1			5		
Marshfield	100	5	Clift	Wm		1		1		1	1		1				5		
Marshfield	100	6	Clift	Joseph Jun	1			1		2			1				5		
Marshfield	100	7	Clift	Nathl	1			1					1				3		
Marshfield	100	8	Rogers	Thomas Junior	1	4	2	1		1			1				10		
Marshfield	100	9	Rogers	Amos		1		1				2	2				6		
Marshfield	100	10	Rogers	Nathl			2	1				1	1	1			6		
Marshfield	100	11	Rogers	Adam			1	1					2	1			5		
Marshfield	100	12	Damon	Obediah				1					1	1			3		
Marshfield	100	13	Damon	Aruanah	1	1		1		2	1	1	1				9		
Marshfield	100	14	Damon	Nathl	3			1		1		2	1				8		
Marshfield	100	15	Eames	Jedediah				1					2				3		
Marshfield	100	16	Eames	John J.	1			1		3			1				6		
Marshfield	100	17	Rogers	Joseph				1		1	1	1		1			5		
Marshfield	100	18	Rogers	Stephen		1		1					1	1			4		
Marshfield	100	19	Rogers	James	1	1		1		3	1		1	1			9		
Marshfield	100	20	Rogers	Asa	2	2		1		2	1		1				9		
Marshfield	100	21	Rogers	Peleg				1				1		1			3		
Marshfield	101	1	Lapham	Daniel				1						1			2		
Marshfield	101	2	Lapham	Sylvanus	1			1		1				1			4		
Marshfield	101	3	Decro	Seth			1	1					1	1			4		
Marshfield	101	4	Porter	John	2	1		1		3	1		1				9		
Marshfield	101	5	Carver	Alison	1	1		1		3			1	1			8		
Marshfield	101	6	Tilden	Wales		1		1				1	1	1			5		
Marshfield	101	7	Mitchel	Sarah			1						1	1			3		
Marshfield	101	8	Jones	John				1					1				2		
Marshfield	101	9	Samson	Aron				1		1				1			3		
Marshfield	101	10	Lapham	Roger	1			1		1			1				4		
Marshfield	101	11	Church	Wm	1			1		1				1			4		
Marshfield	101	12	Church	David	1			1					1				3		
Marshfield	101	13	Mitchel	Rispah			2	1				1	1	1			6		
Marshfield	101	14	Williamson	Samuel	1			1		1			1				4		
Marshfield	101	15	Hatch	David		1				1			1				3		
Marshfield	101	16	Hatch	Benjm				1					1				2		
Marshfield	101	17	Lapham	Adam		1		1					1				3		
Marshfield	101	18	Ewel	Gershom		1		1		1				1			4		
Marshfield	101	19	White	Orphen										1			1		
Marshfield	101	20	Rogers	Samuel			1			1		1		1			4		
Marshfield	101	21	Tilden	Jotham	2			1		1		1	1				6		

36

TOWN	PG#	LN#	LAST NAME	FIRST NAME	FREE WHITE MALES					FREE WHITE FEMALES					TOTAL ALL OTHER	TOTAL SLAVES	TOTALS	DISTRICT/ TOWNSHIP	NOTES
					under 10	10 to 16	16 to 26	26 to 45	45 and over	under 10	10 to 16	16 to 26	26 to 45	45 and over					
Marshfield	102	1	Eames	Amos	1	1			1	1		1		1			6		
Marshfield	102	2	Jones	Amos			1		1	1	2	2	2	1			10		
Marshfield	102	3	Hall	Jane										1			1		
Marshfield	102	4	Hatch	Naomi										1			1		
Marshfield	102	5	Hatch	Jonathan	1	2	2		1			1		1			8		
Marshfield	102	6	Oakman	Tobias					1				1	1			3		
Marshfield	102	7	Oakman	Constant F.		3		1		3			1				8		
Marshfield	102	8	Tilden	Samuel		1	1		1		1			1			5		
Marshfield	102	9	Tilden	Samuel Jun	1			1		3		1	1				7		
Marshfield	102	10	Hall	Timothy				1						1			2		
Marshfield	102	11	Silvester	Jonathan				1		1				1			3		
Marshfield	102	12	Hatch	Amos			1	1				1	1	1			5		
Marshfield	102	13	Hatch	Israel				1				1		1			3		
Marshfield	102	14	Hatch	Joel	1			1		1		1					4		
Marshfield	102	15	Hatch	Anthony	2	2			1	2	1	1	1				10		
Marshfield	102	16	Hatch	Ichobud	1			1					1				3		
Marshfield	102	17	Vinal	Seth				1					1	1			3		
Marshfield	102	18	Sprague	Jonathan		1	1		1	1	1	1		1			7		
Marshfield	102	19	Mitchel	James			1							1			2		
Marshfield	102	20	White	James			1			2			1	1			5		
Marshfield	102	21	White	Joanna										1			1		
Marshfield	103	1	Gray	Frances				1					1	2			4		
Marshfield	103	2	Waterman	Asa Esq	1	2			1	2			1				7		
Marshfield	103	3	Thomas	Briggs		1			1		1	2		2			7		
Marshfield	103	4	Hatch	John			1						1				2		
Marshfield	103	5	Foord	Olive	1	1	1				1	1		1			6		
Marshfield	103	6	Hatch	Charles	2			1			2		1				6		
Marshfield	103	7	Williamson	Nathaniel	4			1		1			1				7		
Marshfield	104	1	Tilden	Elisha	1	1		1		1			1				5		
Marshfield	104	2	Lapham	Stephen				1				1	1	2			5		
Marshfield	104	3	Oakman	Louisa							1			1			2		
Marshfield	104	4	Waterman	Nathl	2			1		2	1		1				7		
Marshfield	104	5	Rogers	Prince				1						1			2		
Marshfield	104	6	Hall	Lemuel				1		1			2				4		
Marshfield	104	7	Lapham	Isaac		1		1		1			1				4		
Marshfield	104	8	Ewel	Christopher	1			1		1			1				4		
Marshfield	104	9	Forde	Asa	1			1				1					3		
Marshfield	104	10	Rogers	Isaac	3			1		1			1				6		
Marshfield	104	11	Forde	Levi		1		1	1			1		1			5		
Marshfield	104	12	Eames	Hannah										1			1		
Marshfield	104	13	Porter	Oliver	2	1			1		1			1			6		
Marshfield	104	14	Waterman	Deborah			1						2				3		
Marshfield	104	15	Chandler	Thomas			3		1				2	1			7		
Marshfield	104	16	Wadsworth	Luke		1	2							2			6		
Marshfield	104	17	Samson	Paul			1	1	1					1			4		
Marshfield	104	18	Bourne	John	2	1			1	1				1			6		
Marshfield	104	19	Dingley	Thomas			1	2	1			2		1			7		

TOWN	PG#	LN#	LAST NAME	FIRST NAME	FREE WHITE MALES under 10	10 to 16	16 to 26	26 to 45	45 and over	FREE WHITE FEMALES under 10	10 to 16	16 to 26	26 to 45	45 and over	TOTAL ALL OTHER	TOTAL SLAVES	TOTALS	DISTRICT/ TOWNSHIP	NOTES
Middleborough	69	1	Atwood	Eli	1			1		2			1				5		
Middleborough	69	2	Alden	John 2d				1		4			1				6		
Middleborough	69	3	Aldrich	Nathan	1			1		2			1				5		
Middleborough	69	4	Alden	John		1		1	1				3	1			7		
Middleborough	69	5	Alden	David				1				1		1			3		
Middleborough	69	6	Alden	Job	1		1	1	1	1	1		1	1			8		
Middleborough	69	7	Allen	John	2				1	1	2	2	1				9		
Middleborough	69	8	Alden	Andrew	2			1				1					4		
Middleborough	69	9	Alden	David Jr	1	1		1				1	1				5		
Middleborough	69	10	Alden	Rufus	1		1		1	2	1			1			7		
Middleborough	69	11	Alden	Elijah	1	2	1		1	2	1	2		1	1		12		
Middleborough	69	12	Aldrich	Joseph	1	1		1						1			4		
Middleborough	69	13	Ashley	Noah	1	1	2		1	1				1			7		
Middleborough	69	14	Allen	Bezalel				1		1			2				4		
Middleborough	69	15	Atwood	Ichabod Jr	3			1					1				5		
Middleborough	69	16	Alden	Earl	1	1	1					1		1			5		
Middleborough	69	17	Atwood	John		1		1		1	1		1				5		
Middleborough	69	18	Alden	Judith Wd									1	1			2		
Middleborough	69	19	Barker	Joseph Revd	3	1		1	2	1		1	1	1			11		
Middleborough	69	20	Bryant	William		1	1	1		1	1	1					6		
Middleborough	69	21	Briggs	Levi	1			1					1				3		
Middleborough	69	22	Briggs	Elisha Dr	1		1						1				3		
Middleborough	69	23	Beals	Solomon	2				1				1				4		
Middleborough	69	24	Wilder	Nathl Junr			1			2		1	1				5		
Middleborough	69	25	Westgard	Jonathan	5	1		1		1		1	1				10		
Middleborough	69	26	Whiting	Ruth Wo									2	1			3		
Middleborough	69	27	Wood	Freeman			1	1		5	2		1	1			11		
Middleborough	69	28	Waterman	Joshua			1		1				1	1			4		
Middleborough	69	29	Williams	Joshua	3			1	1		1		1				7		
Middleborough	69	30	Weston	John Lt					1	1		2	1		1		6		
Middleborough	69	31	Wood	Nelson Lt		1	1						1				3		
Middleborough	69	32	Warner	Joseph				1						1			2		
Middleborough	69	33	Winslow	Benjamin				1					1	1			3		
Middleborough	69	34	Wood	Isaac	2			1		1			1				5		
Middleborough	69	35	Wood	Ephraim				1		1				1			3		
Middleborough	69	36	Wood	Ezra	1			1		1			1				4		
Middleborough	71	1	Benson	Elisha	2	2			1	1	1			1			8		
Middleborough	71	2	Burbank	Thomas	2			1		1			1				5		
Middleborough	71	3	Barrows	Jacob				1		2	1		1				5		
Middleborough	71	4	Bryant	Isaac			1		1			2	1	1			6		
Middleborough	71	5	Booth	Joseph Jun	1		1		1	2				1			6		
Middleborough	71	6	Bryant	Josiah				2				1		1			4		
Middleborough	71	7	Baker	William	2			1					1				4		
Middleborough	71	8	Briggs	Leonard		1		1		5	1		1				9		
Middleborough	71	9	Bennet	Jedediah	1			1		1			1				4		
Middleborough	71	10	Bennet	Edson	1		1						1				3		
Middleborough	71	11	Bennet	Shephard	1			1					1				3		
Middleborough	71	12	Bennet	Elias	1			1	1				1				4		
Middleborough	71	13	Bennet	Nehemh Esqr		1				1		1					4		
Middleborough	71	14	Bennet	Stephen		1	1	1		2	1	2	1	1			10		
Middleborough	71	15	Barrows	Nathl		2	4		1					1			8		
Middleborough	71	16	Briggs	Dean	3			1		1			1				6		
Middleborough	71	17	Barden	John	1	1	2		1	2	1	1		1			10		
Middleborough	71	18	Barden	Solomon				1									1		
Middleborough	71	19	Barden	Ichabod				1									1		
Middleborough	71	20	Barden	Bethiah			1						1				2		
Middleborough	71	21	Briggs	Ebenz				1						1			2		
Middleborough	71	22	Washburn	Thomas	2	2		1		1	1			1			8		
Middleborough	71	23	Wood	Thomas	1			1					1				4		
Middleborough	71	24	Wood	Thomas 2d Cap	2	1		1		1	2		1				8		
Middleborough	71	25	Weston	Zecharh				2		2	1	1	1	1			8		
Middleborough	71	26	Wood	Amos				1				1		1			3		
Middleborough	71	27	Wood	Peter Cap	3	2			2	2			1				10		
Middleborough	71	28	Wood	Anul Lt	3			1		1			1				6		
Middleborough	71	29	Washburn	Solomon		1		1		3	1		1				7		
Middleborough	71	30	Wood	Silvanus	2			1		2			1	1			7		
Middleborough	71	31	Wood	Israel	1	1	2		1			1		1			7		
Middleborough	71	32	Wood	Jacob	3	1		1		1			1				7		
Middleborough	71	33	Wood	Daniel			1						1				2		
Middleborough	71	34	Wood	Silas				1	2				1				4		
Middleborough	71	35	Wood	Timothy	1		1	1		1			1				5		
Middleborough	71	36	Wood	Elnathan		1			1				1	1			4		
Middleborough	71	37	White	Silas		1	1		1			2	1	1			7		
Middleborough	71	38	Wood	Sarah Wo										1			1		
Middleborough	71	39	Washburn	Benjan	3	1	2		1			1	1	1			10		
Middleborough	71	40	Washburn	Judith Wo									1	1			2		
Middleborough	71	41	Weston	Rufus			2		1			1		2			6		
Middleborough	71	42	Washburn	Abiel 2d			1			1			1				3		
Middleborough	71	43	Wilder	Ebenezer			1						1				2		

TOWN	PG#	LN#	HEADS OF HOUSEHOLD		FREE WHITE MALES					FREE WHITE FEMALES					TOTAL ALL OTHER	TOTAL SLAVES	TOTALS	DISTRICT/ TOWNSHIP	NOTES
			LAST NAME	FIRST NAME	under 10	10 to 16	16 to 26	26 to 45	45 and over	under 10	10 to 16	16 to 26	26 to 45	45 and over					
Middleborough	71	44	Wilder	Benariah			1			1		1					3		
Middleborough	72	1	White	Samuel			1			2			1				4		
Middleborough	72	2	White	Joshua Esqr				1					1				2		
Middleborough	72	3	White	Daniel	2	1	1	1		2	1		1				9		
Middleborough	72	4	Wood	Nichols	1	2		1		2	1	1					8		
Middleborough	72	5	Weston	David				1					1				2		
Middleborough	72	6	Weston	David Jr	2			1		2	1	1					7		
Middleborough	72	7	Weston	Seth	2	1		1		2	1		1				8		
Middleborough	72	8	Washburn	Jonathan			2		1	2	2		1				8		
Middleborough	72	9	Winslow	Asa	1			1		4	2		1				9		
Middleborough	72	10	Williams	George			1			3			1				5		
Middleborough	72	11	Washburn	James		3	1				2	2	1		1		10		
Middleborough	72	12	Weston	Thomas		1	1					1	1				4		
Middleborough	72	13	Washburn	Abiel Col	3	1		1		3			2				10		
Middleborough	72	14	Wood	Ebenezer		1		1				2	1				5		
Middleborough	72	15	Wood	Wilkes			1			1		1					3		
Middleborough	72	16	Wood	Gorham			1					1					2		
Middleborough	72	17	Warren	Nathan	3	2		1					1				7		
Middleborough	72	18	Weston	Edmund				1				1	1				3		
Middleborough	72	19	Warren	Silvanus Lt		3		1					1				5		
Middleborough	72	20	Wood	Ichabod Lt	2		2		1	1	1		2				9		
Middleborough	72	21	Wood	Joshua			2	1		1		1					5		
Middleborough	72	22	Wilder	Nath Cap	1	3	2		1	1	2		1				11		
Middleborough	72	23	Wilber	Benjamin	1			1		1	1		1				5		
Middleborough	72	24	White	Bethnael	1		1					1					3		
Middleborough	72	25	Bryant	Jesse				1				1		2			4		
Middleborough	72	26	Bourn	Lemuel		1	1		1		1	2		1			7		
Middleborough	72	27	Bourne	Abner Dr		1	1		1			1		2			6		
Middleborough	72	28	Bourne	Wm Capt			2	1		1			1				5		
Middleborough	72	29	Bryant	Lemuel				1				1					2		
Middleborough	72	30	Burges	Stephen	2	1	1		1	1		1	1	1			9		
Middleborough	72	31	Bennet	William				2					1				3		
Middleborough	72	32	Briggs	George	1		1			1		1					4		
Middleborough	72	33	Burgess	Seth			1						1				2		
Middleborough	72	34	Burrows	Abner				1					2				3		
Middleborough	72	35	Burrows	Abner Jr	2			1		1			1				5		
Middleborough	72	36	Benson	Joshua		1							1				2		
Middleborough	72	37	Benson	John				1				1	1				3		
Middleborough	72	38	Benson	Andrew	2			1		1			1				5		
Middleborough	72	39	Bishop	John			1	1	1		1			1			5		
Middleborough	72	40	Benson	Consider				1					1				2		
Middleborough	72	41	Benson	John 2d	1			1		1			1				4		
Middleborough	72	42	Benson	Ebenz	1		1			1		1					4		
Middleborough	72	43	Blackman	Thomas			1		1				1				3		
Middleborough	72	44	Bourne	Caleb			1			2			1				4		
Middleborough	72	45	Benson	Asa	2	1			1	2		1	1				8		
Middleborough	72	46	Booth	Guilford	1			1		1			1				4		
Middleborough	73	1	Thomson	Isaac Esqr Hon	1	2	1		1	1	2	1	1	1			11		
Middleborough	73	2	Thomson	Molly Wd			1					1	1				3		
Middleborough	73	3	Tinkham	Ebenezer				1					1				2		
Middleborough	73	4	Tinkham	Zebedee		1	1	1				1	1				5		
Middleborough	73	5	Thomas	Solomon	2			1		1	2		1				7		
Middleborough	73	6	Thomas	August	1			1				2					4		
Middleborough	73	7	Thomas	Daniel	3			1		1			1				6		
Middleborough	73	8	Tinkham	Silas			1		1			2	1				6		
Middleborough	73	9	Tinkham	Parience Wo									1				1		
Middleborough	73	10	Tinkham	Jesse	1	2	2		1	1		1		1			9		
Middleborough	73	11	Tinkham	Ebenz 2d	3			1		2			1				7		
Middleborough	73	12	Thomson	Jacob Cap		1		1				2					5		
Middleborough	73	13	Tinkham	Seth				1					1				2		
Middleborough	73	14	Tinkham	Hazuel	2	1		1					1				5		
Middleborough	73	15	Thomson	Thomas	3			1		2			1				7		
Middleborough	73	16	Tinkham	Abigail									1	1			2		
Middleborough	73	17	Thomas	Calvin				1					1				2		
Middleborough	73	18	Thomson	Caleb	3	1	3		1	2	1		2				15		
Middleborough	73	19	Tinkham	James	4		2		1		1	2		1			11		
Middleborough	73	20	Thomas	Zenas		1		1		2	2		1				7		
Middleborough	73	21	Tinkham	Abishaw Capt		1			1			1		1			4		
Middleborough	73	22	Thomas	Nelson Capt	1		1	1		1			1				5		
Middleborough	73	23	Thomas	Abner	1			1		1			1				4		
Middleborough	73	24	Thomas	Zephannah			1	1				3	1				6		
Middleborough	73	25	Tinkham	Isaac		2		1		1	1		1				6		
Middleborough	73	26	Thomas	Joseph		1	2		1	2	1	2	1	1			11		
Middleborough	73	27	Thomas	Isaac				1					1				2		
Middleborough	73	28	Thomas	Isaac 2d	1			1		1			1				4		
Middleborough	73	29	Thomas	Isaac 3d			1					1					2		
Middleborough	73	30	Thomson	John			1			0			1				2		
Middleborough	73	31	Thomson	Ephraim	1			1		1		1					4		
Middleborough	73	32	Tribon	Metzer	1			1									3		

TOWN	PG#	LN#	LAST NAME	FIRST NAME	FREE WHITE MALES					FREE WHITE FEMALES					TOTAL ALL OTHER	TOTAL SLAVES	TOTALS	DISTRICT/ TOWNSHIP	NOTES
					under 10	10 to 16	16 to 26	26 to 45	45 and over	under 10	10 to 16	16 to 26	26 to 45	45 and over					
Middleborough	73	33	Townsend	Silas		1		1		1			1				4		
Middleborough	73	34	Tinkham	Joanna										1			1		
Middleborough	73	35	Thomson	Nathan				1			1			1			3		
Middleborough	73	36	Turner	Caleb Revd		1	1	1				1		2			6		
Middleborough	73	37	Tinkham	Deborah Wo		1	1					1		1			4		
Middleborough	73	38	Thrasher	John	1			1		1			1	1			5		
Middleborough	73	39	Thrasher	Samuel				1									1		
Middleborough	73	40	Vaughan	Joseph	1			1					1				3		
Middleborough	73	41	Vaughan	Nathan			1						1	1			3		
Middleborough	73	42	Vaughan	George Capt	1		2		1		1	1		2			8		
Middleborough	73	43	Vaughan	Peter	3			1		1			1	1			7		
Middleborough	73	44	Vaughan	Daniel 2d	1			1		1			1				4		
Middleborough	73	45	Valentine	John				1						1			2		
Middleborough	73	46	Vaughan	Ebenezer		1	1	1				1		1			5		
Middleborough	73	47	Vaughan	Jabez				2					1				3		
Middleborough	73	48	Vaughan	Elkanah	3			1					1				5		
Middleborough	73	49	Vaughan	Zebulon				1				1		1			3		
Middleborough	73	50	Vaughan	Ephraim W				1		1			1				3		
Middleborough	73	51	Vaughan	David Capt			2		1				2				5		
Middleborough	73	52	Vaughan	Silvanus		1		1		1			1				4		
Middleborough	73	53	Vaughan	Jesse	1				1	2			1				5		
Middleborough	73	54	Vaughan	David Jr	2	2		1		1	1	1					8		
Middleborough	73	55	Vaughan	Joanna Wo									1				1		
Middleborough	73	56	Wood	Zenas Capt	3	1		1		3			1				9		
Middleborough	73	57	Weston	Daniel	2	1		1		1		1					6		
Middleborough	73	58	Weston	Daniel 2d				1		2		1	1				5		
Middleborough	73	59	Wood	Abner Lt				1				2		1	1		5		
Middleborough	73	60	Wood	Abner Junr			1			3		1					5		
Middleborough	73	61	Washburn	Perez	1			1		1			1				4		
Middleborough	74	1	Thomas	Jedediah 2d	1			1		2			1				5		
Middleborough	74	2	Towsend	Abner	1	1		1		1			1				5		
Middleborough	74	3	Thomas	Fear									1				1		
Middleborough	74	4	Tisdael	Isaac			1	1					1				3		
Middleborough	74	5	Thrasher	Job	1			1			1		1				4		
Middleborough	74	6	Thomas	Elisha	3	3		1		3	1		1				12		
Middleborough	74	7	Thrasher	Daniel	1	2	1	1		2			1	1			9		
Middleborough	74	8	Thomas	Israel		1	1	1		1	1		1				6		
Middleborough	74	9	Thomas	Edward		1		1		1			1	1	1		5		
Middleborough	74	10	Thomas	David			2	1					1				4		
Middleborough	74	11	Thomas	Hushar Capt 2d	2			1				1	1				5		
Middleborough	74	12	Tinkham	Peter	1	1			2				1				5		
Middleborough	74	13	Thomas	Enoch 2d	1			1		2	1		1				6		
Middleborough	74	14	Thomas	Hushar		1		1					1				3		
Middleborough	74	15	Tucker	Samuel		1	1	1					1				4		
Middleborough	74	16	Tucker	Daniel	4	3		1		3	1		1				13		
Middleborough	74	17	Thomson	William Capt		2		1		1	1	2		1			8		
Middleborough	74	18	Thomson	Nathl 2d		1			1		1	3		1			7		
Middleborough	74	19	Thomson	Ruth Wo									1				1		
Middleborough	74	20	Thomas	Jonathan	1			1			1	1					4		
Middleborough	74	21	Thomson	Benjn	1			1		2	1		1				6		
Middleborough	75	1	Bent	Zenas	1			1		2			1				5		
Middleborough	75	2	Bent	John				1					1				2		
Middleborough	75	3	Bent	Experience	1	1		1		3		1	1				8		
Middleborough	75	4	Bryant	Seth		1		1					1				3		
Middleborough	75	5	Bryant	Joseph				1					1				2		
Middleborough	75	6	Booth	Benjan	2	1		1		1		1		1			7		
Middleborough	75	7	Briggs	Molbon	4	2		1					1				8		
Middleborough	75	8	Bennet	John		1		1					1				3		
Middleborough	75	9	Bennet	Thomas		1		1		2			1				5		
Middleborough	75	10	Blye	John	3			1		1			1				6		
Middleborough	75	11	Bennet	Hope Wo								1	1				2		
Middleborough	75	12	Briggs	Ebenz 2d	2	1	3		1	1	1	2		1			12		
Middleborough	75	13	Bumpus	Zenos	2			1		2			1				6		
Middleborough	75	14	Bennet	Arthur	2		1					1					4		
Middleborough	75	15	Bryant	John	1			1				2					4		
Middleborough	75	16	Bryant	Hannah 3d									2				2		
Middleborough	75	17	Besse	Joseph				1					1				2		
Middleborough	75	18	Bates	Thomas	1	1	2	1		1	1		1				8		
Middleborough	75	19	Besse	Joseph Jun	3			1		3	1	1					9		
Middleborough	75	20	Bennet	Jacob		1		1		2	1	1	1				7		
Middleborough	75	21	Bennet	Elkanah	1			1		1	1	1	1				6		
Middleborough	75	22	Thomas	Abraham	2			1		1			1				5		
Middleborough	75	23	Thomas	Seth	2		1		1	2	1	1		1			9		
Middleborough	75	24	Thomas	Simeon	2			1		1	1	2	1				9		
Middleborough	75	25	Thomas	Barzilla				1					1				2		
Middleborough	75	26	Thomas	Enoch	1			1			2	4	1				9		
Middleborough	75	27	Thomas	Moses									2				2		
Middleborough	75	28	Thomas	Moses Jur			1		1		1						3		
Middleborough	75	29	Thomas	Jacob			1		1		1						3		

TOWN	PG#	LN#	LAST NAME	FIRST NAME	FREE WHITE MALES					FREE WHITE FEMALES					TOTAL ALL OTHER	TOTAL SLAVES	TOTALS	DISTRICT/ TOWNSHIP	NOTES
					under 10	10 to 16	16 to 26	26 to 45	45 and over	under 10	10 to 16	16 to 26	26 to 45	45 and over					
Middleborough	75	30	Thomas	Henry	2			1		3	1		1				8		
Middleborough	75	31	Thomas	Silvanus Lt			1	1	1		2	1		1			7		
Middleborough	75	32	Thomas	Elijah		1	1	1	1		1		1	1			7		
Middleborough	75	33	Thomas	Churchill	1	1		1		2			1				6		
Middleborough	75	34	Thomas	Jedediah				1				1					2		
Middleborough	75	35	Thomas	Zebedee	1			1		1			1				4		
Middleborough	75	36	Thomas	Eleazer				1						1			2		
Middleborough	75	37	Thomas	Eleazer Jr		2		1		2	1	1	1				8		
Middleborough	75	38	Thomas	Levi		1	1	1		2			1				6		
Middleborough	75	39	Thomas	Perez	2	1	2	1		2	1	1		1			11		
Middleborough	75	40	Thomas	Benjan		1		1			1			1			4		
Middleborough	75	41	Thomas	James	2	2	1	1		2	2	1		1			12		
Middleborough	76	1	Thomas	Ezra	1	1		1		1	3	1					8		
Middleborough	76	2	Thomas	Lemuel				1		2	1		1				5		
Middleborough	76	3	Thomas	Solomon	1			1		2	2		1				7		
Middleborough	76	4	Thomas	Josiah				1		2			1				4		
Middleborough	76	5	Thomas	Samuel	1			1		1	1		1				5		
Middleborough	76	6	Thomas	Jeremiah	2	1		1		2	1		1				8		
Middleborough	76	7	Thomas	Elizabeth Wo									1	1			2		
Middleborough	76	8	Tinkham	Elisha	2		3	1		2	1		1				10		
Middleborough	76	9	Thomas	Silas	3			1				1		1			6		
Middleborough	76	10	Thomson	Nathl			2	1				3		1			7		
Middleborough	76	11	Towsend	John		1		2					2	1			6		
Middleborough	76	12	Townsend	Job				1		3	1		1	1			7		
Middleborough	76	13	Tilson	Silas Lt		1		1					1	1			4		
Middleborough	76	14	Tinkham	Cornelius		1	1	2					1	1			6		
Middleborough	76	15	Tinkham	John Lt	1	2	1	1		1	1	1					8		
Middleborough	76	16	Thomas	Ephraim				1						1			2		
Middleborough	76	17	Tinkham	Levi	2			1		1			2				6		
Middleborough	76	18	Tinkham	Squire	2		1					1					4		
Middleborough	76	19	Thomas	Elkanah	1			1					1				3		
Middleborough	76	20	Thomas	Ebenezer		1		1						1			3		
Middleborough	76	21	Thomas	Peleg				1		3			1				5		
Middleborough	76	22	Tilson	Culverson				1		1			1				3		
Middleborough	76	23	Bisbee	Hopstill	1			1		2		1	1				6		
Middleborough	76	24	Backus	Isaac Revd				1					1	1			3		
Middleborough	76	25	Backus	Simon	3	1		1		1			1				7		
Middleborough	76	26	Briggs	Ebenr 3d Capt	2	1		1		1			1				6		
Middleborough	76	27	Booth	Zebedee	1			1	1			2		1			6		
Middleborough	76	28	Booth	John	1		1	1						1			4		
Middleborough	76	29	Booth	Abiel	1			1		2			1				5		
Middleborough	76	30	Booth	Samuel	3			1					1				5		
Middleborough	76	31	Booth	Abner				1				1					2		
Middleborough	76	32	Briggs	Abiather	3			1		3			1				8		
Middleborough	76	33	Briggs	Ziphanh		1		1				1					3		
Middleborough	76	34	Briggs	Lemuel		1		1			1		1				4		
Middleborough	76	35	Bryant	Jesse Jr				1				1	1				3		
Middleborough	76	36	Booth	Zebedee 2d	4	2		1		2	1		1				11		
Middleborough	76	37	Benson	Isaac	1			1			2		1				5		
Middleborough	76	38	Booth	Joseph					1					1			2		
Middleborough	76	39	Bates	Samuel		1		1		1			1				4		
Middleborough	76	40	Bumpus	Joseph	1		2	1		1	2	2		1			10		
Middleborough	76	41	Bumpus	Joseph 2d	1	2	2	1				1	1				8		
Middleborough	76	42	Bennet	Benjn			1	1									1		
Middleborough	77	1	Cushman	Eliphalet	2	1		1		2		1					7		
Middleborough	77	2	Cushman	Isaac				1			2	1	1				5		
Middleborough	77	3	Cushman	Isaac Jun	3		0	1				1					5		
Middleborough	77	4	Cushman	zebulon	1	1		1		1		1	1				6		
Middleborough	77	5	Clark	Elisha Capt		1	2	1		2		1	1				8		
Middleborough	77	6	Clark	Robert	1	1	4	1			2		1				10		
Middleborough	77	7	Clark	Roger				1			1		1				3		
Middleborough	77	8	Cole	Andrew		1		1					1	1			4		
Middleborough	77	9	Cole	Nathl Lt	2	2		1		1	1		2				9		
Middleborough	77	10	Cushman	David			1			1		1					3		
Middleborough	77	11	Caswell	David	1		2	1		1		2	1				8		
Middleborough	77	12	Caswell	Elkanah				1						1			2		
Middleborough	77	13	Churchill	Isaac	2	1	2	1			2	1	1				10		
Middleborough	77	14	Carver	John Capt		1		1		1			1				4		
Middleborough	77	15	Cobb	Zebedee	1			1				1					3		
Middleborough	77	16	Cobb	Ebenzer			1	1					1	1			4		
Middleborough	77	17	Cobb	Lewis	2			1					1	1			5		
Middleborough	77	18	Clark	Nowls		2		1		1	3	4		1			12		
Middleborough	77	19	Cobb	Birney		1		1				2	1				5		
Middleborough	77	20	Cushman	John			1			1		1	1				4		
Middleborough	77	21	Cobb	Saml Ens		1	1	1				2		1			6		
Middleborough	77	22	Shaw	Elijah	1			2					2				5		
Middleborough	77	23	Soule	James 2d	2	1		1			1		2				7		
Middleborough	77	24	Smith	Zenas				1				1					2		
Middleborough	77	25	Smith	James Jr	1			1		1		1					4		
Middleborough	77	26	Soule	Isaac			3		1			1	2	1			8		

TOWN	PG#	LN#	LAST NAME	FIRST NAME	FREE WHITE MALES					FREE WHITE FEMALES					TOTAL ALL OTHER	TOTAL SLAVES	TOTALS	DISTRICT/ TOWNSHIP	NOTES
					under 10	10 to 16	16 to 26	26 to 45	45 and over	under 10	10 to 16	16 to 26	26 to 45	45 and over					
Middleborough	77	27	Smith	James Lt		2			1	2	1	1		3			10		
Middleborough	77	28	Smith	Jabez			1						1				2		
Middleborough	77	29	Smith	Ebenz Capt	2			1		2	3		1				9		
Middleborough	77	30	Soule	Jacob			1	1	1		3		1				7		
Middleborough	77	31	Standish	Jonathan	2		1						1				4		
Middleborough	77	32	Shaw	Abraham		1		1	1			1	1	1			6		
Middleborough	77	33	Simmons	Margett							1		2				3		
Middleborough	77	34	Smith	John Capt	1		1	1		1			2	1			7		
Middleborough	77	35	Smith	Joseph	3	2		1		1	2		1	1			11		
Middleborough	77	36	Shearman	Nehemh	3	1		1		1	2		1	1			10		
Middleborough	77	37	Shaw	Joshua Capt			1	1		2			1				7		
Middleborough	77	38	Shearman	Henry	1	1			1	2	2	1		1			10		
Middleborough	77	39	Strobridge	William	1	1		1		2			1				6		
Middleborough	77	40	Strobridge	Sarah Wo									1				1		
Middleborough	77	41	Simmons	Noah	1		1						1				3		
Middleborough	77	42	Smith	Joshua	1	1		1		1	2	1	1	1			9		
Middleborough	77	43	Strobridge	Jane Wo									1				1		
Middleborough	78	1	Shaw	Gaius			1			2		1					4		
Middleborough	78	2	Shaw	Joseph	3	1	1	1		1	2		1				10		
Middleborough	78	3	Shaw	James Dr				1		1		1		1			4		
Middleborough	78	4	Shaw	James Jr		1	1	1		2	1		1				7		
Middleborough	78	5	Smith	Daniel		1		1		1				1			4		
Middleborough	78	6	Smith	Daniel Jur	1		1			2		0	1				5		
Middleborough	78	7	Southworth	Seth	1		1	1				1					4		
Middleborough	78	8	Smith	Mary Wo	1							3	1				5		
Middleborough	78	9	Smith	Thomas				1				3	1				5		
Middleborough	78	10	Simmons	Thomas		1		1					1				3		
Middleborough	78	11	Samson	Thankfull									1				1		
Middleborough	78	12	Standish	Joshua	4			1					1				6		
Middleborough	78	13	Samson	Mersbah Wo			1					1		1	1		4		
Middleborough	78	14	Samson	Lazarus			1			1		1					3		
Middleborough	78	15	Spooner	Benjamin		1		1		4	1		1				8		
Middleborough	78	16	Smith	Ezra	1		1					1					3		
Middleborough	78	17	Smith	Abiel			1			1		1					3		
Middleborough	78	18	Spooner	Samuel	2			1		1	1		1				6		
Middleborough	78	19	Samson	Anna Wo			1						1				2		
Middleborough	78	20	Strobridge	Henry	1	1		1		2	1		1				7		
Middleborough	78	21	Sturtevant	Robert		1	1	1					1				4		
Middleborough	78	22	Sturtevant	Robert Jr	1		1						1				4		
Middleborough	78	23	Shaw	David	3	2		1	1				1				8		
Middleborough	78	24	Barrows	Isaac		1		1					1				3		
Middleborough	78	25	Bent	William						1	1		1				3		
Middleborough	78	26	Bennet	Philip	1		1			1		1					4		
Middleborough	78	27	Beirce	Levi			1										1		
Middleborough	78	28	Boes	Bethiah										1			1		
Middleborough	78	29	Bryant	Hannah Wo									1	1			2		
Middleborough	78	30	Blackman	Thomas Jur	1		1						1				3		
Middleborough	78	31	Cornish	William		1		1		2		2	1	1			8		
Middleborough	78	32	Crapo	Spooner	1		1						1				3		
Middleborough	78	33	Cox	Ebenezr	3	2	1	1		1		1	1				10		
Middleborough	78	34	Cushman	Robert		1	1	1		2	1	1	1				8		
Middleborough	78	35	Cobbe	John				1					1				?		
Middleborough	78	36	Cushman	Zenus		1	1	1		1			1				5		
Middleborough	78	37	Cobb	Susanna Wo									1	1			2		
Middleborough	78	38	Cushman	Ichabod	2	0	1	1		2			1				7		
Middleborough	78	39	Churchill	Perez	2	2	1		1		1	1		1			9		
Middleborough	78	40	Churchill	Nelson	1	2		1		2			1				7		
Middleborough	79	1	Caswell	Seth	1			1		2			1				5		
Middleborough	79	2	Chase	Lewis	1			1		2			2				6		
Middleborough	79	3	Cobb	Andrew		1		1				1	1				4		
Middleborough	79	4	Caswell	Jonathan				1				1		1			3		
Middleborough	79	5	Copland	Cyrus	3		1	1					1				6		
Middleborough	79	6	Curtis	Luke					1	3			1				5		
Middleborough	79	7	Cole	Edward	1		1	1		1			1				5		
Middleborough	79	8	Dunham	Joseph	1			1				1	1				4		
Middleborough	79	9	Darling	Benjn			1			1		2	1	1			6		
Middleborough	79	10	Darling	Daniel	1		1			2		1					5		
Middleborough	79	11	Darling	Nathan		1	1	1					1	1			5		
Middleborough	79	12	Duglass	George	1	1		1		1			1				5		
Middleborough	79	13	Duglass	Noah	4			1					1				8		
Middleborough	79	14	Dunham	Jonathan			1						1				2		
Middleborough	79	15	Daggett	Jabez	1			1						1			3		
Middleborough	79	16	Dagg	Peter			1						1				2		
Middleborough	79	17	Dunbar	Samuel				2						1			3		
Middleborough	79	18	Shearman	Job	4	1		1		2			1				9		
Middleborough	79	19	Shaw	Sullivan	2		1			1			1				5		
Middleborough	79	20	Shaw	Jonathan			1			1			1				3		
Middleborough	79	21	Smith	Israel	1		2	1		1	2	2	1				10		
Middleborough	79	22	Shaw	William Capt				1		1			1				3		
Middleborough	79	23	Shaw	William 2d	1		1	1		3		1	1				8		
Middleborough	79	24	Sturtevant	Thomas Dr	3	1	1	1		2	1	2		2			13		
Middleborough	79	25	Shaw	Isaac 2d	2			1					1	1			5		
Middleborough	79	26	Shaw	Mark	1	1		1				1	1				5		
Middleborough	79	27	Severy	Daniel	2	1		1			1		1				6		
Middleborough	79	28	Shaw	Patience Wo			1					1		1			3		
Middleborough	79	29	Shaw	Elkanah			1	1				1		1			4		
Middleborough	79	30	Shaw	Mary Wo									1	1			2		
Middleborough	79	31	Samson	John				1					1	1			3		
Middleborough	79	32	Samson	Nathan	1		1			1		1					4		

TOWN	PG#	LN#	HEADS OF HOUSEHOLD		FREE WHITE MALES					FREE WHITE FEMALES					TOTAL ALL OTHER	TOTAL SLAVES	TOTALS	DISTRICT/ TOWNSHIP	NOTES
			LAST NAME	FIRST NAME	under 10	10 to 16	16 to 26	26 to 45	45 and over	under 10	10 to 16	16 to 26	26 to 45	45 and over					
Middleborough	79	33	Shaw	Samuel	2			1		3		1					7		
Middleborough	79	34	Shaw	John 3d	1	1		1	1	3			1	1			9		
Middleborough	79	35	Samson	Obadiah	1			1									4		
Middleborough	79	36	Shaw	Zephaniah	3		1		1	1	2	2	1	1			12		
Middleborough	79	37	Samson	Samuel	3			1		2			1				7		
Middleborough	79	38	Samson	Thomas	1			1					1				3		
Middleborough	79	39	Shaw	John 2d Lt	3			1		2	2	2	1				11		
Middleborough	79	40	Sears	Leonard	3			1				1	1				6		
Middleborough	80	1	Sears	Earl	1			1						1			3		
Middleborough	80	2	Southworth	Nath	2			1		2	1	1		2			9		
Middleborough	80	3	Southworth	Gideon		1	2		1	1		2	1				8		
Middleborough	80	4	Samson	John Dr	1		1		1	1	1		1				6		
Middleborough	80	5	Samson	Uriah					1				1				4		
Middleborough	80	6	Samson	Isaac	2		1			1			1				5		
Middleborough	80	7	Samson	Elias	2		2	1				1	2				8		
Middleborough	80	8	Smith	Elijah		1	1			1		1					4		
Middleborough	80	9	Samson	Ruth Wo				1						1			2		
Middleborough	80	10	Sharp	Gibbins		1	1					1		1			4		
Middleborough	80	11	Sharp	Gibbins Jr	1		1			2			1				5		
Middleborough	80	12	Samson	Jonathan	1		1			1	3	2	1				9		
Middleborough	80	13	Smith	John 3d	1			1		1			2				5		
Middleborough	80	14	Smith	Thomas			1			3			1				5		
Middleborough	80	15	Shaw	Isaac				1						2			3		
Middleborough	80	16	Snow	Aaron			1	2				1		1			5		
Middleborough	80	17	Soule	Joh Cap	2	2		1	1			1	1	1			9		
Middleborough	80	18	Sprout	Thomas Lt	2			2		2	1		2		1		10		
Middleborough	80	19	Standish	Moses	1		1			3	1		1				7		
Middleborough	80	20	Shaw	Eli	1		1			2			1				5		
Middleborough	80	21	Churchill	Jabez	1	1		2		3	2		2	1			12		
Middleborough	80	22	Cobb	James	2	1	1	1		1	1		1				8		
Middleborough	80	23	Cushman	Joseph		1		1				2	1				5		
Middleborough	80	24	Cushman	Jacob	1		1			2			1				5		
Middleborough	80	25	Cushman	Noah	2		2	1		1		1	1				8		
Middleborough	80	26	Clark	Josiah				2						2			4		
Middleborough	80	27	Clark	Joseph 2d Capt	2		1						1				4		
Middleborough	80	28	Cushman	Elias		1		1					1				3		
Middleborough	80	29	Cox	Elisha				1						1			2		
Middleborough	80	30	Cushman	Joseph 2d			1	1		1			2				5		
Middleborough	80	31	Clark	Abner	4		1	1					1				7		
Middleborough	80	32	Canedy	Wm Capt	1			1				1	1	1			5		
Middleborough	80	33	Clark	Barnabas	1	2		1		1	2	1	1				9		
Middleborough	80	34	Clark	Samuel Dr				1					1	1			3		
Middleborough	80	35	Clark	Joseph Dr	1	1		1		2	1	2	1				9		
Middleborough	80	36	Chace	Benjan			1			1		1					4		
Middleborough	80	37	Canedy	William Jun	1	2		1		2	2		1				9		
Middleborough	80	38	Cole	Nathl 2d	1			1		3			1	1			7		
Middleborough	80	39	Clark	Aniel	2			1					1	1			5		
Middleborough	81	1	Eaton	Nathan	1	1	1		1	3	2			1			10		
Middleborough	81	2	Eaton	Samuel			1		1					1			3		
Middleborough	81	3	Eaton	Enos			1			1			1				3		
Middleborough	81	4	Eaton	Joel Capt			2		1		1	1		1			6		
Middleborough	81	5	Eaton	Jabez		3		1		1			1				6		
Middleborough	81	6	Ellis	Cornelius		2		1			1			1			5		
Middleborough	81	7	Elmes	John				1		1				1			3		
Middleborough	81	8	Eddy	Keziah Wo										1			1		
Middleborough	81	9	Ellis	Lucia Wo										1			1		
Middleborough	81	10	Eddy	Joshua Capt	2	2	5			1	1	2		1			15		
Middleborough	81	11	Eddy	Marcy Wo		1								1			2		
Middleborough	81	12	Eddy	Seth	2			1		1	1		1				6		
Middleborough	81	13	Edminster	Kenney	2	1		1					1	1			6		
Middleborough	81	14	Edson	Abiel	2	2	1		1				1	1			8		
Middleborough	81	15	Ellis	Southworth	1			1		1			1				4		
Middleborough	81	16	Eaton	Elijah		1			1					1			3		
Middleborough	81	17	Eddy	Susanna										2			2		
Middleborough	81	18	Evens	Leonard	1	1	1		1	1				2			7		
Middleborough	81	19	Elmes	Lydia Wo				1						1			2		
Middleborough	81	20	Richmond	John		1		1	1				2	2			7		
Middleborough	81	21	Reed	Nathan	4			1					1				6		
Middleborough	81	22	Richmond	Joseph Capt	2		2	1			1	1	1				8		
Middleborough	81	23	Richmond	Rufus				1						1			2		
Middleborough	81	24	Richmond	Seth	1			1		1			1				4		
Middleborough	81	25	Raymond	Edward		4	2	1	1			1					9		
Middleborough	81	26	Reed	Elijah		2		1		1	2	1	1				8		
Middleborough	81	27	Reed	Samuel	3	1			2	1	1	2		1			11		
Middleborough	81	28	Richmond	Job				1					1				2		
Middleborough	81	29	Richmond	Apollus			1			1			1				3		
Middleborough	81	30	Ransom	Lemuel		1		1				1		1			4		
Middleborough	81	31	Richmond	Stephen				1				1	1	1			4		
Middleborough	81	32	Ramsdell	Seth	3	2		1		2	1		1				10		
Middleborough	81	33	Reed	Bailey	3			1		3	1		1				9		
Middleborough	81	34	Raymond	Joseph	2			1					1	1			5		
Middleborough	81	35	Robins	Samuel	2			1		1	1		1				6		
Middleborough	81	36	Richmond	Edward			1	1	1			1	1	1			6		
Middleborough	81	37	Reed	Charles				1		1		2	1	1			6		
Middleborough	81	38	Reed	Joshua	2			1		2			1				6		
Middleborough	81	39	Rider	Chapman	1			1				1	1				4		
Middleborough	82	1	Ramsdell	William			1			1			1				3		
Middleborough	82	2	Redding	Thankfull										1			1		
Middleborough	82	3	Richmond	Israel	3		3	1		1	2						11		
Middleborough	82	4	Reding	Joseph	1	1			1			1	1				5		

TOWN	PG#	LN#	HEADS OF HOUSEHOLD		FREE WHITE MALES					FREE WHITE FEMALES					TOTAL ALL OTHER	TOTAL SLAVES	TOTALS	DISTRICT/ TOWNSHIP	NOTES
			LAST NAME	FIRST NAME	under 10	10 to 16	16 to 26	26 to 45	45 and over	under 10	10 to 16	16 to 26	26 to 45	45 and over					
Middleborough	82	5	Robins	Seth	1			1					1				3		
Middleborough	82	6	Reed	Joanna Wo									1				1		
Middleborough	82	7	Sparrow	Edward Col	1	1	1		1		1	1		2			8		
Middleborough	82	8	Sparrow	Edward Junr			1	1						1			3		
Middleborough	82	9	Shaw	Chipman	1	3		1		1		1	1				8		
Middleborough	82	10	Shaw	George Dr			1		1					1			3		
Middleborough	82	11	Shaw	Jacob	2	2	2	1				1	1				9		
Middleborough	82	12	Severy	Nathan	1		2						1				4		
Middleborough	82	13	Shaw	George Jr Capt	1	1	1	1		2	1		1				8		
Middleborough	82	14	Shurtliff	Timothy	1	1		1	1	1			1	1			7		
Middleborough	82	15	Shearman	Simeon				1				1	1				3		
Middleborough	82	16	Shearman	Edward				1			1		1				3		
Middleborough	82	17	Simmond	Abraham	1			1		1			1				4		
Middleborough	82	18	Daggett	Seth				1				1	1				3		
Middleborough	82	19	Drake	William	3	1	1	1			1		1				8		
Middleborough	82	20	Daggett	Simeone				1					1				2		
Middleborough	82	21	Daggett	Thomas	1	1		1		1			1				5		
Middleborough	82	22	Duglass	Elisha	1			1		2			1				5		
Middleborough	82	23	Doty	jacob	1			1		1			1				4		
Middleborough	82	24	Duglass	David		1	1		1			3		1			7		
Middleborough	82	25	Duglass	David Jr Capt	1		1					1					3		
Middleborough	82	26	Downing	Joseph				1					1				2		
Middleborough	82	27	Downing	Joshua		3	1	1		1		3		1			10		
Middleborough	82	28	Downing	John	1		1						1				3		
Middleborough	82	29	Duglass	Prudence									1				1		
Middleborough	82	30	Drake	Abigail Wo										1			1		
Middleborough	82	31	Eaton	Joseph				1						1			2		
Middleborough	82	32	Eaton	Solomon	1			1		1			1				4		
Middleborough	82	33	Eaton	Seth	1			1		1		1					4		
Middleborough	82	34	Eaton	Israel	2	2		1			1		1				7		
Middleborough	83	1	Finney	Lewis				1		3		1					5		
Middleborough	83	2	Foster	William				1		1		1					3		
Middleborough	83	3	Filammon	John	1			1		2			1				5		
Middleborough	83	4	Gisban	Deborah Wo										1			1		
Middleborough	83	5	Gammons	Southworth	2			1		1			1				5		
Middleborough	83	6	Gibbs	Elisha		1		1		3			1				6		
Middleborough	83	7	Gammons	John		1	1	1			1	1		1			6		
Middleborough	83	8	Gammons	John Jr		1		1			1	1		1			5		
Middleborough	83	9	Gurney	David Revd		1		1			1	1		1			5		
Middleborough	83	10	Hathaway	Merick	1			1	1				1				4		
Middleborough	83	11	Howland	Isaac				1					1				2		
Middleborough	83	12	Haskins	John				1					2				3		
Middleborough	83	13	Hefford	Ebenezer	3	1		1	1	1	1	4		1			12		
Middleborough	83	14	Howland	Consider	3	2		1		2				1			9		
Middleborough	83	15	Pratt	Wm Capt		3	2	1				1		1			8		
Middleborough	83	16	Pratt	Ludia Wo										1			1		
Middleborough	83	17	Pratt	Kimball				1				1					2		
Middleborough	83	18	Peirce	Job 2d		2		2				2		1			7		
Middleborough	83	19	Peterson	Perez	2			1		2		1	1				7		
Middleborough	83	20	Parker	Micah		1	1	1					1				4		
Middleborough	83	21	Pratt	Nathan	2			1		1			1				5		
Middleborough	83	22	Perkins	Nathan	1			1		1			1				4		
Middleborough	83	23	Peirce	Richard	5	2	1	1				1		1			11		
Middleborough	83	24	Peirce	Elkanah		1		1				1					3		
Middleborough	83	25	Peirce	Freeman			1			1			1				3		
Middleborough	83	26	Peirce	Edmund	1		1						1				3		
Middleborough	83	27	Pickens	Esther Wo								2	2	1			5		
Middleborough	83	28	Paddock	Zachariah				1									1		
Middleborough	83	29	Porter	Oliver	1		1			1			1				4		
Middleborough	83	30	Perkins	Azel	1	1		1		1		1					5		
Middleborough	83	31	Potter	Prince											2		2		
Middleborough	84	1	Rider	Elisha	1	1	2		1	2	1	1		1			10		
Middleborough	84	2	Robins	Moses				1						1			2		
Middleborough	84	3	Robins	Manasseh			1			1		1					3		
Middleborough	84	4	Rider	Robert		3		1						1			5		
Middleborough	84	5	Robins	Benjan	2			1		2			1				6		
Middleborough	84	6	Richmond	Micah		1	1			1		1					4		
Middleborough	84	7	Redding	Luther			1		1		2	4		2			10		
Middleborough	84	8	Rider	Samuel			4		1	2	2	2		1			12		
Middleborough	84	9	Richmond	Elijah	1	1		1				1					4		
Middleborough	84	10	Rider	Benjan			1	1					1				3		
Middleborough	84	11	Ripley	Hezekiah				1		2		1					4		
Middleborough	84	12	Rider	Isaac	2	1		2		3	2		2	1			13		
Middleborough	84	13	Reed	Luke		1		1		1	1	1	1				6		
Middleborough	84	14	Raymond	Joshua				1		2		1					4		
Middleborough	84	15	Reed	Jacob				1					1	1			3		
Middleborough	84	16	Raymond	Samuel		1		1					1	1			4		
Middleborough	84	17	Raymond	Samuel 2d				1			2		1				4		
Middleborough	84	18	Reed	Anna Wo									1				1		
Middleborough	84	19	Reed	Lydia									2	1			3		
Middleborough	84	20	Raymond	Amos			1	1				1		1			4		
Middleborough	84	21	Richmond	Eleazer	1		1	1	1			1	1	1			7		
Middleborough	84	22	Elmes	Elkanah				1									1		
Middleborough	84	23	Elmes	Eliphalet	1	1	1		1	1	2	2	1	1			11		
Middleborough	84	24	Easton	Caesor											3		3		
Middleborough	84	25	Fuller	John	3			1		1	1	2	1				9		
Middleborough	84	26	Fuller	Noah				1		3	2			2			8		
Middleborough	84	27	Foster	Gershom	1	1	1		1				1				10		
Middleborough	84	28	Fuller	Gamalel	1			1		3	1		1	1			8		
Middleborough	84	29	Foster	Thomas				1				1	1				3		

TOWN	PG#	LN#	HEADS OF HOUSEHOLD		FREE WHITE MALES					FREE WHITE FEMALES					TOTAL ALL OTHER	TOTAL SLAVES	TOTALS	DISTRICT/ TOWNSHIP	NOTES
			LAST NAME	FIRST NAME	under 10	10 to 16	16 to 26	26 to 45	45 and over	under 10	10 to 16	16 to 26	26 to 45	45 and over					
Middleborough	84	30	Foster	Peter	1			1		2		1			1		6		
Middleborough	84	31	Finney	Ebenezer				1		2		1					4		
Middleborough	84	32	Faunce	Hannah Wo			1	1						1			3		
Middleborough	84	33	Fuller	Jonatha Dr	1	2			1	1				1			6		
Middleborough	84	34	Freeman	Elisha			1		1	1	1			1			5		
Middleborough	84	35	Freeman	Elisha 2d				1					1				2		
Middleborough	84	36	Freeman	Martin	1			1		2			1				5		
Middleborough	84	37	Freeman	Nathan	3			1	1				1				6		
Middleborough	84	38	Freeman	Benjan	3	1		1		1	1		1				8		
Middleborough	85	1	Hathaway	Levi		1			1	1	1			1			5		
Middleborough	85	2	Hoar	Peter Majr	1	1			1	1		2	1				7		
Middleborough	85	3	Haskins	Joshua	2	2	1		1				1	1			8		
Middleborough	85	4	Harlow	Mary Wo									1	1			2		
Middleborough	85	5	Harlow	John				1						1			2		
Middleborough	85	6	Harlow	Jonathan	1	1	1		1			1	1	1			7		
Middleborough	85	7	Holmes	Ezra	1				1	1			1				4		
Middleborough	85	8	Hunt	Rebecca Wo									1	1			2		
Middleborough	85	9	Hunt	Ephraim		1	1						1				3		
Middleborough	85	10	Holmes	John				1						1			2		
Middleborough	85	11	Hackett	Peleg	1			1		1	1	1					5		
Middleborough	85	12	Haskins	Benjn				1				2		1			4		
Middleborough	85	13	Hall	Jonathan	3	1		1		1			1				7		
Middleborough	85	14	Haskell	Sarah Wo	1					1			2				4		
Middleborough	85	15	Harlow	Ezra Capt	1	1	3		1			2		1			9		
Middleborough	85	16	Hackett	Elijah	1			1	1			1	1				5		
Middleborough	85	17	Hackett	George	1	1		1		1			1				5		
Middleborough	85	18	Hall	Seth	2	1		1		4	1	2	1				12		
Middleborough	85	19	Hathaway	Lazarus			1		1	3	1	3		1			10		
Middleborough	85	20	Hathaway	Joseph			1	2		1				1			5		
Middleborough	85	21	Porter	William Capt	2	1		1		2			1	1			8		
Middleborough	85	22	Porter	Zachariah	1			2		2		1					6		
Middleborough	85	23	Pierre	Job Capt	1	1			1			2		1	1		7		
Middleborough	85	24	Pratt	Thomas	1	1		1				1					4		
Middleborough	85	25	Peirce	Richard Junr	2				1	4				1			8		
Middleborough	85	26	Pickens	Silas	1			1		3			1				6		
Middleborough	85	27	Pickens	Zatto	2			1		2			1				6		
Middleborough	85	28	Pickens	George	1			1		2			1				5		
Middleborough	85	29	Pickens	John	4			1		1	1		2				9		
Middleborough	85	30	Peirce	Silas	1	1	1	1	1	1		2	2	1			11		
Middleborough	85	31	Pratt	Aberdean	1	1		1		1			1				5		
Middleborough	85	32	Pickens	Samuel		1	1	1		1			1				5		
Middleborough	85	33	Peirce	Silas	1			1		1			1				4		
Middleborough	85	34	Peirce	Eleazer	2			1		1		1					5		
Middleborough	85	35	Peirce	Levi		1	1			1		1					4		
Middleborough	85	36	Peirce	Levi 2d	1			1		1		1					4		
Middleborough	85	37	Peirce	Hermon	1			1		2	1		1	1			7		
Middleborough	85	38	Peirce	George			1		1	1		1	1	1			6		
Middleborough	85	39	Peirce	Arodia	2	1	1		1		1		1				7		
Middleborough	86	1	Parris	Isaac	3	1	1		1		1	1	1				9		
Middleborough	86	2	Parris	Samuel		1		1		1				1			4		
Middleborough	86	3	Parris	Moses	1	1	1	1					1				5		
Middleborough	86	4	Peirce	Abrm			1		1	4	2		1				9		
Middleborough	86	5	Peirce	Simeon	2	2		1		2	2		1				10		
Middleborough	86	6	Perkins	Thomas					1	2				1			4		
Middleborough	86	7	Pratt	calvin	1			1					1				3		
Middleborough	86	8	Peirce	Elisha			1			2			1				4		
Middleborough	86	9	Peirce	James Capt	2	1	1		1	1	1	2		1			10		
Middleborough	86	10	Peirce	Betsey Wo	1	2		1			1		1				6		
Middleborough	86	11	Peirce	Abner			1						1				2		
Middleborough	86	12	Pickens	Isaac	1			1		3		1					6		
Middleborough	86	13	Phinney	Jonathan		1	1		2	1		1		1			7		
Middleborough	86	14	Perkins	Jacob	1			1		1		1	1				5		
Middleborough	86	15	Pratt	Abner		1	3		1				1	1			7		
Middleborough	86	16	Peirce	Ephraim	1			1		1			2				5		
Middleborough	86	17	Perkins	Isaac 2d			4		1		1	2		1			9		
Middleborough	86	18	Perkins	Barnabas			1			1		1					3		
Middleborough	86	19	Pratt	Phineas	1			1		4	1		1				8		
Middleborough	86	20	Pratt	Phineas 2d	1			1		3			1				6		
Middleborough	86	21	Pratt	Ebenezer	3	1		1		1	1	1	1				9		
Middleborough	86	22	Pratt	Joseph	2	1		1		2			1				7		
Middleborough	86	23	Paddock	John				1		4	1		1				7		
Middleborough	86	24	Hinds	John	2	2	1	1		2	2		1				11		
Middleborough	86	25	Hour	Job	1	1		1		3	2		1				9		
Middleborough	86	26	Hinds	Leonard		1		1		2		1	1				6		
Middleborough	86	27	Haskell	Elisha		1			1			1		1			4		
Middleborough	86	28	Haskell	Silas	1		1	1		1		2		1			7		
Middleborough	86	29	Haskell	Eli	1	1							1				3		
Middleborough	86	30	Hathaway	Isaac Jun	2			1		2	1		1				7		
Middleborough	86	31	Haskell	Mark	1	1		1		1		1					5		
Middleborough	86	32	Haskell	Zebulon	1		1		1			2		1			6		
Middleborough	86	33	Holloway	Josiah									1				1		
Middleborough	86	34	Holloway	Asa				1		2		1					4		
Middleborough	86	35	Holloway	Isaac				1		3		1	1				6		
Middleborough	86	36	Hoar	William	1			1		3	1		1				7		
Middleborough	86	37	Howland	Rufus			1		1	2			1				5		
Middleborough	86	38	Haskins	Abner	3	1				2			1				7		
Middleborough	86	39	Howland	Ebenezer	1	2		1		4			1				9		
Middleborough	86	40	Hinds	Abinoum Capt	1			1		1			1				4		
Middleborough	86	41	Hathaway	Benjan	2	1		1		3	1		1				9		
Middleborough	87	1	Inglee	Rebecca Wo										2			2		

TOWN	PG#	LN#	LAST NAME	FIRST NAME	Free White Males					Free White Females					TOTAL ALL OTHER	TOTAL SLAVES	TOTALS	DISTRICT/ TOWNSHIP	NOTES
					under 10	10 to 16	16 to 26	26 to 45	45 and over	under 10	10 to 16	16 to 26	26 to 45	45 and over					
Middleborough	87	2	Jackson	Rebecca Wo	1								1				2		
Middleborough	87	3	Jones	Ebenezer			1	1		2	1		1				6		
Middleborough	87	4	Jones	Consider				1				1	1				3		
Middleborough	87	5	Keene	Seth	1	2		1		2	1		1				8		
Middleborough	87	6	Kingman	Abner		1		1					1				3		
Middleborough	87	7	Kingman	John			1	1				1	1				4		
Middleborough	87	8	Keith	Joseph Capt			1	1			1		1				4		
Middleborough	87	9	Keith	Martin	3			1		1			1				6		
Middleborough	87	10	Keith	Cyrus	1	1	1	1		1		1					6		
Middleborough	87	11	Kingsley	Zilpah Wo	1					1			1				3		
Middleborough	87	12	Leonard	George Dr			1	1					1	1			4		
Middleborough	87	13	Leonard	Elkanah	1	1	1	1	1	1			1	1			8		
Middleborough	87	14	Leonard	Joseph				1					1				2		
Middleborough	87	15	Leonard	Joseph 2d		2		1		2			1	1			7		
Middleborough	87	16	Nelson	William Mr		1	1	1			1			1			5		
Middleborough	87	17	Nelson	Hiram			1	1					1				3		
Middleborough	87	18	Nelson	John Col	1		2	1		1			3	1			9		
Middleborough	87	19	Nelson	Thomas		1	1	1				1	1	2			7		
Middleborough	87	20	Nelson	Thos Jr Dr	1			1		2			2				6		
Middleborough	87	21	Nelson	Ebenzr Mr	1	1	1	1		1	1	2	1	1			10		
Middleborough	87	22	Nelson	Isaac		1		1				1	2				5		
Middleborough	87	23	Niles	David	1			1	1				1				4		
Middleborough	87	24	Norcut	John				1					1	1			3		
Middleborough	87	25	Norcut	John Junr	4		1	1				2	1	1			10		
Middleborough	87	26	Niles	Samuel				1	1				1				3		
Middleborough	87	27	Nelson	Saml Revd	1		1	1		1			4	1			9		
Middleborough	87	28	Norcut	Ephraim	2		1			1			1				5		
Middleborough	87	29	Norcut	Elizabeth Wo									1				1		
Middleborough	87	30	Norcut	William				1		1			1				3		
Middleborough	87	31	Norcut	Elijah				1					1				2		
Middleborough	88	1	Oliver	Phebe Wo								1		1			2		
Middleborough	88	2	Oliver	Nathan	2			1		2			1				6		
Middleborough	88	3	Omen	Job				1				1	1				3		
Middleborough	88	4	Perry	Andrew			1	1		1			1				4		
Middleborough	88	5	Pratt	Holmon			1										1		
Middleborough	88	6	Peirce	Abiel Capt				1				2		1			4		
Middleborough	88	7	Peirce	Abiel Jur	2	1		1		1			1				6		
Middleborough	88	8	Pratt	Abiel Wo								2	1				3		
Middleborough	88	9	Peirce	William	3		1	1		1		2	1				9		
Middleborough	88	10	Pratt	Job	4			1		2		1	1				9		
Middleborough	88	11	Perry	Joshua				1					1	2			4		
Middleborough	88	12	Perry	John	2			1		1			2	1			7		
Middleborough	88	13	Paddock	Benjan	1			1				1	1				4		
Middleborough	88	14	Purington	Patience Wo		1	2					2	1	1			7		
Middleborough	88	15	Perkins	Isaac				1						1			2		
Middleborough	88	16	Perry	Elijah Dr		1	1	1				1		1			5		
Middleborough	88	17	Peirce	Eliphalet	1		1	1		3	1		1				8		
Middleborough	88	18	Perkins	Joshua	4	2		1	1				1				9		
Middleborough	88	19	Pratt	Benjamin	1			1			1	2	1				6		
Middleborough	88	20	Hammond	Shubael		1	1	1		2	1	1		1			8		
Middleborough	88	21	Hall	John			1	1		2			1				5		
Middleborough	88	22	Hall	James		2	1	1		2			1				7		
Middleborough	88	23	Hefford	John	2			1					1				4		
Middleborough	88	24	Hoar	Bradock	3			1	1				1				6		
Middleborough	88	25	Hoar	Seth	1		1			1			1				4		
Middleborough	88	26	Haskins	James	5			1		1			1				8		
Middleborough	88	27	Haksins	Job	1			1		1			1				4		
Middleborough	88	28	Haskins	Hannah Wo									2				2		
Middleborough	88	29	Hinds	Ebenzr Revd				1					1				2		
Middleborough	88	30	Hathawway	Gilbert	1		1			1		1					4		
Middleborough	88	31	Haskin	Susanna Wo	2								1				3		
Middleborough	88	32	Howland	Malica	1	1	1	1	1	1	2	2	2				12		
Middleborough	88	33	Howland	William	1			1		2		1					5		
Middleborough	88	34	Harlow	Zenas				1		1			1				3		
Middleborough	88	35	Harlow	Ellie				1		1			1				3		
Middleborough	88	36	Holmes	Fear Wo								1		1			2		
Middleborough	88	37	Holloway	Zephanh				1					1				2		
Middleborough	88	38	Hammond	Christopher	1	2		1		4	1			1			10		
Middleborough	89	1	Leonard	Samuel				1					1	1			3		
Middleborough	89	2	Long	Thomas	1		1			1		1		1			5		
Middleborough	89	3	Leach	John			1	1					1				3		
Middleborough	89	4	Leach	John Jur	1			1		1			1				4		
Middleborough	89	5	LeBaron	Lazarus				1		1			1				3		
Middleborough	89	6	Littlejohn	James	1			1	1				1	1			5		
Middleborough	89	7	Leonard	henry				1					1				2		
Middleborough	89	8	Leonard	Josiah 2d	1			1		3			1	1			7		
Middleborough	89	9	Look	Joseph	1			1					1				3		
Middleborough	89	10	Lucas	Caleb	2	1							1				4		
Middleborough	89	11	Leonard	Moses	1		1	1		1			1	1			6		
Middleborough	89	12	Littlejohn	William	2			1		1				1			5		
Middleborough	89	13	Leonard	Abigail Wo										1			1		
Middleborough	89	14	Leonard	Micah	2	2		1					1	1			7		
Middleborough	89	15	Monson	Robert	1		1						1				3		
Middleborough	89	16	Miller	Jacob		2		1		1			4	1			9		
Middleborough	89	17	Morey	Mary Wo			1						1	1			3		
Middleborough	89	18	Morton	Ichabod Dr	1			1	1	4	1		1				9		
Middleborough	89	19	Morton	Zephaniah		1	1	1		1	1	1		1			7		
Middleborough	89	20	Macomber	Simeon		1	1	1		2		1		1			7		
Middleborough	89	21	Miller	John			1	1					1	1			5		
Middleborough	89	22	Miller	John 2d Cap				1				1		1			3		

46

TOWN	PG#	LN#	LAST NAME	FIRST NAME	FREE WHITE MALES					FREE WHITE FEMALES					TOTAL ALL OTHER	TOTAL SLAVES	TOTALS	DISTRICT/ TOWNSHIP	NOTES
					under 10	10 to 16	16 to 26	26 to 45	45 and over	under 10	10 to 16	16 to 26	26 to 45	45 and over					
Middleborough	89	23	Miller	John 3d	1			1		2			1				5		
Middleborough	89	24	Morton	John Capt	2	1		1		1		1	1				7		
Middleborough	89	25	Miller	Samuel			1	1		1	1	1					5		
Middleborough	89	26	Macomber	Nathl Lt		1		1	1	1	2	2	1	1			10		
Middleborough	89	27	Macomber	Luther	1	1		1		1			1	1			6		
Middleborough	89	28	Morton	Caleb	1			1		2			1				5		
Middleborough	89	29	Morton	Isaac	3			1				1	1				6		
Middleborough	89	30	Miller	Isaac				1									1		
Middleborough	89	31	Macomber	John	3	2		1		2		2	1				11		
Middleborough	89	32	Miller	Seth	1		1	1	1				1				5		
Middleborough	89	33	Moranville	Lewis				1						1			2		
Middleborough	89	34	Miller	Jedediah		2		1				1		1			5		
Middleborough	89	35	Miller	Joseph			1					1					2		
Middleborough	89	36	Miller	Mary										1			1		
Middleborough	89	37	Miller	Lucy										1			1		
Middleborough	89	38	Miller	Peter		3	1		1	3		1		1			10		
Middleborough	89	39	Macomber	Aletha Wo	2					1		1					4		
Middleborough	89	40	Muxsom	Caleb		1	3		1		1	1		1			8		
Middleborough	89	41	Muxsom	Samuel	2	2	1		1	2				1			9		
Middleborough	89	42	Morison	William	1		1		1	1	1	2		1			8		
Middleborough	89	43	Muxsom	Abigail Wo							1	1		1			3		
Middleborough	89	44	McConeley	John	4			1		1		1	1				8		
Middleborough	89	45	Macomber	Lemuel	1		1	1		2	1	2	1				9		
Middleborough	89	46	Macomber	Elijah		2		1			1	1		1			6		
Middleborough	89	47	Macomber	Enoch	2			1		1		1					5		
Middleborough	90	1	Montgomery	Hugh	1			1	1	3	2		2				10		
Middleborough	90	2	Morton	Seth Junr	1	3		1		3		1	1				10		
Middleborough	90	3	Macomber	Joshua				1		3			1				5		
Middleborough	90	4	Morse	Joseph	2			1				1					4		
Middleborough	90	5	Morse	Isaac		2		1					1				4		
Middleborough	90	6	Morse	Isaac Junr		1				2			1				4		
Middleborough	90	7	Morse	Levi		1		1		1			1				4		
Middleborough	90	8	Murdock	John			2	1				1		1			5		
Middleborough	90	9	Murdock	John Jr	3	1		1		1			1				7		
Middleborough	90	10	Miller	Elias			1	1						2			4		
Middleborough	90	11	Miller	Anram		1		1		1		2					5		
Middleborough	90	12	Murdock	Levi		1		1		1			1				4		
Middleborough	90	13	Morton	George	1			1	1	1			1	1			6		
Middleborough	90	14	Morton	John 2d			2			1	1		1				5		
Middleborough	90	15	Munson	Thomas				1			2		1				4		
Middleborough	90	16	Morse	William	1			1			1		1				4		
Middleborough	90	17	McDale	John	1		2			1		1					5		
Middleborough	90	18	Moranville	Lewis Jr			1			1		1					3		
Middleborough	90	19	Murdock	Luther	1			1				1					3		
Middleborough	90	20	McFarland	James			1			1				1			3		
Middleborough	90	21	Leonard	Gideon	1	1		1		1	2		1				7		
Middleborough	90	22	Leonard	Nathan Dr	1	3		1		3	1		1				10		
Middleborough	90	23	Lewis	Lathrop	1	1		1		2		1	1				7		
Middleborough	90	24	Lovell	Joseph	2	1		1		2	1	1	1				9		
Middleborough	90	25	Lovell	Patience Wo									1				1		
Middleborough	90	26	Lovell	Lucy Wo	2			1		2			1				6		
Middleborough	90	27	LeBaron	Levi	1	2		1		2	1		1				8		
Middleborough	90	28	Leonard	Josiah	1			1					1				3		
Middleborough	90	29	Leonard	Nathl	3	1			1	2			1				8		
Middleborough	90	30	Leonard	Nathl 2d	2			1				1	1				5		
Middleborough	90	31	Leonard	Jonathan		1		1		4	2		2	1			11		
Middleborough	90	32	Leonard	George 2d	3	2	1		1	2		2	1				12		
Middleborough	90	33	Leonard	Benjan Capt	1	1	3	1	1		1		2		1		11		
Middleborough	90	34	Lyon	Jedediah		1		1					2				4		
Middleborough	90	35	Leonard	Ephraim	2			1		1			1	1			6		
Middleborough	90	36	Ling	Silvanus	3			1				1					5		
Middleborough	90	37	Leonard	Zadoch	2			1					1				4		
Middleborough	90	38	Leonard	Perez		1			1			1		1			4		
Middleborough	90	39	LeBaron	Japeth		1	1	1		1	1	1		1			7		
Middleborough	90	40	Leonard	Ephraim 2d	1			1				1					3		
Middleborough	90	41	Leonard	Daniel				1		2			1				4		

TOWN	PG#	LN#	LAST NAME	FIRST NAME	FREE WHITE MALES					FREE WHITE FEMALES					TOTAL ALL OTHER	TOTAL SLAVES	TOTALS	DISTRICT/ TOWNSHIP	NOTES
					under 10	10 to 16	16 to 26	26 to 45	45 and over	under 10	10 to 16	16 to 26	26 to 45	45 and over					
Pembroke	31	1	Bonney	Daniel															Tape mark
Pembroke	31	2	Bishop	Nathll		1		1				1		1			5		
Pembroke	31	3	Bisbee	Rheuben			2	2		1		1					6		
Pembroke	31	4	Barker	Isaac	2			2		2			1	1			8		
Pembroke	31	5	Baker	John				1		1				1			3		
Pembroke	31	6	Bailey	Caleb	1			1	1	2	1	1	1				8		
Pembroke	31	7	Briggs	Willm	3	1	1	1	1	1		1		2			11		
Pembroke	31	8	Briggs	Alden	1		3	1	1			1	1	1			9		
Pembroke	31	9	Briggs	Elisha	1		2		1	2	1	1		1			9		
Pembroke	31	10	Barker	Robert			1		1	1			1	1	2		7		
Pembroke	31	11	Baker	Benjn				1									1		
Pembroke	31	12	Briggs	Sampson				1						1			2		
Pembroke	31	13	Bonney	Jonathan	2	1		1		2	1			1			8		
Pembroke	31	14	Bonney	Samll		1	2	1				1		1			6		
Pembroke	31	15	Bates	Benjn	1	2		1		3			1				8		
Pembroke	31	16	Beals	Howland			1	1		1		2		1			6		
Pembroke	31	17	Bonney	Joseph			1		2			2	3	1			9		
Pembroke	31	18	Beals	Isaac	4	1		1			1	1	1				9		
Pembroke	31	19	Bowker	Jamima	2	1						1		1			5		
Pembroke	31	20	Bonney	Lemuel Jun			1			1		1					3		
Pembroke	31	21	Bonney	Lemuel		1		1		1				1			4		
Pembroke	31	22	Buck	Eunice	1	1						2	1	2			7		
Pembroke	31	23	Beals	John				1		3	1			1		3	9		
Pembroke	31	24	Baker	Snow	1			1		3			1	1			7		
Pembroke	31	25	Bonney	Ezekiel	1			1		1	1			1			5		
Pembroke	31	26	Bonney	Nathll	1		1						1				3		
Pembroke	33	1	Bates	Caleb	2	2	1	1		2		1		1			10		
Pembroke	33	2	Bates	Nabby	2								1	1			4		
Pembroke	33	3	Brown	Smith	2	1		1		2	1			2			9		
Pembroke	33	4	Basset	James	2		1	1		1				1			6		
Pembroke	33	5	Bishop	Eliphelet				1						1			2		
Pembroke	33	6	Bradford	Andrew				1					1	1			3		
Pembroke	33	7	Cox	Seth Junr	1			1		1	1		1				5		
Pembroke	33	8	Cox	Ephraim	1			1				1					3		
Pembroke	33	9	Cox	Seth Junr			1	1		1	1	1		1			6		
Pembroke	33	10	Cushing	Nathll	1	1	1	1		2			2	1			9		
Pembroke	33	11	Cushing	Charles	1	1		2		1		1	2				8		
Pembroke	33	12	Collamore	Thos			1	1						2	1		5		
Pembroke	33	13	Cushing	Edward									1		1		2		
Pembroke	33	14	Collamore	Willm		1		1	1	1				1			5		
Pembroke	33	15	Cole	Nathll			2							1			3		
Pembroke	33	16	Cushing	Elijah		1	1	1		1	2	2		1			9		
Pembroke	33	17	Clapp	Dwella	3			1		3		1	1				10		
Pembroke	33	18	Crooker	Daniel			1	1	2					1			5		
Pembroke	33	19	Cushing	Josiah		1		1					1	1	3		7		
Pembroke	33	20	Carrit	Joseph				1						1			2		
Pembroke	33	21	Crooker	Ensign			1					1					2		
Pembroke	33	22	Cushing	Willm		1		1					1				3		
Pembroke	33	23	Chamberlain	Freedom				1						1			2		
Pembroke	34	1	Bigbee	Gamaliel	1	1		1		1	1			1			6		
Pembroke	34	2	Beals	David	1		2		2		1	1	1	1			9		
Pembroke	34	3	Bruster	Willm	1			1		2	1			1			6		
Pembroke	34	4	Barker	B. Isaac	1		1		1	4			1				8		
Pembroke	34	5	Baree	Jacob	1		2	1		1		1	1	1			8		
Pembroke	34	6	Bearee	Isaiah				1						1			2		
Pembroke	34	7	Bonney	Ebenz	1		1		1	2			1				6		
Pembroke	34	8	Barker	Joshua			1		1		1	2		1			6		
Pembroke	34	9	Briggs	Saml	3	1		1		1	2			1			9		
Pembroke	34	10	Bourn	Abel	2	1	1		1	2	1	1	1	1			11		
Pembroke	34	11	Bourn	James Jun	1	1		1		2	2	1	1				9		
Pembroke	34	12	Bourn	James				1		1				1			3		
Pembroke	34	13	Briant	Jacob	2	1		1	1	1	1		1				8		
Pembroke	34	14	Bearse	Benjn		2		1		3				1			7		
Pembroke	34	15	Bearse	Ichabod		1		1			1			1			4		
Pembroke	34	16	Bonney	Noah	2	1	3		1	1	1			1			10		
Pembroke	34	17	Barker	Saml			1				1		2				4		
Pembroke	34	18	Bonney	Josiah	2			1		1			1				5		
Pembroke	34	19	Bonney	James		1		1					1				3		
Pembroke	34	20	Bigbee	Isaac			1		1	1				1			4		
Pembroke	34	21	Baker	Kenelem				1		1	1	1		1			4		
Pembroke	34	22	Berstow	Charles	1		1	1						1			4		
Pembroke	34	23	Berstow	Willm	3			1						1			5		
Pembroke	34	24	Berstow	James Jun	2			1		2	1			1			7		
Pembroke	34	25	Baker	Prissilla		1	1					1		1			4		
Pembroke	34	26	Baker	Abel				1						1			2		
Pembroke	34	27	Bates	Comfort				1			1			1			3		
Pembroke	35	1	Everson	Eunice	2	1	1			3	1	1	1				10		
Pembroke	35	2	Alms	Ansel	1			1		1		1					4		
Pembroke	35	3	Ford	Adam			1		1			1	2	1			6		
Pembroke	35	4	Ford	Willm	1	2		1		3			2	1			10		
Pembroke	35	5	Foster	Micah Jun	2		3			1			1	1			8		
Pembroke	35	6	Foster	Micah			3	1	1			1	1	1			8		
Pembroke	35	7	Ford	Thos				1						2			3		
Pembroke	35	8	Fuller	Seth				1					1	1			3		
Pembroke	35	9	Foster	David				1					1	1			3		
Pembroke	35	10	Ford	James	1			1		1		2	1				6		
Pembroke	35	11	Ford	Henry	2			1				1					4		
Pembroke	35	12	Foster	Lemuel				1					1	1			3		
Pembroke	35	13	Ford	John		1	1		1			1		1			5		
Pembroke	35	14	Fish	Zacheus			1		1					2			4		

| TOWN | PG# | LN# | LAST NAME | FIRST NAME | FREE WHITE MALES | | | | | FREE WHITE FEMALES | | | | | TOTAL ALL OTHER | TOTAL SLAVES | TOTALS | DISTRICT/ TOWNSHIP | NOTES |
					under 10	10 to 16	16 to 26	26 to 45	45 and over	under 10	10 to 16	16 to 26	26 to 45	45 and over					
Pembroke	35	15	Fish	Caleb					1				1				2		
Pembroke	35	16	Fish	Elnathan					1				1	1			3		
Pembroke	35	17	Fish	Isaac		2			1	2			1				6		
Pembroke	35	18	Fish	Thos	1		1	1		1	2		1				7		
Pembroke	35	19	Fish	Hannah			1						1	2			4		
Pembroke	35	20	Ford	Wait			1				2	1	1				6		
Pembroke	35	21	Ford	Lot					1			1	1				3		
Pembroke	36	1	Chamberlin	Freedm Junr	1			1		2	3		1				8		
Pembroke	36	2	Church	Constant		1			1		1		1				4		
Pembroke	36	3	Curtis	Rachel									1				1		
Pembroke	36	4	Cox	James	1				1				2				4		
Pembroke	36	5	Cox	Elias	2		1			1			1				5		
Pembroke	36	6	Curtis	Willm	1		1		1	1	1		1				6		
Pembroke	36	7	Crooker	David Junr	1				1		2	1	1				6		
Pembroke	36	8	Crooker	David					1				2				3		
Pembroke	36	9	Crooker	John	1			1				1					3		
Pembroke	36	10	Crooker	Elijah						2			1				3		
Pembroke	36	11	Cavel	Daniel	1		1					1					3		
Pembroke	36	12	Cole	Margret		2							1				3		
Pembroke	36	13	Damond	Elijah					1				1				2		
Pembroke	36	14	Damond	Elijah Junr	4		1			1			1				7		
Pembroke	36	15	Delano	John	3		1			1			1				6		
Pembroke	36	16	Delano	Willm					1		1			1			3		
Pembroke	36	17	Dwella	Nathan	1		1			2			2				6		
Pembroke	36	18	Dwella	Benjn					1	4	1		1				7		
Pembroke	36	19	Doten	Lemuel	2		1			1			1	1			6		
Pembroke	36	20	Dwella	Jedadiah			1		1		1		1	1			5		
Pembroke	36	21	Dunster	Hannah								2	3				5		
Pembroke	37	1	Hicks	John	2			1		2			1				6		
Pembroke	37	2	Harden	Saml		1		1		1	1			2			6		
Pembroke	37	3	Hathway	Josiah	2			1		3	1		1				8		
Pembroke	37	4	Hall	Job	1			1		1			1				4		
Pembroke	37	5	Howland	Joseph		1			1			2		2			6		
Pembroke	37	6	Hitchcock	Gad	1	2	1		2	3	1	3			2		16		
Pembroke	37	7	Hill	Leonard	1			1					1				3		
Pembroke	37	8	Howland	Daniel	1			1					1				3		
Pembroke	37	9	Howland	Mary						1	2		1				4		
Pembroke	37	10	Hayford	Daniel			1		1			1	1				4		
Pembroke	37	11	House	Saml			1		1			1	1	1			5		
Pembroke	37	12	Hatch	Isaac	2	1		2		2			2	1			10		
Pembroke	37	13	Hall	Jeremiah					1				1	1			3		
Pembroke	37	14	Hall	Bailey			4	1		2	1		1				9		
Pembroke	37	15	Hatch	Josiah		1		1					1	2			5		
Pembroke	37	16	Hatch	Seth			1		1	1	1	1	1				6		
Pembroke	37	17	Hatch	Briggs	2			1		2			1	1			7		
Pembroke	37	18	Hatch	John	2	2			1	1	1		1				8		
Pembroke	37	19	Homes	John		1			1			2	1	1			6		
Pembroke	37	20	Hatch	Harris	2			1		2	3	1	1				10		
Pembroke	38	1	Gurney	Elijah					1				1				2		
Pembroke	38	2	Gould	Willm	1			1		1			2	1			6		
Pembroke	38	3	Gardner	Thos Jun	1	1		1		3			1				7		
Pembroke	38	4	Gardner	Ruth			1				1	1	1				4		
Pembroke	38	5	Gardner	Thos					1		1	1	1				4		
Pembroke	38	6	Gooden	Ameziah	3			1		1		2	1	1			9		
Pembroke	38	7	Glover	James	1	1		1				1		1			5		
Pembroke	38	8	Howland	Thos		1		1						1			3		
Pembroke	38	9	Howland	Prince	1	1	1	1			2	1		1			8		
Pembroke	38	10	Harden	Perry				1			1			1			3		
Pembroke	38	11	Howland	Allen	1		1	1					1				4		
Pembroke	38	12	Howland	Robart	1			1		1				2			5		
Pembroke	38	13	Howland	Luther	1		1					1					3		
Pembroke	38	14	Howland	Daniel	1	1	1	1					1				5		
Pembroke	38	15	Homes	Sarah							1	2	1				4		
Pembroke	38	16	Hatch	Zephaniah				1				1	1				3		
Pembroke	38	17	Hill	Thos	1	1		1				1	2				6		
Pembroke	38	18	Hill	Saml		1		1				1	1				4		
Pembroke	38	19	Hill	Saml Junr	1		1			2	1		1				6		
Pembroke	38	20	Howland	Isaac		1		1				1	1				4		
Pembroke	38	21	Hobart	Isaac		2	1	1		1			1				6		
Pembroke	38	22	Hobart	Thos		1	1				1	1	1				5		
Pembroke	38	23	Harden	Rheuben	1	1			1	3	1	3	1	1			12		
Pembroke	39	1	Keen	Lemuel				1		2		1		1			5		
Pembroke	39	2	Keen	Desiah										1			1		
Pembroke	39	3	Keen	Asa Jun	2			1		2			1				6		
Pembroke	39	4	Keen	Asa					1					2			3		
Pembroke	39	5	Keen	Nathll					1					1			2		
Pembroke	39	6	Keen	Joseph					1				2	1			4		
Pembroke	39	7	Keen	Joseph Jun	1			1		1			1				4		
Pembroke	39	8	Keen	James			1					1					2		
Pembroke	39	9	Lincoln	Levi			1			1			1				3		
Pembroke	39	10	Lowden	Richard			1	1						1			3		
Pembroke	39	11	Levitt	John			1	1						1			3		
Pembroke	39	12	Linsey	James	1			1		2	1		1				6		
Pembroke	39	13	Lapham	Lemuel			1						1				2		
Pembroke	39	14	Lincoln	Lydia										2			2		
Pembroke	39	15	Little	Charles		2	1			2	1	1		1			8		
Pembroke	39	16	Little	Isaac	1		2		1	2	1		1				8		
Pembroke	39	17	Loring	Nathll		2		1	2			2		1			8		
Pembroke	39	18	Lowden	John					1					1			2		
Pembroke	39	19	Levit	Kindsman	3	1		1		1		1	1	1			9		

49

TOWN	PG#	LN#	LAST NAME	FIRST NAME	FREE WHITE MALES					FREE WHITE FEMALES					TOTAL ALL OTHER	TOTAL SLAVES	TOTALS	DISTRICT/ TOWNSHIP	NOTES
					under 10	10 to 16	16 to 26	26 to 45	45 and over	under 10	10 to 16	16 to 26	26 to 45	45 and over					
Pembroke	39	20	Lapham	Caleb		1								1			2		
Pembroke	39	21	McFarland	Foster	3	1		1	1		1		1				8		
Pembroke	39	22	McLathland	Joseph	2	2		1		2				1			8		
Pembroke	40	1	Joselyn	Eleazer	4	2		1		2	1		1				11		
Pembroke	40	2	Joselyn	Francis	1	2		1		3			1				8		
Pembroke	40	3	Joselyn	Sarah									1	1			2		
Pembroke	40	4	Joselyn	W. Saml	1			1				1					3		
Pembroke	40	5	Joselyn	Jacob	2		1			1		1					5		
Pembroke	40	6	Joselyn	Elisha				1		1	1						3		
Pembroke	40	7	Joselyn	Charles Jun	2		1	1		2		1	1				8		
Pembroke	40	8	Joyce	Seth	1			1		1			1				4		
Pembroke	40	9	Joselyn	Isaiah				1					2		2		5		
Pembroke	40	10	Joselyn	B Joseph			1	1					1				3		
Pembroke	40	11	Joselyn	Joseph				1					1				2		
Pembroke	40	12	Joselyn	Henry				1			1	1	1	1			5		
Pembroke	40	13	Joselyn	Henry Jun			1			4			1				6		
Pembroke	40	14	Joselyn	Josiah	1		1	1				1	1	1			5		
Pembroke	40	15	Joselyn	Jabez	1			1		1		1					4		
Pembroke	40	16	Jones	Simeon	2			1		1			1				5		
Pembroke	40	17	Johnson	Isaac	2			1		2			1	1			7		
Pembroke	40	18	Jennings	Nathl	1		1		1	2	2	1		2			10		
Pembroke	40	19	Jacobs	Saml		2		1						1			4		
Pembroke	40	20	Jones	Charls	1			1		1			1				4		
Pembroke	40	21	Keen	Josiah			1	1		4	3	1	1				11		
Pembroke	40	22	Keen	Isaac		1	1	1	1				1	1			6		
Pembroke	40	23	Keen	Galen			1			4		1					6		
Pembroke	41	1	Philips	Lot	1		2		1	2	2	1	2				11		
Pembroke	41	2	Philips	Blany				1				1	1				3		
Pembroke	41	3	Philips	Christopher	1	1	3		1		1		1				8		
Pembroke	41	4	Parris	Benjamen	1	2							1	1			6		
Pembroke	41	5	Perrey	Henry			1	1					1				3		
Pembroke	41	6	Perry	James	1		1			2			1				5		
Pembroke	41	7	Pratt	Joshua	1		1			1		1		1			5		
Pembroke	41	8	Perrey	Seth		1	1	1		1			1				5		
Pembroke	41	9	Pratt	John			1			1		1					3		
Pembroke	41	10	Perry	Barnabas	2		1			2			1				6		
Pembroke	41	11	Perrey	Smal	1		1	1	1	1		2	1	1			9		
Pembroke	41	12	Pierce	Elizabeth	1					1			1				3		
Pembroke	41	13	Pierce	Christopher	1			1	1	1	2			2			8		
Pembroke	41	14	Pierce	Abram				1				1	1				3		
Pembroke	41	15	Ramsdal	Saml	2	1	1	1					1				6		
Pembroke	41	16	Reed	Philip		1						1					2		
Pembroke	41	17	Ramsdal	Garsham	4			2		2			1	1			10		
Pembroke	41	18	Reed	Zadock	1		2		1	2	1	1		1			9		
Pembroke	41	19	Reed	Bela	1			1		1			1				4		
Pembroke	41	20	Reed	Levi	1			1				1					3		
Pembroke	41	21	Randal	Charles	1			1	1	1		1		2			7		
Pembroke	41	22	Ramsdal	Lazerus				1		1				2			4		
Pembroke	41	23	Ramsdal	Charles				1		1	1		1				4		
Pembroke	42	1	McFarland	Deborah									2				2		
Pembroke	42	2	McFarland	Simeon				2					1	1	1		4		
Pembroke	42	3	Mahuren	Isaac	1	1		1		3		1	1	1			9		
Pembroke	42	4	Munro	Henry		1		1		1	2	1		2			8		
Pembroke	42	5	Muro	Joseph	1		1					1					3		
Pembroke	42	6	Magoon	Abner Junr	1			1		1			1				4		
Pembroke	42	7	Magoon	Abner			1		2		5		2				10		
Pembroke	42	8	Magoon	Thos	1				1		2	1	1				6		
Pembroke	42	9	Magoon	Aaron		1	2		1	2	1	2		1			10		
Pembroke	42	10	Magoon	Joseph		1	2		1				1				5		
Pembroke	42	11	Magoon	John			2	2	1			3		1			9		
Pembroke	42	12	Man	Ebenezer	1	1			1	1	1			2			7		
Pembroke	42	13	Man	David	2	3	1		1	1	1	1	1				11		
Pembroke	42	14	Magoon	Isaac		1			1				1				3		
Pembroke	42	15	McFarland	Rebeckah	2								1	1			4		
Pembroke	42	16	Magoon	Seth	1	1		1	1	2			1	1			8		
Pembroke	42	17	Osbourn	George Junr			1				1		1				3		
Pembroke	42	18	Osbourn	Levi		1				1			1				3		
Pembroke	42	19	Osbourn	George		1		1					1				3		
Pembroke	42	20	Oldham	John				1		1			1				3		
Pembroke	42	21	Oldham	David		1		1			2			2			6		
Pembroke	42	22	Oldham	David Junr	1		1			1			1				4		
Pembroke	42	23	Oakham	Allis								1		1			2		
Pembroke	42	24	Osbourn	John	2			1					1				4		
Pembroke	43	1	Silvester	Mathew			2		1	1	1			3	1		9		
Pembroke	43	2	Smith	Josiah	1		3		1			1		1			7		
Pembroke	43	3	Stetson	John			1	1		3			2	1			8		
Pembroke	43	4	Stephens	Edwards	1		1		1			1	1				5		
Pembroke	43	5	Sampson	Stephen	1		1					1					3		
Pembroke	43	6	Stetson	Lot	1	1		1		1	1		1				6		
Pembroke	43	7	Standish	Willm Jun	1		1	1		1		1					5		
Pembroke	43	8	Standish	Willm		1		1			1	1	1	1			6		
Pembroke	43	9	Sampson	Isaiah	2	1	1	1				1	1				7		
Pembroke	43	10	Sampson	Miles	3		1	2		1	1		1	1			10		
Pembroke	43	11	Standish	Miles	2		1	1		3			1				8		
Pembroke	43	12	Shaw	James			1						1				2		
Pembroke	43	13	Stetson	Abner	4		1			1	1		1				8		
Pembroke	43	14	Stetson	Saml				1		1			1				3		
Pembroke	43	15	Sampson	Gideon		1		1					1				3		
Pembroke	43	16	Smith	Nathl			1	1				1			1		4		
Pembroke	43	17	Tolman	Stephen	1					2		2		1			6		

TOWN	PG#	LN#	LAST NAME	FIRST NAME	FREE WHITE MALES					FREE WHITE FEMALES					TOTAL ALL OTHER	TOTAL SLAVES	TOTALS	DISTRICT/ TOWNSHIP	NOTES
					under 10	10 to 16	16 to 26	26 to 45	45 and over	under 10	10 to 16	16 to 26	26 to 45	45 and over					
Pembroke	43	18	Terry	Joseph		2	1	1		4	1		1				10		
Pembroke	43	19	Thomas	Isaac Jun	4				1	1			1				7		
Pembroke	43	20	Tubbs	Nehemiah	1		1					1					3		
Pembroke	43	21	Thomas	Nathl	2		3		1	1	2	1		1			11		
Pembroke	43	22	Thomas	Isaac	1		1		1		2	1	1				7		
Pembroke	43	23	Thomas	John		2	1		2		1	1	1	1	1		9		
Pembroke	43	24	Thomas	Zadoch			2		1		1		1				5		
Pembroke	43	25	Turner	Joshua 2d			1		1		1		1		1		5		
Pembroke	43	26	Turner	Joshua 3d				1				1					2		
Pembroke	43	27	Tailer	Joshua	1		1			1		1					4		
Pembroke	43	28	Tolman	Benjn				1		1			1				3		
Pembroke	43	29	Thomas	Ichabod		1		1		2		1	3				8		
Pembroke	43	30	Turner	Caleb			1			1		1					3		
Pembroke	43	31	Turner	George				1					1	2			4		
Pembroke	43	32	Turner	Joshua				1		1	1	1		1			5		
Pembroke	43	33	Turner	Calven	1	1	3		1	1	1			2			10		
Pembroke	43	34	Turner	Charles	1	1		1				1					4		
Pembroke	43	35	Turner	Elisha	2	2			1	1				1			7		
Pembroke	43	36	Turner	Thomas		1	1	1	1				1	1			6		
Pembroke	43	37	Turner	Job	2	2			1	2	1	2		2			12		
Pembroke	43	38	Tracy	Jacob	2			1			1		1				5		
Pembroke	43	39	Turner	Japhet	1			3				1	1				6		
Pembroke	43	40	Torrey	Willm	1	1		1	1	1	2	1		2			10		
Pembroke	43	41	Turner	Willm	1			1					2				4		
Pembroke	43	42	Tailer	Joseph		1		1	1			1	2				6		
Pembroke	43	43	Tailer	Caleb	1	1	1		1			1		1			6		
Pembroke	43	44	Tailer	Archelous	1		2		1			1		1			6		
Pembroke	43	45	Tubbs	Morris	1	2	2		1	1				1			8		
Pembroke	43	46	Tubbs	Joseph			1		1	1	1						4		
Pembroke	43	47	Turner	John		1	1		1	1	1	1	1				7		
Pembroke	44	1	Wade	Isaac		1	2		1	2		2		1			9		
Pembroke	44	2	White	Jacob	3			1		1			1				6		
Pembroke	44	3	Wade	Levi			1		1					1			3		
Pembroke	44	4	Whiting	Oliver				1	2	1			3	1			8		
Pembroke	44	5	White	Willm	1		3		1		1	1		1			8		
Pembroke	44	6	Whitman	Elijah	2			1		2	2		1				8		
Pembroke	44	7	Witherly	Joseph					1				1	1			3		
Pembroke	44	8	Webb	Saml			1			1	1	1					5		
Pembroke	44	9	White	S. Gideon	2		1		1	2	3	1	1				11		
Pembroke	44	10	Whitman	Kilborn	2	1		1		1			1		1		7		
Pembroke	44	11	Walker	Isaac			2	2		2		1	1				8		
Pembroke	44	12	Walker	John				1		1							2		
Pembroke	44	13	Walker	John Jr	4			1					1				6		
Pembroke	44	14	Winslow	Joseph	1			1		1			1				4		
Pembroke	44	15	Witherly	Josiah	2				1	1	1	3		1			9		
Pembroke	44	16	Witherel	Amos		2			1		1	1		1			6		
Pembroke	44	17	Witherel	Joshua		1	1	1				1		1			5		
Pembroke	44	18	Witherel	Amos Jun			1			1			1				3		
Pembroke	44	19	Brister												2		2		No first name listed
Pembroke	44	20	Caley												6		6		No first name listed
Pembroke	44	21	Gundery	Richard											6		6		
Pembroke	44	22		Dick											4		4		No last name listed
Pembroke	44	23	Ramsford	John	2	2		1		2	1		1				9		
Pembroke	44	24	Ramsdal	Simeon					1		2			1			4		
Pembroke	44	25	Randal	Mercy	2				1	2			1				6		
Pembroke	44	26	Ramsdal	Anna							1		2				3		
Pembroke	44	27	Reed	Willm					1			1		1			3		
Pembroke	44	28	Randal	John	1			1		1		1					4		
Pembroke	44	29	Shaw	Amous		1			1					1			3		
Pembroke	44	30	Soper	Nathl		1		1				1	1				4		
Pembroke	44	31	Soper	Isaac	2			1		2			3	1			9		
Pembroke	44	32	Soper	Alexander	1				1				1	1			4		
Pembroke	44	33	Shearman	Elisha				1		2			1	1			5		
Pembroke	44	34	Stetson	Abel	1				1				3	1			6		
Pembroke	44	35	Standish	Amos		2			1				1	1			5		
Pembroke	44	36	Stephens	Nathan			1		1			1	1	1			5		
Pembroke	44	37	Smith	Joseph	3		1		1	1	3		1				10		
Pembroke	44	38	Stetson	Jeremiah Jr	1	1		1		1	1	1					6		
Pembroke	44	39	Stetson	Jeremiah		1			1				2	1			5		
Pembroke	44	40	Studley	Benjn	2		1	1		2	1			2			9		
Pembroke	44	41	Sampson	Jonathan	2			1		4			1				8		
Pembroke	44	42	Spear	Chrisehina		1						1		1			3		
Pembroke	44	43	Salmon	Peter		2			1	1			1		1		6		
Pembroke	44	44	Stetson	Thos	2			1	1			2		1			7		
Pembroke	44	45	Sturtivant	Levi	2		1	1		1			1				6		
Pembroke	44	46	Standish	Willm		1		1				1			1		4		
Pembroke	44	47	Setetson	Susa							2	1	1				4		

TOWN	PG#	LN#	LAST NAME	FIRST NAME	FREE WHITE MALES					FREE WHITE FEMALES					TOTAL ALL OTHER	TOTAL SLAVES	TOTALS	DISTRICT/ TOWNSHIP	NOTES
					under 10	10 to 16	16 to 26	26 to 45	45 and over	under 10	10 to 16	16 to 26	26 to 45	45 and over					
Plimton	19	1	Soule	Ebenezer				1		2	1	2		1			7		
Plimton	19	2	Soule	Asaph	1	1	1		1			2		1			7		
Plimton	19	3	Bonney	Isaac	1	1	2	1				2	1				8		
Plimton	19	4	Bonney	Ebenezer			1	1						1			3		
Plimton	19	5	Harlow	Nathaniel				1					1				2		
Plimton	19	6	Perkins	Luke	1			1		1			1				4		
Plimton	19	7	Harlow	Sarah								1	2	1			4		
Plimton	19	8	Harlow	Levi	3	2		1		1			1				8		
Plimton	19	9	Wright	Joseph	2	2		1					1				7		
Plimton	19	10	Bagnall	Spinks				1		2			1				4		
Plimton	19	11	Leonard	Eliphalet				1					1				2		
Plimton	19	12	Leonard	Henry	1				1					1			3		
Plimton	19	13	Lamson	Deborah		1						1		1			3		
Plimton	19	14	Ripley	William				1						1			2		
Plimton	19	15	Lamson	Gideon	1	1		1		2	2	2	1				10		
Plimton	19	16	Fuller	Philamon	3	3	1	1					1	1			10		
Plimton	19	17	Bisbee	George	1	1	3		1	2		1		1			10		
Plimton	19	18	Cushman	Zacheriah		1		2		2	1	1	1				8		
Plimton	19	19	Cushman	Oliver	1			1		2			1				5		
Plimton	19	20	Wright	Chandler	1			1		2			1				5		
Plimton	19	21	Wright	Billa	2	1		1		2	1		1				8		
Plimton	19	22	Dean	Ebenezer		1	1	1	1				1	1			6		
Plimton	19	23	Ricket	Samuel		1		1					1	1			4		
Plimton	19	24	Ricket	Isaac	3	1		1		1	3		1				10		
Plimton	20	1	Ricket	Simeon	1	1		1		2			1				6		
Plimton	20	2	Carver	Nathaniel				1			1		1				3		
Plimton	20	3	Holmes	Ebenezer	1			1		1			1				4		
Plimton	20	4	Churchill	James				1	1	1	2	1					6		
Plimton	21	1	Samson	Peleg		1		1	1		1		1				6		
Plimton	21	2	Bisbee	John	2			1		1				1			5		
Plimton	21	3	Bisbee	Ischecar	1			1		1			1				4		
Plimton	21	4	Ellis	Samuel			1						1				2		
Plimton	21	5	Bisbee	Noah		1	2		1	1	1			1			8		
Plimton	21	6	Bisbee	Elijah		1	2		2	1	2			2			10		
Plimton	21	7	Perkins	Jonah	2		1		1		1		1				6		
Plimton	21	8	Perkins	Bezimel			1		1			1	1				4		
Plimton	21	9	Wright	Levi	1			1		2			1				5		
Plimton	21	10	Hooker	Asaph		1		1		2			1				5		
Plimton	21	11	Shurtlif	Elkanah	1			1				1	1				4		
Plimton	21	12	Wright	Sarah									2				2		
Plimton	21	13	Samson	George	3	2	2		1	1			1				10		
Plimton	21	14	Samson	Philamon	1			1		2	2		1				7		
Plimton	21	15	Loring	Melzer	2	1	2		1	1			1				8		
Plimton	21	16	Cooper	Richard		1		1		2	2		1				7		
Plimton	21	17	Loring	Simeon	1			1		1			1				4		
Plimton	21	18	Wright	Ebenezer		1		1				3		1			6		
Plimton	21	19	Waterman	Thomas		1		1					1	1			4		
Plimton	21	20	Ripley	Timothy		1	1	1	1			1	3		1		9		
Plimton	21	21	Ripley	Ezekiel	1			1		3			1				7		
Plimton	21	22	Cushman	Benjamin			1	1					2	1			5		
Plimton	21	23	Cuchman	Jacob	1			1					1				3		
Plimton	21	24	Ripley	Josiah			2	1		1			1				5		
Plimton	21	25	Loring	Hannah								2			1		3		
Plimton	22	1	Parker	Oliver	1		2	1		1		1					6		
Plimton	22	2	Bosworth	Isaac	2			1					1				4		
Plimton	22	3	Weston	Noah				1			1	3	1				6		
Plimton	22	4	Weston	Zadock		1		1		1	2		1				6		
Plimton	22	5	Bishop	William				1		3			1	2			7		
Plimton	22	6	Ellis	Joel		1		1					1				3		
Plimton	22	7	Ellis	Stephen		3		1		1	1			1			7		
Plimton	22	8	Pratt	Joshua		1		1					1	1			4		
Plimton	22	9	Ellis	Willard	3	1		1		1		1	1				8		
Plimton	22	10	Nye	Jonathan		1	1	1		1		1		1			6		
Plimton	22	11	Cobb	Lemuel			1	1					1				3		
Plimton	22	12	Thomas	Noah		1		1	1	2			1				6		
Plimton	22	13	Bradford	Calvin		2		1		1	1	3	1				9		
Plimton	22	14	Cushman	Deborah								1		1			2		
Plimton	22	15	Cushman	William	3		1						1	1			7		
Plimton	22	16	Soule	Daniel	2			1		1	2		1				7		
Plimton	22	17	Bradford	Samuel	2	1	1		1			2		1			8		
Plimton	22	18	Bradford	Levi	1		1	1	1			1	1	1			7		
Plimton	22	19	Wright	Samuel				1		1	1	2					5		
Plimton	22	20	Wright	Peleg		1							1				2		
Plimton	22	21	Wright	Jacob				1						1			2		
Plimton	22	22	Bradford	Gideon	2	1	3	1		1			1				9		
Plimton	22	23	Sherman	Asa	2	2		1		2		1					8		
Plimton	22	24	Wright	Isaac	2	1		1		2	1		1				8		
Plimton	22	25	Cobb	Rowland	2	1				2	1		1				8		
Plimton	22	26	Bradford	Daniel			2						1				3		

TOWN	PG#	LN#	LAST NAME	FIRST NAME	FREE WHITE MALES under 10	10 to 16	16 to 26	26 to 45	45 and over	FREE WHITE FEMALES under 10	10 to 16	16 to 26	26 to 45	45 and over	TOTAL ALL OTHER	TOTAL SLAVES	TOTALS	DISTRICT/ TOWNSHIP	NOTES
Plimton	23	1	Churchill	Isaac			2	1						1			4		
Plimton	23	2	Stetson	Caleb		1		1		1	3			2			8		
Plimton	23	3	Churchill	William				1						1			2		
Plimton	23	4	Churchill	Joseph	2	1		1			1		1				6		
Plimton	23	5	Cushing	Isaac	1			1		1		1					4		
Plimton	23	6	Magoun	James	1	1		1		1	1						5		
Plimton	23	7	Bradford	Elizabeth				1					1	1			3		
Plimton	23	8	Bradford	John		1		1		2	1	2		1			8		
Plimton	23	9	Bradford	Peleg	3			1		2			1				7		
Plimton	23	10	Bradford	William	1			1		3			1				6		
Plimton	23	11	Churchill	Jacob	1			1		1			1				4		
Plimton	23	12	Perkins	Zepheniah	1		1	1					1	1			5		
Plimton	23	13	Churchill	Joshua	1			1					1				3		
Plimton	23	14	Perkins	Luke				1			1			1			3		
Plimton	23	15	Nye	Elias	3			1			2			1			7		
Plimton	23	16	Churchill	Elias	1			1		2	2	1		1			8		
Plimton	23	17	Holmes	Zacheus			1				1	1	1				4		
Plimton	23	18	Churchill	Nathaniel				1						1			2		
Plimton	23	19	Churchill	Levi	1		1						1				3		
Plimton	23	20	Ripley	Isaiah		1	2	1					2	1			7		
Plimton	23	21	Chandler	Josiah		2		1					2	1			6		
Plimton	23	22	Chandler	Arthur	1	1		1		2	2		1				8		
Plimton	23	23	Samson	Rebecca									1	1			2		
Plimton	23	24	Parker	Jonathan		1		1	1					1			4		
Plimton	23	25	Parker	Polacarpus			1					1	1				3		
Plimton	23	26	Crooker	Benjamin	2			1		2	1		1				7		
Plimton	24	1	Parker	Betsey				1					1	3			5		
Plimton	24	2	Perkins	Seth	2		1	1		2			1				7		
Plimton	24	3	Finney	Ichabod				1						1			2		
Plimton	24	4	Finney	Barnabas	1			1					1				3		
Plimton	24	5	Churchill	Thomas	1	1		1		1			1				5		
Plimton	24	6	Bisbee	Abner			1			1		1					3		
Plimton	24	7	Churchill	Zadock		1				1		1					3		
Plimton	24	8	Churchill	Ebenezer				1			1		1				3		
Plimton	24	9	Churchill	Alferd			1			2		1					4		
Plimton	24	10	Bisbee	Abner		1		1		1				2			5		
Plimton	24	11	Churchill	Prince	1			1		3			1				6		
Plimton	24	12	Holmes	Francis		1	1	1			1	2		1			7		
Plimton	24	13	Holmes	Peleg	1		1			1			1				4		
Plimton	24	14	Standish	Sadrich				1			1	2		1			5		
Plimton	24	15	Standish	Sadrich	1		1						1				3		
Plimton	24	16	Churchill	Andrew	1			1					1				3		
Plimton	24	17	Sturtevant	Nehemiah		1		1		1		2		1			6		
Plimton	24	18	Loring	Jacob		2		1		2			1				6		
Plimton	24	19	Soule	Zacheus	1			1		1			1				4		
Plimton	24	20	Soule	Ephraim				1						1			2		
Plimton	24	21	Thomas	Jabez			1			1		1					3		
Plimton	24	22	Chandler	Zebeda		2		1		3			1				7		
Plimton	24	23	Standish	Ebenezer	1	1	1						1				4		
Plimton	24	24	Bartlett	Silvanus	2	1	2		1	2	1	1		1			11		
Plimton	24	25	Samson	Thomas		1		1		1				1			4		
Plimton	24	26	Soule	Aaron	1			1					1				3		
Plimton	24	27	Randall	Onisamus		1		1		1	1	1	1				6		
Plimton	26	1	Hall	Abner	2			1		1			1				5		
Plimton	26	2	Bryant	Levi	2		1	1		3	2	1	1	1			12		
Plimton	26	3	Bryant	Luther			1			4			1				6		
Plimton	26	4	Bryant	Dorothy	1	1	1			4	2	1	1				11		
Plimton	26	5	Harlow	James		2		1					1				4		
Plimton	26	6	Bryant	Benjamin		1		1				1	1	1			5		
Plimton	26	7	Wright	John				1		1			1				3		
Plimton	26	8	Everson	Joseph	2			1					1				4		
Plimton	26	9	Bonney	Nathaniel		1				1		1					3		
Plimton	26	10	Bonney	Nathaniel		1		1						1			3		
Plimton	26	11	Bonney	Joseph	3	2		1	1		1		1				9		
Plimton	26	12	Bryant	Zenas	1	2		1		3			1	1			9		
Plimton	26	13	Bartlett	Isaac	2			1					1				4		
Plimton	26	14	Cushing	Seth		1	1	1					3	1			7		
Plimton	26	15	Cushing	James			1			1		1					3		
Plimton	26	16	Loring	Ezekiel	1	3	1			3		2	1	1	1		14		
Plimton	26	17	Weston	Jabez	2	2		1				1	1	1			8		
Plimton	26	18	Bonney	Seth			1			1			1				3		
Plimton	26	19	Lobdall	Ebenezer	1	3		1		1		3	1				10		
Plimton	26	20	Wright	Ebenezer	2	1		1					1	1			6		
Plimton	26	21	Gannett	Thomas				1						1			2		
Plimton	26	22	Loring	Caleb		1		1					1				4		
Plimton	26	23	Perkins	John	3	1	1	1				2	2				10		
Plimton	26	24	Harlow	Mary			1				2	1		1			5		
Plimton	26	25	Churchill	Daniel	1			1					1				3		
Plimton	26	26	Churchill	Josiah	1			1		2			1				5		

TOWN	PG#	LN#	LAST NAME	FIRST NAME	M under 10	M 10-16	M 16-26	M 26-45	M 45+	F under 10	F 10-16	F 16-26	F 26-45	F 45+	TOTAL ALL OTHER	TOTAL SLAVES	TOTALS	DISTRICT/ TOWNSHIP	NOTES
Plymouth	1	1	Thacher	James		1		1		1	2		2				7		
Plymouth	1	2	Hayward	Nathan			1	1		1		1	1	1	1		7		
Plymouth	1	3	White	Joanna										2			2		
Plymouth	1	4	Morton	Seth	1		1			1		1		1			5		
Plymouth	1	5	Warren	James			1	1				1	2				5		
Plymouth	1	6	Turner	David			1			1			1				3		
Plymouth	1	7	Watson	George		1	1	1			1		1	1			6		
Plymouth	1	8	Spooner	Ephraim		1	1	1			1		1	1			6		
Plymouth	1	9	Taylor	Mary	3					2			3				8		
Plymouth	1	10	Bartlett	Ephraim			1						1				2		
Plymouth	1	11	Pope	Thomas	2		1					1		1			5		
Plymouth	1	12	Drew	Benjamin		2		1		1			1				5		
Plymouth	1	13	Warren	Henry	3	1		1		1	1		2				9		
Plymouth	1	14	Jackson	Nathaniel			1	1		1	1						5		
Plymouth	1	15	Jackson	Henry	1		1						1				3		
Plymouth	1	16	Banks	Isaac			1						1				2		
Plymouth	1	17	Sears	Barthll		1							1				2		
Plymouth	1	18	Dickson	John			1	1		1		1					4		
Plymouth	1	19	Churchill	Lewis	2			1		2			1				6		
Plymouth	1	20	Hitchill	Ebenezer	1			1		1			1				4		
Plymouth	1	21	Robbins	Samuel	2	2	1		1								6		
Plymouth	3	1	Holmes	Martha	1		1					1					3		
Plymouth	3	2	Nelson	Ebenezer	1	1		1		2			1	1			7		
Plymouth	3	3	Nelson	Ebenezer		1			1		1		1	1			5		
Plymouth	3	4	Rider	Job	2	1		1					1	2			7		
Plymouth	3	5	Nelson	Joseph W.		1		1				1	1	1			5		
Plymouth	3	6	Westcoat	Benjamin	2	1		1		2	1		1	1			9		
Plymouth	3	7	Hall	William	1			1		4			1				7		
Plymouth	3	8	Holmes	Rowland	1			1		1			1				4		
Plymouth	3	9	Robbins	Seth	1			1					1				3		
Plymouth	3	10	Whiting	Abraham	1			1		1		1		1			5		
Plymouth	3	11	Nelson	Lemuel				1			1	1	1				4		
Plymouth	3	12	Cobb	Lemuel	1	1	2	1				2		1			8		
Plymouth	3	13	Faunce	Thaddeus	1	2	2	1				1		1			8		
Plymouth	3	14	Lavery	Betsy	1						1	1					3		
Plymouth	3	15	River	Joseph			1			1		1					3		
Plymouth	3	16	Holmes	Ebenezer	1			1				1		1			4		
Plymouth	3	17	Holmes	Samuel			1			2		1		1			5		
Plymouth	3	18	Robbins	Samuel	2		1			2		1					7		
Plymouth	3	19	Drew	Seth	1		1			2	1		1				6		
Plymouth	3	20	Macumber	Elijah	1	1						1					3		
Plymouth	3	21	Austin	Richard	2	1		1		3			1				8		
Plymouth	3	22	Samson	Stephen				1			1	1	1				4		
Plymouth	3	23	Harlow	Amaziah			1	1		1	1						4		
Plymouth	4	1	Morton	Edward		1	1	1		1	1		1	1			7		
Plymouth	4	2	Jennings	Joseph	1		1	1		1			1				5		
Plymouth	4	3	Prince	Eunice		1		1		1	1		2		2		8		
Plymouth	4	4	Morton	Osborne	1		1	1		1		1	1	1			7		
Plymouth	4	5	Burbank	John	2		1	1					1	1			6		
Plymouth	4	6	Rogers	Silvanus			1			1		1					3		
Plymouth	4	7	Burbank	Samuel	1			1			1	2					5		
Plymouth	4	8	LeBaron	James		1							2				3		
Plymouth	4	9	Nelson	Hezekiah	1		1	1		2	1	1	1	1			9		
Plymouth	4	10	Robbins	Benjamin	1	1	1			4			1				8		
Plymouth	4	11	Robbins	William	3	2	1				1		1				8		
Plymouth	4	12	Robbins	Nathaniel			1					1					2		
Plymouth	4	13	Lavery	Nehemiah	2		1			2		1					6		
Plymouth	4	14	Cobb	Cornelius		1		1				2		1			5		
Plymouth	4	15	Cobb	Job				1			1			2			4		
Plymouth	4	16	Hall	Luke	2	1		1		2	1		1				8		
Plymouth	4	17	Polden	Thomas	2			1					1				4		
Plymouth	4	18	Raymond	Clarke		1		1					1	1			4		
Plymouth	4	19	Holmes	Nathaniel		1		1		1			1	1			5		
Plymouth	4	20	Tincolm	Hezekiah				1					1	1			3		
Plymouth	4	21	Robbins	Charles	3			1					1	1			6		
Plymouth	5	1	Dellano	Avery	1			1	3				1				6		
Plymouth	5	2	Bartlett	Elkanah			1	1		2	1			1			6		
Plymouth	5	3	Mathews	Thomas	1		1	1					1	1			5		
Plymouth	5	4	Drew	Lemuel	1	2	3	1					1	1			9		
Plymouth	5	5	Kean	William	2	1	1				1	1	1	1			8		
Plymouth	5	6	Davie	Solomon	3	1		1		1	1		1				8		
Plymouth	5	7	Davie	Ebenezer	1		1						1				3		
Plymouth	5	8	Ricket	Anselm	1		1					1					3		
Plymouth	5	9	Howard	Ebenezer	1		2			2		1	1				7		
Plymouth	5	10	Landman	Peter	4		1			1	2		1				9		
Plymouth	5	11	Rider	Seth			1					1	1				3		
Plymouth	5	12	Doten	Daniel		1	1			1		2					5		
Plymouth	5	13	Clarke	Benjamun		2		1			1		1				5		
Plymouth	5	14	Landman	Sarah	1	1											4		

TOWN	PG#	LN#	LAST NAME	FIRST NAME	FREE WHITE MALES					FREE WHITE FEMALES					TOTAL ALL OTHER	TOTAL SLAVES	TOTALS	DISTRICT/ TOWNSHIP	NOTES
					under 10	10 to 16	16 to 26	26 to 45	45 and over	under 10	10 to 16	16 to 26	26 to 45	45 and over					
Plymouth	5	15	Bartlett	Benjamun		1		1						1			3		
Plymouth	5	16	Nelson	Thomas				1		1			1	1			4		
Plymouth	5	17	Bacon	George			1						1	1			3		
Plymouth	5	18	Brewster	Job	2		1	1		1	1		1				7		
Plymouth	5	19	Brewster	America			1						1				2		
Plymouth	5	20	Drew	Lemuel		1	1	1		2			3				8		
Plymouth	5	21	Bartlett	Thomas	1		1			1			1				4		
Plymouth	5	22	Collings	James	3			1		3			1				8		
Plymouth	5	23	Holmes	Richard	1	1	1			2	1	4		1			12		
Plymouth	5	24	Brewster	Ellis			1			1			1				3		
Plymouth	6	1	Tibble	Joseph		2	1		1			1	1	1			7		
Plymouth	6	2	Douglas	John	1			1		3			1	1			7		
Plymouth	6	3	Allen	William			1			2		1					4		
Plymouth	6	4	Allen	John	1			1	1	1	1		1				6		
Plymouth	6	5	O'Larrie	Edmund	4			1				1	1				7		
Plymouth	6	6	Coye	William		1			1			1	1				4		
Plymouth	6	7	Goodwin	William	1	2	1	1		2			1		1		9		
Plymouth	6	8	Goodwin	Timothy		1	1		1	1	1	1	1				7		
Plymouth	6	9	Thomas	Joshua	1	2			1	1	1		1		2		9		
Plymouth	6	10	Lothrop	Isaac			1	2					1	1			5		
Plymouth	6	11	Thomas	William		1		2						1			4		
Plymouth	6	12	Howland	Joseph				1						1			2		
Plymouth	6	13	Thomas	Nathaniel			1			1	1		1				4		
Plymouth	6	14	Hammatt	Priscilla	2		2			2	1		1				8		
Plymouth	6	15	Holmes	Joseph			1			1	1	4		1			8		
Plymouth	6	16	Barnes	Joseph		1		1		1			1				4		
Plymouth	6	17	Bacon	David	2	1			1	1		3	1				9		
Plymouth	6	18	Torrey	Thomas	3	1			1	1			1				7		
Plymouth	6	19	Obrien	James		2	1		1				1				5		
Plymouth	6	20	Barrett	Hannah		1				2			1				4		
Plymouth	6	21	Torrey	Joshua				1		1			1				3		
Plymouth	6	22	Burbank	Joseph				1			1			1			3		
Plymouth	6	23	Nicholson	Hannah	2	1	2			2		3	1				11		
Plymouth	7	1	Hedge	Barnabas				1					1		2		4		
Plymouth	7	2	Hedge	Barnabas Jr	2		1	1		1			1				7		
Plymouth	7	3	Kendall	James Revd		2		1			1	2					6		
Plymouth	7	4	Churchill	Barnabas		1			1	2			1				5		
Plymouth	7	5	Bradford	Josiah				1				1	1				3		
Plymouth	7	6	LeBaron	William				1			1	4					6		
Plymouth	7	7	LeBaron	Isaac			1			1				2			5		
Plymouth	7	8	Bartlett	Zacheus	1		1	1					2				5		
Plymouth	7	9	Dolen	Isaac			1	1					1	2			5		
Plymouth	7	10	Symmes	Isaac	1		1						1				3		
Plymouth	7	11	Weston	William	1	1		1		1	1	1	1				7		
Plymouth	7	12	Torence	Thomas				1		2	1		1				5		
Plymouth	7	13	Simmonds	Lemuel	1		1		1	1	1	2		1			8		
Plymouth	7	14	Churchill	Sarah	1	1				1				1			4		
Plymouth	7	15	Drew	Benjamin Jr		2		1		2			1		1		7		
Plymouth	7	16	Weston	Lewis	1		1					1					3		
Plymouth	7	17	Croswell	Joseph	1				1				1				4		
Plymouth	7	18	Dinan	Rebecca								1	1	2			4		
Plymouth	7	19	Crandon	Benjamin		1		1		5	1	1		1			10		
Plymouth	7	20	Massey	Stephen	4	2			1	2	1	1	1				12		
Plymouth	7	21	Dolen	Jabez			1				1	1	1				4		
Plymouth	7	22	Finney	Josiah	1		1	1		2	1	2	1				9		
Plymouth	7	23	Weston	William	1			2		2	2		1	2			10		
Plymouth	7	24	Cotton	Roseter	2	2		1		1	1		1				8		
Plymouth	7	25	Rogers	William	1	1		1		1			1				5		
Plymouth	7	26	Jackson	Samuel	3	1	1	1			1	1	1				9		
Plymouth	7	27	Jackson	Samuel			1	1	1			1		1			5		
Plymouth	7	28	Jackson	Daniel	5	1		1			1		1				9		
Plymouth	8	1	Holmes	George				1						1			2		
Plymouth	8	2	Bradford	Thomas		1						1					2		
Plymouth	8	3	Dunham	Robert		1		1		1	2			2			7		
Plymouth	8	4	Warren	David	1			1		1		1	1				5		
Plymouth	8	5	Shaw	Ichabod	1			1			1	1	2	1			7		
Plymouth	8	6	Shaw	Southworth		1				1		1					3		
Plymouth	8	7	Goodwin	Thomas	1	1	1		1	2		2		1			9		
Plymouth	8	8	Symmes	Joanna		1						1		3			5		
Plymouth	8	9	Randell	Ruth	2	1				1			1				5		
Plymouth	8	10	Bailey	Benjamin	2			1		1			2				6		
Plymouth	8	11	Goddard	Benjamin			1			3			1				5		
Plymouth	8	12	Bartlett	John		1		1		1		1					4		
Plymouth	8	13	Reap	John M	2			1		1		1					5		
Plymouth	8	14	Richmond	Salome		1	1			1			1	1			6		
Plymouth	8	15	Kempton	Zacheus	3	1			1	1	2	1	1				10		
Plymouth	8	16	LeBaron	Bartlett					1	1	2		1				5		
Plymouth	8	17	Polder	George		1						1		1			3		
Plymouth	8	18	Diman	David	1	1		1	1	2			2	1			10		

TOWN	PG#	LN#	LAST NAME	FIRST NAME	M under 10	M 10 to 16	M 16 to 26	M 26 to 45	M 45 and over	F under 10	F 10 to 16	F 16 to 26	F 26 to 45	F 45 and over	TOTAL ALL OTHER	TOTAL SLAVES	TOTALS	DISTRICT/ TOWNSHIP	NOTES
Plymouth	8	19	Bartlett	Joshua				1		1		1		1			4		
Plymouth	8	20	Diman	Josiah	2		1	1		1			1	1			7		
Plymouth	8	21	Sturtevant	William				2		3			1				6		
Plymouth	8	22	Holmes	Nathaniel	1			1		1			1				4		
Plymouth	8	23	Cotton	Josiah	1				1	1	1	1	1				6		
Plymouth	8	24	Lewis	Nathaniel	2				1	2			2				7		
Plymouth	8	25	Cole	Samuel					1						1		2		
Plymouth	9	1	Roberts	Robert				1			1		1				3		
Plymouth	9	2	Brown	Lemuel	1	1		1		1		1					5		
Plymouth	9	3	Goodwin	Nathaniel		1			1		2	1		2	1		8		
Plymouth	9	4	Davis	William		1	2	1				1	2				7		
Plymouth	9	5	Wethrell	Thomas		1		1	1	1		1	1				6		
Plymouth	9	6	Bradford	Sally		1		1					1	1			4		
Plymouth	9	7	Bartlett	Dorothy		1							1	1			3		
Plymouth	9	8	Bartlett	George	1				1	1				1			4		
Plymouth	9	9	Hall	Asa	2			1		1			1				5		
Plymouth	9	10	Hammall	Lucy						2			1	1			4		
Plymouth	9	11	Jackson	Thomas				1					1				2		
Plymouth	9	12	Jackson	William	2			1		1		1	2	1			9		
Plymouth	9	13	Jackson	William H.			1	1	1			1		1	2		7		
Plymouth	9	14	Straffens	William	2			1					1	1			5		
Plymouth	9	15	Fitzgerald	John	1				1				1				3		
Plymouth	9	16	Watson	William		1		1				1	1				4		
Plymouth	9	17	Bailey	Eliphalet	4			1				1	1		1		8		
Plymouth	9	18	Bramhall	Benjamin	3	1		1		2			1				8		
Plymouth	9	19	Reed	Nathan		1		1		1			1				4		
Plymouth	9	20	Bramhall	Silvanus	1			1				1					3		
Plymouth	9	21	Wethrell	Thomas	1			1				1					3		
Plymouth	9	22	Cobb	Ebenezer				1						1			2		
Plymouth	9	23	Holmes	Zepheniah	1			1				1	1				4		
Plymouth	9	24	Tufts	Jonathan	2				1	2		1	1				7		
Plymouth	9	25	Churchill	John		1	1						1	1			4		
Plymouth	9	26	Virgin	John	2		1	1					1				5		
Plymouth	9	27	Brown	Robert		1			1	2			1				5		
Plymouth	9	28	Cobb	Nehemiah			1	1	1				1				4		
Plymouth	10	1	Jackson	Charles		1	1	1		1			1				5		
Plymouth	10	2	Jackson	Thomas	3	1			1	1	1		1				8		
Plymouth	10	3	Jackson	Sarah							1	2	1	1			5		
Plymouth	10	4	Callon	John	1			1		2			1				5		
Plymouth	10	5	Russell	John	1	2		1		1			1				6		
Plymouth	10	6	Bradford	Charles	3	1		1				1	2				8		
Plymouth	10	7	Bagnall	Richard	2	1		1		1	1		1				7		
Plymouth	10	8	Kyes	Oliver	1			1		1			1				4		
Plymouth	10	9	Holmes	William	4		1	1		1		1	2	1			11		
Plymouth	10	10	Holmes	Richard			1	1	1	2	1	1	1	1			9		
Plymouth	10	11	Gale	Noah	4	3		1					2				10		
Plymouth	10	12	Churchill	Elizabeth	1					1		1	1	1			5		
Plymouth	10	13	Crowell	Jonathan		1				1			1				3		
Plymouth	10	14	Turner	Lothrop	2			1		3	1	1					9		
Plymouth	10	15	Drew	James	1			1					1	1			4		
Plymouth	10	16	Cushing	Mathew	1			1		1	1		1				5		
Plymouth	10	17	Bartlett	Peabody	2			1					1				4		
Plymouth	10	18	Rider	William					1	2	1	1	1				6		
Plymouth	10	19	Drew	David		3			1	1			1				6		
Plymouth	10	20	Clarke	John	1			1		1			1				4		
Plymouth	10	21	Tribble	Joseph				1					1				2		
Plymouth	10	22	Luce	Ebenezer				1				1	1				3		
Plymouth	10	23	Barnes	William	2	1		1					1				5		
Plymouth	10	24	Strattens	George	2			1					1				4		
Plymouth	10	25	Marshall	Barsheba						1	1		1				3		
Plymouth	10	26	Bartlett	James		1		1		4	1		2				9		
Plymouth	10	27	Faunce	Thomas				1						3			4		
Plymouth	10	28	Robbins	Jane			3							2			5		
Plymouth	11	1	Morton	Benjamin	2			1		2	2		1				8		
Plymouth	11	2	Bearse	Ichabod				1		2		1					4		
Plymouth	11	3	Holmes	Mary		1		2		2	2		3				10		
Plymouth	11	4	Shurlliff	Lydia										2			2		
Plymouth	11	5	Lamson	George			1		1	2		1					5		
Plymouth	11	6	Bradford	William	1		1			1		1	1				5		
Plymouth	11	7	Spooner	Nathaniel	3	2		1		1		2	1	1	1		12		
Plymouth	11	8	Breck	Moses			2	1		2		1					6		
Plymouth	11	9	Ripley	Nathaniel		1		1	1				1	2			6		
Plymouth	11	10	Polden	Jonas	2			1		2			1				6		
Plymouth	11	11	Churchill	Benjamin		1			1					1			3		
Plymouth	11	12	Sherman	Samuel	2			1		1			1				5		
Plymouth	11	13	Robbins	Mercy	1	1						1		1			4		
Plymouth	11	14	Morton	Cary		1		1						1			3		
Plymouth	11	15	Holmes	Elnathan		1		1				1		1			4		
Plymouth	11	16	Holmes	Ichabod		1	3	1			1		1	1			8		

TOWN	PG#	LN#	LAST NAME	FIRST NAME	FREE WHITE MALES under 10	10 to 16	16 to 26	26 to 45	45 and over	FREE WHITE FEMALES under 10	10 to 16	16 to 26	26 to 45	45 and over	TOTAL ALL OTHER	TOTAL SLAVES	TOTALS	DISTRICT/ TOWNSHIP	NOTES
Plymouth	11	17	Bradford	Nathaniel	1		2		1	1	1		1				7		
Plymouth	11	18	Cooper	Benjamin	1			1		2			1				5		
Plymouth	11	19	Simmons	Bennet	1			1		2				1			5		
Plymouth	11	20	Holmes	Elnathan Jr	1		2	1		1	2		1	1			9		
Plymouth	11	21	Warren	Benjamin					2			1		1			4		
Plymouth	11	22	Kempton	John				1	1				2	1			5		
Plymouth	11	23	Traske	Joseph					1				1	1			3		
Plymouth	11	24	Bradford	Lemuel	3			1		1	1		1				7		
Plymouth	11	25	Bartlett	David			1			2			1				4		
Plymouth	11	26	Bartlett	Stephen				1		1	1	1					4		
Plymouth	11	27	Holmes	Ephraim			1					1					2		
Plymouth	11	28	Bradford	*			2		1	2		2		1			8		
Plymouth	12	1	Leonard	William	1			1		3			1				6		
Plymouth	12	2	Lucas	Levi	2			1					1				4		
Plymouth	12	3	Burbank	Priscilla			2						2	1			5		
Plymouth	12	4	Washburn	Prince	1	1		1		1			1				5		
Plymouth	12	5	Burbank	Ezra	2			1		2			1				6		
Plymouth	12	6	Washburn	Nathaniel				1		1			1				3		
Plymouth	12	7	Bramhall	Silvanus	1			1				1					3		
Plymouth	12	8	Holmes	Nathaniel	1			1		1		1	1				5		
Plymouth	12	9	Cooper	Joseph	2	1		1					1				5		
Plymouth	12	10	Morton	george	1	1		1		2	1		1	2			9		
Plymouth	12	11	Ellis	Nathaniel	3			1		2	1		1				8		
Plymouth	12	12	Everson	Ephraim				1		2			1				4		
Plymouth	12	13	Davie	Ichabod				1		2	1	1					5		
Plymouth	12	14	Holmes	Anselm				1		1		1					3		
Plymouth	12	15	Robbins	Anselm	5		1	1				1	1				9		
Plymouth	12	16	Cooper	Richard		1	1	1					1				4		
Plymouth	12	17	Darling	Polly									2				2		
Plymouth	12	18	Nicholson	Seth	3			1		3			1	1			9		
Plymouth	12	19	Holmes	Abner		1						1					2		
Plymouth	12	20	Dotten	John	1			1		1			1				4		
Plymouth	12	21	Rogers	Thomas	2			1				1					4		
Plymouth	12	22	Atwood	Thomas				1		1		1	1				4		
Plymouth	12	23	Dotten	James					1	1		2		1			5		
Plymouth	12	24	Bartlett	Hannah						2			1	1			4		
Plymouth	12	25	Clarke	Nathaniel	1	1		1		1	1		1				6		
Plymouth	12	26	Harlow	Zacheus	3			1		1	2	1	1				9		
Plymouth	12	27	Bradford	Ruth		2	1			1			1				5		
Plymouth	12	28	Obrien	Joseph	1		1					1					3		
Plymouth	13	1	Harvey	Jonathan	1		1			1		1					4		
Plymouth	13	2	Polden	Jonathan		1			1					1	1		4		
Plymouth	13	3	Churchill	Daniel				1		2		1					4		
Plymouth	13	4	Churchill	Heman	1			1		1		1					4		
Plymouth	13	5	Bartlett	Trueman	1		1			1		1					4		
Plymouth	13	6	Finney	Ezra			1			1		1					3		
Plymouth	13	7	Churchill	Rufus	1			1					1				3		
Plymouth	13	8	Hurtins	William	1		1	1	1	4	1	1	1				11		
Plymouth	13	9	Bartlett	Amasa				1	1	3	1		1				7		
Plymouth	13	10	Finney	Seth	1		1					1					3		
Plymouth	13	11	Farmer	Thomas	2			1		3			1				7		
Plymouth	13	12	Smith	Sarah									2				2		
Plymouth	13	13	Holbrook	Eliphalet		1	2		1	1		1		1			7		
Plymouth	13	14	Churchill	Charles	1			1		1			1				4		
Plymouth	13	15	Samson	Jonathan		1			1			2	1				5		
Plymouth	13	16	Brewster	William	1			1				1	1				4		
Plymouth	13	17	Attwood	John		1	1					1					3		
Plymouth	13	18	Churchill	Stephen		1			1	2	1			1	1		7		
Plymouth	13	19	Rogers	Abigail		1	1						1				3		
Plymouth	13	20	Rogers	Samuel			1			1		1					3		
Plymouth	13	21	Thomas	Isaac	1			1		2		1	1				6		
Plymouth	13	22	Holmes	Thomas	2		2	1				1					6		
Plymouth	13	23	Barnes	Corben					1	2	3		1				7		
Plymouth	13	24	Cushing	James	1		1					1	1				4		
Plymouth	13	25	Barnes	Corben Jr	2	1	1	1		2			1				8		
Plymouth	13	26	Barnes	Lemuel				1					1	2			4		
Plymouth	13	27	Barnes	Benjamin		1	2	1	1	1	1	1					8		
Plymouth	13	28	Barnes	Bradford		1						2					3		
Plymouth	14	1	Robbins	James			2			1		1					4		
Plymouth	14	2	Bartlett	Freeman	3	1		1					1				6		
Plymouth	14	3	Herring	Wyatt	2			1					1	1			5		
Plymouth	14	4	Jackson	Woodward			1					1	1				3		
Plymouth	14	5	Churchill	Branch				1				1	1	2			5		
Plymouth	14	6	Freeman	Samuel				1					1				2		
Plymouth	14	7	Bartlett	Jesse	2			1				1		2			6		
Plymouth	14	8	Bartlett	Silvanus				1				1	1	1			4		
Plymouth	14	9	Torrey	John	2	1	1	1				1	2				8		
Plymouth	14	10	Otis	Barnabas		2		1				1	1				5		
Plymouth	14	11	Lothrop	David					1			1		1			3		
Plymouth	14	12	Nelson	William	1		1	1		2			1				6		

TOWN	PG#	LN#	LAST NAME	FIRST NAME	FREE WHITE MALES under 10	10 to 16	16 to 26	26 to 45	45 and over	FREE WHITE FEMALES under 10	10 to 16	16 to 26	26 to 45	45 and over	TOTAL ALL OTHER	TOTAL SLAVES	TOTALS	DISTRICT/ TOWNSHIP	NOTES
Plymouth	14	13	Washburn	Thomas	1			1			1		1				4		
Plymouth	14	14	Bishop	John	1	1			1					1	1		5		
Plymouth	14	15	Crombie	Calvin		1	1	1		2		2			1		8		
Plymouth	14	16	Crombie	William			1		1			2		1			5		
Plymouth	14	17	Seymour	Benjamin	2			2		2	1	1	1				9		
Plymouth	14	18	Bartlett	Amasa			2			3			1				6		
Plymouth	14	19	Crombie	William	2		1	1		2		1					7		
Plymouth	14	20	Rogers	Thomas		1			1			1		1			4		
Plymouth	14	21	Sturtevant	Silvanus	1			1		2			1				5		
Plymouth	14	22	Wilkens	Samuel	1		1	2		2			1				7		
Plymouth	14	23	Dike	Anthony	1	2	2		1	5			1				12		
Plymouth	14	24	Inglee	Solomon	2	2	1	2		1	1		1				10		
Plymouth	14	25	Packard	Zadock	2			1		1	1		1				6		
Plymouth	14	26	Bradford	Pelham			2			1		1					4		
Plymouth	14	27	Allen	Timothy	3			1		2		1					8		
Plymouth	14	28	Dunbar	John D	3		1	1			2		1				8		
Plymouth	14	29	Bates	David		1		1			1			1			4		
Plymouth	15	1	Brattles	Samuel	2			1	6	3			2	11			23		
Plymouth	15	2	Brattles	Samuel Jr	3			1		1			1				6		
Plymouth	15	3	Stephens	John	2	1		1		2			1				7		
Plymouth	15	4	Stephens	William		2			1	1		1		2			7		
Plymouth	15	5	Davie	William		1	1		1			1		1			5		
Plymouth	15	6	Bartlett	Ephraim		2	1	1				1		1			6		
Plymouth	15	7	Churchill	Elizabeth	1	1				1	1		1				5		
Plymouth	15	8	Samson	Ebenezer	1			1	2	1	2	3	2				10		
Plymouth	15	9	Finney	Daniel			1			3		1					5		
Plymouth	15	10	Covington	Mary						1		1		1			3		
Plymouth	15	11	Hempton	Oliver			1			1			1				3		
Plymouth	15	12	Holmes	Silvanus				1						1			2		
Plymouth	15	13	Harlow	Nathaniel			1	1		1		1					4		
Plymouth	15	14	Rogers	George			1			1		1					3		
Plymouth	15	15	Harlow	Seth			1				1	1	1				5		
Plymouth	15	16	Rogers	John			1							1			2		
Plymouth	15	17	Harlow	Seth B.	1		1				1		1				4		
Plymouth	15	18	Carver	Josiah	1		1			1	1		1				5		
Plymouth	15	19	Paty	John	1	2	1	1		1		1	1				8		
Plymouth	15	20	Harlow	Ezra	1			1		2			1				5		
Plymouth	15	21	Doten	Joseph	1			1		2			1				5		
Plymouth	15	22	Holmes	Chandler	1			1		1			1				4		
Plymouth	15	23	Rider	Seth	1	1		1		2	1		1				7		
Plymouth	15	24	Holmes	David		1		1		1		1		1			5		
Plymouth	15	25	Doten	Nathaniel		2		1						1			4		
Plymouth	15	26	Silvester	Nathaniel	2			1		1			1	3			8		
Plymouth	15	27	Silvester	John	1			1		1			1				4		
Plymouth	15	28	Paty	Thomas	2		1						1				4		
Plymouth	15	29	Churchill	Samuel				1			1		1				3		
Plymouth	15	30	Holmes	Corrthial	2	1	1		1		1	2		1			9		
Plymouth	16	1	Churchill	Hannah						2	1		1				4		
Plymouth	16	2	Harlow	Lewis	1		1	1		1		1					5		
Plymouth	16	3	Barnes	Isaac	1		1	1		2	1		1	1			8		
Plymouth	16	4	Luce	Seth				1					1				2		
Plymouth	16	5	Bartlett	Henry	2			1		1			2				6		
Plymouth	16	6	Bryant	Caleb	2			1			1		1				5		
Plymouth	16	7	Perkins	George		1						1					2		
Plymouth	16	8	Bradford	Samuel		1		1		1	1		1				5		
Plymouth	16	9	Harlow	Lothrop			2							1			3		
Plymouth	16	10	Harlow	Lazarus			1				1	1	1				4		
Plymouth	16	11	Harlow	Jesse		1	1	1					1				4		
Plymouth	16	12	Carver	Nathaniel	1			1		2	1	1	1				7		
Plymouth	16	13	Bartlett	Thomas			1			1			1				3		
Plymouth	16	14	Barnes	Hannah								1		1			2		
Plymouth	16	15	Warner	Benjamin	3			1		1			1				6		
Plymouth	16	16	Holmes	Joseph			1			4			1	1			7		
Plymouth	16	17	Durfey	Richard	1			1	1				1	1			7		
Plymouth	16	18	Barnes	William	2	1		1		1			1				6		
Plymouth	16	19	Goddard	Daniel	2			1					1				4		
Plymouth	16	20	Leonard	Thomas				1		3			1	2			7		
Plymouth	16	21	Greene	John	1			1					1				3		
Plymouth	16	22	Davie	Betsey						2			1				3		
Plymouth	16	23	Faunce	Barnabas		1				1			1				3		
Plymouth	16	24	Sargent	William		1				2			1				4		
Plymouth	16	25	Harlow	Hannah		1				1			1				3		
Plymouth	16	26	Davie	William Jr			1			1	1	1					3		
Plymouth	16	27	Holmes	Samuel	3	2	1				1		1				8		
Plymouth	16	28	Harlow	Jesse Jr	2	1		1		2	2		1				9		
Plymouth	16	29	Harlow	Ephraim	2			1		1			1				5		
Plymouth	17	1	Bartlett	Thomas				1				1					2		
Plymouth	17	2	Bartlett	Joseph		1	1	1						1			4		
Plymouth	17	3	Bartlett	Nathaniel	1			1		2			1				5		
Plymouth	17	4	Holmes	Barnabas	2	1	2		1	2		1	1	1			11		
Plymouth	17	5	Doten	William	1	1			1	1	2	1		2			9		
Plymouth	17	6	Morton	Ichabod Jr		1		1		3	1		2				8		
Plymouth	17	7	Morton	Ichabod			1	1		1			1	2			6		
Plymouth	17	8	Bartlett	Samuel			1				1		1	2			5		
Plymouth	17	9	Churchill	Jabez			1						1	2			4		
Plymouth	17	10	Howes	Silvanus				1				1		1			3		
Plymouth	17	11	Bartlett	Anselm	3	1				1			1				7		
Plymouth	17	12	Howland	Sarah	1					1	1		1				4		
Plymouth	17	13	Sears	Willard		2	1		1	2				1			7		

TOWN	PG#	LN#	LAST NAME	FIRST NAME	M under 10	M 10 to 16	M 16 to 26	M 26 to 45	M 45 and over	F under 10	F 10 to 16	F 16 to 26	F 26 to 45	F 45 and over	TOTAL ALL OTHER	TOTAL SLAVES	TOTALS	DISTRICT/ TOWNSHIP	NOTES
Plymouth	17	14	Churchill	Nathaniel			1			1	1	1		1			5		
Plymouth	17	15	Whiting	Joseph	2		1				1	1					5		
Plymouth	17	16	Whiting	Ephraim	3		1					1	1	1			7		
Plymouth	17	17	Morton	Samuel	1		1			2			1				5		
Plymouth	17	18	Finney	George			1			1		1					3		
Plymouth	17	19	Finney	Clarke			1			2		2	1				6		
Plymouth	17	20	Finney	Elizabeth		1	1					1	1	1			5		
Plymouth	17	21	Whiting	Levi		1	1			1			1				4		
Plymouth	17	22	Finney	Lydia		1				1			1	1			4		
Plymouth	17	23	Holbrook	Hannah		1								1			2		
Plymouth	17	24	Finney	John			1		1	1	1			1			5		
Plymouth	17	25	Leach	Lemuel			1		1	1	1			1			5		
Plymouth	17	26	Finney	Robert				1		3			1				5		
Plymouth	17	27	Clarke	William	1		2		1	2				1			7		
Plymouth	17	28	Clarke	Nathaniel				1					1	1			3		
Plymouth	17	29	Morey	Silas	3	1		1		2	1		1				9		
Plymouth	17	30	Clarke	John	2		1			2		1	1				7		
Plymouth	18	1	Hackel	Zadoch	1		1			2			1				5		
Plymouth	18	2	Davie	Robert	1		1			2		1	1				6		
Plymouth	18	3	Churchill	Amaziah			1			1	2		1				5		
Plymouth	18	4	Holmes	Ellis	1		1			3			1				6		
Plymouth	18	5	Holmes	Eleazer		1	1	1		2	1	1		3			10		
Plymouth	18	6	Holmes	Ichabod	1			1						1			3		
Plymouth	18	7	Shaw	Ichabod			1				1		1				3		
Plymouth	18	8	Luce	Crosby	1	2			1	2	1	1		1			9		
Plymouth	18	9	Morton	Eleazer	2	1	2		1		2		1				9		
Plymouth	18	10	Faunce	Hannah	2					1		2	2	1			8		
Plymouth	18	11	Bartlett	Nathaniel	1	1		1		1			1				5		
Plymouth	18	12	Churchill	Elizabeth		1	2			2	1		1				7		
Plymouth	18	13	Dunham	William	2		1			1	1		2	1			8		
Plymouth	18	14	Albertson	Rufus	1		1			2	2		1				7		
Plymouth	18	15	Shurlliff	Isaac			1						1	1			3		
Plymouth	18	16	Reed	James	2		1			2			1				6		
Plymouth	18	17	Hathaway	Silas	2		2	1		1		1	1				8		
Plymouth	18	18	Dunham	Elijah		1			1	2		1	1				6		
Plymouth	18	19	Ricket	Samuel	2	1		1		2			2				8		
Plymouth	18	20	Drew	Samuel	1	1			1	1		1		1			6		
Plymouth	18	21	Bartlett	Joseph Jr	4		2			2			1	1			10		
Plymouth	18	22	Dunham	John	1		1			3	1		1				7		
Plymouth	18	23	Nicols	Moses	3	1	1			1	1	1	1				9		
Plymouth	18	24	Bartlett	John	1		1			1			1				4		
Plymouth	18	25	Paty	Silvanus	1	1	1			2			1				6		
Plymouth	18	26	Churchill	Thaddeus			2		1			2		1			6		
Plymouth	18	27	Morton	Thomas	1	1	1	1	1	3	1		2				11		
Plymouth	18	28	Churchill	Solomon	1	2				1		1	1				7		
Plymouth	18	29	Sears	Thomas			1			1			1				3		
Plymouth	19	1	Bramshall	George		1				1		1	1				4		
Plymouth	19	2	Saunders	Bella	1				1	3			1				6		
Plymouth	19	3	Holmes	Andrew	2		1			1			1				5		
Plymouth	19	4	Holmes	Jeremiah			1	1				1		1			4		
Plymouth	19	5	Morton	William Jr		1	1			2			1				5		
Plymouth	19	6	Holmes	Nathaniel		1		1				2		1			5		
Plymouth	19	7	Holmes	Gilbert		1		1		2				1			5		
Plymouth	19	8	Corvett	Jesse	2			1					1	1			5		
Plymouth	19	9	Perry	John	2		1			2			1				6		
Plymouth	19	10	Clarke	Zoeth			2	2		1		1	1				7		
Plymouth	19	11	Dunham	George	3	2	1				1		1	1			9		
Plymouth	19	12	Lucas	Anselm			1	1		1			1				6		
Plymouth	19	13	Lucas	Bela	1	1	1	1		1	1			2			8		
Plymouth	19	14	Jackson	Isaac	1			1			2	2		1			7		
Plymouth	19	15	Jackson	Ransome			1				1	1					3		
Plymouth	19	16	Ripley	Thadeus		1		1		4			1	1			8		
Plymouth	19	17	Barrows	Zadock			2	1									3		
Plymouth	19	18	Barrows	Asa	2		1			3			1				7		
Plymouth	19	19	Brattles	Caleb	1		1					1					3		
Plymouth	19	20	Foster	Daniel	2		1			3			1				6		
Plymouth	19	21	Dunham	Ichabod	1	1		1	1	1			1	1			7		
Plymouth	19	22	Holmes	Bartlett		1			1			1		2			5		
Plymouth	19	23	Harlow	James	1				1					1			3		
Plymouth	19	24	Harlow	Anselm					1					1			2		
Plymouth	19	25	Bartlett	James			1			3			1	1			6		
Plymouth	19	26	Clarke	James	2	1		1		3	1		1				9		
Plymouth	19	27	Holbrook	Gideon			1	1		1	3		1				7		
Plymouth	20	1	Clarke	Nathaniel			1			1		1					3		
Plymouth	20	2	Finney	Elkanah	1		1					1					3		
Plymouth	20	3	Morton	Josiah	1	2		1		2			2				8		
Plymouth	20	4	Howland	Isaac	4	2	1		1				1				9		
Plymouth	20	5	Doten	Stephen Jr			1		1	4	3		1				10		
Plymouth	20	6	Doten	Stephen		1		1	1				1	1			5		
Plymouth	20	7	Doten	John	1		1			1			1				4		
Plymouth	20	8	Morton	Rebecca	1	1				2			1				5		
Plymouth	20	9	Morton	Ezekiel			1		1	1	1	1					5		
Plymouth	20	10	Morton	Caleb			1						1				2		
Plymouth	20	11	Finney	Caleb				3					1	2			6		
Plymouth	20	12	Whiting	Benjamin	1		1			1			1				4		
Plymouth	20	13	Finney	Solomon	1		1						1				3		
Plymouth	20	14	Leach	Lemuel	2		1			1			1	1			6		
Plymouth	20	15	Howland	Abraham	1		1			1		1					4		
Plymouth	20	16	Howland	Jacob			1			1				1			3		
Plymouth	20	17	Harlow	Ezra			1		1					1			3		

Census table — Plymouth

TOWN	PG#	LN#	LAST NAME	FIRST NAME	M <10	M 10-16	M 16-26	M 26-45	M 45+	F <10	F 10-16	F 16-26	F 26-45	F 45+	TOTAL ALL OTHER	TOTAL SLAVES	TOTALS	DISTRICT/TOWNSHIP	NOTES
Plymouth	20	18	Morton	Thomas		2		1		2	3	1					9		
Plymouth	20	19	Rider	Samuel		1		1		1		1		1			5		
Plymouth	20	20	Whiting	Nathan	1		1			1			1				4		
Plymouth	20	21	Rider	Joshua			1						1				2		
Plymouth	20	22	Leonard	Phillip			1	1					1	1			4		
Plymouth	20	23	Leonard	Warren	1		1			1			1				4		
Plymouth	20	24	Swift	John	1		2	1		1	2	1		3			11		
Plymouth	20	25	Swift	John Jr	1		1			1		1					4		
Plymouth	20	26	Raymond	Nathaniel	2		1	1		1	1	1	1				8		
Plymouth	20	27	Raymond	Nathaniel Jr			1					1					2		
Plymouth	20	28	Washburn	Seth	1			1						1			3		
Plymouth	20	29	Ricket	Eleazer				1						1			2		
Plymouth	21	1	Blackmore	Branch		1	1	1	1			1	1	1			7		
Plymouth	21	2	Blackmore	John	3	1		1					1				6		
Plymouth	21	3	Clarke	Josiah		3		1		3	1	1	1				10		
Plymouth	21	4	Bates	Hannah		1							2	1			4		
Plymouth	21	5	Johnson	Joseph	1			1		1	1		1				5		
Plymouth	21	6	Harlow	James	1	1		1		1	1	1	1				7		
Plymouth	21	7	Cornish	Samuel	1			1					1				3		
Plymouth	21	8	Cornish	David				1		3			1				5		
Plymouth	21	9	Holmes	Barnabas				1		2			1				4		
Plymouth	21	10	Cornish	Josiah	1	1		1		1	1		2				7		
Plymouth	21	11	Bartlett	John		1		1						1			3		
Plymouth	21	12	Harlow	Isaac		3		1						1			5		
Plymouth	21	13	Shaw	Silvanus		1		1					1	1			4		
Plymouth	21	14	Clarke	Lothrop	2	1	1	1		2			1				8		
Plymouth	21	15	Holmes	Barnabas	2	3	1	1		2			1				10		
Plymouth	21	16	Bates	Samuel		1		1		1	2		1				6		
Plymouth	21	17	Bartlett	Runa			1			2			1				4		
Plymouth	21	18	Vallier	Simeon		2	1	1		4			1				9		
Plymouth	21	19	Holmes	James			1	1				3		1			6		
Plymouth	21	20	Morey	Silvanus	2			1		2			1				6		
Plymouth	21	21	Morey	Cornelius	2	2		1		1	1		1				8		
Plymouth	21	22	Clarke	Seth	2			1		2			1				6		
Plymouth	21	23	Clarke	Ruth		2	1						1				4		
Plymouth	21	24	Cornish	Thomas			1			1			2	1			5		
Plymouth	21	25	Cornish	John			4	1			1	1		1			8		
Plymouth	21	26	Cornish	Benjamin				1						1			2		
Plymouth	22	1	Lucas	Wiliam	4	2		1		1	1		1				10		
Plymouth	22	2	Clarke	John	1	1		1		3		1	1				8		
Plymouth	22	3	Clarke	James				1		1				1			3		
Plymouth	22	4	Clarke	Seth	2	1		1		2			1				7		
Plymouth	22	5	Holmes	Seth		1	3	1				1		2	1		9		
Plymouth	22	6	Holmes	Seth	1			1		1	1	1					5		
Plymouth	22	7	Holmes	Stephen				1		1			1				3		
Plymouth	22	8	Holmes	Elkanah				1						2			3		
Plymouth	22	9	Johnson	Hannah		1	1					1	1	1			5		
Plymouth	22	10	Harlow	Reuben	1		1	1		3			1				7		
Plymouth	22	11	Johnson	Jacob				1		1							2		
Plymouth	22	12	Bartlett	Joseph	4	3		2		1	2	1	1				15		
Plymouth	22	13	Bartlett	George	1	1		1		3			1				7		
Plymouth	22	14	Bartlett	Nathaniel				1						1			2		
Plymouth	22	15	Barrows	Ebenezer	1			1		2			1				5		
Plymouth	22	16	Bartlett	Nathaniel Jr	4	3		1				1	1				10		
Plymouth	22	17	Bartlett	Lemuel		2		1		1	1		1				6		
Plymouth	22	18	Bartlett	Abner	1	2	2	1		1	2	1		1			11		
Plymouth	22	19	Bartlett	Amasa	1	1							1				3		
Plymouth	22	20	Bartlett	Rufus	1	1							1	1			4		
Plymouth	22	21	Laurence	Daniel	1	1		1		4	1	1	1	1	2		13		
Plymouth	22	22	Bartlett	Francis	3			1		1			1				6		
Plymouth	22	23	Bartlett	Andrew				1		1	1	1		1			5		
Plymouth	22	24	Bartlett	Hosea			1			1		1					3		
Plymouth	22	25	Holmes	Jeremiah	2		1	1		1			1	1			7		
Plymouth	22	26	Bartlett	James		1		1		1			1				4		
Plymouth	22	27	Bartlett	William		1		1		3	1	1					7		
Plymouth	22	28	Bartlett	Rebecca	1					2			1				4		
Plymouth	22	29	Hovey	Ivory Revd				1						3			4		
Plymouth	23	1	Besse	Robert	3			1					1				5		
Plymouth	23	2	Besse	Barzilla				1				1		1			3		
Plymouth	23	3	Besse	Andrew			1			4		1					6		
Plymouth	23	4	Besse	Nathaniel			1			2		1					4		
Plymouth	23	5	Bumpus	Joseph				1						1			2		
Plymouth	23	6	Wing	Jonathan		2		1		1	1			1			6		
Plymouth	23	7	Caswell	Zenas	2		1							1			4		
Plymouth	23	8	Raymond	Caleb	2			1						1			4		
Plymouth	23	9	Mantor	Prince	1		1			1				1			4		
Plymouth	23	10	Pearce	Richard		2		1		1				1			5		
Plymouth	23	11	Pearce	Richard Jr	1		1			1			1				4		
Plymouth	23	12	Castle	Thomas	3			1				2	1				7		
Plymouth	23	13	Samson	Joseph	1		1	2		1			1				6		
Plymouth	23	14	Burges	William	2	2		1		2	1	1	1				11		
Plymouth	23	15	Doten	Lemuel	1	1	1			1	1	1	1				7		
Plymouth	23	16	Wright	Joshua	1	1	1	2	1	1	2	1	1				11		
Plymouth	23	17	Samson	Mary		1	1					4		1			7		
Plymouth	23	18	Pearce	Jesse	2	2		1				1	1				7		
Plymouth	23	19	Burges	John	2	2		1		3	2		1				11		
Plymouth	23	20	Raymond	Lemuel	2			1		1		1					5		
Plymouth	23	21	Thrasher	George	3			1		4	2		1				11		
Plymouth	23	22	Parsons	William	1			1		3	2		1				8		
Plymouth	23	23	Wright	Samuel		3		1		1	1		1				7		

TOWN	PG#	LN#	LAST NAME	FIRST NAME	FREE WHITE MALES					FREE WHITE FEMALES					TOTAL ALL OTHER	TOTAL SLAVES	TOTALS	DISTRICT/TOWNSHIP	NOTES
					under 10	10 to 16	16 to 26	26 to 45	45 and over	under 10	10 to 16	16 to 26	26 to 45	45 and over					
Plymouth	23	24	Holmes	Jonathan					1					1			2		
Plymouth	23	25	Carpenter	Thomas		1			1				2	1			5		
Plymouth	24	1	Cornish	George		1	1			5	1		1				9		
Plymouth	24	2	Gammons	Benjamin			1		1	1	1		1				5		
Plymouth	24	3	Cornish	Nathaniel					1			1		1	2		5		
Plymouth	24	4	Cornish	Benjamin	2			1		1			1				5		
Plymouth	24	5	Harlow	Joseph	2		2	1					1				6		
Plymouth	24	6	Harlow	Thomas				1		1		1					3		
Plymouth	24	7	Ellis	Jerusha		1	1					1	1				4		
Plymouth	24	8	Ellis	William	3			1		1			1				6		
Plymouth	24	9	Ellis	Barnabas	1		1		1	1		1		1			6		
Plymouth	24	10	Churchill	Sally	1	1				1				1			4		
Plymouth	24	11	Ellis	Francis	1		1					1					3		
Plymouth	24	12	Raymond	Asa				1		3			1				5		
Plymouth	24	13	Norris	Samuel	1			1		1			1				4		
Plymouth	24	14	Ellis	Reuben	1			1					1				3		
Plymouth	24	15	Wadsworth	Christopher			1		1					1			3		
Plymouth	24	16	Brattles	Benjamin			1			1		1					3		
Plymouth	24	17	Briggs	Isaac		2	1		1	1	2		1				8		
Plymouth	24	18	Briggs	Reuben			1						1				2		
Plymouth	24	19	Bates	Joseph	2	2	1	1		3	1		1				11		
Plymouth	24	20	Thrasher	Jonathan	1	3		1		2	1		1				9		
Plymouth	24	21	Holmes	Robert			1						1				2		
Plymouth	24	22	Swift	Jacob		1			1			2		1			5		
Plymouth	24	23	Swift	Phineas	1	1		1				2	1	1			7		
Plymouth	24	24	Ellis	George	2	1	1		1	2	1			1			9		
Plymouth	24	25	Chubbock	John		2			1	3	1	1		1			9		
Plymouth	24	26	Chubbock	Timothy		1	2		1			1		1			6		
Plymouth	24	27	Chubbock	Benjamin	1	1			1	1				1			5		
Plymouth	24	28	Chubbock	Ephraim	2			1		1			1				5		
Plymouth	24	29	Besse	Benjamin		1			1			1		1			4		
Plymouth	26	1	Allen	John	2	2	1		1	1			1				8		
Plymouth	26	2	Wright	James	1		1			1		1					4		
Plymouth	26	3	Westcoat	Joseph	2			1		1			1				5		
Plymouth	26	4	Burges	Nathan	3			1		1			1				6		
Plymouth	26	5	Burges	Thomas		2		1		4	1	2	1				11		
Plymouth	26	6	Raymond	Ezekiel	2		2	1	1				1	1	1		9		
Plymouth	26	7	Watson	John	1	1	2		1	1	1	1	2				10		
Plymouth	26	8	Hoyt	Israel	1	1			1	1			1				5		
Plymouth	26	9	Hollis	Samuel	1			1		1			1				4		
Plymouth	26	10	Douglas	John	4	1	2		1	1	1			1			11		
Plymouth	26	11		Plato Negro											6		6		
Plymouth	26	12		Prince Negro											7		7		
Plymouth	26	13		Cato Negro											2		2		
Plymouth	26	14		Dolphin Negro											8		8		

TOWN	PG#	LN#	HEADS OF HOUSEHOLD		FREE WHITE MALES					FREE WHITE FEMALES					TOTAL ALL OTHER	TOTAL SLAVES	TOTALS	DISTRICT/ TOWNSHIP	NOTES
			LAST NAME	FIRST NAME	under 10	10 to 16	16 to 26	26 to 45	45 and over	under 10	10 to 16	16 to 26	26 to 45	45 and over					
Rochester	105	1	Pope	Seth	2	2	2		1	1	1			1			10		
Rochester	105	2	Peirce	Asa	1			1		2	1		1	1			7		
Rochester	105	3	Peirce	Joshua		1		1		3			1				6		
Rochester	105	4	Randal	Ebr	2			1		1			1				5		
Rochester	105	5	Raymond	Stephen				1					1				2		
Rochester	105	6	Randal	Thomas	1			1		2			1	1			8		
Rochester	105	7	Randal	Job	2	1		1		2	1		1				8		
Rochester	105	8	Randal	Lewis		1	1	1	1	1	1			1			7		
Rochester	105	9	Ruggles	Polly						1			1	1			3		
Rochester	105	10	Reed	Wm				1				2	1	1			5		
Rochester	105	11	Rider	David	3	1	2	1	1	1	1	1	1				12		
Rochester	105	12	Randal	Jethro	1	1		1		3		1		1			8		
Rochester	105	13	Randal	Saml	3			1					1				5		
Rochester	105	14	Randal	Seth	1	1	1	1				2		1			7		
Rochester	105	15	Reed	Mary									1	1			2		
Rochester	105	16	Ruggles	Elisha	4	2	1	1		1	1	2	1	1			14		
Rochester	105	17	Randal	John			2					2	1				5		
Rochester	105	18	Randal	Leml		2	1		1	1	3		2				10		
Rochester	105	19	Rider	Saml	3		1		1	1	2		1				9		
Rochester	105	20	Ruggles	Nathl	1	1	1	1	1	3	1	1	1				11		
Rochester	105	21	Rogers	Moosen				1				1					2		
Rochester	105	22	Randal	David			2		1			1		1			5		
Rochester	105	23	Rogers	Ebr	1			1					1				3		
Rochester	105	24	Reed	Ichabod	1	1	1	1		2	1	3	1				11		
Rochester	105	25	Reynolds	Isaac	2			1		1			1				5		
Rochester	105	26	Russell	Stephen	1				1			1		1			4		
Rochester	105	27	Snow	Thomas	2	2	1			2	1		1				9		
Rochester	105	28	*	*	*	*	*	*	*	*	*	*	*	*			*		Tape Mark
Rochester	105	29	Smith	Elijah	1		1			1							3		
Rochester	105	30	Sherman	Joseph	1			1		1		1		1			5		
Rochester	105	31	Sherman	Richard	1	1		1		1			1				5		
Rochester	105	32	Smith	Wm	1	1	1		1					1			5		
Rochester	105	33	Smith	John				1						1			2		
Rochester	105	34	Snow	Jonn	3	1		1	1	1	1	1	1	1			11		
Rochester	105	35	Smith	Henry	1			1				1		1			4		
Rochester	105	36	Simmons	John			1		1	1		1		1			5		
Rochester	105	37	Snow	Hannah		1		1		1	3		1				7		
Rochester	105	38	Snow	Susanna	1	1								1			3		
Rochester	105	39	Stuart	Thankful										1			1		
Rochester	105	40	Sherman	Wm		2	1		1				1				6		
Rochester	105	41	Sherman	Joshua		2	1		1	1	2		1				8		
Rochester	105	42	Soper	Alexr	2	1	1		1	2	1	2		2			12		
Rochester	105	43	Simmons	John	2	1		1		1	1		1				7		
Rochester	105	44	Sherman	Abigail		1						1	1	1			4		
Rochester	105	45	Sherman	Cornelius	1			1		2	1		1				6		
Rochester	105	46	Sherman	Thos	2			1		2		1	1				7		
Rochester	105	47	Sherman	Joshua 2d	4		1	1		1	1	1					9		
Rochester	105	48	Sturtevant	Charles	2	1	1		3	2	1	1	1	1			13		
Rochester	105	49	Sears	Nathan		1	1	1		1	1			1			6		
Rochester	105	50	Shattalar	Hannah	*	*	*	*	*	*	*	*	*	*			*		Tape Mark
Rochester	105	51	*	*	*	*	*	*	*	*	*	*	*	*			*		Tape Mark
Rochester	105	52	*	*	*	*	*	*	*	*	*	*	*	*			*		Tape Mark
Rochester	105	53	*	*	*	*	*	*	*	*	*	*	*	*			*		Tape Mark
Rochester	105	54	*worth	*		1	1	1						1			4		Tape Mark
Rochester	105	55	Snow	*		1				1		1					3		Tape Mark
Rochester	105	56	Snow	Joshua	3			1		1			1				6		
Rochester	105	57	Snow	Bowman				1						1			2		
Rochester	105	58	Snow	James	2			1	1				1				5		
Rochester	105	59	Snow	Joseph				1						1			2		
Rochester	105	60	Snow	Prince	3			1		2			1				7		
Rochester	105	61	Snow	Rebecca	1							1	1	1			4		
Rochester	105	62	Stevens	Noah	1	1		1		1	1			1			6		
Rochester	105	63	Swift	Saml	1			1		1			1				4		
Rochester	105	64	Snow	Ebr				1		3	1	1	1	1			8		
Rochester	105	65	Shaw	Ambrose	2	1	1		1	1	1	1		1			9		
Rochester	105	66	Sherman	Thos 2d	2			1		2			1				6		
Rochester	105	67	Standish	Isaiah	1	1						1		1			5		
Rochester	105	68	Swift	James	1	4	1	1		1	1	1	1	2			13		
Rochester	105	69	Sherman	John		2	2	1	1	1	1	2	1				12		
Rochester	105	70	Snow	Saml	1		1	1					1				4		
Rochester	105	71	Tinkham	Charles		2		1		1	1	1		1			7		
Rochester	105	72	Tinkham	Peter				1						1			2		
Rochester	105	73	Tinkham	Abrm		1						1					2		
Rochester	105	74	Tinkham	Eliza		1				1	1	1		1			5		
Rochester	105	75	Trip	Jesse				1					1	1			3		
Rochester	105	76	Temple	Saml	1			1						1			3		
Rochester	105	77	Trip	Jesse Jr	3			1		1			1				6		
Rochester	105	78	Torey	Joseph	1			1				1					3		
Rochester	106	1	Nye	Wm Jr	3	2		1		1	1		1				9		
Rochester	106	2	Nichols	Asa	3			1					1				5		
Rochester	106	3	Nye	Nathan	1		1	1		2	2	1	1				9		
Rochester	106	4	Nye	John				1				1		1			3		
Rochester	106	5	Nye	Bars	2	1		1				1					5		
Rochester	106	6	Negro	Thos											3		3		
Rochester	106	7	Nye	Geo	2	2		1		1	1	1	1				9		
Rochester	106	8	Nye	Stephen		1		1				1					3		
Rochester	106	9	Oliver	Susanna									1				1		
Rochester	106	10	Pitcher	Thos	2	2		1		1			2				8		
Rochester	106	11	Peirce	Wm	3			1					1				5		
Rochester	106	12	Parker	Polly	1								1				2		

TOWN	PG#	LN#	LAST NAME	FIRST NAME	FREE WHITE MALES					FREE WHITE FEMALES					TOTAL ALL OTHER	TOTAL SLAVES	TOTALS	DISTRICT/ TOWNSHIP	NOTES
					under 10	10 to 16	16 to 26	26 to 45	45 and over	under 10	10 to 16	16 to 26	26 to 45	45 and over					
Rochester	106	13	Parker	Ebr			2		1		1		1	1			6		
Rochester	106	14	Parlow	Jesse	4			1	1	2			1	1			10		
Rochester	106	15	Parlow	Thomas	3		1	1				2	2				9		
Rochester	106	16	Parlow	Wm				1									1		
Rochester	106	17	Parlow	David	1			1				1	1				4		
Rochester	106	18	Peirce	Saml	1	1	1	1				1	1				6		
Rochester	106	19	Perkins	Benjn	3	2	2	1		1	1	1	1				12		
Rochester	106	20	Peckham	David		1	1	1	1	1	1	3		1			10		
Rochester	106	21	Phelps	Edward											3		3		
Rochester	106	22	Pease	Theos Jr				1					1				2		
Rochester	106	23	Pease	Theos				1				3		1			5		
Rochester	106	24	Pease	Asa					1				3		1		5		
Rochester	106	25	Paine	Epm	1		1						1				3		
Rochester	106	26	Pope	Seth Jr			1						1				2		
Rochester	107	1	Mendal	Moses	*	*	*	1	*	*	*	*	*	*	*	*	1		Tape mark
Rochester	107	2	Morton	Bartlett	*	*	*	1	*	3							4		
Rochester	107	3	Morse	Melatiah	1		1					1					3		
Rochester	107	4	Mendel	Danl	3			1		1			1				6		
Rochester	107	5	Morse	Joshua		1	1	1				2	1				6		
Rochester	107	6	Mendal	Caleb	1	1	1	1				1	1				6		
Rochester	107	7	Morse	John			2	1			1	2	1				7		
Rochester	107	8	Mendal	Abner	2			1					1				4		
Rochester	107	9	Millard	John				1	1				1	1			4		
Rochester	107	10	Mondal	Seth	1		3		1	1	3	1	1	1			12		
Rochester	107	11	Mendel	Ebr	1			1		1			1				4		
Rochester	107	12	Moore	Jonn	2			1				2	1				6		
Rochester	107	13	Mendal	Timo	2			1		2			1	1			7		
Rochester	107	14	Manhal	Allen	1	1		1				1	2	2			8		
Rochester	107	15	Merry	Wm	1		1			1			2				5		
Rochester	107	16	Mitchel	Calvin		1	2	1					1				5		
Rochester	107	17	Mathews	Nathan		1	1		1	2	1	1	1				8		
Rochester	107	18	Mendel	David				1		3	1	1	1				7		
Rochester	107	19	Mendel	Jonn		1		1		2		1					5		
Rochester	107	20	Mead	Zacheus	2	1		1	1	3	3	1	1	1			14		
Rochester	107	21	Muggs	Caleb	1			1					1				3		
Rochester	107	22	Muggs	Ebr	1			1	1	3			1				7		
Rochester	107	23	Martin	Abigail		1							1	1			3		
Rochester	107	24	Mendel	Barse	1			1					1	1			4		
Rochester	107	25	Morell	John		1	1			1			1				4		
Rochester	107	26	Mann	Joseph	2			1		1	1		1				6		
Rochester	107	27	Hammit	Shubael		1	1			1			1				4		
Rochester	107	28	Trip	Peleg			1	1		1			1				4		
Rochester	107	29	Tobey	Thos		2		1		1	1		1				6		
Rochester	107	30	Thacher	Lot	3	3	2	1		2		2	1				14		
Rochester	107	31	Vaughan	Danl	2	2	1		1	1	1		1				10		
Rochester	107	32	Wing	Joseph		1		1					3	1			6		
Rochester	107	33	Wing	Elisha				1		1			1				3		
Rochester	107	34	White	Justes	1	1		1		3	1		1				8		
Rochester	107	35	Wing	Philip	3	1		1		1	2		1				9		
Rochester	107	36	Wing	John Jr	1	1		1	1	2			1				7		
Rochester	107	37	Winslow	Nathan	1	1		1					1				4		
Rochester	107	38	Winslow	Dorcas			1	1		1				1	1		5		
Rochester	107	39	Winslow	Leml	1			1				1	1				4		
Rochester	107	40	Winslow	Micah				1					1				2		
Rochester	107	41	Wing	Buffer	2		1	1		1	1		1				7		
Rochester	107	42	Wingate	Wanton	1	1	1	1		3		1	1				9		
Rochester	107	43	Whitridge	Peleg	1		1						1				3		
Rochester	107	44	Winslow	Benjn	2	1	1		1	1		1	1				8		
Rochester	107	45	Whitridge	Joseph			1						1				2		
Rochester	107	46	Whitridge	Thos		1			1					1			3		
Rochester	107	47	Whitridge	Wm		1	1						1				3		
Rochester	107	48	Whitman	Richard	1			1					1				3		
Rochester	107	49	Wilber	Owen		1		1		5		1					8		
Rochester	108	1	Hall	George	3			1		1	1						6		
Rochester	108	2	Holmes	Church	2			1		1	1			1			6		
Rochester	108	3	Jenne	Joseph			2			3			1				6		
Rochester	108	4	Jenne	Nathan		1		1		1			1				4		
Rochester	108	5	Jenne	Lettes	2			1		1			1				6		
Rochester	108	6	Jucket	Peter					1				1				2		
Rochester	108	7	Keen	John			2	1	1	1		1	1	1			8		
Rochester	108	8	King	Molly	2									2	2		6		
Rochester	108	9	King	John	1	2	1		1			1	1				8		
Rochester	108	10	King	Geo					1				1	1			3		
Rochester	108	11	King	Nathl		1		1	1	1	1	1					6		
Rochester	108	12	King	Ebr	4	2		1		1			1	1			10		
Rochester	108	13	Killy	Amos				1				3	1	1	1		7		
Rochester	108	14	Luce	Rowland	3	1	2	1		1	1	1	1	1			12		
Rochester	108	15	Luce	Stephen				1					1				2		
Rochester	108	16	Luce	Bars			1	1						1			3		
Rochester	108	17	Look	Allice										2			2		
Rochester	108	18	Look	John	3	1		1		1			1				7		
Rochester	108	19	Look	Henry	2			1		1			1				5		
Rochester	108	20	Look	Savory				1				2	1				4		
Rochester	108	21	Leavit	Joseph Jr	1			1		1		1					4		
Rochester	108	22	Leavit	Joseph		1		1				1		1			4		
Rochester	108	23	Lumbard	Mary	2					1	1		1				5		
Rochester	108	24	Lincoln	Sherman	2			1	1	1			2				7		
Rochester	108	25	Luce	Lucy		1				1			1				3		
Rochester	108	26	Lincoln	John				1					1				2		
Rochester	108	27	Morse	*		1		1		2	2						6		Tape mark

TOWN	PG#	LN#	HEADS OF HOUSEHOLD		FREE WHITE MALES					FREE WHITE FEMALES					TOTAL ALL OTHER	TOTAL SLAVES	TOTALS	DISTRICT/ TOWNSHIP	NOTES
			LAST NAME	FIRST NAME	under 10	10 to 16	16 to 26	26 to 45	45 and over	under 10	10 to 16	16 to 26	26 to 45	45 and over					
Rochester	108	28	Maxham	Thomas	1			1	1	1				1			5		
Rochester	109	1	Haskell	Abigail	*	*	*	*	*	*	*	*	*	*	*		*		
Rochester	109	2	Handy	Freeman			1				2	1	1				5		
Rochester	109	3	Haskell	Nathl	2		2		1	1	2	3		1			12		
Rochester	109	4	Hammit	John	2				1						1		4		
Rochester	109	5	Hammit	Shubael	1			1					1				3		
Rochester	109	6	Hammit	John Jr			1						1				2		
Rochester	109	7	Hammond	Nathl			1		1		1		1	1			5		
Rochester	109	8	Hammond	David					1					1			2		
Rochester	109	9	Hammond	Noah	2			1					1	2			6		
Rochester	109	10	Hammond	Stafford			1			1				1			3		
Rochester	109	11	Hammond	Benjn		2	1		1		2	1		1			8		
Rochester	109	12	Hammond	Hursnewel			1		1					1			3		
Rochester	109	13	Hammond	James	2			1		1	1	1					6		
Rochester	109	14	Hammond	Josiah					1					1			2		
Rochester	109	15	Hammond	Gidn	1	1		1		1			1	1			6		
Rochester	109	16	Hammond	Benjn	3			1					1				5		
Rochester	109	17	Hammond	Huldah									2				2		
Rochester	109	18	Hammond	Timo	2			1		2		1	1	1			8		
Rochester	109	19	Hammond	Nathl Jr	2			1		1			1				5		
Rochester	109	20	Hammond	John			1	1			1		1				4		
Rochester	109	21	Hovey	Danl			1	1			1	1					4		
Rochester	109	22	Hammond	Nathl 2	1			1		1		1					5		Name scratched out
Rochester	109	23	Hammond	Ebr		1	1	1			2	1		1			7		
Rochester	109	24	Hatch	Benjn	2		1	1	1		2		1	1			9		
Rochester	109	25	Hammond	Jesse		1		1		4		1					7		
Rochester	109	26	Higgins	Heman	2		1	1		1	1		1				7		
Rochester	109	27	Hall	Luther	1	1		1		1		3		1			8		
Rochester	109	28	Holmes	Bethia	1		1						2	1			5		
Rochester	110	1	Handy	Edward	3			1		1	2		1				8		
Rochester	110	2	Heller	John				1						1			2		
Rochester	110	3	Heller	Benjn			1					1					2		
Rochester	110	4	Heller	Timoy		1	1	1		2	1		1	1			8		
Rochester	110	5	Heller	David		1		1		1		1	1	1			6		
Rochester	110	6	Heller	Jonn	4		1			1		1	1				8		
Rochester	110	7	Holmes	Ebr	1		2		2	2			1				8		
Rochester	110	8	Heller	Moses				2					1				3		
Rochester	110	9	Heller	Isaac	2		1					1					4		
Rochester	110	10	Hathaway	Eunice	2	2				1	2		1	2			10		
Rochester	110	11	Haskell	David		1	1	1				2		1			6		
Rochester	110	12	Haskell	Timo			2	1		1	2		1				7		
Rochester	110	13	Hathaway	Peleg	2		1			1			1				5		
Rochester	110	14	Hall	Solomon	1	1	2		1	1	1	2	2	1			12		
Rochester	110	15	Haskins	Thomas	1			1					2				4		
Rochester	110	16	Hammlin	Phebe	1	1				1			1				4		
Rochester	110	17	Hammond	Ebr	2			1					1				4		
Rochester	110	18	Hammond	Seth	2			1					1				4		
Rochester	110	19	Hammond	Pollypus	1	1		1		2			1				6		
Rochester	110	20	Hammond	Suylvanus	1	2		1		1			1				6		
Rochester	110	21	Haskell	Zebr	1		2		1	2			1	1			8		
Rochester	110	22	Hammond	Aaron				1			1		1				3		
Rochester	110	23	Holmes	Saml	3			1		1	1	1	1				8		
Rochester	110	24	Hatch	Lucy						1				2			3		
Rochester	110	25	Hall	John			1		1					1			4		
Rochester	110	26	Holland	Richard			1		1					1			3		
Rochester	110	27	Harte	Dory		1				1		1	1	1			5		
Rochester	110	28	Haskell	Jesse	1			2				1		1	1		6		
Rochester	110	29	Haskell	Lot	1			1		4			1		1		8		
Rochester	111	1	Dexter	Ephm		2		1		1	2	1		1			8		
Rochester	111	2	Dexter	Caleb		1		1			2		1				5		
Rochester	111	3	Dexter	Ebenzr	1		1			1		1					4		
Rochester	111	4	Doten	Zephh			1			1	1		1				4		
Rochester	111	5	Davis	Nicholas	2		1	1		1	2	1		1			9		
Rochester	111	6	Ellis	Thomas			1		1	2	1	1	1				7		
Rochester	111	7	Ellis	Malachi	2	1	1			1	1	2		1			9		
Rochester	111	8	Ellis	Joel	2			1	1	3		1		1			9		
Rochester	111	9	Edwards	Joseph	1	1			1	1		2		1			7		
Rochester	111	10	Elmes	Walter	2				1	1	1		1				6		
Rochester	111	11	Ellis	Joel Junr	2	1			1	1	1		1				7		
Rochester	111	12	Fuller	Zeba	2			1		3	1			1			8		
Rochester	111	13	Fuller	Israel	1	1	1		1	2	1	1					9		
Rochester	111	14	Foster	James Junr	1	1	1	1					1		1		6		
Rochester	111	15	Foster	James	2			1	1	1		1	1	1			8		
Rochester	111	16	Gurney	Levi			1		1		1			1			4		
Rochester	111	17	Gurney	Benjm		1	1	1		2	1	1	1				8		
Rochester	111	18	Gurney	Leml			1		1		1			1			4		
Rochester	111	19	Gurney	Leml Jr			1			1		1					3		
Rochester	111	20	Gammons	Leml	3		1			1			1				6		
Rochester	111	21	Gorham	Jabez	2		1	1		3		1		1			9		
Rochester	111	22	Gibbs	Thankful			1				2		1				4		
Rochester	111	23	Greene	Bars	3			1		1		1		1			7		
Rochester	111	24	Greene	Richard	1			1		1		1		1			5		
Rochester	111	25	Hammond	Edward	1		3		1	1		1	1	1			9		
Rochester	111	26	Hammond	Stephen	1			1					1				3		
Rochester	111	27	Hammond	Nathl 3	2			1					1				4		
Rochester	111	28	Fuller	Seth	1			1		4	1		1				8		
Rochester	111	29	Handy	Silas	2			1		1			1				5		
Rochester	111	30	Handy	Jonn	1	1			1	2				1			6		
Rochester	112	1	Cushman	Cephas	2	2	3	1	1	2	2	3		1			17		
Rochester	112	2	Dexter	John Jr	1	1	1		1		1		1	1			7		

TOWN	PG#	LN#	LAST NAME	FIRST NAME	FREE WHITE MALES under 10	10 to 16	16 to 26	26 to 45	45 and over	FREE WHITE FEMALES under 10	10 to 16	16 to 26	26 to 45	45 and over	TOTAL ALL OTHER	TOTAL SLAVES	TOTALS	DISTRICT/ TOWNSHIP	NOTES
Rochester	112	3	Dexter	John				1	1				2	1			5		
Rochester	112	4	Dexter	Thankfull							2	1					3		
Rochester	112	5	Dexter	Philip	1			1			1	1					4		
Rochester	112	6	Doty	Joseph	1		3	1	1	1	1	1		1			10		
Rochester	112	7	Delano	Harper		1	1		1	2	1			1			7		
Rochester	112	8	Delano	Stephen		2			1	3		1		1			8		
Rochester	112	9	Delano	Jabez	2	1	1		1	2	1			1			9		
Rochester	112	10	Delano	Jabez Jr	1		1						1				3		
Rochester	112	11	Doty	Jerahmeel	2	1		1		2	1		1	1			9		
Rochester	112	12	Doty	Silas	3	1		1		1			1				7		
Rochester	112	13	Dexter	Elijah	1		2		1	2	2			1			10		
Rochester	112	14	Davis	Timo	1	1	1	1		3	1		1				9		
Rochester	112	15	Dexter	Elias			1			1			1				3		
Rochester	112	16	Dexter	Jabez			1							1			2		
Rochester	112	17	Dexter	Elisha	2		1			3	1		1				8		
Rochester	112	18	Dexter	Sarah	1								2				3		
Rochester	112	19	Dexter	Noah	2		1	1		3			1	1			9		
Rochester	112	20	Dexter	Benjm			1	1					1	1			4		
Rochester	112	21	Dillingham	David	2		1	1		3			1				8		
Rochester	112	22	Davis	Joseph	2			1		3		1	1				8		
Rochester	112	23	Dexter	David	3		1		1		1	2	1				9		
Rochester	112	24	Dexter	Reubin	1			1		1			1				4		
Rochester	112	25	Dexter	Sarah			1						3				4		
Rochester	112	26	Dexter	Edward			1			1		1					3		
Rochester	113	1	Cannon	Nathan	*	*	*	*	*	*	*	*	*	*	*		*		Tape mark
Rochester	113	2	Cushing	Nathl	*	*	*	*	*	*	*	*	*	1	*		1		Tape mark
Rochester	113	3	Cole	John	*	*	*	*	*	*	*	*	1	1	+		2		Tape mark
Rochester	113	4	Cundal	Enoch	1	1		1		1		1					5		
Rochester	113	5	Cushman	Ezekiel	3		1	1		3			1				9		
Rochester	113	6	Clap	Kenolm			1			1	1		1				3		
Rochester	113	7	Cole	Archippus				1			2	1	1				5		
Rochester	113	8	Clifton	Timo		1		1		4	2		1				9		
Rochester	113	9	Clap	Nathl			1		1		1	2		1			6		
Rochester	113	10	Cook	Thomas	1		1		1	1	1	2		1			8		
Rochester	113	11	Cale	Thomas	2		1				1		1				5		
Rochester	113	12	Clark	Elijah			1			1			1				3		
Rochester	113	13	Crossman	Annah	3		1					1					5		
Rochester	113	14	Cowing	Seth	1		1	1			4		1				8		
Rochester	113	15	Cannon	Ebenzr	1		1	1	1	1		2	1				8		
Rochester	113	16	Cowing	Lot				1					1				2		
Rochester	113	17	Crapo	Nichs	2	2		1		3		3	1				12		
Rochester	113	18	Crapo	Lot			1			1		1	1				4		
Rochester	113	19	Crapo	Abm		1	1	1		2							5		
Rochester	113	20	Crapo	John				1		2		2					6		
Rochester	113	21	Coomer	Crissully		1				1			1				3		
Rochester	113	22	Coomer	Perez	1		1			1		1					4		
Rochester	113	23	Coomer	Caleb	1			1				3	1				6		
Rochester	113	24	Chaddock	Calvin	2		1		1	1	1	1	1				8		
Rochester	113	25	Clark	Willard	2			1	1	1	1		1	1			8		
Rochester	113	26	Cobb	Oliver	1	1	1	1		1	1		1				7		
Rochester	114	1	Bolles	Reubin	1		1	1		2			1				6		
Rochester	114	2	Bowland	Remember									1	4			5		
Rochester	114	3	Bisbee	Hopestill		1	2	1	1		1	1		1			8		
Rochester	114	4	Butler	James	1		1	1		1			2	2			9		
Rochester	114	5	Cannon	Ebenzr Jr	2			1		3			1				7		
Rochester	114	6	Clark	Willm	1	1		1		3			1	1			8		
Rochester	114	7	Clark	James	1	1			1		1	1		1			6		
Rochester	114	8	Clark	Nathan			1			1	1	1					4		
Rochester	114	9	Clayton	Savory	3		1			2	1		1				8		
Rochester	114	10	Caswell	Elijah	1			1		1	2			1			6		
Rochester	114	11	Caswell	Elisha	1			1				1					3		
Rochester	114	12	Caswell	Thomas	1	2	1		1	3		3		1			12		
Rochester	114	13	Cobb	Isaiah	1			1		1			1				4		
Rochester	114	14	Chamberlin	Philip			1			1			1				3		
Rochester	114	15	Clark	Malatiah		1				4	1	2	1				10		
Rochester	114	16	Clark	Leml	1		1	1		2	1	1	2	1			10		
Rochester	114	17	Crapo	Wm	2	3	1	1	1	2		1	1	2			14		
Rochester	114	18	Clark	Isaac	1	1		1				1	1				5		
Rochester	114	19	Clark	Nathl		1	2		1			2	1	1			8		
Rochester	114	20	Cowing	Israel	2			1		1			1				5		
Rochester	114	21	Clark	John	1				1	3	2	1	1				9		
Rochester	114	22	Cowing	Zadock				1	1		1	1		1			5		
Rochester	114	23	Cowing	Asahel			2		1			1		2			6		
Rochester	114	24	Church	Jonn	2	1	1		1	1		1	1	1			9		
Rochester	114	25	Church	Earl	1			2			1	1	1	1			7		
Rochester	115	1	Bates	Moses			1	1				1	1				4		
Rochester	115	2	Bolles	Saml				1		1		2	3	1			8		
Rochester	115	3	Bates	Lydia		1	1				1			1			4		
Rochester	115	4	Briggs	Nathl		1		1		1		2		1			6		
Rochester	115	5	Bolles	Ebenr	1	1	3		1	2	1	1		1			11		
Rochester	115	6	Brownell	James			1		1	1		1	2	1			7		
Rochester	115	7	Barteman	Davenport		1	1	1		1		1	1				7		
Rochester	115	8	Bennet	Jonn	1			1					1				3		
Rochester	115	9	Besse	Nathl					1			3	1				5		
Rochester	115	10	Besse	Joshua	1			1		4	1		1				8		
Rochester	115	11	Barlow	Seth			1		1				1				3		
Rochester	115	12	Barlow	George			1		1			1		1			4		
Rochester	115	13	Barlow	George Jr	1		1					1					3		
Rochester	115	14	Barstow	Benjn			1					1					2		
Rochester	115	15	Barstow	Gideon		1		1	1			1		1			5		

65

TOWN	PG#	LN#	HEADS OF HOUSEHOLD LAST NAME	FIRST NAME	FREE WHITE MALES under 10	10 to 16	16 to 26	26 to 45	45 and over	FREE WHITE FEMALES under 10	10 to 16	16 to 26	26 to 45	45 and over	TOTAL ALL OTHER	TOTAL SLAVES	TOTALS	DISTRICT/ TOWNSHIP	NOTES
Rochester	115	16	Barstow	Wilson	2		1	1		1	1		1				7		
Rochester	115	17	Barstow	Gidn Jr	3		3	1		1	1	1	1				11		
Rochester	115	18	Beard	John		1	2		1					1			5		
Rochester	115	19	Bolles	Amzh	1			1	1			2	1	1			7		
Rochester	115	20	Bradford	Oliver	2	3		1		3	1	1	1				12		
Rochester	115	21	Bennet	John 2d		1	1		1		1			1			5		
Rochester	115	22	Bennet	Levy					1					1			2		
Rochester	115	23	Briggs	Elijah	1		1		1			2	1	1			7		
Rochester	115	24	Bennet	John	3			1	1			1	1	1			8		
Rochester	115	25	Bisbee	Ezra	1	1		1			1		1				5		
Rochester	115	26	Braley	Russel			3		1			1		1			6		
Rochester	115	27	Braley	Elijah	1	1	1		1			1		1			6		
Rochester	116	1	Blankinship	Seth	1		1	1		1			1				5		
Rochester	116	2	Briggs	Seth	1			1		1	1		1				5		
Rochester	116	3	Briggs	Elisha	1		1		1	1	1		1				6		
Rochester	116	4	Blankinship	Paul	2			1		2	1		1				7		
Rochester	116	5	Blankinship	Wm	1			1		2	1		1				6		
Rochester	116	6	Briggs	Arnold	3			1		1	1		1				7		
Rochester	116	7	Burges	Wm				1				2	1				4		
Rochester	116	8	Bates	Jonn			2		1	2	1	1	1				8		
Rochester	116	9	Briggs	Elisha 2d	1	1			1	1	1	1	1				7		
Rochester	116	10	Bowman	Simeon		1			1				1				3		
Rochester	116	11	Bishop	Henry			1	1	1	1		1		1			6		
Rochester	116	12	Bosworth	Nehemiah	2	1		1	1			1		1			7		
Rochester	116	13	Briggs	John			2	1	1			1	1	1			7		
Rochester	116	14	Briggs	Cornelius	2			1		1		1					5		
Rochester	116	15	Bassett	Joseph			1		1	1	1		1				5		
Rochester	116	16	Bolles	Benjn			1		1			1	1				4		
Rochester	116	17	Bassett	Perez			1			1		1					3		
Rochester	116	18	Blackwell	Seth				1	1				1	1			4		
Rochester	116	19	Bonney	Saml				1		1		1	1	1			5		
Rochester	116	20	Blackwell	Caleb				1		1		1	1				4		
Rochester	116	21	Blackmore	Salisbury	2	2	3		1	2		3	1				14		
Rochester	116	22	Briggs	Nathan	2		1	1	1	1	2	3	1				12		
Rochester	116	23	Bolles	Isaac		1	1		1		1			1	1		6		
Rochester	116	24	Bassett	Eleanor									1	2			3		
Rochester	116	25	Bassett	John	1		1						2	1			5		
Rochester	116	26	Bassett	Thos Capt	4	2	2	1				1		1			11		
Rochester	117	1	Allen	Western				1		2			1				4		
Rochester	117	2	Allen	Ruth						2			1				3		
Rochester	117	3	Allen	Justes	2		1					1					4		
Rochester	117	4	Allen	Joshua	1			1				1	1				4		
Rochester	117	5	Ames	Seth		1		1				1	1				4		
Rochester	117	6	Arnold	Seth			2	1				1					4		
Rochester	117	7	Atsett	John		1		2				1					4		
Rochester	117	8	Atsett	Philip				1				1					2		
Rochester	117	9	Arnold	John	1			1				1					3		
Rochester	117	10	Ashley	John		2	1	1		1	2		1				8		
Rochester	117	11	Allen	George	1	1	3	1	1	2	1	1		1			12		
Rochester	117	12	Allen	Oliver	2			1					2	1			6		
Rochester	117	13	Arnold	Samuel		1		1					2	1			5		
Rochester	117	14	Blankinship	Perez			1			1		1	2	1			6		
Rochester	117	15	Barden	Stephen		1		1					2				4		
Rochester	117	16	Barden	Fredrick	1		1	1		1			1	1			6		
Rochester	117	17	Blankinship	Peleg	1		1					1					3		
Rochester	117	18	Blankinship	Charles	1	2			1	2			1				7		
Rochester	117	19	Blankinship	George	1	2			1	1			1		2		8		
Rochester	117	20	Briggs	Silas	1			1		1	1		1				5		
Rochester	117	21	Baker	Joshua				1	1	1	1	1	1	1			7		
Rochester	117	22	Bolles	Hosea		2	1		1				1				5		
Rochester	117	23	Blankinship	James				1					2				3		

TOWN	PG#	LN#	LAST NAME	FIRST NAME	FREE WHITE MALES					FREE WHITE FEMALES					TOTAL ALL OTHER	TOTAL SLAVES	TOTALS	DISTRICT/ TOWNSHIP	NOTES
					under 10	10 to 16	16 to 26	26 to 45	45 and over	under 10	10 to 16	16 to 26	26 to 45	45 and over					
Scituate	119	1	Turner	Charles Jun	4			1		2			1	1	1		10		
Scituate	119	2	Turner	Joseph					1								1		
Scituate	119	3	Copeland	Ebenezer	1	1			1	2			1	2			8		
Scituate	119	4	Barstow	Thomas	1		1	1		2	2		2				9		
Scituate	119	5	Briggs	William		1			1	1		1		2			6		
Scituate	119	6	Church	Thomas					1	2	2		1				6		
Scituate	119	7	Soper	Anna										1			1		
Scituate	119	8	Stetson	Ephraim	1		1		1	2	3	1		1			10		
Scituate	119	9	Stodder	Melzar			1				2		1				4		
Scituate	119	10	Silvester	John	2	1		1		1	2		1				8		
Scituate	119	11	Haskins	William	1			1	1			1					4		
Scituate	119	12	Stetson	Silas	4			1		1		1	1				8		
Scituate	119	13	Stetson	Micah	3	1	1		1	3	2		1				12		
Scituate	119	14	Stetson	Elizabeth									1	2			3		
Scituate	119	15	Copeland	William	1	1			1	3	1	1	1				9		
Scituate	119	16	James	William	1	1			1		1	2	1				7		
Scituate	119	17	Ewell	Gershom		1			1	2	1	2		1			8		
Scituate	119	18	Jacobs	Lemuel		2		1		1	1		1				6		
Scituate	119	19	Jacobs	John					1			1		1			3		
Scituate	119	20	James	Elisha		1		1	1		1		1				5		
Scituate	119	21	Southworth	Thos	1			1			1						3		
Scituate	119	22	Chittenden	Ruth			1			2	1			1			5		
Scituate	119	23	Talman	Joseph		1			1	1		2	1	1			7		
Scituate	119	24	Cushing	Nathl	4	1		1			1		1	1			9		
Scituate	119	25	Stetson	Lydia									2		1		3		
Scituate	119	26	Colman	Thomas					1				1				2		
Scituate	119	27	Curtis	Samuel Junr			2		1	1	1	1	2	2	1		11		
Scituate	121	1	Turner	Abner					1				1	1			3		
Scituate	121	2	Tower	Mathew	1		1	1		1	2		1				7		
Scituate	121	3	Stetson	Snow	1			1		2	1		1				6		
Scituate	121	4	Sprague	Asher		1		1		1			1	1			5		
Scituate	121	5	Winslow	Nathl Junr			1			2		1					4		
Scituate	121	6	Randall	Sarah										1			1		
Scituate	121	7	Tolman	Chas			2		1	1	1	1		1			7		
Scituate	121	8	Wright	Jesse	1		1		1			1	1				5		
Scituate	121	9	Tolman	Samuel	2	1		1			1		2	1			8		
Scituate	121	10	Winslow	Nathaniel		2			1		1	2		2			8		
Scituate	121	11	Palmer	Nehemiah					1			1		1			3		
Scituate	121	12	Castle	Susanna									1				1		
Scituate	121	13	Turner	Israel		2			1	1	2		1				7		
Scituate	121	14	Cushing	Thomas		1		1		2		1	1				6		
Scituate	121	15	Collamore	Benjm			2		1	2	1		2				8		
Scituate	121	16	Silvester	Thos Junr		1	1		1	2		2		2			9		
Scituate	121	17	Ewell	John		1				2			1				4		
Scituate	121	18	Stetson	Benjamin	1			1	1	3		1					7		
Scituate	121	19	Daman	Luther	1			1		1		1					4		
Scituate	121	20	Nash	John	1			1		1			1				4		
Scituate	121	21	Torrey	Caleb		1		1		1				2			5		
Scituate	121	22	Lane	Benjm	1		1	1		4			1				8		
Scituate	121	23	Torrey	Isaac			1	1				1		1			4		
Scituate	122	1	Taylor	Richard		1				2			1				4		
Scituate	122	2	Lapham	Abigail										1			1		
Scituate	122	3	Brooks	Willm	2	2	1		1		1	4		1			12		
Scituate	122	4	Ruggles	Thomas	2	1		1		1	2	1	1				9		
Scituate	122	5	Ruggles	John					1				1				2		
Scituate	122	6	Wilson	Abigail								2					2		
Scituate	122	7	Stetson	Stephen			3	1			1	2	1				8		
Scituate	122	8	Stetson	Abner		1	2	1					1				5		
Scituate	122	9	Ford	Micah		2						3	1				7		
Scituate	122	10	Stetson	Mathew			1	1			1						3		
Scituate	122	11	Palmer	Lydia									2				2		
Scituate	122	12	Leavitt	Gad	4			1		1			1				7		
Scituate	122	13	Church	Lemuel		1	1		1	1			1				5		
Scituate	122	14	Barstow	Elijah	1	1		1			1	1	2	1			8		
Scituate	122	15	Palmer	Jane									2				2		
Scituate	122	16	Donnell	Samuel	2			2		1		1	1				7		
Scituate	122	17	Stockbridge	Stephen					1			1	1				3		
Scituate	122	18	Thompson	Hesther									4				4		
Scituate	122	19	Wheeler	Willm W.		1			1			1					3		
Scituate	122	20	Palmer	Benjamin					1			1		1			3		
Scituate	122	21	Foster	Freeman	1		1					1					3		
Scituate	122	22	Waterman	Deborah								1	1				2		
Scituate	122	23	Waterman	Samuel		1		1		1	1	1					5		
Scituate	122	24	Tolman	John	2	2		1				1	1	1			8		
Scituate	123	1	Lambert	Zaccheus					1	1	1			1			4		
Scituate	123	2	Bourne	Melatiah					1			1					2		
Scituate	123	3	Clapp	Constant		1			1				1				3		
Scituate	123	4	Clapp	William					1			4		1			6		
Scituate	123	5	Clapp	John			1	1				1		1			4		

67

TOWN	PG#	LN#	LAST NAME	FIRST NAME	FREE WHITE MALES under 10	10 to 16	16 to 26	26 to 45	45 and over	FREE WHITE FEMALES under 10	10 to 16	16 to 26	26 to 45	45 and over	TOTAL ALL OTHER	TOTAL SLAVES	TOTALS	DISTRICT/ TOWNSHIP	NOTES
Scituate	123	6	Curtis	Experience				1						2			3		
Scituate	123	7	Curtis	Peleg	1	1		1				1	1				5		
Scituate	123	8	Rose	Reuben			1	1			1	2		1			6		
Scituate	123	9	Barrell	Luther	2			1		2			1		1		7		
Scituate	123	10	Barrell	Noah	2			1		1	3	1		1			9		
Scituate	123	11	Barrell	James				1					1				2		
Scituate	123	12	Jones	John	1	1	1		1	1		1	1	1			8		
Scituate	123	13	Bowker	Bejamin			1		1		2	1	1	1	1		8		
Scituate	123	14	Otis	Ephraim		2			1	1		1		1	1		7		
Scituate	123	15	Lapham	Charles	1			1		1		1					4		
Scituate	123	16	Turner	Elijah Esq	1	1	1		1	1		1	2	2			11		
Scituate	123	17	Howard	Perez	3			1						2			6		
Scituate	123	18	Stodder	Edward		1							1				2		
Scituate	123	19	Lincoln	Solomon	2			1		1	1		1				7		
Scituate	123	20	Bourne	Sherjeshul				1			2	1	1		1		6		
Scituate	123	21	Lincoln	James		1	1	1		1		1		1			6		
Scituate	123	22	Hatch	John	1	1		1	1				1				5		
Scituate	123	23	Foster	Samuel	3			1				1	1				7		
Scituate	124	1	Barnes	David Revd			1	1					1	1			4		
Scituate	124	2	Silvester	Elisha			1	1				1		2			5		
Scituate	124	3	Randall	Hannah										3			3		
Scituate	124	4	Turner	Seth	1	2			1	1			2	1			8		
Scituate	124	5	Torrey	George	2	2		1		1	1	1	1				9		
Scituate	124	6	Sampson	Araunah	1			1		1	2	1	1				7		
Scituate	124	7	Randall	Zipporah										1			1		
Scituate	124	8	Church	William				1						1			2		
Scituate	124	9	Jordan	Nathl		1	2	1						1			5		
Scituate	124	10	Souther	Laban		1	1						1				3		
Scituate	124	11	Oldham	Jonathan			1	1						1			3		
Scituate	124	12	House	Coomes	1			1		1			1				4		
Scituate	124	13	Silvester	Fruitful Negro											8		8		
Scituate	124	14	Lapham	Thomas				2						3			5		
Scituate	124	15	Turner	Nathaniel	1		1	1		3			1				7		
Scituate	124	16	Brooks	Hannah							1	1	1				3		
Scituate	124	17	Humphris	Edward				1						1			2		
Scituate	124	18	Carlow	William	1		2	1			1	2		1	1		9		
Scituate	124	19	Wilder	Joanna										2			2		
Scituate	124	20	Lapham	Michael			1			2			1				4		
Scituate	124	21	Kent	David				1					2				4		
Scituate	124	22	Kent	Samuel		2	1		1				1				5		
Scituate	124	23	Lapham	Thos Junr		1		1		3	1		1	1			8		
Scituate	125	1	Studley	William		1		1					1				3		
Scituate	125	2	Stetson	Isaac				1				1	1				3		
Scituate	125	3	Brooks	Nathl Junr	2	1		1		1			1	1			7		
Scituate	125	4	Brooks	Nathl		1		1									2		
Scituate	125	5	Damon	Edward Junr		1							1				2		
Scituate	125	6	Stetson	Gideon				1									1		
Scituate	125	7	Benson	Joseph	1		2	1		1	2	1		1			9		
Scituate	125	8	Totman	Sarah										1			1		
Scituate	125	9	Bowker	Ruth								1		1			2		
Scituate	125	10	Barrell	Bartlett	1		1			1			1		1		5		
Scituate	125	11	Bowker	Dimeck	2		1						1				4		
Scituate	125	12	Turner	William Esq				1		1		1		1			4		
Scituate	125	13	Barrell	Martha	2		1			1	1		1				7		
Scituate	125	14	Barrell	William		1		1			2	3		1			8		
Scituate	125	15	Cushing	James Jr				2					1	1	1		5		
Scituate	125	16	Simmons	Peleg				1						1			2		
Scituate	125	17	Cobun	Saul Negro											6		6		
Scituate	125	18	Randall	Samuel		1				1		4		1			8		
Scituate	125	19	Gammett	Seth	3			1		2			1				7		
Scituate	125	20	Clapp	Samuel				1									1		
Scituate	125	21	Frane	Bethiah										1			1		
Scituate	125	22	Jacobs	James		1	1	1		1	1		1		2		8		
Scituate	125	23	Silvester	Sarah									2				2		
Scituate	126	1	Woodworth	John	1			1		2	1		1				6		
Scituate	126	2	Jordan	David	1	2	2	1		1	2	2		1			12		
Scituate	126	3	Esllo	Nathaniel	1			1						1			3		
Scituate	126	4	Cushing	George				1			1	1		2			5		
Scituate	126	5	Cushing	Nathan Honble			1	1			1	2	1		2		8		
Scituate	126	6	Turner	Harris	1			1		1		1					4		
Scituate	126	7	Cushing	Willm Honble				1					1		5		7		
Scituate	126	8	Bowker	Lazarus		1	1	1		2	2		1				8		
Scituate	126	9	Clapp	Silvanus		2		1				3	1	1			8		
Scituate	126	10	Damon	Calvin	1	1	2	1		2	1	2	1				11		
Scituate	126	11	Osborn	Ebenz		1							1				2		
Scituate	126	12	Rose	Laban	2			1		2			1				6		
Scituate	126	13	Carlow	Bille			1			3			1	1			6		
Scituate	126	14	Cushing	Ellis	1					1			1				3		
Scituate	126	15	Cushing	Pickels Jun	2		2	1		1							7		

68

TOWN	PG#	LN#	LAST NAME	FIRST NAME	FREE WHITE MALES under 10	10 to 16	16 to 26	26 to 45	45 and over	FREE WHITE FEMALES under 10	10 to 16	16 to 26	26 to 45	45 and over	TOTAL ALL OTHER	TOTAL SLAVES	TOTALS	DISTRICT/ TOWNSHIP	NOTES
Scituate	126	16	Briggs	James Junr			2	1	1				2				6		
Scituate	126	17	Briggs	Joseph	2		1						1				4		
Scituate	126	18	Briggs	James		1		1					2				4		
Scituate	126	19	Jacobs	Walter			1	1		1		1					4		
Scituate	126	20	Curtis	James				1					1				2		
Scituate	126	21	Turner	John	1			1		1			1	1			5		
Scituate	126	22	Freeman	Lemuel Negro											5		5		
Scituate	126	23	Silvester	Thomas				1					1				2		
Scituate	127	1	Silvester	Israel		1	1	1				1	1	1			7		
Scituate	127	2	Wethrell	Josiah		1							1				2		
Scituate	127	3	Hooper	Betty									2				2		
Scituate	127	4	Jacobs	Joshu Junr		1		1		2	1		1				6		
Scituate	127	5	Simmons	Leah								1	1				2		
Scituate	127	6	Simmons	Charles	3			1					1				5		
Scituate	127	7	Damon	Juda									2				2		
Scituate	127	8	Simmons	Samuel	3	1		1		1			2				8		
Scituate	127	9	Northey	Mary									1	1			2		
Scituate	127	10	Northey	Robert	1					2			1				5		
Scituate	127	11	Totman	Stephen	3	1				2	1	1		1			10		
Scituate	127	12	Jacobs	Susanna			1						1				2		
Scituate	127	13	Damon	Joshua	1	1		1		2	2	1	1				9		
Scituate	127	14	Damon	Simeon	1	1			1	3	2		1				9		
Scituate	127	15	Sparrell	James	3	1	1	1				2	1				9		
Scituate	127	16	Curtis	Elijah	1			1		3	1		1	1	1		9		
Scituate	127	17	Tildon	Thatcher	3		1			1			1				6		
Scituate	127	18	Turner	Elisha		1		1		1			1				4		
Scituate	127	19	Foster	John		1	1		1			2					5		
Scituate	127	20	Otis	James	1	1		1	1				3	1			8		
Scituate	127	21	James	Hannah									1				1		
Scituate	127	22	James	John	3	1		1		2			1				8		
Scituate	127	23	Briggs	John				1					2	2			5		
Scituate	127	24	Briggs	Elisha		1				4			1				6		
Scituate	128	1	Jacobs	Mary									1				1		
Scituate	128	2	Jacobs	Joshua				1				1	1				3		
Scituate	128	3	Rogers	Walter		1	1			3			1				6		
Scituate	128	4	Withington	John		1		1				1	1				4		
Scituate	128	5	Jacobs	Deborah									1	1			2		
Scituate	128	6	Bailey	Adams		1		1					1	1			4		
Scituate	128	7	Stodder	Hezekiah Junr	2	1	1		1	2	2	1	1				11		
Scituate	128	8	Collamore	Enoch	1	2	3		1		1	1	1	1	1		11		
Scituate	128	9	Farrow	Abiel	4	1		1	1	1	1		1				10		
Scituate	128	10	Prouty	William			3	1	1			2	1	1			9		
Scituate	128	11	Stodder	Hezekiah	1			1			1	1	1				6		
Scituate	128	12	Prouty	David		1	1		1	1		1	1				6		
Scituate	128	13	Whiting	Benja	2			1					1				4		
Scituate	128	14	Whiting	Ezekiel				1				3	1				5		
Scituate	128	15	Whiting	Archelaus		1						1					2		
Scituate	128	16	Gardner	Elizabeth							1	1	1				3		
Scituate	128	17	Stodder	Obadiah	3	1							1				6		
Scituate	128	18	Whiting	Galen	2		1						1				4		
Scituate	128	19	Neal	Joseph	2				1	1			1				5		
Scituate	128	20	Gardner	David				1					1				2		
Scituate	128	21	Silvester	Jacob	2	1			2				2				7		
Scituate	128	22	Silvester	Margarett		2	1						1				4		
Scituate	128	23	Gross	Elijah			1						1				2		
Scituate	129	1	Stockbridge	Samuel		1	1	1				1	1	1			6		
Scituate	129	2	Stockbridge	Saml Junr		1		1				1					3		
Scituate	129	3	Hooper	Sarah									1				1		
Scituate	129	4	Turner	Jonathan			1		1			2					4		
Scituate	129	5	Hiland	William				1					1				2		
Scituate	129	6	Cole	James junr		1		1		1			1				4		
Scituate	129	7	Clapp	Elijah	1		1	1				2	2				7		
Scituate	129	8	Hiland	Mary									1				1		
Scituate	129	9	Briggs	Benja Junr	3			1		3			1				8		
Scituate	129	10	Merritt	Consider	2	2	1		1	1	1	2	1				11		
Scituate	129	11	Elmes	Samuel	1			1		2		1					5		
Scituate	129	12	Litchfield	Frany									1				1		
Scituate	129	13	Litchfield	Abner				1		2			1				4		
Scituate	129	14	Elmes	Joseph	1	1		1	1	3			1	1			9		
Scituate	129	15	Litchfield	Daniel		2		1	1		1	1		1			7		
Scituate	129	16	Litchfield	Francis				1		2			1				4		
Scituate	129	17	Clapp	Alexander	4			1			1		1				7		
Scituate	129	18	Litchfield	James				1					1				2		
Scituate	129	19	Litchfield	Silas	1			1		1			1				4		
Scituate	129	20	Litchfield	John	1				1	3			1				6		
Scituate	129	21	Whitcomb	Sarah		1							1		1		3		
Scituate	129	22	Whitcomb	John		1	3	1			1		1				7		
Scituate	129	23	Cowin	Job				1					1	1			3		
Scituate	129	24	Bates	Cornelius						1	1		1				5		

69

TOWN	PG#	LN#	HEADS OF HOUSEHOLD		FREE WHITE MALES					FREE WHITE FEMALES					TOTAL ALL OTHER	TOTAL SLAVES	TOTALS	DISTRICT/ TOWNSHIP	NOTES
			LAST NAME	FIRST NAME	under 10	10 to 16	16 to 26	26 to 45	45 and over	under 10	10 to 16	16 to 26	26 to 45	45 and over					
Scituate	129	25	Hiland	Samuel	1	1	2	1		3			1				9		
Scituate	130	1	Nichols	Noah				1			2	2		2			7		
Scituate	130	2	Standley	Mary								2		2			4		
Scituate	130	3	Freeman	Prince Negro											4		4		
Scituate	130	4	Cole	Charles	1	1			1	1	2	1	1				8		
Scituate	130	5	Damon	Galin	3		1	1		1	1		1				8		
Scituate	130	6	Studley	Olive									2				2		
Scituate	130	7	Esllo	Nathl Junr			2						1				3		
Scituate	130	8	Turner	Rowland	2	2		1				2	1				8		
Scituate	130	9	Hatch	Jonathan				1				1	1	1			4		
Scituate	130	10	Torrey	James	1	2	1	1		3	1		1		1		11		
Scituate	130	11	Litchfield	Amos		2	1						1				4		
Scituate	130	12	Bryant	Joshua	1	2	3	1		1			1				9		
Scituate	130	13	Sears	Peter	1					1	2	1	2				8		
Scituate	130	14	Bowker	Edmond			1	1				1	1				4		
Scituate	130	15	Bowker	Warren	1		1					1					3		
Scituate	130	16	Bowker	John				1					2				3		
Scituate	130	17	Bowker	Elijah	3	1		1		2			1				8		
Scituate	130	18	Otis	Ignatius			1	1				4	1				7		
Scituate	130	19	Daman	John			2	1			2	1	1				7		
Scituate	130	20	Wright	James			1	1		3			1				6		
Scituate	130	21	Daman	Stephen		1		2					1				4		
Scituate	130	22	Damon	Isaac	1			1					3		1		6		
Scituate	130	23	Brown	Alijah				1			1		1				3		
Scituate	130	24	Stockbridge	James			3	1	1		1		1	1			8		
Scituate	130	25	Stodder	Seth	1		1	1	1	1			2				7		
Scituate	131	1	Merritt	Seth	3	2		1		1	1		1				9		
Scituate	131	2	Pierce	Seth			1	1	1			1	1				5		
Scituate	131	3	Wade	Mary									3				3		
Scituate	131	4	Vinal	Lydia			1						1				2		
Scituate	131	5	Sutton	Ray		1							1				2		
Scituate	131	6	Sutton	Hannah									1				1		
Scituate	131	7	Vinal	Nathl	1	2		1		3	1	1	1				10		
Scituate	131	8	Bailey	Abner	1	1		1			1	3		1			8		
Scituate	131	9	Vinal	Mary									1				1		
Scituate	131	10	Bailey	Caleb	2			1		2			1				6		
Scituate	131	11	Vinal	Israel				1		2							3		
Scituate	131	12	Gannett	Samuel	1			1					1				3		
Scituate	131	13	Mott	Stephen	1	1		1		2	1	1	1				8		
Scituate	131	14	Downs	Ruth		1	1						2	1			5		
Scituate	131	15	Pierce	Mathew		1	2	1		1			1				6		
Scituate	131	16	Bailey	Israel		1	1			3			1				6		
Scituate	131	17	Wade	Jotham			1			4			1				6		
Scituate	131	18	Tilden	Sarah									2				2		
Scituate	131	19	Russell	Eunice		1							1	1			3		
Scituate	131	20	Bozworth	Eunice	1								1				2		
Scituate	131	21	Otis	Paul	2		1						1	1	1		6		
Scituate	131	22	Hayden	Daniel	2	1					1	1	1	1			8		
Scituate	131	23	Pierce	Calvin		1	1	1				1	1	1			6		
Scituate	131	24	Studley	Lewis	3			1		1	1		1				7		
Scituate	133	1	Damon	Zadock	3	3		1				2	1				10		
Scituate	133	2	Damon	Hannah		1						1	2		2		6		
Scituate	133	3	Brown	Mary									1	1			2		
Scituate	133	4	Brown	Jonathan			1			2			1				4		
Scituate	133	5	Stetson	James	3	1		1		1	1		1				8		
Scituate	133	6	Jenkins	Thomas		1		1					1				3		
Scituate	133	7	Hatch	Jonathan Junr	3			1		2			2				8		
Scituate	133	8	Mann	Josiah		1		1		1	1	1					5		
Scituate	133	9	Grandison	Cuff Negro											3		3		
Scituate	133	10	Cushing	Pickels		1		1			1	1	2	1			7		
Scituate	133	11	Cushing	Joseph	2		1			3			1				7		
Scituate	133	12	Nichols	Meriam	1		1	1		1			1				5		
Scituate	133	13	Litchfield	Lucinda	1							1					2		
Scituate	133	14	Bawker	Gershom	1	2	1		1	2		1	1				9		
Scituate	133	15	Pencin	Simeon		2	1		1			2	1				7		
Scituate	133	16	Merritt	John				2				1	2				5		
Scituate	133	17	Nash	Joseph		1		1				2	1		1		6		
Scituate	133	18	Nash	Solon	2			1		1			1				5		
Scituate	133	19	Hayden	Peleg	1	1		1		1	1		1				7		
Scituate	133	20	Jenkins	James		1	1	1		1	1	1	1				7		
Scituate	133	21	Jenkins	Calvin	2	1		1		3	1	1	1	1			11		
Scituate	133	22	Merritt	Nehemiah	1			1		1	1		1	1			6		
Scituate	133	23	Merritt	Gamaliel	2	1		1		1	2	1	1				9		
Scituate	133	24	Hammond	Experience	1	2	1			2		1	1				8		
Scituate	133	25	Jones	Samuel P	4	1	1				2	1	1				10		
Scituate	133	26	Clapp	Leonard	1		1			1			1	2			6		
Scituate	133	27	Coleman	David			1					1					2		
Scituate	133	28	Otis	David	2	1		1	1	2	2	3	1				13		
Scituate	133	29	Otis	Abijah	2			1		2		1					6		
Scituate	133	30	Otis	Prince									1				1		

TOWN	PG#	LN#	HEADS OF HOUSEHOLD — LAST NAME	FIRST NAME	FREE WHITE MALES under 10	10 to 16	16 to 26	26 to 45	45 and over	FREE WHITE FEMALES under 10	10 to 16	16 to 26	26 to 45	45 and over	TOTAL ALL OTHER	TOTAL SLAVES	TOTALS	DISTRICT/ TOWNSHIP	NOTES
Scituate	133	31	Russell	John	1			1		1	2		1	1			7		
Scituate	133	32	Cole	Asahel		1	2	1				1	1	1			7		
Scituate	133	33	Jackson	Jonathan			1	1	1				2	1			6		
Scituate	133	34	Otis	Mary								1		1			2		
Scituate	133	35	Cudworth	Rachel										2			2		
Scituate	133	36	Cudworth	Jopth			3		1	2	2	1		1			10		
Scituate	133	37	Holmes	Kezia										2			2		
Scituate	133	38	Curtis	John					1			2		1			4		
Scituate	133	39	Curtis	John Junr				1					1				2		
Scituate	133	40	Curtis	Samuel				1	1			1	1	1			5		
Scituate	133	41	Elmes	Ebenezer W.	2			1		4	1		1				9		
Scituate	133	42	Lincoln	Hannah										2			2		
Scituate	133	43	Stetson	Benjn Junr	1			1		1			1				4		
Scituate	133	44	Webb	Paul				1						1			2		
Scituate	133	45	Wade	Mercy		1	1			1	2		1				6		
Scituate	133	46	Wade	Nathl Junr	2	1		1		2	2		1				9		
Scituate	133	47	Wade	Nathl				1					1				2		
Scituate	133	48	Webb	Barnabas	1	2			1	3	1	1	1				10		
Scituate	133	49	Curtis	Gamaliel		1			1	2	1		1				6		
Scituate	133	50	Clapp	Thomas			1			1		1					3		
Scituate	134	1	Clapp	Deborah			1						1				2		
Scituate	134	2	Clapp	Zilphe					1				1		3		5		
Scituate	134	3	Clapp	Augustus			1	2					2				5		
Scituate	134	4	Bailey	Abner Junr	1		1					1					3		
Scituate	134	5	Bates	Caleb	1		1			1		1					4		
Scituate	134	6	Nash	James	1		1			2	2						6		
Scituate	134	7	Stockbridge	Charles	1			1		1	3		1				7		
Scituate	134	8	Clapp	Lewis	1			1		2	1		1	1			7		
Scituate	134	9	Stodder	Canturbury			1							1			2		
Scituate	134	10	Hatch	Samuel			1						1	3	1		6		
Scituate	134	11	Shearman	Otis	2		1						1				4		
Scituate	134	12	Northey	Bettey	1		1			1	2		1				6		
Scituate	134	13	Briggs	Benjamin			1	1				1	1				4		
Scituate	134	14	Mann	Jonathan		1	1	1				2		1			6		
Scituate	134	15	Merritt	Daniel	3	2		1					1				7		
Scituate	134	16	Withrell	Simeon		1	1		1	2	1	3	1				10		
Scituate	134	17	Daman	Silvanus		1	1	1	1	3	2		2				11		
Scituate	134	18	Northey	Elizabeth							1		1				2		
Scituate	134	19	Hawland	Consider	1		1	1					1				4		
Scituate	134	20	Studley	Amasa				1									1		
Scituate	134	21	Briggs	Judith						3	1	3		1			8		
Scituate	134	22	Collier	Isaac		1	2		1	2	1	3		1			11		
Scituate	134	23	Cudworth	John	2	1	2		1	2	1	1	1				11		
Scituate	134	24	Bailey	Paul		1	1	1				1		1			5		
Scituate	134	25	Cudworth	Israel		2		1		2			1				6		
Scituate	134	26	Cudworth	John Junr			1			1			2				4		
Scituate	134	27	Mott	Atwood				1				1		2			4		
Scituate	134	28	Collier	Jonathan	2		1			2	1		1				7		
Scituate	134	29	Otis	John	2	1		1		3	1	2	1				11		
Scituate	134	30	Wade	Charlotte	1	1				1	2		1				6		
Scituate	134	31	Litchfield	Abner H.	4	1	1	1		1	1	1	1				11		
Scituate	134	32	Litchfield	Lawrence	2	3	1	1		2		1	1				11		
Scituate	134	33	Litchfield	Priscilla								1	1				2		
Scituate	134	34	Vinal	Nathl Junr	1		1			1	1	1					5		
Scituate	134	35	Litchfield	Rhoda								1	1				2		
Scituate	134	36	Merritt	Caleb			1					1	1				3		
Scituate	134	37	Sutton	Abner		1	2		1		1	2	1				8		
Scituate	134	38	Litchfield	Elisha		1		1					1				3		
Scituate	134	39	Litchfield	Nathaniel	1		1			1		1					4		
Scituate	134	40	Clapp	Peggy	3								1				4		
Scituate	134	41	Pierce	Martha										1			1		
Scituate	134	42	Price	Noah	1	1		2				1	1				6		
Scituate	134	43	Daman	Reuben	2	1	1	1		1	1	1	1				9		
Scituate	134	44	Studley	John	1	2		1		3	1		1	1			10		
Scituate	135	1	Jenkins	Caleb	2			1		2			1				6		
Scituate	135	2	Jenkins	Samuel				1			1	1	1				4		
Scituate	135	3	Jenkins	Charles	4	1					1	1					8		
Scituate	135	4	Nash	Joseph Junr	1		1					2					4		
Scituate	135	5	Cole	David				1			1		1				3		
Scituate	135	6	Curtis	Eli Junr	1	1		1		2			1				6		
Scituate	135	7	Vinal	Stephen	2		1			1			1				5		
Scituate	135	8	Vinal	William	2	1		1			1	1		1			7		
Scituate	135	9	Vinal	Judith			1						2	1			4		
Scituate	135	10	Curtis	Samuel 3d			1		1	3		1	1	1			8		
Scituate	135	11	Coleman	Joseph Junr	1		1			4			1				7		
Scituate	135	12	Dweller	Sally								1	1				2		
Scituate	135	13	Jenkins	Gideon	3	1	2		1	1	1	1	1				11		
Scituate	135	14	Young	Gideon	1		1			2			1				5		
Scituate	135	15	Young	Joshua	1	2	1	1	1	2		2		1			11		
Scituate	135	16	Young	Ezekiel					1		1		1				3		
Scituate	135	17	Turner	Nathl Junr		1		1		3		1	1				7		
Scituate	135	18	Baker	Nathl			1			1		1					3		
Scituate	135	19	Turner	James			2		2			1	1	1			7		
Scituate	135	20	Jenkins	Gera		1						2		1			5		
Scituate	135	21	James	Benja		1	1					1					3		
Scituate	135	22	Fish	Ziba							1			1			2		
Scituate	135	23	Coleman	Joseph		1		1	1	2	2		1	1			9		
Scituate	135	24	Chubbuck	David	1	3		1		3			1		1		10		
Scituate	135	25	Hayden	Luther							1	1	1				3		

TOWN	PG#	LN#	HEADS OF HOUSEHOLD		FREE WHITE MALES					FREE WHITE FEMALES					TOTAL ALL OTHER	TOTAL SLAVES	TOTALS	DISTRICT/ TOWNSHIP	NOTES
			LAST NAME	FIRST NAME	under 10	10 to 16	16 to 26	26 to 45	45 and over	under 10	10 to 16	16 to 26	26 to 45	45 and over					
Scituate	135	26	Collier	Isaac Junr	2			1					1				4		
Scituate	135	27	Merritt	Asahel	2			1					1				4		
Scituate	135	28	Merritt	Elizabeth									1	1			2		
Scituate	135	29	Vinal	Jonathan	1				1				1	1			4		
Scituate	135	30	Bailey	Ebenz	3			1		2			1	1			8		
Scituate	135	31	Merritt	Amos	4	1			1		1	1	1				9		
Scituate	135	32	Williams	John					2					1			3		
Scituate	135	33	Peirce	Hayward Esqr	2	3			1	1	1	1	1				10		
Scituate	135	34	Doane	John	1			1		1		1	1				5		
Scituate	135	35	Parker	Eleazer			1	1		2				2			6		
Scituate	135	36	Litchfield	Rowland	1	1	1	1		2	2		1				9		
Scituate	135	37	Curtis	Charles	1			1					1				3		
Scituate	135	38	Litchfield	Stephen	1			1	1	1		2					6		
Scituate	135	39	Mann	Deborah					1				1	2			4		
Scituate	135	40	Mann	Susanna										1			1		
Scituate	135	41	Mann	David					1					1			2		
Scituate	135	42	Litchfield	Job					1	1				1			3		
Scituate	135	43	Vinal	Levi	3	1			1	1	1		1	1			9		
Scituate	135	44	Vinal	Ignatius					1	1			1				3		
Scituate	135	45	Vinal	Job	3	2			1	1	2		1				10		
Scituate	135	46	Litchfield	Thomas				1	1			2	2	1			7		
Scituate	135	47	Litchfield	Eleazer	2	1	1	1		1	2		1				9		
Scituate	135	48	Daman	Josiah	2	1	1	1		2	1	1	1				10		
Scituate	135	49	Litchfield	Simeon	4			1		2			1				8		
Scituate	135	50	Daman	Elizabeth	2	2	1	1					1				7		
Scituate	136	1	Cook	Robert	4	1		1		2	1	2	1				12		
Scituate	136	2	Litchfield	Ward	3	2	1	1		1			1				9		
Scituate	136	3	Tilden	John	3		1	1		1		1	1				8		
Scituate	136	4	Otis	Joshua					1				1	1			3		
Scituate	136	5	Otis	Joshua Junr			2	1		2			1				6		
Scituate	136	6	Elmes	Robert		1	1	2	1			1		2			8		
Scituate	136	7	Jenkins	Samuel Junr				1		1			1				3		
Scituate	136	8	Webb	Seth	1			1					1				3		
Scituate	136	9	Tilden	Abigail			1					2		1			4		
Scituate	136	10	Tilden	Amos	1			1		2			1				5		
Scituate	136	11	Mann	John	2		1	1		2	1						7		
Scituate	136	12	White	Timothy	2			1		1			1		1		6		
Scituate	136	13	White	Sarah	1			1					1	1			4		
Scituate	136	14	Thomas	Nehemiah Revd	1			1		2	1		1				6		
Scituate	136	15	Merritt	Israel				1		3		1					5		
Scituate	136	16	Jenkins	Abigail				1			1			1			3		
Scituate	136	17	Jenkins	Daniel	2		1	1	1				1				6		
Scituate	136	18	Otis	Ensign		1		1	1	3			1				6		
Scituate	136	19	Curtis	Nehemiah	1			1					1				3		
Scituate	136	20	Young	Stephen	1			1		1			1				4		
Scituate	136	21	Coleman	Thomas Junr				1			1		1				3		
Scituate	136	22	Vinal	Asa	1	1		1		3			1				7		
Scituate	136	23	Prouty	Caleb	2		2		1		1			1			7		
Scituate	136	24	Vinal	Lemuel			1			1	1	1		1			5		
Scituate	136	25	Merritt	Ensign				1		1				2			4		
Scituate	136	26	Merritt	Malichi	1			1		4			1				7		
Scituate	136	27	Merritt	Noah	2			1		1	1		1				6		
Scituate	136	28	Jenkins	Eli	1			1					1				3		
Scituate	136	29	Dunbar	David					2					1			3		
Scituate	136	30	Little	James		1		1		1		1	1				5		
Scituate	136	31	Barker	Benjamin	1				2				1	2			6		
Scituate	136	32	Clapp	James	2	1	1	1		2	1	1	1				10		
Scituate	136	33	Dunbar	Jesse	2			1		1		1	1				6		
Scituate	136	34	Young	Joseph		2	1		1	2	1		1				8		
Scituate	136	35	Monson	Nehemiah	2			1		1			1				5		
Scituate	136	36	Ray	Caleb	2			1			1		1				5		
Scituate	136	37	Morton	John				1						1			2		
Scituate	136	38	Hiland	Rebecca							1		1				2		
Scituate	136	39	Woodworth	Benjn		1	1		1			2	1				6		
Scituate	136	40	Bryant	Samuel				1									1		
Scituate	136	41	Jenkins	Oliver			1			2	1		1				5		
Scituate	136	42	Curtis	Eli			1							1			2		
Scituate	136	43	Bates	Reuben			1				1		1				3		
Scituate	136	44	Burnett	Thomas W.			1			2		1					4		
Scituate	136	45	Mann	Deborah		1							1	1			3		
Scituate	136	46	Otis	Phebe							1	1	1				3		
Scituate	136	47	Otis	John Junr	1			1					1				3		
Scituate	136	48	Vinal	William Junr	1	1		2			1	1	1				7		
Scituate	136	49	Jenkins	Elijah	1			1		2			1	1			6		
Scituate	136	50	Otis	Prince		1	1		1				1				4		

TOWN	PG#	LN#	LAST NAME	FIRST NAME	FREE WHITE MALES under 10	10 to 16	16 to 26	26 to 45	45 and over	FREE WHITE FEMALES under 10	10 to 16	16 to 26	26 to 45	45 and over	TOTAL ALL OTHER	TOTAL SLAVES	TOTALS	DISTRICT/ TOWNSHIP	NOTES
Wareham	109	1	Briggs	Hallet	1	2			1	1	1		1				7		
Wareham	109	2	Benson	Jabez			1	1	1			1	1				5		
Wareham	109	3	Briggs	Eli		1	1	1	2		2	1		1			9		
Wareham	109	4	Briggs	Jesse	2	1				2	1			2			9		
Wareham	109	5	Benson	Levi	2				2	2		1		2			9		
Wareham	109	6	Bumpus	Noah			1			1		1	2				5		
Wareham	109	7	Bumpus	Asa	2			1		2			1				6		
Wareham	109	8	Briggs	Saml	1	1	2		1		1	3		2			11		
Wareham	109	9	Barrows	Isaac			2		1			3		1			7		
Wareham	109	10	Burges	Elisha	2	1	2	1	1		1	3		1			12		
Wareham	109	11	Bumpus	Benjn		1			1		1	1		1			5		
Wareham	109	12	Bumpus	Lot	3	3		1	1	1		1	1				11		
Wareham	109	13	Bumpus	Mary							1	1	1	1			4		
Wareham	109	14	Bumpus	Jere		2	1		2	1		2		1			9		
Wareham	109	15	Barrows	Abishai	1		1			1		1					4		
Wareham	109	16	Barrows	Thos			1					1					2		
Wareham	109	17	Bumpus	Eliphalet	1		1					1					3		
Wareham	109	18	Bates	Bars	2	1			1								4		
Wareham	109	19	Barrows	*					1								1		
Wareham	109	20	Be*	*										1			1		
Wareham	109	21	Wilkins	Mabel				1					1				2		
Wareham	109	22	Wing	Stephen		2	1	1				2	1				7		
Wareham	110	1	*	*	*	*	*	*	*	*	*	*	*	*	*		*		
Wareham	110	2	*	John	*	*	*	*	*	*	*	*	*	*	*		*		
Wareham	110	3	*	*	*	*	*	*	*	*	*	*	*	*	*		*		
Wareham	110	4	Baker	Thomas	*	*	*	*	*	*	*	*	*	*	*		*		
Wareham	110	5	Bourne	Ebenz	2	1	1		1			1	1				7		
Wareham	110	6	*	*	3	1		1			1		1				7		
Wareham	110	7	*	*	2	2	*	*	*	*	*	*	*	1			5		
Wareham	110	8	Briggs	Benjm 2	3	1			1	1			1				7		
Wareham	110	9	Besse	Silas	3	1	2	1		2	1		1				11		
Wareham	110	10	Besse	David		1	4	1	1	2	2	1	1				13		
Wareham	110	11	Bumpus	James	2	2		1	1	1	1		1				9		
Wareham	110	12	Bumpus	Joseph	2	1	1	1				2		1			8		
Wareham	110	13	Besse	Jabez				1			1		1				3		
Wareham	110	14	Bumpus	Jonn	3			1		1			1				6		
Wareham	110	15	Bumpus	Prince	1	2	1		1	1	1			1			8		
Wareham	110	16	Burges	James		1	1	1		2			1				6		
Wareham	110	17	Crocker	Wadsworth	1			1				1					3		
Wareham	110	18	Crocker	Kenslem	1	1		1	1	1			1				6		
Wareham	110	19	Crocker	Timo	2		1		2	4	2		1				12		
Wareham	110	20	Crapo	Micah	2		1		2				1				6		
Wareham	110	21	Conant	Wm	1	3		1		1			1	1			8		
Wareham	110	22	Everet	Noble	2	2			1	2	2	1	1				11		
Wareham	110	23	Edwards	John	1		1						1				3		
Wareham	110	24	Eddy	Kezia	1			1	1	1	1		1				6		
Wareham	110	25	Ellis	Danl	2			1		3	1		1				8		
Wareham	110	26	Fearing	John	1					2		1	2	1			9		
Wareham	110	27	Fearing	Moses	1	1		1		1	1	1					7		
Wareham	111	1	Fearing	David		1	1	1		3	1	1	1		1		10		
Wareham	111	2	Fearing	Benjm	2	1	3		1	3	1		1	1	1		14		
Wareham	111	3	Fearing	Israel		2		1		1		1		1	1		7		
Wareham	111	4	Fearing	Israel Jr		1			1	1	1	1	1	1			7		
Wareham	111	5	Fearing	Wm	1			1				1					3		
Wareham	111	6	Gibbs	Joshua	3	3			1	1	1		1				10		
Wareham	111	7	Gibbs	Abrm	1		1	1		1			1				5		
Wareham	111	8	Gibbs	John		1		1	1		1			1			5		
Wareham	111	9	Gibbs	John Jr	2	1	2		1		1	1		2			10		
Wareham	111	10	Gibbs	Chloe	2	1					1	2	1				7		
Wareham	111	11	Gibbs	Jonan	3		1		1	1	2	2		1			11		
Wareham	111	12	Gibbs	Joseph	1	1		1		2	1		1				7		
Wareham	111	13	Gurney	George	1	1		1		2	1		1				7		
Wareham	111	14	Howard	Enos		1	2		2		1		1	1			8		
Wareham	111	15	Hilchborn	Salisbury					1					1			2		
Wareham	111	16	Hathaway	David	2		1		1	1	1		1				7		
Wareham	111	17	Hathaway	Savoy	1	2		1					1	2			7		
Wareham	111	18	Hathaway	Salathiel	3	1		1		1	2		1				9		
Wareham	111	19	Hathaway	Arthur		1		1	1	1	1			3			7		
Wareham	111	20	Kendricks	Huldah		1	1			1		1		1			5		
Wareham	111	21	Leonard	Archippus	1	1		1		2	1	1	1				8		
Wareham	111	22	Lincoln	Rufus	3	2			1		1		1				8		
Wareham	112	1	Maxhie	Andrew	1	2	1		1		2	1		1			9		
Wareham	112	2	Morey	Benjm		2			1				1				4		
Wareham	112	3	Maxham	Reubin	3		3		1		1	2		1			11		
Wareham	112	4	Maxham	David		1			1		1	1		1			5		
Wareham	112	5	Nye	Jabez		1			1	1	1			1			5		
Wareham	112	6	Nye	David			1		2			1		1	1		6		
Wareham	112	7	Norris	Oliver	1				1					1			3		
Wareham	112	8	Olliver	Peter												6	6		

73

TOWN	PG#	LN#	LAST NAME	FIRST NAME	FREE WHITE MALES					FREE WHITE FEMALES					TOTAL ALL OTHER	TOTAL SLAVES	TOTALS	DISTRICT/ TOWNSHIP	NOTES
					under 10	10 to 16	16 to 26	26 to 45	45 and over	under 10	10 to 16	16 to 26	26 to 45	45 and over					
Wareham	112	9	Perry	David	1			1	1	1			1	1			6		
Wareham	112	10	Pease	Cors	2	1	2		1	1			1	1			9		
Wareham	112	11	Pine	Wm				1						1			2		
Wareham	112	12	Swift	Lemuel		1	2		1	1	1	1		1			8		
Wareham	112	13	Scott	Primus											4		4		
Wareham	112	14	Stevens	Mary	2		1			1		1	1				6		
Wareham	112	15	Sturtevant	Leml	2	1		1		2	1		1				8		
Wareham	112	16	Sturtevant	Rowland				2						3			5		
Wareham	112	17	Sampson	Ichabod		2	1		2	1		2		1			9		
Wareham	112	18	Swift	Asa		3	3		1			1	1				9		
Wareham	112	19	Savory	Samuel	2	1		1	1	1	1		2	1			10		
Wareham	112	20	Savory	Saml Jr	1	1			2	1	2	3		1			11		
Wareham	112	21	Swift	Enoch	1			1	1			1	1	1			6		
Wareham	112	22	Smith	Peter	1			1					1				3		
Wareham	112	23	Smith	Chloe	2	2							1				5		
Wareham	112	24	Saunders	Nathl			1			2			1				4		
Wareham	112	25	Saunders	Joseph		1			1	1	2		1				6		
Wareham	113	1	Sturtevant	Jonan	3			1						1			5		
Wareham	113	2	Swift	Micah				1		1				1			3		
Wareham	113	3	Swift	Wm			1						1				2		
Wareham	113	4	Sturtevant	David	1		1			2			1				5		
Wareham	113	5	Swift	Jonah			1	1		1	1		1	1			6		
Wareham	113	6	Swift	Elisha	1		2		1	2			1				7		
Wareham	113	7	Swift	Jesse			1	2	1			3		1			8		
Wareham	113	8	Sturtevant	Joseph		1	1		1				2	1			6		
Wareham	113	9	Sturtevant	Heman			1			1		1					3		
Wareham	113	10	Smith	Jonah	2	1		1		1				1			6		
Wareham	113	11	Savory	Thomas		1	1		1			1		1			5		
Wareham	113	12	Savory	Isaac	1	2	1		1	1	1	1		1			9		
Wareham	113	13	Taber	Admiral	3		1	1		3	2			1			11		
Wareham	113	14	White	Edward	1		1	1	1	1	1	1	1				8		
Wareham	113	15	White	Ebz	1		1	1		1	1						5		
Wareham	113	16	White	Nathl	1	1			1				2				5		
Wareham	113	17	Young	Zacheus	1			1					1	1			4		
Wareham	113	18	Young	Solomon	1			1		1			1	1			5		
Wareham	113	19	Young	Henry	1	1	1	1	2	1		1					8		
Wareham	113	20	Young	John	3			1					1				5		

TOWN	PG#	LN#	LAST NAME	FIRST NAME	FWM under 10	FWM 10 to 16	FWM 16 to 26	FWM 26 to 45	FWM 45 and over	FWF under 10	FWF 10 to 16	FWF 16 to 26	FWF 26 to 45	FWF 45 and over	TOTAL ALL OTHER	TOTAL SLAVES	TOTALS	DISTRICT/ TOWNSHIP	NOTES
Rochester	105	28	*	*	*	*	*	*	*	*	*	*	*	*			*		Tape Mark
Rochester	105	51	*	*	*	*	*	*	*	*	*	*	*	*			*		Tape Mark
Rochester	105	52	*	*	*	*	*	*	*	*	*	*	*	*			*		Tape Mark
Rochester	105	53	*	*	*	*	*	*	*	*	*	*	*	*			*		Tape Mark
Wareham	110	1	*	*	*	*	*	*	*	*	*	*	*	*	*		*		
Wareham	110	3	*	*	*	*	*	*	*	*	*	*	*	*	*		*		
Wareham	110	6	*	*	3	1		1		1		1					7		
Wareham	110	7	*	*	2	2	*	*	*	*	*	*	*	1			5		
Wareham	110	2	*	John	*	*	*	*	*	*	*	*	*	*	*		*		
Rochester	105	54	*worth	*		1	1		1					1			4		Tape Mark
Abington	42	1	Adams	*				1				1					2		
Kingston	29	41	Adams	Ebenezer		1	3		1		2		1	1			9		
Kingston	29	31	Adams	Franis		1			2	2	2			1			8		
Kingston	29	26	Adams	John		1	1		1					1			4		
Kingston	29	38	Adams	John					1					1			2		
Kingston	29	14	Adams	Joseph			2		1		1			1			5		
Kingston	29	39	Adams	Melzer		2	3		1			1		1			8		
Kingston	29	40	Adams	Rufus	1			1					1				3		
Duxbury	101	8	Addington	Cloe									1	1			2		
Plymouth	18	14	Albertson	Rufus	1			1		2	2		1				7		
Duxbury	94	18	Alden	Abigail							2	2		1			5		
Bridgewater	49	31	Alden	Alexander	1		1	1		1			1				5		
Bridgewater	49	30	Alden	Amasa		1						1					2		
Duxbury	93	13	Alden	Amharst		1		1		1			1	1			5		
Middleborough	69	8	Alden	Andrew	2			1				1					4		
Bridgewater	49	32	Alden	Asahel	1	1		1		1		1					5		
Bridgewater	58	25	Alden	Caleb	2			1		3		1	1				8		
Middleborough	69	5	Alden	David					1			1		1			3		
Middleborough	69	9	Alden	David Jr	1	1		1			1		1				5		
Middleborough	69	16	Alden	Earl	1	1	1					1		1			5		
Bridgewater	58	26	Alden	Eleazer					1					2			3		
Bridgewater	58	27	Alden	Eleazer Junr	1		2	1				1	1				6		
Middleborough	69	11	Alden	Elijah	1	2	1		1	2	1	2		1	1		12		
Bridgewater	68	29	Alden	Ezra	1		1					1					3		
Bridgewater	68	27	Alden	Isaac	2			1				1	1				5		
Bridgewater	68	28	Alden	Isaac Junr				1		2			1				4		
Middleborough	69	6	Alden	Job	1		1	1	1	1	1		1	1			8		
Middleborough	69	4	Alden	John		1		1	1				3	1			7		
Middleborough	69	2	Alden	John 2d				1		4			1				6		
Bridgewater	68	26	Alden	Jonathan		1	1		1		1			1			5		
Bridgewater	58	24	Alden	Joseph	1	1	3		1	1	2			1			10		
Bridgewater	62	1	Alden	Joseph 2d			1			2		1					4		
Bridgewater	58	28	Alden	Joshua		1			1	1			1				4		
Duxbury	94	24	Alden	Josiah	2	1		1		2	1		1				8		
Duxbury	95	23	Alden	Judah Esquire	1	2			2	2	1	2	1				11		
Middleborough	69	18	Alden	Judith Wd								1	1				2		
Duxbury	94	25	Alden	Lydia							2	2					4		
Bridgewater	68	24	Alden	Nathan					1		1			1			3		
Bridgewater	68	25	Alden	Nathan Junr	1	1	1		1	1		2					8		
Bridgewater	49	29	Alden	Noah			1			2			1				4		
Bridgewater	58	23	Alden	Oliver		1		1				1		1			4		
Middleborough	69	10	Alden	Rufus	1		1		1	2	1			1			7		
Abington	42	2	Alden	Saml		1	1	1		1	1			1			7		
Bridgewater	62	3	Alden	Sarah	2	1				1		1					5		
Bridgewater	58	29	Alden	Seth		1	2						1				4		
Bridgewater	49	28	Alden	Solomon					1				1				2		
Bridgewater	58	30	Alden	Solomon Junr	1	1	1	1		1	1		2				8		
Duxbury	94	23	Alden	Wrestling				1		1			3	5			10		
Middleborough	69	12	Aldrich	Joseph	1	1		1					1				4		
Middleborough	69	3	Aldrich	Nathan	1		1			2		1					5		
Bridgewater	49	33	Aldridge	Daniel		1		2	1	2		1	2				9		
Bridgewater	49	34	Aldridge	James				1					1				2		
Bridgewater	47	2	Alger	Abiezer		1	1	2		2		2	1				9		
Bridgewater	62	8	Alger	Daniel	1			1		2		1	1				6		
Bridgewater	47	5	Alger	Ebenezer	2			1		2			1	1	1		8		
Bridgewater	47	4	Alger	Edmund		2		2	1	2		1					8		
Bridgewater	47	7	Alger	Huldah	3						1		1				5		
Bridgewater	47	1	Alger	James			1		1			2		2			6		
Bridgewater	58	33	Alger	James 2d	2		1		1	1	2	1		1			9		
Bridgewater	58	34	Alger	James 3d	2			1		1			2				6		
Bridgewater	47	3	Alger	Joseph	3		1			3	1		1				9		
Bridgewater	47	6	Alger	Nathan	2			1		1			1	1			6		
Bridgewater	68	31	Allen	Asahel			1	1				1	1	1			5		
Bridgewater	68	35	Allen	Barza				1		1		2					4		
Bridgewater	58	32	Allen	Benjamin	2			1				1					4		
Middleborough	69	14	Allen	Bezalel				1		1			2				4		
Bridgewater	68	32	Allen	David	2		2	1	1	1	1	1					10		
Rochester	117	11	Allen	George	1	1	3	1	1	2	1	1		1			12		
Bridgewater	68	33	Allen	Isaac			2		1	1		1	1				6		
Middleborough	69	7	Allen	John	2				1	1	2	2	1				9		
Plymouth	6	4	Allen	John	1			1	1		1	1		1			6		
Plymouth	26	1	Allen	John	2	2	1		1		1			1			8		
Bridgewater	68	34	Allen	Joseph		1	1		1	1		1					5		
Rochester	117	4	Allen	Joshua	1			1					1				4		

TOWN	PG#	LN#	LAST NAME	FIRST NAME	FREE WHITE MALES					FREE WHITE FEMALES					TOTAL ALL OTHER	TOTAL SLAVES	TOTALS	DISTRICT/ TOWNSHIP	NOTES
					under 10	10 to 16	16 to 26	26 to 45	45 and over	under 10	10 to 16	16 to 26	26 to 45	45 and over					
Rochester	117	3	Allen	Justes	2			1					1				4		
Bridgewater	67	11	Allen	Mary									1	1			2		
Bridgewater	68	36	Allen	Matthew			1			4	2		1	1			9		
Bridgewater	58	31	Allen	Oliver	2	1		1		1			1				6		
Rochester	117	12	Allen	Oliver	2			1					2	1			6		
Bridgewater	68	37	Allen	Pratt	2		1			1		1					5		
Rochester	117	2	Allen	Ruth						2			1				3		
Bridgewater	68	30	Allen	Simeon	1	1	1		1					2			6		
Plymouth	14	27	Allen	Timothy	3			1		2	1		1				8		
Rochester	117	1	Allen	Western				1		2			1				4		
Plymouth	6	3	Allen	William			1			2		1					4		
Duxbury	95	18	Allyn	John Rvd	2			1		1	1		1				6		
Pembroke	35	2	Alms	Ansel	1			1		1			1				4		
Bridgewater	47	15	Ames	Abiah			1					1		1			3		
Bridgewater	47	8	Ames	Abiel	2			1		1	1		2	1			8		
Bridgewater	58	38	Ames	Alexander	2			1		3			1				7		
Bridgewater	58	40	Ames	Bezer	3			1		2			1				7		
Bridgewater	62	6	Ames	Daniel		1	2	1	1				2	1			8		
Bridgewater	47	16	Ames	James	2			1			1		1	1			6		
Bridgewater	47	9	Ames	John		3	1	1	2	1	1	2		1			12		
Bridgewater	47	10	Ames	John Junr			1			1		1					3		
Bridgewater	47	12	Ames	Jonathan	3	2		1		1	1		1				9		
Bridgewater	58	35	Ames	Joseph	1	1	1		1	1	1	2		1			9		
Bridgewater	47	11	Ames	Joshua		2		1		2			1	2			8		
Bridgewater	47	14	Ames	Nathaniel				1					1				2		
Bridgewater	62	5	Ames	Noah			2	1		1			1				5		
Bridgewater	58	42	Ames	Seth	1			1					1				3		
Rochester	117	5	Ames	Seth			1		1		1		1				4		
Bridgewater	58	37	Ames	Simeon		1			1		1		2				5		
Bridgewater	58	36	Ames	Solomon	1			1	1			2		1	2		8		
Bridgewater	58	39	Ames	Solomon Junr	2			1					1				4		
Bridgewater	47	13	Ames	Thomas				1			1		1	1			4		
Bridgewater	62	4	Ames	Timothy	1			1		2	1		1				6		
Bridgewater	58	43	Andrews	Gideon	2			1		1			1				5		
Bridgewater	58	41	Andrews	Silas			1						1	1			3		
Bridgewater	47	17	Angier	John			1					2					3		
Bridgewater	68	23	Angier	Samuel		1			1				1	1	2		6		
Carver	12	23	Apling	John	1	1	1	1			1		1				6		
Duxbury	103	10	Arnold	Dako			1			1		1					3		
Duxbury	103	8	Arnold	Edward		1	1	1				1		1			5		
Abington	42	3	Arnold	H. Thos.	3		1		1				1				6		
Rochester	117	9	Arnold	John	1			1				1					3		
Rochester	117	13	Arnold	Samuel		1		1					2	1			5		
Rochester	117	6	Arnold	Seth			2	1					1				4		
Duxbury	103	9	Arnold	Wm				1					1				2		
Bridgewater	47	18	Ash	Henry				1					1				2		
Rochester	117	10	Ashley	John		2	1	1		1	2		1				8		
Middleborough	69	13	Ashley	Noah	1	1	2		1	1			1				7		
Bridgewater	65	13	Ashport	Cuff											5		5		
Rochester	117	7	Atsett	John		1		2					1				4		
Rochester	117	8	Atsett	Philip			1						1				2		
Carver	12	12	Attwood	Caleb	1	1			1	2	2	2	1				10		
Carver	9	11	Attwood	Francis			1			1		1					3		
Carver	5	3	Attwood	John	1			1		3		1					6		
Carver	8	17	Attwood	John			1		2				1				4		
Plymouth	13	17	Attwood	John		1	1					1					3		
Carver	8	22	Attwood	Joseph	2		2		1	2	1		1				9		
Carver	8	21	Attwood	Joshua	4			1					1				6		
Carver	8	20	Attwood	Nathaniel	1	1		1	1	2	1		1	1			9		
Carver	8	19	Attwood	Samuel		2	1	1		3	2		1				10		
Carver	5	4	Attwood	William			2	1		1			1				5		
Middleborough	69	1	Atwood	Eli	1			1		2			1				5		
Middleborough	69	15	Atwood	Ichabod Jr	3			1					1				5		
Middleborough	69	17	Atwood	John		1		1		1		1	1				5		
Plymouth	12	22	Atwood	Thomas			1			1		1	1				4		
Bridgewater	65	14	Augustus	Casar											2		2		
Plymouth	3	21	Austin	Richard	2	1		1		3			1				8		
Middleborough	76	24	Backus	Isaac Revd					1				1	1			3		
Middleborough	76	25	Backus	Simon	3	1		1		1			1				7		
Plymouth	6	17	Bacon	David	2			1		1		3	1				9		
Plymouth	5	17	Bacon	George			1						1	1			3		
Bridgewater	57	1	Bacon	John			1			3			1				5		
Bridgewater	59	27	Badger	William				1		1	1	1		1			5		
Plymouth	10	7	Bagnall	Richard	2	1				1	1	1	1				7		
Plimton	19	10	Bagnall	Spinks			1			2			1				4		
Scituate	131	8	Bailey	Abner	1	1			1		1	3		1			8		
Scituate	134	4	Bailey	Abner Junr	1		1					1					3		
Scituate	128	6	Bailey	Adams		1		1					1	1	1		4		
Plymouth	8	10	Bailey	Benjamin	2			1		1			2				6		
Pembroke	31	6	Bailey	Caleb	1			1	1	2	1	1	1				8		
Scituate	131	10	Bailey	Caleb	2			1		2			1				6		
Hanover	128	4	Bailey	Calvin	2		1	1		1			1				6		
Hanover	128	15	Bailey	Charles	2			1		2			1				8		

TOWN	PG#	LN#	LAST NAME	FIRST NAME	FREE WHITE MALES					FREE WHITE FEMALES					TOTAL ALL OTHER	TOTAL SLAVES	TOTALS	DISTRICT/ TOWNSHIP	NOTES
					under 10	10 to 16	16 to 26	26 to 45	45 and over	under 10	10 to 16	16 to 26	26 to 45	45 and over					
Scituate	135	30	Bailey	Ebenz	3			1		2			1	1			8		
Plymouth	9	17	Bailey	Eliphalet	4			1			1		1		1		8		
Hanover	130	6	Bailey	George		3	1		1		1	1		1			8		
Scituate	131	16	Bailey	Israel			1	1		3			1				6		
Abington	41	18	Bailey	Jack											6		6		
Hanover	128	5	Bailey	John					2					1			3		
Hanover	130	23	Bailey	John Junr		1	3		1	1	2			1	1		10		
Scituate	134	24	Bailey	Paul		1	1		1			1		1			5		
Hanover	130	7	Bailey	Stephen	1	1	1	1		1			3	1			10		
Pembroke	34	26	Baker	Abel				1					1				2		
Pembroke	31	11	Baker	Benjn			1										1		
Marshfield	98	3	Baker	Bradbery			1					2	1				4		
Duxbury	91	5	Baker	Celia							1	1	1				3		
Marshfield	93	18	Baker	Charles		1	1		1			1		1			5		
Marshfield	93	12	Baker	Charles Jun				1		1			1				3		
Duxbury	97	14	Baker	Dotty	4			1					1				6		
Duxbury	103	14	Baker	Elijah	1	2	1		1		1	1		1			8		
Marshfield	98	4	Baker	Henry			1						1				2		
Duxbury	104	1	Baker	John		1			1	1				1			4		
Marshfield	95	1	Baker	John					1					1			2		
Pembroke	31	5	Baker	John					1	1				1			3		
Marshfield	93	6	Baker	Joshua				1				1	1				3		
Rochester	117	21	Baker	Joshua				1	1	1	1	1	1				7		
Pembroke	34	21	Baker	Kenelem				1		1	1		1				4		
Scituate	135	18	Baker	Nathl				1		1			1				3		
Pembroke	34	25	Baker	Prissilla		1	1				1		1				4		
Duxbury	91	7	Baker	Samuel				1					1				2		
Marshfield	95	2	Baker	Scolly	1	1		1		2			1				6		
Pembroke	31	24	Baker	Snow	1				1	3			1	1			7		
Duxbury	103	18	Baker	Thomas		1			1					1			3		
Wareham	110	4	Baker	Thomas	*	*	*	*	*	*	*	*	*	*	*		*		
Marshfield	96	10	Baker	William					1					1			2		
Middleborough	71	7	Baker	William	2			1				1					4		
Marshfield	96	11	Baker	William Jun	2			1		1			1				5		
Plymouth	1	16	Banks	Isaac				1				1					2		
Middleborough	71	20	Barden	Bethiah			1							1			2		
Rochester	117	16	Barden	Fredrick	1		1	1		1			1	1			6		
Middleborough	71	19	Barden	Ichabod					1								1		
Middleborough	71	17	Barden	John	1	1	2		1	2	1	1		1			10		
Middleborough	71	18	Barden	Solomon				1									1		
Rochester	117	15	Barden	Stephen		1		1					2				4		
Pembroke	34	5	Baree	Jacob	1			2	1	1		1	1	1			8		
Pembroke	34	4	Barker	B. Isaac	1		1		1	4			1				8		
Scituate	136	31	Barker	Benjamin	1				2				1	2			6		
Pembroke	31	4	Barker	Isaac	2			2		2		1	1				8		
Middleborough	69	19	Barker	Joseph Revd	3	1		1	2	1	1		1	1			11		
Pembroke	34	8	Barker	Joshua			1		1		1	2		1			6		
Pembroke	31	10	Barker	Robert			1		1	1			1	1	2		7		
Pembroke	34	17	Barker	Saml			1					1		2			4		
Rochester	115	12	Barlow	George			1		1			1		1			4		
Rochester	115	13	Barlow	George Jr	1		1					1					3		
Rochester	115	11	Barlow	Seth			1		1				1				3		
Plymouth	13	27	Barnes	Benjamin		1	2	1	1		1	1	1				8		
Plymouth	13	28	Barnes	Bradford			1					2					3		
Plymouth	13	23	Barnes	Corben					1		2	3		1			7		
Plymouth	13	25	Barnes	Corben Jr	2	1	1	1		2			1				8		
Scituate	124	1	Barnes	David Revd			1		1			1	1				4		
Plymouth	16	14	Barnes	Hannah							1		1				2		
Plymouth	16	3	Barnes	Isaac	1		1	1		2	1		1	1			8		
Plymouth	6	16	Barnes	Joseph		1		1		1			1				4		
Plymouth	13	26	Barnes	Lemuel					1				1	2			4		
Plymouth	10	23	Barnes	William	2	1		1				1					5		
Plymouth	16	18	Barnes	William	2	1		1		1			1				6		
Bridgewater	68	38	Barrel	James		1		1			1	1	1				7		
Bridgewater	68	39	Barrel	Joshua	1	2	1		1			1		1			7		
Bridgewater	61	38	Barrel	William			1		1				1	1			4		
Scituate	125	10	Barrell	Bartlett	1			1		1			1		1		5		
Hanover	123	3	Barrell	Elisha			1		1			2		2			6		
Scituate	123	11	Barrell	James					1					1			2		
Scituate	123	9	Barrell	Luther	2			1		2			1		1		7		
Scituate	125	13	Barrell	Martha	2		1			1	1	1		1			7		
Scituate	123	10	Barrell	Noah	2			1		1	3	1		1			9		
Scituate	125	14	Barrell	William			1		1		2	3		1			8		
Plymouth	6	20	Barrett	Hannah		1				2							4		
Wareham	109	19	Barrows	*					1								1		
Wareham	109	15	Barrows	Abishai	1		1			1		1					4		
Carver	9	7	Barrows	Andrew	2	2			1		1	2		1			9		
Plymouth	19	18	Barrows	Asa	2			1		3			1				7		
Carver	8	2	Barrows	Carver			2	1					1				4		
Plymouth	22	15	Barrows	Ebenezer	1			1		2			1				5		
Middleborough	78	24	Barrows	Isaac		1			1				1				3		
Wareham	109	9	Barrows	Isaac			2		1			3		1			7		
Middleborough	71	3	Barrows	Jacob				1		2	1		1				5		
Carver	7	14	Barrows	James	1			1		1			1				4		
Carver	11	7	Barrows	James	3			1			3		1				8		

TOWN	PG#	LN#	LAST NAME	FIRST NAME	FREE WHITE MALES under 10	10 to 16	16 to 26	26 to 45	45 and over	FREE WHITE FEMALES under 10	10 to 16	16 to 26	26 to 45	45 and over	TOTAL ALL OTHER	TOTAL SLAVES	TOTALS	DISTRICT/ TOWNSHIP	NOTES
Bridgewater	57	11	Barrows	Joseph	1			1		2			1				5		
Carver	10	14	Barrows	Joshua	1			1		1			1				4		
Middleborough	71	15	Barrows	Nathl		2	4		1					1			8		
Carver	12	6	Barrows	Peleg	3	1	2		1	1		1	1				10		
Wareham	109	16	Barrows	Thos			1					1					2		
Plymouth	19	17	Barrows	Zadock			2	1									3		
Rochester	115	14	Barstow	Benjn			1					1					2		
Hanover	130	4	Barstow	Daniel		1		1	2	1	1	3	1	1			11		
Scituate	122	14	Barstow	Elijah	1	1		1			1	1	2	1			8		
Rochester	115	15	Barstow	Gideon		1		1	1			1		1			5		
Rochester	115	17	Barstow	Gidn Jr	3		3	1		1	1	1	1				11		
Duxbury	104	26	Barstow	James				1						1			2		
Hanover	132	16	Barstow	John B.	4			1		2	2	1	1				11		
Duxbury	99	20	Barstow	Joseph	4	2			1	1			1				9		
Scituate	119	4	Barstow	Thomas	1		1		1	2	2		2				9		
Rochester	115	16	Barstow	Wilson	2		1	1		1	1		1				7		
Rochester	115	7	Barteman	Davenport		1	1	1	1		1		1	1			7		
Plymouth	22	18	Bartlett	Abner	1	2	2		1	1	2	1		1			11		
Plymouth	13	9	Bartlett	Amasa			1	1		3	1		1				7		
Plymouth	14	18	Bartlett	Amasa			2			3			1				6		
Plymouth	22	19	Bartlett	Amasa	1		1					1					3		
Plymouth	22	23	Bartlett	Andrew				1		1	1	1		1			5		
Plymouth	17	11	Bartlett	Anselm	3	1		1		1			1				7		
Plymouth	5	15	Bartlett	Benjamun		1			1					1			3		
Bridgewater	47	20	Bartlett	David	1		1			1		1					4		
Plymouth	11	25	Bartlett	David			1			2		1					4		
Plymouth	9	7	Bartlett	Dorothy			1					1		1			3		
Plymouth	5	2	Bartlett	Elkanah			1	1		2	1		1				6		
Plymouth	1	10	Bartlett	Ephraim			1						1				2		
Plymouth	15	6	Bartlett	Ephraim			2	1	1			1		1			6		
Plymouth	22	22	Bartlett	Francis	3			1		1			1				6		
Plymouth	14	2	Bartlett	Freeman	3	1							1				6		
Plymouth	9	8	Bartlett	George	1			1			1						4		
Plymouth	22	13	Bartlett	George	1	1		1			3		1				7		
Plymouth	12	24	Bartlett	Hannah						2		1	1				4		
Plymouth	16	5	Bartlett	Henry	2			1		1			2				6		
Plymouth	22	24	Bartlett	Hosea			1			1		1					3		
Plimton	26	13	Bartlett	Isaac	2		1					1					4		
Plymouth	10	26	Bartlett	James		1		1		4	1		2				9		
Plymouth	19	25	Bartlett	James			1			3		1	1				6		
Plymouth	22	26	Bartlett	James		1		1				1		1			4		
Plymouth	14	7	Bartlett	Jesse	2		1					1		2			6		
Kingston	29	42	Bartlett	John		2		1		1		2		1			7		
Plymouth	8	12	Bartlett	John		1		1		1	1						4		
Plymouth	18	24	Bartlett	John	1			1		1			1				4		
Plymouth	21	11	Bartlett	John			1	1					1				3		
Kingston	29	43	Bartlett	Joseph			1			1		1					3		
Plymouth	17	2	Bartlett	Joseph		1	1	1					1				4		
Plymouth	22	12	Bartlett	Joseph	4	3		2		1	2	1	1	1			15		
Plymouth	18	21	Bartlett	Joseph Jr	4			2		2		1	1				10		
Plymouth	8	19	Bartlett	Joshua			1			1		1		1			4		
Plymouth	22	17	Bartlett	Lemuel		2		1		1	1		1				6		
Plymouth	17	3	Bartlett	Nathaniel	1			1		2			1				5		
Plymouth	18	11	Bartlett	Nathaniel	1	1		1		1			1				5		
Plymouth	22	14	Bartlett	Nathaniel				1					1				2		
Plymouth	22	16	Bartlett	Nathaniel Jr	4	3		1			1		1				10		
Plymouth	10	17	Bartlett	Peabody	2			1					1				4		
Kingston	29	15	Bartlett	Peleg			1	1		1		1	1				5		
Kingston	29	44	Bartlett	Rana		1	1					1	1	1			5		
Plymouth	22	28	Bartlett	Rebecca	1					2			1				4		
Plymouth	22	20	Bartlett	Rufus	1		1					1		1			4		
Plymouth	21	17	Bartlett	Runa			1			2			1				4		
Bridgewater	47	19	Bartlett	Samuel					1				1	1			3		
Plymouth	17	8	Bartlett	Samuel			1				1		1	2			5		
Plimton	24	24	Bartlett	Silvanus	2	1	2		1	2	1	1					11		
Plymouth	14	8	Bartlett	Silvanus				1			1	1	1				4		
Plymouth	11	26	Bartlett	Stephen			1			1	1	1					4		
Plymouth	5	21	Bartlett	Thomas	1			1		1			1				4		
Plymouth	16	13	Bartlett	Thomas			1			1		1					3		
Plymouth	17	1	Bartlett	Thomas				1				1					2		
Plymouth	13	5	Bartlett	Trueman	1		1			1		1					4		
Plymouth	22	27	Bartlett	William		1			1	3		1	1				7		
Plymouth	7	8	Bartlett	Zacheus	1		1	1				2					5		
Duxbury	96	7	Barton	John	2	1	1	1					1				6		
Hanover	125	24	Bass	Benjamin	1	1	1		1		1	1	2	2			10		
Hanover	129	2	Bass	Benjamin Junr	2			1		1			1				5		
Pembroke	33	4	Basset	James	2		1		1	1				1			6		
Kingston	29	30	Basset	Zeleach				2					1				3		
Bridgewater	57	5	Bassett	Caleb	1	3		1		3		1	1				10		
Rochester	116	24	Bassett	Eleanor									1	2			3		
Rochester	116	25	Bassett	John	1		1					2	1				5		
Bridgewater	57	2	Bassett	Joseph				1			2		1				4		
Rochester	116	15	Bassett	Joseph		1		1	1	1	1			1			5		
Bridgewater	57	3	Bassett	Joseph 2d	2	2	3			1	1	1	1				11		
Bridgewater	57	4	Bassett	Joseph 3d	2			1		1			1				5		

TOWN	PG#	LN#	LAST NAME	FIRST NAME	FREE WHITE MALES					FREE WHITE FEMALES					TOTAL ALL OTHER	TOTAL SLAVES	TOTALS	DISTRICT/ TOWNSHIP	NOTES
					under 10	10 to 16	16 to 26	26 to 45	45 and over	under 10	10 to 16	16 to 26	26 to 45	45 and over					
Rochester	116	17	Bassett	Perez			1			1		1					3		
Rochester	116	26	Bassett	Thos Capt	4	2	2	1			1		1				11		
Wareham	109	18	Bates	Bars	2	1			1								4		
Hanover	129	16	Bates	Benjamin				1		1							2		
Pembroke	31	15	Bates	Benjn	1	2		1		3			1				8		
Pembroke	33	1	Bates	Caleb	2	2	1	1		2	1		1				10		
Scituate	134	5	Bates	Caleb	1			1		1			1				4		
Bridgewater	68	41	Bates	Christopher	2	2		1		2			1				8		
Hanover	129	13	Bates	Clement	2	1			1	1	1		1				7		
Pembroke	34	27	Bates	Comfort					1		1			1			3		
Scituate	129	24	Bates	Cornelius		1		1		1	1		1				5		
Plymouth	14	29	Bates	David		1		1				1		1			4		
Hanover	129	11	Bates	Doughty	1	1		1		2			1				6		
Abington	42	4	Bates	Eleazer		1			2					2			5		
Abington	42	27	Bates	Eleazer 2d			1	3					1	1			6		
Hanover	125	17	Bates	Enos			1										1		
Hanover	129	12	Bates	Gamaliel	3	1	1		1	1	1	2	1	1			12		
Plymouth	21	4	Bates	Hannah		1						2	1				4		
Abington	42	6	Bates	James		1		1					1				4		
Rochester	116	8	Bates	Jonn			2		1	2	1	1		1			8		
Abington	42	22	Bates	Joseph				1						2			3		
Hanover	129	4	Bates	Joseph				1						1			2		
Plymouth	24	19	Bates	Joseph	2	2	1	1		3	1		1				11		
Hanover	125	8	Bates	Joseph N.	2	1		1		2			1				7		
Hanover	125	16	Bates	Joshua	1			1					1				3		
Abington	42	5	Bates	Josiah				1		1		1	1				4		
Rochester	115	3	Bates	Lydia		1	1				1			1			4		
Rochester	115	1	Bates	Moses		1	1					1	1				4		
Pembroke	33	2	Bates	Nabby	2							1	1				4		
Hanover	125	13	Bates	Paul	2			1					1	1			5		
Scituate	136	43	Bates	Reuben				1		1				1			3		
Middleborough	76	39	Bates	Samuel		1		1		1		1					4		
Plymouth	21	16	Bates	Samuel		1		1		1	2		1				6		
Duxbury	95	15	Bates	Seth	2			1		2			1				6		
Hanover	125	7	Bates	Seth		1		1		1	2	1	1				7		
Hanover	129	15	Bates	Thomas	2			1				1					4		
Middleborough	75	18	Bates	Thomas	1	1	2		1	1	1		1				8		
Scituate	133	14	Bawker	Gershom	1	2	1		1	2	1		1				9		
Wareham	109	20	Be*	*									1				1		
Kingston	30	42	Beal	David	1	2	1		1	1		3	1				12		
Abington	42	17	Beals	Benjm			2	1					2	1			6		
Pembroke	34	2	Beals	David	1		2	2		1	1	1	1				9		
Pembroke	31	16	Beals	Howland			1	1		1			2	1			6		
Bridgewater	62	17	Beals	Isaac	1		4			1	1	1					8		
Pembroke	31	18	Beals	Isaac	4	1		1			1	1	1				9		
Bridgewater	62	16	Beals	Japhet	1	1		1					1	1			5		
Bridgewater	62	14	Beals	Jeremiah		1	1		1	2			1				7		
Pembroke	31	23	Beals	John				1		3	1		1		3		9		
Bridgewater	68	40	Beals	Jonathan				1						1			2		
Abington	42	31	Beals	Melzer	1			1			1		1				4		
Abington	42	32	Beals	Noah	1	1	2		1	2	1		1				9		
Middleborough	69	23	Beals	Solomon	2			1					1				4		
Abington	42	13	Beals	Zelotus	2			1					1				4		
Halifax	17	10	Bearce	Andrew				1						1			2		
Bridgewater	68	42	Bearce	Job	1		2	1		2	1	1					9		
Kingston	29	27	Bearce	John			1	1					4	1			7		
Rochester	115	18	Beard	John		1	2	1						1			5		
Pembroke	34	6	Bearee	Isaiah				1						1			2		
Pembroke	34	14	Bearse	Benjn		2		1		3				1			7		
Pembroke	34	15	Bearse	Ichabod		1		1		1				1			4		
Plymouth	11	2	Bearse	Ichabod			1			2	1						4		
Middleborough	78	27	Beirce	Levi			1										1		
Middleborough	75	14	Bennet	Arthur	2		1					1					4		
Middleborough	76	42	Bennet	Benjn		1	1										1		
Abington	42	29	Bennet	E. Nathl		1		1		3	1		1				7		
Middleborough	71	10	Bennet	Edson	1		1						1				3		
Middleborough	71	12	Bennet	Elias	1			1	1					1			4		
Middleborough	75	21	Bennet	Elkanah	1			1		1	1	1	1				6		
Abington	42	28	Bennet	George	2			1		1		1	1	1			7		
Abington	42	14	Bennet	Hannah									1	1			2		
Middleborough	75	11	Bennet	Hope Wo									1	1			2		
Middleborough	75	20	Bennet	Jacob		1		1		2	1	1	1				7		
Bridgewater	49	25	Bennet	James											2		2		
Middleborough	71	9	Bennet	Jedediah	1				1		1			1			4		
Abington	42	30	Bennet	John	1			1		3			1				6		
Middleborough	75	8	Bennet	John		1		1					1				3		
Rochester	115	24	Bennet	John	3			1	1			1	1	1			8		
Rochester	115	21	Bennet	John 2d		1	1		1		1			1			5		
Rochester	115	8	Bennet	Jonn	1			1				1					3		
Rochester	115	22	Bennet	Levy				1						1			2		
Middleborough	71	13	Bennet	Nehemh Esqr		1			1		1		1				4		
Middleborough	78	26	Bennet	Philip	1			1		1			1				4		
Middleborough	71	11	Bennet	Shephard	1			1					1				3		
Middleborough	71	14	Bennet	Stephen		1	1	1		2	1	2	1	1			10		
Middleborough	75	9	Bennet	Thomas		1		1		2			1				5		

TOWN	PG#	LN#	HEADS OF HOUSEHOLD		FREE WHITE MALES					FREE WHITE FEMALES					TOTAL ALL OTHER	TOTAL SLAVES	TOTALS	DISTRICT/ TOWNSHIP	NOTES
			LAST NAME	FIRST NAME	under 10	10 to 16	16 to 26	26 to 45	45 and over	under 10	10 to 16	16 to 26	26 to 45	45 and over					
Middleborough	72	31	Bennet	William					2				1				3		
Middleborough	72	38	Benson	Andrew	2			1		1			1				5		
Middleborough	72	45	Benson	Asa	2	1			1	2		1	1				8		
Middleborough	72	40	Benson	Consider				1						1			2		
Bridgewater	57	8	Benson	David	1	1		1		4	1	3	1				12		
Bridgewater	57	7	Benson	Ebenezer	1	1		1					1				4		
Middleborough	72	42	Benson	Ebenz	1		1			1		1					4		
Middleborough	71	1	Benson	Elisha	2	2		1		1	1		1				8		
Middleborough	76	37	Benson	Isaac	1			1			2		1				5		
Wareham	109	2	Benson	Jabez		1	1	1			1	1					5		
Middleborough	72	37	Benson	John				1			1		1				3		
Middleborough	72	41	Benson	John 2d	1			1		1			1				4		
Bridgewater	57	9	Benson	Jonah	1	1		1		2	1	1	2	1			10		
Bridgewater	57	6	Benson	Jonathan		1	1	1			1	1		1			6		
Scituate	125	7	Benson	Joseph	1		2	1		1	2	1		1			9		
Middleborough	72	36	Benson	Joshua		1								1			2		
Wareham	109	5	Benson	Levi	2				2	2		1		2			9		
Middleborough	75	3	Bent	Experience	1	1		1		3		1	1				8		
Middleborough	75	2	Bent	John				1						1			2		
Duxbury	97	23	Bent	Lot	1		3		1	1		2	1	1			10		
Middleborough	78	25	Bent	William				1			1			1			3		
Middleborough	75	1	Bent	Zenas	1			1		2			1				5		
Carver	5	1	Berry	John	1			1		1			1				4		
Pembroke	34	22	Berstow	Charles	1		1	1					1				4		
Pembroke	34	24	Berstow	James Jun	2			1		2	1		1				7		
Pembroke	34	23	Berstow	Willm	3			1					1				5		
Plymouth	23	3	Besse	Andrew				1		4			1				6		
Plymouth	23	2	Besse	Barzilla				1				1	1				3		
Plymouth	24	29	Besse	Benjamin		1		1				1		1			4		
Wareham	110	10	Besse	David		1	4	1	1		2	2	1	1			13		
Wareham	110	13	Besse	Jabez				1				1		1			3		
Rochester	115	10	Besse	Joshua	1			1		4	1		1				8		
Plymouth	23	4	Besse	Nathaniel				1		2			1				4		
Rochester	115	9	Besse	Nathl				1				3	1				5		
Plymouth	23	1	Besse	Robert	3			1					1				5		
Wareham	110	9	Besse	Silas	3	1	2	1		2	1			1			11		
Middleborough	75	17	Besse	Joseph				1					1				2		
Middleborough	75	19	Besse	Joseph Jun	3			1		1	3		1				9		
Abington	42	25	Bicknell	Jacob			4	1		1	1	1		1			9		
Abington	42	23	Bicknell	Luke	1	2	2	2		1	1	1		2			12		
Abington	42	24	Bicknell	Nathl 2d	1		1						1				3		
Bridgewater	47	45	Biganeer	John Frederic				1							2		3		
Pembroke	34	1	Bigbee	Gamaliel	1	1				1	1		1				6		
Pembroke	34	20	Bigbee	Isaac			1			1	1		1				4		
Plimton	24	6	Bisbee	Abner			1			1		1					3		
Plimton	24	10	Bisbee	Abner		1		1		1				2			5		
Carver	7	10	Bisbee	Asaph	2	2	1			1	1		1				8		
Plimton	21	6	Bisbee	Elijah		1	2		2	1	2			2			10		
Rochester	115	25	Bisbee	Ezra	1	1		1			1	1	1				5		
Plimton	19	17	Bisbee	George	1	1	3		1	2		1		1			10		
Rochester	114	3	Bisbee	Hopestill		1	2	1	1		1	1		1			8		
Middleborough	76	23	Bisbee	Hopstill	1			1		2		1	1				6		
Plimton	21	3	Bisbee	Ischecar	1			1				1	1				4		
Bridgewater	67	5	Bisbee	John	4	1	1			2	1	1	1	1			13		
Plimton	21	2	Bisbee	John	2			1		1			1				5		
Carver	10	10	Bisbee	Jonah	1	1		1		1			1				5		
Plimton	21	5	Bisbee	Noah		1	2		1	1	1	1		1			8		
Pembroke	31	3	Bisbee	Rheuben			2	2		1		1					6		
Pembroke	33	5	Bishop	Eliphelet				1					1				2		
Rochester	116	11	Bishop	Henry		1	1	1		1		1		1			6		
Middleborough	72	39	Bishop	John		1	1	1		1			1				5		
Plymouth	14	14	Bishop	John	1	1		1					1		1		5		
Pembroke	31	2	Bishop	Nathll		1	1	1				1	1				5		
Plimton	22	5	Bishop	William			1			3			1	2			7		
Middleborough	72	43	Blackman	Thomas			1	1					1				3		
Middleborough	78	30	Blackman	Thomas Jur	1		1					1					3		
Plymouth	21	1	Blackmore	Branch		1	1	1			1	1	1				7		
Plymouth	21	2	Blackmore	John	3	1	1						1				6		
Rochester	116	21	Blackmore	Salisbury	2	2	3		1	2		3		1			14		
Rochester	116	20	Blackwell	Caleb				1		1		1	1				4		
Rochester	116	18	Blackwell	Seth			1	1					1	1			4		
Bridgewater	50	28	Blakeley	William				1					1				2		
Abington	42	11	Blanchard	Adam			2	1		3			1				7		
Abington	42	33	Blanchard	Adam Jr	2			1		2		1	1				7		
Abington	42	9	Blanchard	Dean			1	1		2		1					5		
Abington	42	10	Blanchard	Eli	1			1					1				3		
Abington	42	8	Blanchard	Jesse	1			1				1	1				4		
Abington	42	12	Blanchard	Thos Jrn	3	1		1			1		1				7		
Rochester	117	18	Blankinship	Charles	1	2			1	2			1				7		
Rochester	117	19	Blankinship	George	1	2			1	1			1		2		8		
Rochester	117	23	Blankinship	James				1						2			3		
Rochester	116	4	Blankinship	Paul	2			1		2	1		1				7		
Rochester	117	17	Blankinship	Peleg	1			1					1				3		
Rochester	117	14	Blankinship	Perez			1			1		1	2	1			6		
Rochester	116	1	Blankinship	Seth	1		1	1		1			1				5		

TOWN	PG#	LN#	LAST NAME	FIRST NAME	FREE WHITE MALES					FREE WHITE FEMALES					TOTAL ALL OTHER	TOTAL SLAVES	TOTALS	DISTRICT/ TOWNSHIP	NOTES
					under 10	10 to 16	16 to 26	26 to 45	45 and over	under 10	10 to 16	16 to 26	26 to 45	45 and over					
Rochester	116	5	Blankinship	Wm	1			1		2	1		1				6		
Bridgewater	57	10	Blossom	Barnabas				1		3	1	1	1	1			8		
Middleborough	75	10	Blye	John	3			1		1							6		
Middleborough	78	28	Boes	Bethiah										1			1		
Rochester	115	19	Bolles	Amzh	1			1	1		2	1	1				7		
Rochester	116	16	Bolles	Benjn			1		1		1		1				4		
Rochester	115	5	Bolles	Ebenr	1	1	3		1	2	1	1		1			11		
Rochester	117	22	Bolles	Hosea		2	1		1				1				5		
Rochester	116	23	Bolles	Isaac		1	1		1	1			1	1	1		6		
Rochester	114	1	Bolles	Reubin	1		1	1		2			1				6		
Rochester	115	2	Bolles	Saml				1		1		2	3	1			8		
Bridgewater	67	12	Bolton	Betty									1	1			2		
Bridgewater	57	12	Bolton	David	1			1		1			1				4		
Bridgewater	57	13	Bolton	John	1	1		1		3			1				7		
Bridgewater	67	13	Bolton	Joseph				1		2				1			4		
Bridgewater	50	29	Bolton	Philip				1	1	1			1				3		
Pembroke	31	1	Bonney	Daniel															Tape mark
Plimton	19	4	Bonney	Ebenezer			1		1				1				3		
Pembroke	34	7	Bonney	Ebenz	1		1		1	2			1				6		
Pembroke	31	25	Bonney	Ezekiel	1			1		1	1			1			5		
Plimton	19	3	Bonney	Isaac	1	1	2	1			2		1				8		
Pembroke	34	19	Bonney	James		1			1					1			3		
Pembroke	31	13	Bonney	Jonathan	2	1			1	2	1			1			8		
Pembroke	31	17	Bonney	Joseph			1		2			2	3	1			9		
Plimton	26	11	Bonney	Joseph	3	2		1	1	1			1				9		
Pembroke	34	18	Bonney	Josiah	2			1		1			1				5		
Pembroke	31	21	Bonney	Lemuel			1		1	1				1			4		
Pembroke	31	20	Bonney	Lemuel Jun			1		1	1		1					3		
Pembroke	31	26	Bonney	Nathll	1		1					1					3		
Plimton	26	9	Bonney	Nathaniel			1			1		1					3		
Plimton	26	10	Bonney	Nathaniel		1			1				1				3		
Pembroke	34	16	Bonney	Noah	2	1	3		1	1	1			1			10		
Rochester	116	19	Bonney	Saml				1	1	1		1	1	1			6		
Pembroke	31	14	Bonney	Saml1		1	2		1			1		1			6		
Plimton	26	18	Bonney	Seth			1			1		1					3		
Bridgewater	67	6	Bonney	William	2			1		1			2				6		
Middleborough	76	29	Booth	Abiel	1			1		2			1				5		
Middleborough	76	31	Booth	Abner			1					1					2		
Middleborough	75	6	Booth	Benjan	2	1			1	1		1		1			7		
Middleborough	72	46	Booth	Guilford	1			1		1			1				4		
Middleborough	76	28	Booth	John	1		1							1			4		
Middleborough	76	38	Booth	Joseph				1						1			2		
Middleborough	71	5	Booth	Joseph Jun	1		1		1	2				1			6		
Middleborough	76	30	Booth	Samuel	3			1					1				5		
Middleborough	76	27	Booth	Zebedee	1			1	1		2		1				6		
Middleborough	76	36	Booth	Zebedee 2d	4	2		1		2	1		1				11		
Halifax	15	22	Bosworth	Asaph	2			1		2			1				6		
Duxbury	97	20	Bosworth	Benjm	2		2	1		2		1	1				9		
Halifax	15	16	Bosworth	David	2	1		1		3			1				8		
Halifax	15	21	Bosworth	Hannah	2	1					2		1				6		
Halifax	17	9	Bosworth	Ichabod			1		1	1				1			4		
Plimton	22	2	Bosworth	Isaac	2		1						1				4		
Halifax	16	20	Bosworth	James	2		1		1	1	1		1	1			8		
Halifax	15	15	Bosworth	John	3			1					1				5		
Halifax	15	20	Bosworth	John			2		1					1			4		
Rochester	116	12	Bosworth	Nehemiah	2	1		1	1			1		1			7		
Halifax	16	1	Bosworth	Richard	4	1	2		1	1	2	1		2			14		
Halifax	16	2	Bosworth	Salah	2	1	1	1		1	1		1	2			10		
Halifax	13	20	Bosworth	Waterman				1		4	1		1				7		
Pembroke	34	10	Bourn	Abel	2		1		1	2	1	1	1				11		
Pembroke	34	12	Bourn	James				1		1				1			3		
Pembroke	34	11	Bourn	James Jun	1	1		1		2	2	1					9		
Middleborough	72	26	Bourn	Lemuel		1	1		1	1	2			1			7		
Marshfield	93	8	Bourn	Rouse	2					2							6		
Marshfield	94	18	Bourn	Thomas			1			2			1				4		
Middleborough	72	27	Bourne	Abner Dr		1	1		1			1		2			6		
Middleborough	72	44	Bourne	Caleb			1			2			1				4		
Halifax	18	18	Bourne	Ebenezer				1		3	2		1				7		
Wareham	110	5	Bourne	Ebenz	2	1	1		1			1	1				7		
Marshfield	104	18	Bourne	John	2	1		1		1			1				6		
Scituate	123	2	Bourne	Melatiah				1					1				2		
Halifax	15	13	Bourne	Newcomb	2			1		1			1				5		
Scituate	123	20	Bourne	Sherjeshul					1			2	1	1	1		6		
Middleborough	72	28	Bourne	Wm Capt			2	1		1			1				5		
Scituate	123	13	Bowker	Bejamin			1		1	2	1	1	1		1		8		
Scituate	125	11	Bowker	Dimeck	2			1				1					4		
Scituate	130	14	Bowker	Edmond			1	1				1	1				4		
Scituate	130	17	Bowker	Elijah	3	1				2			1				8		
Pembroke	31	19	Bowker	Jamima	2	1						1	1				5		
Scituate	130	16	Bowker	John				1						2			3		
Scituate	126	8	Bowker	Lazarus			1	1		2	2		1				8		
Abington	42	7	Bowker	Liberty	1		1			1			1				4		
Bridgewater	61	40	Bowker	Nelson	1		1			1		1					4		
Scituate	125	9	Bowker	Ruth							1			1			2		

TOWN	PG#	LN#	LAST NAME	FIRST NAME	FREE WHITE MALES					FREE WHITE FEMALES					TOTAL ALL OTHER	TOTAL SLAVES	TOTALS	DISTRICT/ TOWNSHIP	NOTES
					under 10	10 to 16	16 to 26	26 to 45	45 and over	under 10	10 to 16	16 to 26	26 to 45	45 and over					
Scituate	130	15	Bowker	Warren	1		1						1				3		
Rochester	114	2	Bowland	Remember									1	4			5		
Rochester	116	10	Bowman	Simeon		1		1					1				3		
Scituate	131	20	Bozworth	Eunice	1								1				2		
Plymouth	11	28	Bradford	*			2		1	2		2		1			8		
Pembroke	33	6	Bradford	Andrew				1					1	1			3		
Plimton	22	13	Bradford	Calvin		2		1		1	1	3	1				9		
Plymouth	10	6	Bradford	Charles	3	1		1				1	2				8		
Duxbury	95	8	Bradford	Daniel				1		1			1				3		
Plimton	22	26	Bradford	Daniel			2						1				3		
Kingston	29	22	Bradford	David		1			1			1		1			4		
Kingston	29	24	Bradford	Elisha					1					1	2		4		
Plimton	23	7	Bradford	Elizabeth				1					1	1			3		
Kingston	29	50	Bradford	Ellis	2			1	1			1	1	2			8		
Duxbury	95	19	Bradford	Gamaliel Esq			1	1	1	1			2	2			8		
Plimton	22	22	Bradford	Gideon	2	1	3		1		1			1			9		
Kingston	30	27	Bradford	Israel		1				3	1		1				7		
Kingston	29	45	Bradford	James		2	2		1			1		1			7		
Kingston	29	46	Bradford	John			1	1	1				1	2			6		
Plimton	23	8	Bradford	John		1			1	2	1	2		1			8		
Plymouth	7	5	Bradford	Josiah					1			1	1				3		
Plymouth	11	24	Bradford	Lemuel	3			1	1	1		1					7		
Kingston	29	28	Bradford	Levi	1	2		1		1		1	1				7		
Plimton	22	18	Bradford	Levi	1		1	1	1			1	1	1			7		
Duxbury	102	20	Bradford	Lewis	1	2	1	1		1			1				7		
Plymouth	11	17	Bradford	Nathaniel	1		2		1	1		1	1				7		
Rochester	115	20	Bradford	Oliver	2	3			1	3	1	1	1				12		
Plimton	23	9	Bradford	Peleg	3			1		2			1				7		
Plymouth	14	26	Bradford	Pelham			2			1		1					4		
Plymouth	12	27	Bradford	Ruth		2	1			1				1			5		
Plymouth	9	6	Bradford	Sally		1		1				1	1				4		
Duxbury	99	1	Bradford	Samuel	1	1		1	1		1	1		1			7		
Plimton	22	17	Bradford	Samuel	2	1	1		1			2		1			8		
Plymouth	16	8	Bradford	Samuel		1		1		1			2	1			5		
Duxbury	99	2	Bradford	Seth			1		1	1			2	1			6		
Duxbury	99	7	Bradford	Seth Jun			1			2			1				4		
Kingston	29	47	Bradford	Silvanus	3				1		2	1	1				8		
Kingston	29	48	Bradford	Stetson		1	2		1				2	2			8		
Plymouth	8	2	Bradford	Thomas			1						1				2		
Plimton	23	10	Bradford	William	1			1		3			1				6		
Plymouth	11	6	Bradford	William	1		1			1		1	1				5		
Duxbury	97	15	Bradford	Zadoch	1	1		1		1			2				6		
Rochester	115	27	Braley	Elijah	1	1	1		1			1		1			6		
Rochester	115	26	Braley	Russel			3		1			1		1			6		
Plymouth	9	18	Bramhall	Benjamin	3	1		1		2			1				8		
Plymouth	9	20	Bramhall	Silvanus	1			1					1				3		
Plymouth	12	7	Bramhall	Silvanus	1			1					1				3		
Plymouth	19	1	Bramshall	George			1			1			1	1			4		
Bridgewater	59	24	Brattles	Asa			1			3			1				5		
Plymouth	24	16	Brattles	Benjamin			1			1			1				3		
Plymouth	19	19	Brattles	Caleb	1			1					1				3		
Bridgewater	62	15	Brattles	Samuel	3			1		1	2		1	1			9		
Plymouth	15	1	Brattles	Samuel	2			1	6	3			2	11			23		
Plymouth	15	2	Brattles	Samuel Jr	3			1		1			1				6		
Plymouth	11	8	Breck	Moses			2	1		2			1				6		
Bridgewater	59	25	Brett	Abigail			1					1		1			3		
Bridgewater	62	18	Brett	Amasa	2			1		1	1		1				6		
Bridgewater	62	19	Brett	Calvin	2	1		1		2			1				7		
Bridgewater	47	21	Brett	Daniel	1	1		1		1			1				5		
Bridgewater	62	12	Brett	Isaac			2		1		1			1			5		
Bridgewater	62	13	Brett	Joseph	1			1				1					3		
Bridgewater	62	9	Brett	Samuel					1				1	1			3		
Bridgewater	62	10	Brett	Samuel Jun		1	1		1	1	1	2		1			8		
Bridgewater	59	26	Brett	Susanna			1					1	1				3		
Bridgewater	67	7	Brett	Uriah				1		2			1				4		
Bridgewater	62	11	Brett	William		3		1		2			1	1			8		
Plymouth	5	19	Brewster	America			1						1				2		
Duxbury	98	21	Brewster	Cyrus	1			1					1				3		
Kingston	27	9	Brewster	Eliha			2		1				1				4		
Plymouth	5	24	Brewster	Ellis			1		1	1			1				3		
Kingston	29	6	Brewster	Fear						2			1	3			6		
Kingston	27	23	Brewster	Isaac			1		1				1	1			4		
Plymouth	5	18	Brewster	Job	2			1	1	1	1		1				7		
Duxbury	94	17	Brewster	Joseph	2	1	1		1	2		2		1			10		
Duxbury	94	14	Brewster	Joshua	2	1		1		2			1				7		
Duxbury	102	4	Brewster	Joshua	1	1		1		2	2		1				8		
Duxbury	102	18	Brewster	Nathan			1	1						1			3		
Kingston	27	24	Brewster	Pelham			1			1		1					3		
Kingston	27	20	Brewster	Rebecca	1								1				2		
Kingston	29	25	Brewster	Thomas			1		1	1		1	1	1			6		
Plymouth	13	16	Brewster	William	1			1				1	1				4		
Kingston	30	50	Brewster	Wrestling				1						2			3		
Kingston	29	1	Brewster	Wrestling Jr		1		1					2				4		
Pembroke	34	13	Briant	Jacob	2	1		1	1	1		1	1				8		

TOWN	PG#	LN#	LAST NAME	FIRST NAME	FREE WHITE MALES under 10	10 to 16	16 to 26	26 to 45	45 and over	FREE WHITE FEMALES under 10	10 to 16	16 to 26	26 to 45	45 and over	TOTAL ALL OTHER	TOTAL SLAVES	TOTALS	DISTRICT/TOWNSHIP	NOTES
Middleborough	76	32	Briggs	Abiather	3			1		3			1				8		
Halifax	18	4	Briggs	Abigail					1					2			3		
Pembroke	31	8	Briggs	Alden	1		3	1	1		1	1	1				9		
Rochester	116	6	Briggs	Arnold	3			1		1	1		1				7		
Scituate	129	9	Briggs	Benja Junr	3			1		3			1				8		
Scituate	134	13	Briggs	Benjamin			1	1					1	1			4		
Wareham	110	8	Briggs	Benjm 2	3	1		1		1			1				7		
Rochester	116	14	Briggs	Cornelius	2			1		1		1					5		
Middleborough	71	16	Briggs	Dean	3			1		1			1				6		
Middleborough	76	26	Briggs	Ebenr 3d Capt	2	1		1		1			1				6		
Middleborough	71	21	Briggs	Ebenz					1					1			2		
Middleborough	75	12	Briggs	Ebenz 2d	2	1	3	1		1	1	2		1			12		
Wareham	109	3	Briggs	Eli		1	1	1	2		2	1					9		
Rochester	115	23	Briggs	Elijah	1		1		1			2	1	1			7		
Pembroke	31	9	Briggs	Elisha	1		2		1	2	1	1		1			9		
Rochester	116	3	Briggs	Elisha	1		1		1	1				1			6		
Scituate	127	24	Briggs	Elisha			1			4			1				6		
Rochester	116	9	Briggs	Elisha 2d	1	1			1	1	1	1	1				7		
Middleborough	69	22	Briggs	Elisha Dr	1		1						1				3		
Hanover	126	19	Briggs	Ezra			2	1					1	1			5		
Hanover	127	23	Briggs	Ezra	2			1	1	2			1				7		
Bridgewater	67	4	Briggs	George		1			1					2			4		
Middleborough	72	32	Briggs	George	1		1			1		1					4		
Wareham	109	1	Briggs	Hallet	1	2			1	1	1		1				7		
Plymouth	24	17	Briggs	Isaac		2	1		1	1	2		1				8		
Scituate	126	18	Briggs	James		1			1			2					4		
Scituate	126	16	Briggs	James Junr			2	1	1					2			6		
Wareham	109	4	Briggs	Jesse	2	1			1	2	1			2			9		
Halifax	17	12	Briggs	John					1			1		1			3		
Rochester	116	13	Briggs	John			2	1	1			1	1	1			7		
Scituate	127	23	Briggs	John					1			2	2				5		
Scituate	126	17	Briggs	Joseph	2		1						1				4		
Scituate	134	21	Briggs	Judith						3	1	3		1			8		
Middleborough	76	34	Briggs	Lemuel		1		1			1		1				4		
Middleborough	71	8	Briggs	Leonard		1		1		5	1		1				9		
Middleborough	69	21	Briggs	Levi	1			1					1				3		
Middleborough	75	7	Briggs	Molbon	4	2		1					1				8		
Rochester	116	22	Briggs	Nathan	2		1	1	1	1		2	3	1			12		
Rochester	115	4	Briggs	Nathl		1		1		1		2		1			6		
Halifax	18	6	Briggs	Rebecca	1						1	1		1			4		
Plymouth	24	18	Briggs	Reuben			1					1					2		
Abington	42	20	Briggs	Richard	4	2			1		1		1	1			10		
Wareham	109	8	Briggs	Saml	1	1	2		1		1	3		2			11		
Pembroke	34	9	Briggs	Saml	3	1		1		1	2	1					9		
Pembroke	31	12	Briggs	Sampson			1							1			2		
Halifax	17	13	Briggs	Seth			1			1		1					3		
Rochester	116	2	Briggs	Seth	1			1		1	1		1				5		
Rochester	117	20	Briggs	Silas	1				1	1	1		1				5		
Scituate	119	5	Briggs	William		1			1	1		1		2			6		
Pembroke	31	7	Briggs	Willm	3	1	1	1	1	1	1		2				11		
Middleborough	76	33	Briggs	Ziphanh		1		1					1				3		
Pembroke	44	19	Brister												2		2		No first name listed
Scituate	124	16	Brooks	Hannah							1		1	1			3		
Hanover	127	20	Brooks	Joseph		1		1			3	1	2				8		
Scituate	125	4	Brooks	Nathl		1		1									2		
Scituate	125	3	Brooks	Nathl Junr	2	1			1	1			1	1			7		
Hanover	127	21	Brooks	Samuel					1			1		1			3		
Scituate	122	3	Brooks	Willm	2	2	1		1		1	4		1			12		
Scituate	130	23	Brown	Alijah					1		1			1			3		
Duxbury	97	17	Brown	Amos		1		1		2	1		1				6		
Bridgewater	67	3	Brown	Charles	1			1		1		1					4		
Abington	42	21	Brown	Daniel	1		2	1		1		1	1				7		
Bridgewater	67	2	Brown	Isaac	2	1		1		1			1				6		
Bridgewater	67	1	Brown	John		1	1		1				1	1			5		
Scituate	133	4	Brown	Jonathan				1		2			1				4		
Plymouth	9	2	Brown	Lemuel	1			1		1		1					5		
Duxbury	95	17	Brown	Lydia										1			1		
Scituate	133	3	Brown	Mary									1	1			2		
Bridgewater	61	39	Brown	Nathaniel		1			1	1				1			4		
Plymouth	9	27	Brown	Robert		1			1			2		1			5		
Abington	42	19	Brown	Saml		1	1	1	1	2			1	1	2		10		
Pembroke	33	3	Brown	Smith	2	1			1	2	1			2			9		
Abington	42	18	Brown	Woodbridge	2	1		1				2	1				7		
Rochester	115	6	Brownell	James			1		1	1		1	2	1			7		
Pembroke	34	3	Bruster	Willm	1			1		2	1						6		
Plimton	26	6	Bryant	Benjamin			1	1			1	1	1				5		
Plymouth	16	6	Bryant	Caleb	2			1			1		1				5		
Plimton	26	4	Bryant	Dorothy	1	1	1			4	2	1	1				11		
Middleborough	75	16	Bryant	Hannah 3d										2			2		
Middleborough	78	29	Bryant	Hannah Wo								1	1				2		
Middleborough	71	4	Bryant	Isaac			1		1			2	1	1			6		
Middleborough	72	25	Bryant	Jesse				1				1		2			4		
Middleborough	76	35	Bryant	Jesse Jr				1				1	1				3		
Middleborough	75	15	Bryant	John	1			1					2				4		

83

TOWN	PG#	LN#	LAST NAME	FIRST NAME	M under 10	M 10 to 16	M 16 to 26	M 26 to 45	M 45 and over	F under 10	F 10 to 16	F 16 to 26	F 26 to 45	F 45 and over	TOTAL ALL OTHER	TOTAL SLAVES	TOTALS	DISTRICT/ TOWNSHIP	NOTES
Middleborough	75	5	Bryant	Joseph					1					1			2		
Scituate	130	12	Bryant	Joshua	1	2	3		1	1				1			9		
Middleborough	71	6	Bryant	Josiah				2				1		1			4		
Middleborough	72	29	Bryant	Lemuel				1						1			2		
Plimton	26	2	Bryant	Levi	2		1	1		3	2	1	1	1			12		
Plimton	26	3	Bryant	Luther				1		4			1				6		
Kingston	29	49	Bryant	Peleg	2			1		2		1	2				8		
Scituate	136	40	Bryant	Samuel				1									1		
Middleborough	75	4	Bryant	Seth		1	1							1			3		
Middleborough	69	20	Bryant	William		1	1	1		1	1	1					6		
Plimton	26	12	Bryant	Zenas	1	2		1		3		1	1				9		
Bridgewater	59	23	Bryant	Calvin	1			1		3		1					6		
Bridgewater	62	21	Bryant	Job	1		2	1		1	1		1				6		
Bridgewater	59	22	Bryant	Job S	1			1		2			1				5		
Bridgewater	62	22	Bryant	Nathaniel	1			1		4			1				7		
Bridgewater	62	20	Bryant	Philip	1		1	1		1		1		2			8		
Pembroke	31	22	Buck	Eunice	1	1						2	1	2			7		
Wareham	109	7	Bumpus	Asa	2		1			2			1				6		
Carver	11	11	Bumpus	Benjamin	2		1			1			1				5		
Wareham	109	11	Bumpus	Benjn		1					1	1		1			5		
Carver	11	12	Bumpus	Daniel	3		1			2	1		1				8		
Carver	11	9	Bumpus	Edward	1	1	1						1				4		
Wareham	109	17	Bumpus	Eliphalet	1		1						1				3		
Wareham	110	11	Bumpus	James	2	2	1	1		1	1		1				9		
Wareham	109	14	Bumpus	Jere		2	1	2		1		2	1				9		
Carver	11	10	Bumpus	John	1		1						1				3		
Wareham	110	14	Bumpus	Jonn	3		1			1			1				6		
Middleborough	76	40	Bumpus	Joseph	1		2	1		1	2	2		1			10		
Plymouth	23	5	Bumpus	Joseph				1						1			2		
Wareham	110	12	Bumpus	Joseph	2	1	1						2				8		
Middleborough	76	41	Bumpus	Joseph 2d	1	2	2	1				1	1				8		
Wareham	109	12	Bumpus	Lot	3	3	1	1		1	1		1				11		
Wareham	109	13	Bumpus	Mary							1	1	1	1			4		
Wareham	109	6	Bumpus	Noah			1			1		1	2				5		
Wareham	110	15	Bumpus	Prince	1	2	1			1		1		1			8		
Carver	11	13	Bumpus	Thankful	1					1		1					3		
Middleborough	75	13	Bumpus	Zenos	2		1			2			1				6		
Plymouth	12	5	Burbank	Ezra	2		1			2			1				6		
Plymouth	4	5	Burbank	John	2	1	1					1	1				6		
Plymouth	6	22	Burbank	Joseph				1			1			1			3		
Plymouth	12	3	Burbank	Priscilla			2					2	1				5		
Plymouth	4	7	Burbank	Samuel	1		1			1	2						5		
Middleborough	71	2	Burbank	Thomas	2		1			1			1				5		
Carver	7	15	Burden	Gashum			1			1			1				3		
Wareham	109	10	Burges	Elisha	2	1	2	1	1		1	3		1			12		
Duxbury	96	2	Burges	Jacob	3	1	1	1		1		1	1				9		
Wareham	110	16	Burges	James		1	1	1		1			1				6		
Plymouth	23	19	Burges	John	2	2		1		3	2		1				11		
Plymouth	26	4	Burges	Nathan	3		1			1			1				6		
Duxbury	94	16	Burges	Ruth									1	1			2		
Middleborough	72	30	Burges	Stephen	2	1	1		1	1		1	1	1			9		
Plymouth	26	5	Burges	Thomas		2		1		4	1	2	1				11		
Plymouth	23	14	Burges	William	2	2		1		1	1	1	1	1			11		
Rochester	116	7	Burges	Wm			1					2		1			4		
Middleborough	72	33	Burgess	Seth			1						1				2		
Scituate	136	44	Burnett	Thomas W.			1			2		1					4		
Bridgewater	50	26	Burr	Calvin	1	1		1		1		1					5		
Bridgewater	50	27	Burr	Elijah	3		1	1		2		1	1				9		
Bridgewater	50	25	Burr	John	2			1		1			1				5		
Abington	42	15	Burrel	Benony	2	1		1		3	1	1					9		
Abington	42	16	Burrel	Isaac			2	1	1	1			1				6		
Abington	42	26	Burrel	John	1	1	1	1			1	1	1				7		
Middleborough	72	34	Burrows	Abner				1					2				3		
Middleborough	72	35	Burrows	Abner Jr	2			1		1			1				5		
Rochester	114	4	Butler	James	1	1		1	1	1			2	2			9		
Bridgewater	67	9	Byram	David	2			1		2			1				6		
Bridgewater	67	8	Byram	Josiah				1		1	1	1		1			5		
Bridgewater	67	10	Byram	Matilda						1	1		1				3		
Rochester	113	11	Cale	Thomas	2		1			1			1				5		
Pembroke	44	20	Caley												6		6		No first name listed
Plymouth	10	4	Callon	John	1			1			2		1				5		
Middleborough	80	37	Canedy	William Jun	1	2		1		2	2		1				9		
Middleborough	80	32	Canedy	Wm Capt	1			1				1	1	1			5		
Rochester	113	15	Cannon	Ebenzr	1		1	1		1			2	1			8		
Rochester	114	5	Cannon	Ebenzr Jr	2		1			1			2	1			7		
Rochester	113	1	Cannon	Nathan	*	*	*	*	*	*	*	*	*	*	*		*		Tape mark
Scituate	126	13	Carlow	Bille			1			3			1	1			6		
Scituate	124	18	Carlow	William	1		2	1		1	2		1	1	1		9		
Plymouth	23	25	Carpenter	Thomas		1		1				2	1				5		
Bridgewater	60	5	Carr	Daniel				1				1	2				4		
Bridgewater	60	6	Carr	Daniel Junr		1				1			1				3		
Bridgewater	60	4	Carr	Thomas				1				1	1				3		
Pembroke	33	20	Carrit	Joseph				1						1			2		
Halifax	18	20	Carter	Benjamin M.				1				1		1			3		

84

TOWN	PG#	LN#	LAST NAME	FIRST NAME	FREE WHITE MALES under 10	10 to 16	16 to 26	26 to 45	45 and over	FREE WHITE FEMALES under 10	10 to 16	16 to 26	26 to 45	45 and over	TOTAL ALL OTHER	TOTAL SLAVES	TOTALS	DISTRICT/TOWNSHIP	NOTES
Hanover	123	9	Carter	Seth	3			1		2			1				7		
Hanover	123	1	Carthell	Theoph					1	1				1			3		
Marshfield	101	5	Carver	Alison	1	1		1		3			1	1			8		
Bridgewater	57	14	Carver	Eleazer					1		1	3	1	1	1		7		
Bridgewater	60	33	Carver	John		1		1				2		1			5		
Middleborough	77	14	Carver	John Capt			1	1		1				1			4		
Marshfield	93	2	Carver	Joshua	1		1	2				1		1			6		
Plymouth	15	18	Carver	Josiah	1			1		1	1	1					5		
Plimton	20	2	Carver	Nathaniel				1			1		1				3		
Plymouth	16	12	Carver	Nathaniel	1			1		2	1	1	1				7		
Duxbury	101	5	Carver	Zadoch	3			1						1			5		
Bridgewater	59	40	Cary	Daniel	1	1		1		1		3	1				8		
Bridgewater	57	15	Cary	Eleazer			2	1			1	1	1				6		
Bridgewater	57	16	Cary	Eliphalet		1		1						2			4		
Bridgewater	67	14	Cary	Ephraim	1		2	1		1				1			6		
Bridgewater	59	33	Cary	Howard	2	2	1	1		1	1		1				9		
Bridgewater	59	31	Cary	James			1				1						2		
Bridgewater	59	28	Cary	Jonathan				1						2			3		
Bridgewater	59	30	Cary	Jonathan Junr	3	1		1		4	2		1				12		
Bridgewater	67	16	Cary	Mary										3			3		
Bridgewater	59	29	Cary	Moses			2	1		2	1			1			7		
Bridgewater	59	32	Cary	Simeon				1						1	1		3		
Scituate	121	12	Castle	Susanna									1				1		
Plymouth	23	12	Castle	Thomas	3			1		2			1				7		
Middleborough	77	11	Caswell	David	1		2	1		1		2	1				8		
Rochester	114	10	Caswell	Elijah	1			1		1	2			1			6		
Rochester	114	11	Caswell	Elisha	1			1				1					3		
Middleborough	77	12	Caswell	Elkanah					1					1			2		
Middleborough	79	4	Caswell	Jonathan					1		1			1			3		
Middleborough	79	1	Caswell	Seth	1			1		2			1				5		
Rochester	114	12	Caswell	Thomas	1	2	1		1	3		3		1			12		
Plymouth	23	7	Caswell	Zenas	2			1					1				4		
Halifax	15	11	Causell	Sherebral		2		1		2	2	2					9		
Pembroke	36	11	Cavel	Daniel	1		1					1					3		
Middleborough	80	36	Chace	Benjan	1		1			1		1					4		
Rochester	113	24	Chaddock	Calvin	2			1		1	1	1	1		1		8		
Pembroke	33	23	Chamberlain	Freedom				1						1			2		
Bridgewater	67	15	Chamberlin	Benjamin				1			1	2	1				5		
Pembroke	36	1	Chamberlin	Freedm Junr	1			1		2	3		1				8		
Bridgewater	67	21	Chamberlin	Isaac	3			1		2			2	2			10		
Abington	42	45	Chamberlin	John	1	1	3		1	1	3	1	1				12		
Bridgewater	67	19	Chamberlin	Joseph	1	1		1				1		1			5		
Hanover	125	21	Chamberlin	Josiah	1			1		1	2		1				6		
Bridgewater	67	17	Chamberlin	Lewis	1		1						1				3		
Bridgewater	67	18	Chamberlin	Nathaniel				1				1		1			3		
Rochester	114	14	Chamberlin	Philip			1			1			1				3		
Bridgewater	67	20	Chamberlin	Thomas		1	1			3	1		1				7		
Duxbury	93	8	Chandler	Abel	2			1		2	1	2	1				9		
Duxbury	104	20	Chandler	Anna										3			3		
Duxbury	94	12	Chandler	Aron	1			1		1		1					4		
Duxbury	96	17	Chandler	Aron	1			1		1			1				4		
Plimton	23	22	Chandler	Arthur	1	1		1		2	2		1				8		
Duxbury	101	24	Chandler	Asa		1	1	1			1						5		
Duxbury	101	18	Chandler	Asa Jun	2			1		2		1		2			8		
Duxbury	99	3	Chandler	Bisbe	1	1			1	2	2		1				8		
Duxbury	101	23	Chandler	Daniel			1					1					2		
Duxbury	99	21	Chandler	Ezekiel			1	1						1			3		
Duxbury	93	17	Chandler	Henery	2			1					1				4		
Duxbury	102	15	Chandler	Howard	4			1			1		1				7		
Duxbury	101	17	Chandler	Ira	3			1		1			1				6		
Plimton	23	21	Chandler	Josiah		2			1			2		1			6		
Kingston	29	35	Chandler	Mary		1	1				1	1		1			5		
Duxbury	102	1	Chandler	Peleg	1			1		3			1				6		
Duxbury	101	22	Chandler	Phillip		2		1			1	1		1			6		
Duxbury	99	8	Chandler	Samuel		1		2		3	1	3		1			11		
Duxbury	102	13	Chandler	Seva				1		1	2	2		1			7		
Halifax	17	14	Chandler	Simeon		1				1		1					3		
Duxbury	102	6	Chandler	Stephen			1			2			1				4		
Duxbury	102	7	Chandler	Thomas				1					1	1			3		
Marshfield	104	15	Chandler	Thomas			3	1					2	1			7		
Duxbury	94	15	Chandler	Thomas Jun			1			1		1					3		
Duxbury	102	10	Chandler	Wadsworth	1			1				1		1			4		
Plimton	24	22	Chandler	Zebeda		2		1		3			1				7		
Carver	8	9	Chase	Consider			1	1						1			3		
Carver	8	10	Chase	Levi	4	1		1		1			1				8		
Middleborough	79	2	Chase	Lewis	1			1		2			2				6		
Hanover	128	22	Chatman	John	3			1		1			1				6		
Bridgewater	59	39	Cheeseman	Noah			1					1					2		
Bridgewater	59	38	Cheeseman	Samuel			1		1	2		1		1			6		
Scituate	119	22	Chittenden	Ruth			1			2	1			1			5		
Plymouth	24	27	Chubbock	Benjamin	1	1			1	1				1			5		
Plymouth	24	28	Chubbock	Ephraim	2			1		1			1				5		
Plymouth	24	25	Chubbock	John		2			1	3	1	1		1			9		
Plymouth	24	26	Chubbock	Timothy		1	2		1				1	1			6		
Scituate	135	24	Chubbuck	David	1	3		1		3			1		1		10		
Abington	42	48	Chubuck	James	3	2			1	1	1		1	1			10		
Abington	42	49	Chubuck	Jeremiah	1				1	1			1	1			5		

TOWN	PG#	LN#	LAST NAME	FIRST NAME	FREE WHITE MALES					FREE WHITE FEMALES					TOTAL ALL OTHER	TOTAL SLAVES	TOTALS	DISTRICT/ TOWNSHIP	NOTES
					under 10	10 to 16	16 to 26	26 to 45	45 and over	under 10	10 to 16	16 to 26	26 to 45	45 and over					
Pembroke	36	2	Church	Constant		1			1		1			1			4		
Marshfield	101	12	Church	David	1			1			1						3		
Rochester	114	25	Church	Earl	1		2				1	1	1	1			7		
Rochester	114	24	Church	Jonn	2	1	1		1	1	1		1	1			9		
Scituate	122	13	Church	Lemuel		1	1		1		1			1			5		
Scituate	119	6	Church	Thomas					1	2	2		1				6		
Hanover	126	10	Church	Timothy	2			1			1	1					5		
Scituate	124	8	Church	William					1				1				2		
Marshfield	101	11	Church	Wm	1			1		1			1				4		
Duxbury	97	22	Churchel	Peleg	2	1		1		2			1				7		
Duxbury	97	21	Churchel	Stephen	1		2	1					1				5		
Plimton	24	9	Churchill	Alferd		1				2		1					4		
Plymouth	18	3	Churchill	Amaziah			1			1	2	1					5		
Plimton	24	16	Churchill	Andrew	1		1					1					3		
Plymouth	7	4	Churchill	Barnabas		1		1			2			1			5		
Plymouth	11	11	Churchill	Benjamin		1		1						1			3		
Plymouth	14	5	Churchill	Branch				1				1		1	2		5		
Plymouth	13	14	Churchill	Charles	1		1			1				1			4		
Bridgewater	61	41	Churchill	Cornelius		1					1						2		
Plimton	26	25	Churchill	Daniel	1		1						1				3		
Plymouth	13	3	Churchill	Daniel			1			2		1					4		
Abington	42	34	Churchill	David	1		1					1					3		
Plimton	24	8	Churchill	Ebenezer			1		1			1				3		
Bridgewater	50	42	Churchill	Eleazer	1		1		3	1	1					7		
Plimton	23	16	Churchill	Elias	1		1		2	2	1		1			8		
Plymouth	10	12	Churchill	Elizabeth	1				1	1		1	1			5		
Plymouth	15	7	Churchill	Elizabeth	1	1			1	1		1				5		
Plymouth	18	12	Churchill	Elizabeth		1	2		2	1		1				7		
Bridgewater	60	1	Churchill	Ephraim	1			1				1	1			4		
Bridgewater	60	2	Churchill	Ephraim Junr			1				1	1				3		
Plymouth	16	1	Churchill	Hannah						2	1	1				4		
Plymouth	13	4	Churchill	Heman	1		1		1			1				4		
Middleborough	77	13	Churchill	Isaac	2	1	2	1			2	1	1			10		
Plimton	23	1	Churchill	Isaac			2	1					1			4		
Carver	8	14	Churchill	Jabez	1		1		1	3	1		1			8		
Middleborough	80	21	Churchill	Jabez	1	1		2		3	2		2	1		12		
Plymouth	17	9	Churchill	Jabez			1						1	2			4		
Plimton	23	11	Churchill	Jacob	1		1			1			1				4		
Bridgewater	60	3	Churchill	James			1				1		1				3		
Plimton	20	4	Churchill	James				1		1	2	1		1			6		
Plymouth	9	25	Churchill	John		1	1						1	1			4		
Plimton	23	4	Churchill	Joseph	2	1		1			1			1			6		
Plimton	23	13	Churchill	Joshua	1		1						1				3		
Plimton	26	26	Churchill	Josiah	1		1		2			1				5		
Abington	42	35	Churchill	Levi		1	1				1					3		
Plimton	23	19	Churchill	Levi	1		1				1					3		
Plymouth	1	19	Churchill	Lewis	2		1		2			1				6		
Plimton	23	18	Churchill	Nathaniel			1					1						
Plymouth	17	14	Churchill	Nathaniel			1		1	1	1		1			5		
Middleborough	78	40	Churchill	Nelson	1	2	1		2			1				7		
Middleborough	78	39	Churchill	Perez	2	2	1	1		1	1		1			9		
Plimton	24	11	Churchill	Prince	1		1		3			1				6		
Plymouth	13	7	Churchill	Rufus	1		1					1				3		
Plymouth	24	10	Churchill	Sally	1	1			1			1				4		
Plymouth	15	29	Churchill	Samuel			1		1		1					3		
Plymouth	7	14	Churchill	Sarah	1	1			1			1				4		
Plymouth	18	28	Churchill	Solomon	1	2	1		1		1	1				7		
Plymouth	13	18	Churchill	Stephen		1		1			2	1	1	1		7		
Plymouth	18	26	Churchill	Thaddeus			2	1			2		1			6		
Plimton	24	5	Churchill	Thomas	1	1		1		1			1			5		
Plimton	23	3	Churchill	William				1					1			2		
Plimton	24	7	Churchill	Zadock		1			1		1				3		
Bridgewater	61	45	Clap	Caesar											2		2		
Rochester	113	6	Clap	Kenolm		1				1		1					3		
Rochester	113	9	Clap	Nathl		1	1			1	2		1			6		
Scituate	129	17	Clapp	Alexander	4		1			1		1				7		
Scituate	134	3	Clapp	Augustus		1	2					2				5		
Scituate	123	3	Clapp	Constant		1		1				1				3		
Scituate	134	1	Clapp	Deborah		1					1					2		
Pembroke	33	17	Clapp	Dwella	3	1		1		3		1	1			10		
Scituate	129	7	Clapp	Elijah	1		1	1			2		2			7		
Scituate	136	32	Clapp	James	2	1	1	1		2	1	1	1			10		
Scituate	123	5	Clapp	John			1	1			1		1			4		
Scituate	133	26	Clapp	Leonard	1		1		1			1	2			6		
Scituate	134	8	Clapp	Lewis	1		1		2	1		1	1			7		
Hanover	123	4	Clapp	Michael	1		1		3			1				6		
Scituate	134	40	Clapp	Peggy	3							1				4		
Scituate	125	20	Clapp	Samuel				1								1		
Scituate	126	9	Clapp	Silvanus		2		1			3	1	1			8		
Scituate	133	50	Clapp	Thomas		1			1		1					3		
Scituate	123	4	Clapp	William			1			4		1				6		
Scituate	134	2	Clapp	Zilphe			1					1		1	3	5		
Middleborough	80	31	Clark	Abner	4		1	1				1				7		
Middleborough	80	39	Clark	Aniel	2		1			1	1					5		

TOWN	PG#	LN#	HEADS OF HOUSEHOLD		FREE WHITE MALES					FREE WHITE FEMALES					TOTAL ALL OTHER	TOTAL SLAVES	TOTALS	DISTRICT/ TOWNSHIP	NOTES
			LAST NAME	FIRST NAME	under 10	10 to 16	16 to 26	26 to 45	45 and over	under 10	10 to 16	16 to 26	26 to 45	45 and over					
Middleborough	80	33	Clark	Barnabas	1	2		1		1	2	1	1				9		
Hanover	132	8	Clark	Belcher	3		2		1		2		1				9		
Duxbury	102	17	Clark	Elias	1			1		2				1			5		
Rochester	113	12	Clark	Elijah			1			1			1				3		
Middleborough	77	5	Clark	Elisha Capt		1	2		1	2		1	1				8		
Hanover	132	7	Clark	Hannah		2							1				3		
Rochester	114	18	Clark	Isaac	1	1		1				1		1			5		
Rochester	114	7	Clark	James	1	1			1		1	1					6		
Rochester	114	21	Clark	John	1				1	3	2	1	1				9		
Abington	42	39	Clark	Jonathan	1		1		1	1	2			1			7		
Middleborough	80	27	Clark	Joseph 2d Capt	2		1						1				4		
Middleborough	80	35	Clark	Joseph Dr	1	1			1	2	1	2	1				9		
Middleborough	80	26	Clark	Josiah				2					2				4		
Rochester	114	16	Clark	Leml	1		1	1		2	1	1	2	1			10		
Rochester	114	15	Clark	Malatiah		1		1		4	1	2	1				10		
Hanover	130	10	Clark	Mary									1				1		
Rochester	114	8	Clark	Nathan			1			1	1	1					4		
Hanover	126	1	Clark	Nathaniel			1	1					1		1		4		
Rochester	114	19	Clark	Nathl		1	2		1			2	1	1			8		
Middleborough	77	18	Clark	Nowls		2		1		1	3	4		1			12		
Middleborough	77	6	Clark	Robert	1	1	4		1	2			1				10		
Middleborough	77	7	Clark	Roger			1			1		1					3		
Middleborough	80	34	Clark	Samuel Dr				1				1	1				3		
Rochester	113	25	Clark	Willard	2		1	1		1	1		1	1			8		
Rochester	114	6	Clark	Willm	1	1		1		3			1	1			8		
Halifax	17	19	Clarke	Alice	2					1			1				4		
Bridgewater	57	18	Clarke	Benjamin	3			1				1		1			6		
Plymouth	5	13	Clarke	Benjamun		2		1		1			1				5		
Plymouth	19	26	Clarke	James	2	1		1		3	1		1				9		
Plymouth	22	3	Clarke	James					1	1				1			3		
Plymouth	10	20	Clarke	John	1			1		1			1				4		
Plymouth	17	30	Clarke	John	2			1		2		1	1				7		
Plymouth	22	2	Clarke	John	1	1		1		3		1	1				8		
Plymouth	21	3	Clarke	Josiah			3		1	3	1	1	1				10		
Plymouth	21	14	Clarke	Lothrop	2	1	1	1		2			1				8		
Plymouth	12	25	Clarke	Nathaniel	1	1		1		1	1		1				6		
Plymouth	17	28	Clarke	Nathaniel				1				1	1				3		
Plymouth	20	1	Clarke	Nathaniel		1				1		1					3		
Plymouth	21	23	Clarke	Ruth		2	1						1				4		
Plymouth	21	22	Clarke	Seth	2			1		2			1				6		
Plymouth	22	4	Clarke	Seth	2	1		1		2			1				7		
Plymouth	17	27	Clarke	William	1		2		1	2				1			7		
Plymouth	19	10	Clarke	Zoeth		2	2			1		1	1				7		
Rochester	114	9	Clayton	Savory	3		1			2	1		1				8		
Bridgewater	67	24	Clift	Adna Winslow			1			2	2		1				6		
Marshfield	99	10	Clift	Bethia			1						1	1			3		
Marshfield	100	3	Clift	Joseph				1					1				2		
Marshfield	100	6	Clift	Joseph Jun	1		1			2			1				5		
Bridgewater	67	25	Clift	Nathaniel			1			1		1					3		
Marshfield	100	7	Clift	Nathl	1			1					1				3		
Marshfield	100	4	Clift	Wills				1		1	1	1		1			5		
Marshfield	100	5	Clift	Wm		1			1	1	1		1				5		
Rochester	113	8	Clifton	Timo		1		1		4	2		1				9		
Middleborough	79	3	Cobb	Andrew		1		1			1		1				4		
Carver	10	23	Cobb	Barnabas	2			1		3		1	1				8		
Carver	10	24	Cobb	Benjamin	2	2	1	1			1	1	1				9		
Middleborough	77	19	Cobb	Birney			1		1			2		1			5		
Plymouth	4	14	Cobb	Cornelius		1			1			2		1			5		
Kingston	27	22	Cobb	Ebenezer				1					1				2		
Plymouth	9	22	Cobb	Ebenezer				1					1				2		
Middleborough	77	16	Cobb	Ebenzer			1	1					1	1			4		
Abington	42	36	Cobb	Edward			1			1			1				3		
Carver	10	19	Cobb	Isaac	1	1		1	1	2	1		1				8		
Rochester	114	13	Cobb	Isaiah	1			1		1			1				4		
Middleborough	80	22	Cobb	James	2	1	1	1		1	1		1				8		
Plymouth	4	15	Cobb	Job				1		1				2			4		
Abington	42	38	Cobb	John	2	2	1	1		2			2				10		
Kingston	27	21	Cobb	John		1	2	1		1	1	1	1				8		
Carver	7	17	Cobb	Joseph		1		1		1				1			4		
Plimton	22	11	Cobb	Lemuel		1	1						1				3		
Plymouth	3	12	Cobb	Lemuel	1	1	2		1			2		1			8		
Middleborough	77	17	Cobb	Lewis	2			1					1	1			5		
Carver	7	3	Cobb	Nehemiah	1	1	1		1		2		1	1			8		
Plymouth	9	28	Cobb	Nehemiah			1	1	1				1				4		
Rochester	113	26	Cobb	Oliver	1	1	1	1		1	1		1				7		
Plimton	22	25	Cobb	Rowland	2	1		1		2	1		1				8		
Middleborough	77	21	Cobb	Saml Ens		1	1		1			2		1			6		
Kingston	27	18	Cobb	Seth				1		1		1					3		
Kingston	29	9	Cobb	Stephen	2			1		1			1				5		
Middleborough	78	37	Cobb	Susanna Wo									1	1			2		
Carver	7	7	Cobb	Timothy		1	2		1			1		1			6		
Carver	7	8	Cobb	William				1	1				1	1			4		
Middleborough	77	15	Cobb	Zebedee	1		1					1					3		
Middleborough	78	35	Cobbe	John				1					1				2		
Scituate	125	17	Cobun	Saul Negro											6		6		

TOWN	PG#	LN#	LAST NAME	FIRST NAME	FREE WHITE MALES					FREE WHITE FEMALES					TOTAL ALL OTHER	TOTAL SLAVES	TOTALS	DISTRICT/ TOWNSHIP	NOTES
					under 10	10 to 16	16 to 26	26 to 45	45 and over	under 10	10 to 16	16 to 26	26 to 45	45 and over					
Bridgewater	55	17	Codner	Samuel											9		9		
Middleborough	77	8	Cole	Andrew		1			1				1	1			4		
Rochester	113	7	Cole	Archippus					1			2	1	1			5		
Scituate	133	32	Cole	Asahel		1	2	1				1	1	1			7		
Carver	10	18	Cole	Betsey		1	1				1			1			4		
Scituate	130	4	Cole	Charles	1	1			1	1		2	1	1			8		
Scituate	135	5	Cole	David				1				1		1			3		
Middleborough	79	7	Cole	Edward	1		1	1		1			1				5		
Bridgewater	59	37	Cole	Ephraim	2	2		1			1		1				7		
Scituate	129	6	Cole	James junr		1			1		1			1			4		
Carver	7	6	Cole	Job	1	1			1	2	2	1		1			9		
Rochester	113	3	Cole	John	*	*	*	*	*	*	*	*	1	1	+		2		Tape mark
Carver	12	21	Cole	Joshua	1			1						1			3		
Carver	10	5	Cole	Lemuel		1		1		2		1		1			6		
Carver	10	6	Cole	Lemuel	3	1			1			1		1			7		
Pembroke	36	12	Cole	Margret			2							1			3		
Middleborough	80	38	Cole	Nathl 2d	1			1		3			1	1			7		
Middleborough	77	9	Cole	Nathl Lt	2	2		1		1	1		2				9		
Pembroke	33	15	Cole	Nathll			2							1			3		
Plymouth	8	25	Cole	Samuel				1							1		2		
Carver	7	16	Cole	Sarah								1		2			3		
Scituate	133	27	Coleman	David			1					1					2		
Scituate	135	23	Coleman	Joseph		1		1	1	2	2		1	1			9		
Scituate	135	11	Coleman	Joseph Junr	1			1		4			1				7		
Scituate	136	21	Coleman	Thomas Junr			1				1		1				3		
Scituate	121	15	Collamore	Benjm			2	1		2	1		2				8		
Scituate	128	8	Collamore	Enoch	1	2	3		1			1	1		1	1	11		
Pembroke	33	12	Collamore	Thos				1					2	1	1		5		
Pembroke	33	14	Collamore	Willm		1	1	1		1			1				5		
Scituate	134	22	Collier	Isaac		1	2		1	2	1	3		1			11		
Scituate	135	26	Collier	Isaac Junr	2			1				1					4		
Scituate	134	28	Collier	Jonathan	2			1		2		1					7		
Plymouth	5	22	Collings	James	3			1		3			1				8		
Scituate	119	26	Colman	Thomas				1					1				2		
Abington	42	46	Colson	John		1		1					1				3		
Bridgewater	50	30	Colwell	Ebenezer	1	1	1	1			1		2				7		
Bridgewater	60	29	Conant	Andrew	1		1					1					3		
Bridgewater	57	20	Conant	Elias		1	1	1					1				4		
Bridgewater	60	25	Conant	Ezra	1	2	1	1				1	2				8		
Bridgewater	60	36	Conant	Joanna									2				2		
Bridgewater	57	22	Conant	John				1					1				2		
Bridgewater	60	24	Conant	John Junr		1		1	1	1			1				5		
Bridgewater	49	36	Conant	Martin	1	1			2		1						5		
Bridgewater	60	28	Conant	Nathaniel				1			2		1				4		
Bridgewater	57	19	Conant	Peter	1	1	2	1		1	1	1					8		
Bridgewater	57	21	Conant	Phineas	1	1	1			1	1		1				6		
Bridgewater	60	27	Conant	Silvanus		1		1				2	1	1			6		
Wareham	110	21	Conant	Wm	1	3		1		1			1	1			8		
Bridgewater	60	26	Conant	Zenas				1			1	1		1			4		
Kingston	30	1	Cook	Amos	1	1	1		1	2	2	1		2			11		
Kingston	29	53	Cook	Elkanah		2		1		1			1				5		
Bridgewater	50	40	Cook	John				1			1			1			3		
Kingston	29	11	Cook	John	2	1		1		1			1				6		
Kingston	30	6	Cook	Josiah		1	1		1	1	1	2	1	1			9		
Abington	42	47	Cook	Levi	3	2	1	1		1	1	1	1				11		
Kingston	29	52	Cook	Mary		1	1	3						1			6		
Kingston	30	2	Cook	Robert		1	3	1	1				1	1			8		
Scituate	136	1	Cook	Robert	4	1		1		2	1	2	1				12		
Kingston	30	34	Cook	Silvanus		1		1				2	1	2			7		
Rochester	113	10	Cook	Thomas	1		1	1		1		1	2	1			8		
Rochester	113	23	Coomer	Caleb	1			1				3		1			6		
Rochester	113	21	Coomer	Crissully		1						1		1			3		
Rochester	113	22	Coomer	Perez	1		1						1	1			4		
Duxbury	98	13	Coomer	Wm	1	1		1					1	1			5		
Plymouth	11	18	Cooper	Benjamin	1			1		2			1				5		
Plymouth	12	9	Cooper	Joseph	2	1		1					1				5		
Kingston	27	16	Cooper	Nathaniel	1	1		1		3	1		1				8		
Plimton	21	16	Cooper	Richard		1		1		2	2	1					7		
Plymouth	12	16	Cooper	Richard		1	1	1						1			4		
Kingston	27	13	Cooper	Thomas				1						1			2		
Bridgewater	50	39	Copeland	Anselm			1		1				1				3		
Bridgewater	50	36	Copeland	Asa	3		1			1		1	1				7		
Bridgewater	50	37	Copeland	Caleb	3		1	1		3		1	1				10		
Bridgewater	60	35	Copeland	Daniel	1		1	1		1	2	1		1			8		
Bridgewater	50	34	Copeland	Ebenezer	1	1		1						1			4		
Scituate	119	3	Copeland	Ebenezer	1	1		1		2			1	2			8		
Bridgewater	50	35	Copeland	Ebenezer Jun			1			1							2		
Bridgewater	50	31	Copeland	Jonathan				1					2	1			4		
Bridgewater	50	32	Copeland	Jonathan Jun	3	1	1	1		1	1		1				9		
Bridgewater	50	33	Copeland	Joseph		1		1				2	1	1			6		
Bridgewater	50	38	Copeland	Salmon	1	1	1						1				4		
Scituate	119	15	Copeland	William	1	1		1		3		1	1	1			9		
Middleborough	79	5	Copland	Cyrus	3		1	1					1				6		
Plymouth	21	26	Cornish	Benjamin				1						1			2		

TOWN	PG#	LN#	LAST NAME	FIRST NAME	FREE WHITE MALES					FREE WHITE FEMALES					TOTAL ALL OTHER	TOTAL SLAVES	TOTALS	DISTRICT/ TOWNSHIP	NOTES
					under 10	10 to 16	16 to 26	26 to 45	45 and over	under 10	10 to 16	16 to 26	26 to 45	45 and over					
Plymouth	24	4	Cornish	Benjamin	2			1		1			1				5		
Plymouth	21	8	Cornish	David				1		3		1					5		
Plymouth	24	1	Cornish	George		1				5	1		1				9		
Plymouth	21	25	Cornish	John			4		1		1	1		1			8		
Plymouth	21	10	Cornish	Josiah	1	1		1		1	1		2				7		
Plymouth	24	3	Cornish	Nathaniel					1		1		1	1	2		5		
Plymouth	21	7	Cornish	Samuel	1			1				1					3		
Plymouth	21	24	Cornish	Thomas				1		1			2	1			5		
Middleborough	78	31	Cornish	William		1		1		2		2	1	1			8		
Plymouth	19	8	Corvett	Jesse	2				1			1	1				5		
Plymouth	8	23	Cotton	Josiah	1			1		1	1	1	1				6		
Plymouth	7	24	Cotton	Roseter	2	2		1		1	1		1				8		
Plymouth	15	10	Covington	Mary						1		1	1				3		
Scituate	129	23	Cowin	Job					1				1	1			3		
Bridgewater	60	30	Cowin	Joseph			1		1		1	4	1	1			9		
Rochester	114	23	Cowing	Asahel			2		1			1		2			6		
Rochester	114	20	Cowing	Israel	2			1		1			1				5		
Rochester	113	16	Cowing	Lot					1					1			2		
Rochester	113	14	Cowing	Seth	1			1	1				4		1		8		
Rochester	114	22	Cowing	Zadock				1	1		1	1		1			5		
Middleborough	78	33	Cox	Ebenezr	3	2	1	1		1		1	1				10		
Pembroke	36	5	Cox	Elias	2			1		1			1				5		
Middleborough	80	29	Cox	Elisha					1				1				2		
Pembroke	33	8	Cox	Ephraim	1			1				1					3		
Pembroke	36	4	Cox	James	1				1				2				4		
Pembroke	33	7	Cox	Seth Junr	1			1		1	1		1				5		
Pembroke	33	9	Cox	Seth Junr				1	1	1	1		1	1			6		
Plymouth	6	6	Coye	William		1			1			1	1				4		
Bridgewater	59	42	Crafts	John	1			1					1				3		
Bridgewater	59	41	Crafts	Thomas	1	1		1		2	1		1				7		
Bridgewater	67	23	Crandell	Ezra			1			1		1					3		
Plymouth	7	19	Crandon	Benjamin						5	1	1	1				10		
Bridgewater	50	41	Crane	John	1			1		3			1	1			7		
Bridgewater	49	35	Crane	Jonathan	1			1	1	1		1		1			6		
Bridgewater	60	31	Crane	Samuel					1								1		
Rochester	113	19	Crapo	Abm		1	1	1		2							5		
Rochester	113	20	Crapo	John	1				1	2			2				6		
Rochester	113	18	Crapo	Lot				1			1		1	1			4		
Wareham	110	20	Crapo	Micah	2		1		2			1					6		
Rochester	113	17	Crapo	Nichs	2	2		1		3			3	1			12		
Middleborough	78	32	Crapo	Spooner	1	1							1				3		
Rochester	114	17	Crapo	Wm	2	3	1	1	1	2		1	1	2			14		
Carver	10	8	Crocker	Heman	3	1			1	1	2			1			9		
Wareham	110	18	Crocker	Kenslem	1	1		1	1	1			1				6		
Carver	10	9	Crocker	Mercy	2								1				3		
Wareham	110	19	Crocker	Timo	2		1		2	4	2		1				12		
Wareham	110	17	Crocker	Wadsworth	1			1					1				3		
Plymouth	14	15	Crombie	Calvin		1	1	1		2		2			1		8		
Plymouth	14	16	Crombie	William		1		1		2			1				5		
Plymouth	14	19	Crombie	William	2		1	1		2		1					7		
Plimton	23	26	Crooker	Benjamin	2				1	2	1		1				7		
Pembroke	33	18	Crooker	Daniel					1	1	2			1			5		
Pembroke	36	8	Crooker	David					1					2			3		
Pembroke	36	7	Crooker	David Junr	1				1		2	1		1			6		
Pembroke	36	10	Crooker	Elijah						2			1				3		
Pembroke	33	21	Crooker	Ensign				1				1					2		
Halifax	15	19	Crooker	James	2			1		1		1					5		
Pembroke	36	9	Crooker	John	1			1				1					3		
Bridgewater	61	44	Crooker	Pero											2		2		
Hanover	132	13	Crooker	Tilden			2		1	2	2		1				8		
Bridgewater	57	17	Crooker	Zenas	1		2	1		3			1	1			9		
Rochester	113	13	Crossman	Annah	3			1					1				5		
Bridgewater	59	34	Croswell	Benjamin					1					1			2		
Plymouth	7	17	Croswell	Joseph	1				1	1			1				4		
Plymouth	10	13	Crowell	Jonathan			1			1		1					3		
Plimton	21	23	Cuchman	Jacob	1				1				1				3		
Scituate	134	25	Cudworth	Israel		2		1		2			1				6		
Scituate	134	23	Cudworth	John	2	1	2		1	2	1	1	1				11		
Scituate	134	26	Cudworth	John Junr				1		1			2				4		
Scituate	133	36	Cudworth	Jopth			3		1	2	2	1		1			10		
Scituate	133	35	Cudworth	Rachel										2			2		
Rochester	113	4	Cundal	Enoch	1	1		1		1		1					5		
Hanover	127	25	Curtis	Amos				1					2	1			4		
Hanover	128	3	Curtis	Anna		2	1			1		1	1	2			8		
Hanover	126	14	Curtis	Barker				1						1			2		
Bridgewater	59	36	Curtis	Barnabas		2	1		1	1		2	2	2			11		
Hanover	126	20	Curtis	Calvin			1		1		1						3		
Scituate	135	37	Curtis	Charles	1			1					1				3		
Scituate	136	42	Curtis	Eli					1					1			2		
Scituate	135	6	Curtis	Eli Junr	1	1		1		2			1				6		
Hanover	126	21	Curtis	Elienm			1		1			1		1			4		
Scituate	127	16	Curtis	Elijah	1			1		3	1		1	1	1		9		
Hanover	132	2	Curtis	Elisha		1			1		1			1			4		
Hanover	132	3	Curtis	Elisha Junr	1			1				1		1			4		
Scituate	123	6	Curtis	Experience				1						2			3		
Scituate	133	49	Curtis	Gamaliel		1		1		2	1		1				6		

TOWN	PG#	LN#	HEADS OF HOUSEHOLD		FREE WHITE MALES					FREE WHITE FEMALES					TOTAL ALL OTHER	TOTAL SLAVES	TOTALS	DISTRICT/ TOWNSHIP	NOTES
			LAST NAME	FIRST NAME	under 10	10 to 16	16 to 26	26 to 45	45 and over	under 10	10 to 16	16 to 26	26 to 45	45 and over					
Scituate	126	20	Curtis	James					1					1			2		
Hanover	127	16	Curtis	Jesse		1			1					1			3		
Hanover	127	15	Curtis	Job					2					1			3		
Hanover	128	9	Curtis	John			1	1		1			1				4		
Scituate	133	38	Curtis	John					1				2	1			4		
Scituate	133	39	Curtis	John Junr			1						1				2		
Abington	42	43	Curtis	Joshua	4			1		1	1		1				8		
Hanover	126	12	Curtis	Lemuel		1	1	1	1				2	1			7		
Middleborough	79	6	Curtis	Luke					1	3			1				5		
Hanover	126	13	Curtis	Malzar Esq	1	1	2		1			2		1			8		
Scituate	136	19	Curtis	Nehemiah	1			1					1				3		
Scituate	123	7	Curtis	Peleg	1	1						1		1			5		
Hanover	127	17	Curtis	Phebe									1				1		
Hanover	126	22	Curtis	Prince					1			2					3		
Pembroke	36	3	Curtis	Rachel										1			1		
Hanover	132	20	Curtis	Reuben			2							1			3		
Hanover	132	5	Curtis	Reuben Junr	1		1						1				3		
Abington	42	44	Curtis	Rufus			4	1					1	1			7		
Scituate	133	40	Curtis	Samuel			1	1				1	1	1			5		
Scituate	135	10	Curtis	Samuel 3d			1			3		1	1	1			7		
Scituate	119	27	Curtis	Samuel Junr			2		1	1	1	2	2	1			11		
Bridgewater	67	22	Curtis	Simeon	2		2	1		3	1		1				10		
Hanover	126	11	Curtis	Simon	2	2		1		2			1				8		
Bridgewater	59	35	Curtis	Theophilus	3			1		2			1				7		
Pembroke	36	6	Curtis	Willm	1		1	1		1	1		1				6		
Duxbury	103	29	Curtis	Wm			1			3			1				5		
Halifax	15	6	Cushing	Benjamin	1			1			2			1			5		
Abington	42	41	Cushing	Brackley	2		1										3		
Pembroke	33	11	Cushing	Charles	1	1		2		1		1	2				8		
Pembroke	33	13	Cushing	Edward									1	1			2		
Kingston	30	4	Cushing	Elijah		2	2	1					1	1			7		
Pembroke	33	16	Cushing	Elijah			1	1	1	1		2	2	1			9		
Scituate	126	14	Cushing	Ellis	1							1	1				3		
Abington	42	40	Cushing	Ezra	1	1	1		1				1				6		
Abington	42	37	Cushing	Ezra Junr			1						1				2		
Scituate	126	4	Cushing	George				1				1	1	2			5		
Plimton	23	5	Cushing	Isaac	1			1		1			1				4		
Plimton	26	15	Cushing	James				1		1			1				3		
Plymouth	13	24	Cushing	James	1		1						1	1			4		
Scituate	125	15	Cushing	James Jr				2					1	1	1		5		
Scituate	133	11	Cushing	Joseph	2		1			3			1				7		
Duxbury	98	8	Cushing	Joshua				1					1				2		
Duxbury	98	5	Cushing	Joshua Jun	1		1	1		3		1	1				8		
Pembroke	33	19	Cushing	Josiah		1		1				1	1	3			7		
Plymouth	10	16	Cushing	Mathew	1		1			1	1		1				5		
Scituate	126	5	Cushing	Nathan Honble		1		1			1	2	1	2			8		
Rochester	113	2	Cushing	Nathl	*	*	*	*	*	*	*	*	1	*			1		Tape mark
Scituate	119	24	Cushing	Nathl	4			1		1			1	1			9		
Pembroke	33	10	Cushing	Nathll	1	1	1	1				2	2	1			9		
Scituate	133	10	Cushing	Pickels		1		1				1	1	2	1		7		
Scituate	126	15	Cushing	Pickels Jun	2		2	1		1			1				7		
Hanover	132	4	Cushing	Ruth	1		1			1		2	1				6		
Kingston	29	51	Cushing	Seth	1			1		2			1				5		
Plimton	26	14	Cushing	Seth		1	1	1				3		1			7		
Scituate	121	14	Cushing	Thomas		1		1				1	1				6		
Pembroke	33	22	Cushing	Willm		1		1					1				3		
Scituate	126	7	Cushing	Willm Honble									1	1		5	7		
Abington	42	42	Cushing	Zattue	1		1			3	1		1				7		
Plimton	21	22	Cushman	Benjamin			1	1					2	1			5		
Rochester	112	1	Cushman	Cephas	2	2	3	1	1	2	2	3		1			17		
Middleborough	77	10	Cushman	David		1						1	1				3		
Plimton	22	14	Cushman	Deborah									1	1			2		
Kingston	30	3	Cushman	Ebenezer		2	2	1				1	2	1			9		
Middleborough	80	28	Cushman	Elias		1		1					1				3		
Middleborough	77	1	Cushman	Eliphalet	2	1						2		1			7		
Rochester	113	5	Cushman	Ezekiel	3		1	1		3			1				9		
Duxbury	100	2	Cushman	Ezra	1		1						1				3		
Duxbury	94	7	Cushman	George	1	1	1			4	1		1				9		
Middleborough	78	38	Cushman	Ichabod	2	0	1	1		2			1				7		
Middleborough	77	2	Cushman	Isaac				1				2	1				5		
Middleborough	77	3	Cushman	Isaac Jun	3	0	1						1				5		
Middleborough	80	24	Cushman	Jacob	1		1			2			1				5		
Kingston	29	18	Cushman	James	3		2	1		2			1				10		
Middleborough	77	20	Cushman	John		1						1	1				4		
Middleborough	80	23	Cushman	Joseph		1		1				2		1			5		
Middleborough	80	30	Cushman	Joseph 2d			1	1		1			2				5		
Duxbury	100	1	Cushman	Joshua		1		1						1			3		
Middleborough	80	25	Cushman	Noah	2		2	1		1		1	1				8		
Plimton	19	19	Cushman	Oliver	1		1			2			1				5		
Middleborough	78	34	Cushman	Robert		1	1	1		2	1	1	1				8		
Bridgewater	60	32	Cushman	Thomas	2			1				1		2			6		
Bridgewater	60	34	Cushman	William				1						1			2		
Plimton	22	15	Cushman	William	3		1	1					1	1			7		
Plimton	19	18	Cushman	Zacheriah		1			2	2	1	1					8		

TOWN	PG#	LN#	LAST NAME	FIRST NAME	FREE WHITE MALES					FREE WHITE FEMALES					TOTAL ALL OTHER	TOTAL SLAVES	TOTALS	DISTRICT/ TOWNSHIP	NOTES
					under 10	10 to 16	16 to 26	26 to 45	45 and over	under 10	10 to 16	16 to 26	26 to 45	45 and over					
Middleborough	77	4	Cushman	zebulon	1	1		1		1		1	1				6		
Middleborough	78	36	Cushman	Zenus		1	1		1	1			1				5		
Middleborough	79	16	Dagg	Peter			1					1					2		
Middleborough	79	15	Daggett	Jabez	1			1					1				3		
Middleborough	82	18	Daggett	Seth				1				1	1				3		
Middleborough	82	20	Daggett	Simeone				1					1				2		
Middleborough	82	21	Daggett	Thomas	1	1		1		1			1				5		
Bridgewater	60	10	Dailey	Lewis	1	1		1		2	2		1	1			9		
Bridgewater	49	3	Dale	Silence				1					1	1			3		
Scituate	135	50	Daman	Elizabeth	2	2	1	1					1				7		
Scituate	130	19	Daman	John		2		1				2	1				7		
Scituate	135	48	Daman	Josiah	2	1	1	1		2	1	1	1				10		
Scituate	121	19	Daman	Luther	1			1		1		1					4		
Scituate	134	43	Daman	Reuben	2	1	1	1		1	1	1	1				9		
Scituate	134	17	Daman	Silvanus		1	1	1	1	3	2		2				11		
Scituate	130	21	Daman	Stephen		1			2					1			4		
Abington	39	8	Dammond	Joseph				1					1				2		
Marshfield	100	13	Damon	Aruanah	1	1		1		2	1	1	1	1			9		
Scituate	126	10	Damon	Calvin	1	1	2	1		2	1	2	1				11		
Scituate	125	5	Damon	Edward Junr		1							1				2		
Scituate	130	5	Damon	Galin	3		1	1		1	1		1				8		
Scituate	133	2	Damon	Hannah		1						1		2	2		6		
Scituate	130	22	Damon	Isaac	1			1						3	1		6		
Scituate	127	13	Damon	Joshua	1	1		1		2	2	1	1				9		
Scituate	127	7	Damon	Juda										2			2		
Marshfield	100	14	Damon	Nathl	3			1		1	2		1				8		
Marshfield	100	12	Damon	Obediah				1				1		1			3		
Scituate	127	14	Damon	Simeon	1	1		1		3	2		1				9		
Scituate	133	1	Damon	Zadock	3	3		1				2		1			10		
Pembroke	36	13	Damond	Elijah				1					1				2		
Pembroke	36	14	Damond	Elijah Junr	4		1			1			1				7		
Bridgewater	60	39	Darling	Benjamin	1			1		1			1	1			5		
Middleborough	79	9	Darling	Benjn				1		1		2	1	1			6		
Middleborough	79	10	Darling	Daniel	1		1			2		1					5		
Middleborough	79	11	Darling	Nathan			1	1	1				1	1			5		
Plymouth	12	17	Darling	Polly										2			2		
Duxbury	99	4	Darling	Samuel	3	1		1		3		1					9		
Abington	41	19	Darte	Anthony											3		3		
Plymouth	16	22	Davie	Betsey						2			1				3		
Plymouth	5	7	Davie	Ebenezer	1			1					1				3		
Plymouth	12	13	Davie	Ichabod				1		2	1	1					5		
Plymouth	18	2	Davie	Robert	1			1		2	1	1					6		
Plymouth	5	6	Davie	Solomon	3	1			1	1	1						8		
Plymouth	15	5	Davie	William		1	1		1				1	1			5		
Plymouth	16	26	Davie	William Jr			1			1		1					3		
Rochester	112	22	Davis	Joseph	2			1		3		1	1				8		
Kingston	30	28	Davis	Martha	1	2	1			2				1			7		
Rochester	111	5	Davis	Nicholas	2		1	1		1	2	1		1			9		
Rochester	112	14	Davis	Timo	1	1	1	1		3	1		1				9		
Kingston	30	40	Davis	Timothy	1			1					1				3		
Plymouth	9	4	Davis	William		1	2	1					1	2			7		
Kingston	30	8	Dawes	Ebenezer		1			1	2	2	3		1			10		
Bridgewater	67	26	Dawes	Nathan		1			1	1		1	1				5		
Duxbury	91	12	Day	John			1			1		1					3		
Plimton	19	22	Dean	Ebenezer		1	1	1				1		1			6		
Bridgewater	49	40	Deane	Abiel	2	1		1		2	2			1			9		
Marshfield	101	3	Decro	Seth			1	1				1	1				4		
Duxbury	96	14	Delano	Asa	1			1		1			1				4		
Duxbury	104	16	Delano	Charles			1			3			1				5		
Duxbury	93	14	Delano	Cornelius		3		1						1			5		
Rochester	112	7	Delano	Harper		1	1	1		2	1			1			7		
Duxbury	104	14	Delano	Ichobud	1			1		6	2	1					11		
Duxbury	99	11	Delano	Isaac	1	1		1		3	2	1					9		
Rochester	112	9	Delano	Jabez	2	1	1		1	2	1			1			9		
Rochester	112	10	Delano	Jabez Jr	1		1						1				3		
Duxbury	93	21	Delano	Jepther	1			1		1	1	1	1	1			7		
Duxbury	101	6	Delano	John		1	2	1	1			1	2	1			9		
Pembroke	36	15	Delano	John	3			1		1			1				6		
Duxbury	96	12	Delano	Judah				1						2			3		
Duxbury	98	24	Delano	Luther				1						1			2		
Duxbury	93	15	Delano	Lydia									3	2			5		
Duxbury	96	10	Delano	Malachi				1						1			2		
Duxbury	98	22	Delano	Nathl	1	2		1		1			1	1			7		
Duxbury	96	15	Delano	Phillip	1		1	1		2	1		1				7		
Duxbury	104	21	Delano	Rheuben	1			1		2			1	1			6		
Duxbury	95	9	Delano	Samuel			1	1				2		1			6		
Duxbury	95	14	Delano	Samuel Jun	2		1	1		2		1	1				8		
Rochester	112	8	Delano	Stephen		2			1	3		1		1			8		
Duxbury	100	18	Delano	Sylv				1		1			1	1			4		
Pembroke	36	16	Delano	Willm				1			1			1			3		
Duxbury	102	3	Delano	Zenus	1	1		1		2		1					6		
Plymouth	5	1	Dellano	Avery	1			1		3			1				6		
Rochester	112	20	Dexter	Benjm			1		1				1	1			4		
Rochester	111	2	Dexter	Caleb		1			1		2		1				5		
Rochester	112	23	Dexter	David	3		1		1			1	2	1			9		
Rochester	111	3	Dexter	Ebenzr	1					1		1					4		
Rochester	112	26	Dexter	Edward				1		1		1					3		

TOWN	PG#	LN#	HEADS OF HOUSEHOLD LAST NAME	FIRST NAME	FWM under 10	FWM 10 to 16	FWM 16 to 26	FWM 26 to 45	FWM 45 and over	FWF under 10	FWF 10 to 16	FWF 16 to 26	FWF 26 to 45	FWF 45 and over	TOTAL ALL OTHER	TOTAL SLAVES	TOTALS	DISTRICT/ TOWNSHIP	NOTES
Rochester	112	15	Dexter	Elias			1			1			1				3		
Rochester	112	13	Dexter	Elijah	1		2		1	2	1	2		1			10		
Rochester	112	17	Dexter	Elisha	2			1		3	1		1				8		
Rochester	111	1	Dexter	Ephm		2		1		1	2	1		1			8		
Rochester	112	16	Dexter	Jabez			1							1			2		
Rochester	112	3	Dexter	John			1	1					2	1			5		
Rochester	112	2	Dexter	John Jr	1	1	1		1		1		1	1			7		
Rochester	112	19	Dexter	Noah	2		1	1		3			1	1			9		
Rochester	112	5	Dexter	Philip	1			1			1		1				4		
Rochester	112	24	Dexter	Reubin	1		1			1			1				4		
Rochester	112	18	Dexter	Sarah	1								2				3		
Rochester	112	25	Dexter	Sarah			1						3				4		
Rochester	112	4	Dexter	Thankfull							2		1				3		
Bridgewater	60	11	Dickerman	Manaseh	2	1			1	4		2					10		
Bridgewater	60	12	Dickerman	Samuel			1			1		1					3		
Plymouth	1	18	Dickson	John			1	1		1		1					4		
Plymouth	14	23	Dike	Anthony	1	2	2		1	5		1					12		
Bridgewater	60	7	Dill	James	3			1		2		1					7		
Kingston	27	12	Dillano	Joshua			1		1		1	2		1			6		
Rochester	112	21	Dillingham	David	2		1	1		3			1				8		
Plymouth	8	18	Diman	David	1	1		1	1	2	1		2	1			10		
Plymouth	8	20	Diman	Josiah	2		1	1		1		1		1			7		
Plymouth	7	18	Dinan	Rebecca							1	1	2				4		
Marshfield	93	1	Dingley	*	1			1		2			1				5		Tape Mark
Duxbury	91	27	Dingley	Abner	1				1				1	1			4		
Duxbury	91	28	Dingley	Abner Jun	2		1	1		1	2		1				8		
Duxbury	91	24	Dingley	J*				1						1			2		
Marshfield	98	9	Dingley	Jacob	2		1			2			1				6		
Marshfield	94	20	Dingley	Jebez			1	1			1		1				4		
Duxbury	91	25	Dingley	John	2			1		1			1				5		
Marshfield	104	19	Dingley	Thomas			1	2	1			2		1			7		
Scituate	135	34	Doane	John	1		1		1	1		1					5		
Bridgewater	60	41	Doggett	Mark	3		1				1	1					6		
Carver	9	23	Dolen	Ebenezer	2		1			3			1				7		
Carver	9	24	Dolen	Edward	1		1			1			1				4		
Plymouth	7	9	Dolen	Isaac			1	1					1	2			5		
Plymouth	7	21	Dolen	Jabez			1			1	1	1					4		
Carver	8	6	Dolen	Thomas			1	1		2				1			5		
Scituate	122	16	Donnell	Samuel	2		2		1			1	1				7		
Hanover	127	9	Dorman	Eills		1	1	1	1		1	1		1			7		
Hanover	127	10	Dorman	Ezra	2	1			1	2		1		1			8		
Hanover	129	7	Dorman	Leah							1		1				2		
Plymouth	5	12	Doten	Daniel			1	1		1			2				5		
Kingston	27	19	Doten	Jacob				1			1		1				3		
Plymouth	20	7	Doten	John	1			1		1			1				4		
Plymouth	15	21	Doten	Joseph	1		1			2			1				5		
Pembroke	36	19	Doten	Lemuel	2		1			1			1	1			6		
Plymouth	23	15	Doten	Lemuel	1	1	1		1	1			1	1			7		
Plymouth	15	25	Doten	Nathaniel			2		1				1				4		
Plymouth	20	6	Doten	Stephen		1			1	1			1	1			5		
Plymouth	20	5	Doten	Stephen Jr			1		1	4	3		1				10		
Plymouth	17	5	Doten	William	1	1		1		1	2	1		2			9		
Rochester	111	4	Doten	Zephh			1			1	1			1			4		
Plymouth	12	23	Dotten	James				1		1		2		1			5		
Plymouth	12	20	Dotten	John	1			1		1			1				4		
Middleborough	82	23	Doty	jacob	1			1		1			1				4		
Rochester	112	11	Doty	Jerahmeel	2	1		1		2	1		1	1			9		
Rochester	112	6	Doty	Joseph	1		3	1	1	1	1	1		1			10		
Rochester	112	12	Doty	Silas	3	1		1		1			1				7		
Plymouth	6	2	Douglas	John	1		1			3		1	1				7		
Plymouth	26	10	Douglas	John	4	1	2		1	1	1			1			11		
Middleborough	82	28	Downing	John	1		1					1					3		
Middleborough	82	26	Downing	Joseph				1					1				2		
Middleborough	82	27	Downing	Joshua		3	1	1		1		3		1			10		
Scituate	131	14	Downs	Ruth		1	1						2	1			5		
Middleborough	82	30	Drake	Abigail Wo									1				1		
Middleborough	82	19	Drake	William	3	1	1	1		1			1				8		
Kingston	30	43	Drew	Abijah	2	2			1	4		2	1				12		
Plymouth	1	12	Drew	Benjamin		2		1	1				1				5		
Plymouth	7	15	Drew	Benjamin Jr		2		1		2			1		1		7		
Duxbury	94	4	Drew	Charles	2			1		2	1		1				7		
Kingston	30	47	Drew	Cornelius		2	1			1	1		1				6		
Plymouth	10	19	Drew	David		3		1	1					1			6		
Kingston	30	46	Drew	Dorothy	1	1				1		2	1				6		
Duxbury	97	5	Drew	Isaac	4	1		2		3	2			1			15		
Kingston	30	44	Drew	James		1			1			1		1			4		
Plymouth	10	15	Drew	James	1			1				1	1				4		
Halifax	18	7	Drew	Job		2			1	1		1		1			6		
Duxbury	94	11	Drew	Joseph			1	1			1	1	1				5		
Kingston	29	10	Drew	Judah	1				1		1	1					4		
Plymouth	5	4	Drew	Lemuel	1	2	3				1		1	1			9		
Plymouth	5	20	Drew	Lemuel		1	1	1		2			3				8		
Kingston	30	29	Drew	Nehemiah				1		1	1	1					4		
Carver	12	14	Drew	Nicholas	1		1					1					3		
Duxbury	94	2	Drew	Reuben	2			1		1							6		

TOWN	PG#	LN#	LAST NAME	FIRST NAME	FREE WHITE MALES					FREE WHITE FEMALES					TOTAL ALL OTHER	TOTAL SLAVES	TOTALS	DISTRICT/ TOWNSHIP	NOTES
					under 10	10 to 16	16 to 26	26 to 45	45 and over	under 10	10 to 16	16 to 26	26 to 45	45 and over					
Kingston	30	7	Drew	Samuel		1			1	1				1			4		
Plymouth	18	20	Drew	Samuel	1	1			1	1		1		1			6		
Kingston	29	21	Drew	Seth		1	1				1	1		1			6		
Plymouth	3	19	Drew	Seth	1			1		2	1			1			6		
Kingston	30	48	Drew	Stephen			1	1		4		1	1				8		
Duxbury	94	3	Drew	Syls	1				1			3	1	1			7		
Halifax	15	18	Drew	Thomas	1	1	1		1			2		2			8		
Kingston	30	38	Drew	William	1		1	1		1	1	1					6		
Kingston	30	45	Drew	Zenas		1	1	1				3	1	1			8		
Middleborough	82	24	Duglass	David		1	1		1			3		1			7		
Middleborough	82	25	Duglass	David Jr Capt	1		1					1					3		
Middleborough	82	22	Duglass	Elisha	1				1	2			1				5		
Middleborough	79	12	Duglass	George	1	1		1		1			1				5		
Middleborough	79	13	Duglass	Noah	4			1		2			1				8		
Middleborough	82	29	Duglass	Prudence									1				1		
Bridgewater	49	1	Dunbar	Barnabas	4	2	2	1	1	4	2	1	1	1			19		
Scituate	136	29	Dunbar	David				2					1				3		
Bridgewater	60	15	Dunbar	Ebenezer	2	2		1		1			1				7		
Bridgewater	49	39	Dunbar	Eliab	2			1		1			1				5		
Bridgewater	60	38	Dunbar	Elias			5					1					6		
Bridgewater	60	13	Dunbar	Jacob				1					1				2		
Bridgewater	60	14	Dunbar	Jacob Junr				1		1	1		1				4		
Halifax	13	6	Dunbar	Jane			3				1			2			6		
Bridgewater	49	38	Dunbar	Jesse				1			2		1				4		
Scituate	136	33	Dunbar	Jesse	2			1		1		1	1				6		
Plymouth	14	28	Dunbar	John D	3		1	1		2			1				8		
Bridgewater	60	16	Dunbar	Lemuel	2			1		1			1				5		
Bridgewater	60	37	Dunbar	Peter	2	2			1	1		1		1			8		
Bridgewater	49	37	Dunbar	Samuel				1		3			1				5		
Middleborough	79	17	Dunbar	Samuel					2				1				3		
Bridgewater	49	2	Dunbar	Silas	2	1			1					1			5		
Bridgewater	50	43	Dunbar	Simeon	1	2	1		1			1		1			7		
Abington	39	7	Dunbar	Stephen				1	1					3			5		
Carver	12	19	Dunham	Caleb				1		2		1					4		
Abington	39	2	Dunham	Cornelus		2	1	1		1		1		2			8		
Carver	11	16	Dunham	Ebenezer	2			1		1	1	1					6		
Plymouth	18	18	Dunham	Elijah		1			1	2		1	1				6		
Plymouth	19	11	Dunham	George	3	2		1			1		1	1			9		
Plymouth	19	21	Dunham	Ichabod	1	1	1	1				1	1	1			7		
Carver	8	7	Dunham	Israel		1	1	1		1			1				5		
Carver	12	18	Dunham	John		1		1					1				3		
Plymouth	18	22	Dunham	John	1			1		3	1		1				7		
Middleborough	79	14	Dunham	Jonathan				1					1				2		
Middleborough	79	8	Dunham	Joseph	1			1		1			1				4		
Carver	12	20	Dunham	Mary		2		1		3			1	1			8		
Plymouth	8	3	Dunham	Robert			1		1	1	2			2			7		
Kingston	27	14	Dunham	Silas	1	2			1	3	3		1				11		
Halifax	15	9	Dunham	William					1					1			2		
Plymouth	18	13	Dunham	William	2			1		1	1		2	1			8		
Pembroke	36	21	Dunster	Hannah								2	3				5		
Plymouth	16	17	Durfey	Richard	1			1	1	2			1	1			7		
Pembroke	36	18	Dwella	Benjn			1			4	1		1				7		
Pembroke	36	20	Dwella	Jedadiah		1		1			1		1	1			5		
Pembroke	36	17	Dwella	Nathan	1			1		2			2				6		
Scituate	135	12	Dweller	Sally									1	1			2		
Hanover	125	18	Dwelley	Aaron	1			1				1					3		
Hanover	128	11	Dwelley	Joshua	1			1		2		1					5		
Hanover	128	13	Dwelley	Lemuel	1			2				1	1	1			6		
Hanover	125	26	Dwelley	Melzar	2			1		1		1					5		
Abington	39	3	Dyer	Bela	1	1	1	1		2	1	2	1	1			11		
Abington	39	1	Dyer	Christopher	1	1		1		3	1		1				8		
Abington	39	4	Dyer	Jacob			1	1						1			3		
Abington	39	5	Dyer	Jacob Jun			1					1					2		
Abington	39	6	Dyer	James		1	1		1		1	1		1			6		
Bridgewater	60	40	Dyer	Jason		1	1					1	2	2			7		
Bridgewater	60	42	Dyer	John		1	1		1	1	1		1	1	1		7		
Bridgewater	60	8	Dyke	Samuel		1		1					1	1			4		
Bridgewater	60	9	Dyke	Samuel Junr	1	2			1			3	2				9		
Marshfield	102	1	Eames	Amos	1	1			1	1		1		1			6		
Duxbury	91	6	Eames	Benjamin	3	1	1		1	1	1	1		1			10		
Bridgewater	60	18	Eames	Elisha		1		1		1			1				4		
Marshfield	104	12	Eames	Hannah										1			1		
Duxbury	103	23	Eames	Isaac	2			1					1				4		
Marshfield	100	15	Eames	Jedediah			1							2			3		
Marshfield	100	16	Eames	John J.	1			1		3			1				6		
Bridgewater	60	17	Eames	Josiah		1			1					1			3		
Marshfield	93	14	Eames	Rebeckah	1								1				2		
Duxbury	91	23	Eames	Wm															Tape Mark
Middleborough	84	24	Easton	Caesor											3		3		
Kingston	28	20	Eaton	Benjamin				1					1				2		
Middleborough	81	16	Eaton	Elijah		1			1				1				3		
Middleborough	81	3	Eaton	Enos				1		1			1				3		
Middleborough	82	34	Eaton	Israel	2	2		1			1		1				7		
Middleborough	81	5	Eaton	Jabez		3			1	1			1				6		
Kingston	30	10	Eaton	Job					1					1			2		
Middleborough	81	4	Eaton	Joel Capt			2		1		1	1		1			6		

TOWN	PG#	LN#	LAST NAME	FIRST NAME	FREE WHITE MALES under 10	10 to 16	16 to 26	26 to 45	45 and over	FREE WHITE FEMALES under 10	10 to 16	16 to 26	26 to 45	45 and over	TOTAL ALL OTHER	TOTAL SLAVES	TOTALS	DISTRICT/TOWNSHIP	NOTES
Middleborough	82	31	Eaton	Joseph					1					1			2		
Kingston	30	11	Eaton	Lot					2		1		1	1			5		
Middleborough	81	1	Eaton	Nathan	1	1	1		1		3	2		1			10		
Middleborough	81	2	Eaton	Samuel			1		1					1			3		
Middleborough	82	33	Eaton	Seth	1			1		1			1				4		
Middleborough	82	32	Eaton	Solomon	1			1		1				1			4		
Bridgewater	59	1	Eddy	Azor		1		1						1			3		
Middleborough	81	10	Eddy	Joshua Capt	2	2	5		1	1	1	2		1			15		
Wareham	110	24	Eddy	Kezia	1			1	1	1	1		1				6		
Middleborough	81	8	Eddy	Keziah Wo										1			1		
Middleborough	81	11	Eddy	Marcy Wo		1								1			2		
Middleborough	81	12	Eddy	Seth	2			1		1	1			1			6		
Middleborough	81	17	Eddy	Susanna									2				2		
Middleborough	81	13	Edminster	Kenney	2	1		1					1	1			6		
Middleborough	81	14	Edson	Abiel	2	2	1		1				1	1			8		
Bridgewater	60	43	Edson	Benjamin	3				1				1	1			6		
Bridgewater	60	44	Edson	Cyrus			1			2			1				4		
Bridgewater	57	23	Edson	David		2		1		4			1	1	1		10		
Bridgewater	57	24	Edson	Ebenezer				1					1				2		
Bridgewater	60	19	Edson	Ichabod		1		1					1	1			4		
Bridgewater	60	22	Edson	James				1					1				2		
Bridgewater	67	27	Edson	Joel	2	2	1	1	1				3	1			11		
Bridgewater	60	23	Edson	Josiah		1			1	2		1	3	1			9		
Bridgewater	49	7	Edson	Liberas	2	1		1		1			1	1			7		
Bridgewater	49	41	Edson	Lucy			1	1		2	1	1					6		
Bridgewater	57	25	Edson	Martha									1	1			2		
Bridgewater	49	9	Edson	Mary		1				1				1			3		
Bridgewater	49	6	Edson	Noah	4	2		1		1			1				9		
Bridgewater	49	8	Edson	Rebecca									2				2		
Bridgewater	49	4	Edson	Samuel				1					1				2		
Bridgewater	49	5	Edson	Samuel Jun		2		1				2		1			6		
Bridgewater	60	21	Edson	Seth	2	1		1		3	1		1		1		10		
Bridgewater	60	20	Edson	William	1	1		1		3			1				7		
Wareham	110	23	Edwards	John	1		1					1					3		
Rochester	111	9	Edwards	Joseph	1	1		1		1		2		1			7		
Hanover	132	9	Eells	Ruth		1	4	1						2			8		
Hanover	132	15	Eells	William				1		1		1		1			5		
Abington	39	9	Elkins	Robert	2	3		1		1			1				8		
Plymouth	24	9	Ellis	Barnabas	1		1		1	1		1		1			6		
Hanover	130	16	Ellis	Clark	1	1	1		1			1	1				6		
Middleborough	81	6	Ellis	Cornelius		2		1			1			1			5		
Wareham	110	25	Ellis	Danl	2			1		3	1			1			8		
Bridgewater	49	42	Ellis	Ebenezer	2	1	2		1		1	1		1			9		
Plymouth	24	11	Ellis	Francis	1		1					1					3		
Plymouth	24	24	Ellis	George	2	1		1		2	1			1			9		
Plymouth	24	7	Ellis	Jerusha		1	1					1		1			4		
Plimton	22	6	Ellis	Joel		1		1						1			3		
Rochester	111	8	Ellis	Joel	2			1	1	3			1	1			9		
Rochester	111	11	Ellis	Joel Junr	2	1			1	1		1		1			7		
Carver	8	18	Ellis	Joseph			2	1	1			2		1			7		
Middleborough	81	9	Ellis	Lucia Wo										1			1		
Rochester	111	7	Ellis	Malachi	2	1	1		1	1		2		1			9		
Hanover	130	13	Ellis	Mordecai	1	1	1	2	1	1			1	1			9		
Hanover	130	17	Ellis	Mordecai Junr	2			1		2	1	3		1			10		
Plymouth	12	11	Ellis	Nathaniel	3		1			2	1		1				8		
Plymouth	24	14	Ellis	Reuben	1		1						1				3		
Plimton	21	4	Ellis	Samuel		1						1					2		
Middleborough	81	15	Ellis	Southworth	1		1			1			1				4		
Plimton	22	7	Ellis	Stephen		3		1		1	1		1				7		
Rochester	111	6	Ellis	Thomas		1		1		2	1	1	1				7		
Plimton	22	9	Ellis	Willard	3	1		1		1			1	1			8		
Plymouth	24	8	Ellis	William	3		1			1			1				6		
Scituate	133	41	Elmes	Ebenezer W.	2		1			4	1		1				9		
Middleborough	84	23	Elmes	Eliphalet	1	1	1		1	1	2	2	1	1			11		
Middleborough	84	22	Elmes	Elkanah				1									1		
Middleborough	81	7	Elmes	John				1		1			1				3		
Scituate	129	14	Elmes	Joseph	1	1		1	1	3			1	1			9		
Middleborough	81	19	Elmes	Lydia Wo					1					1			1		
Scituate	136	6	Elmes	Robert		1	1	2	1				1	2			8		
Scituate	129	11	Elmes	Samuel	1					2		1					5		
Rochester	111	10	Elmes	Walter	2			1		1	1		1				6		
Scituate	126	3	Esllo	Nathaniel	1			1					1				3		
Scituate	130	7	Esllo	Nathl Junr			2						1				3		
Hanover	125	1	Estes	Benjamin		1	1			1		1					4		
Hanover	129	22	Estes	Joseph			1			1		1					3		
Hanover	130	1	Estes	Mary	1	1	1				2		1				6		
Hanover	128	25	Estes	Robert				1				1	1	1	1		4		
Hanover	129	25	Estes	Zaccheus	5	2		1				1					10		
Hanover	128	24	Estes	Zilpah				1				1	1	1	1		4		
Bridgewater	49	20	Evan	Thomas											10		10		
Middleborough	81	18	Evens	Leonard	1	1	1		1	1			2				7		
Wareham	110	22	Everet	Noble	2	2			1	2	2	1	1				11		
Kingston	30	9	Everson	Ebenezer		1	1		1	2	1	1	1	1			9		
Plymouth	12	12	Everson	Ephraim				1		2			1				4		
Pembroke	35	1	Everson	Eunice	2	1	1			3	1	1	1				10		

TOWN	PG#	LN#	LAST NAME	FIRST NAME	FREE WHITE MALES					FREE WHITE FEMALES					TOTAL ALL OTHER	TOTAL SLAVES	TOTALS	DISTRICT/ TOWNSHIP	NOTES
					under 10	10 to 16	16 to 26	26 to 45	45 and over	under 10	10 to 16	16 to 26	26 to 45	45 and over					
Kingston	30	12	Everson	Joseph			1	1		2		1	1				6		
Plimton	26	8	Everson	Joseph	2			1					1				4		
Kingston	30	13	Everson	Samuel			1						1				2		
Kingston	30	14	Everson	Seth	1			1		2	1	2	1	2			10		
Kingston	30	41	Everson	Silvanus			2		1	2	1			1			7		
Marshfield	97	21	Ewel	Christopher	1			1		1			1				4		
Marshfield	104	8	Ewel	Christopher	1			1		1			1				4		
Marshfield	101	18	Ewel	Gershom			1		1		1			1			4		
Marshfield	99	9	Ewel	James	2			1		3			1				7		
Marshfield	97	14	Ewel	Jedediah	1				1			1	1	2			6		
Marshfield	99	8	Ewel	Job		2	2		1	2	2			1			10		
Marshfield	97	19	Ewel	Joseph	1	1		1		1		1	1				6		
Marshfield	97	15	Ewel	Seth				1			1			1			3		
Scituate	119	17	Ewell	Gershom		1		1		2	1	2		1			8		
Scituate	121	17	Ewell	John		1				2			1				4		
Abington	39	18	Farer	Benja				1						1			2		
Plymouth	13	11	Farmer	Thomas	2			1		3			1				7		
Scituate	128	9	Farrow	Abiel	4	1		1	1	1	1		1				10		
Plymouth	16	23	Faunce	Barnabas			1						1				3		
Kingston	30	17	Faunce	Benjamin	1			1		1			1				4		
Carver	7	5	Faunce	Daniel			2		1			2		1			6		
Kingston	28	17	Faunce	Eleazer			2		1	1	1		1				6		
Kingston	30	24	Faunce	Elijah	1	2		1		1			1	1			7		
Plymouth	18	10	Faunce	Hannah	2					1		2	2	1			8		
Middleborough	84	32	Faunce	Hannah Wo			1	1						1			3		
Kingston	30	15	Faunce	John	1			1	2		1	1	2	3			11		
Kingston	30	16	Faunce	Lydia			1						1	1			3		
Duxbury	100	21	Faunce	Susanna		1	1						1	1			4		
Plymouth	3	13	Faunce	Thaddeus	1	2		1		2			1	1			8		
Plymouth	10	27	Faunce	Thomas				1						3			4		
Kingston	28	22	Faunce	Tilden			1						1				2		
Abington	39	11	Faxon	Elisha	1		1	1		1		1	1				6		
Halifax	18	8	Faxon	elisha	2				1	1	2	2		2			10		
Bridgewater	67	29	Faxon	Samuel	1	1		1		1	2		1	1			8		
Wareham	111	2	Fearing	Benjm	2	1	3		1	3	1		1	1	1		14		
Wareham	111	1	Fearing	David		1	1	1		3	1	1	1		1		10		
Wareham	111	3	Fearing	Israel		2		1		1		1		1	1		7		
Wareham	111	4	Fearing	Israel Jr		1			1	1	1	1	1	1			7		
Wareham	110	26	Fearing	John	1		1	1		2		1	2	1			9		
Wareham	110	27	Fearing	Moses	1	1		1		1	1	1	1				7		
Bridgewater	59	8	Fearing	Noah				1		1	2	1					5		
Wareham	111	5	Fearing	Wm	1			1					1				3		
Bridgewater	57	30	Field	Barzillai	1			2		1			1				6		
Bridgewater	57	35	Field	Daniel	1	1		1		1							4		
Bridgewater	57	29	Field	Jabez					2		1		1	1			5		
Bridgewater	57	27	Field	Richard			1		1	2	2	2	1				9		
Bridgewater	57	28	Field	William	2			1		1			1				5		
Middleborough	83	3	Filammon	John	1			1		2			1				5		
Bridgewater	49	13	Fillebrown	James	2	2		1		2		1	1				9		
Plimton	24	4	Finney	Barnabas	1			1					1				3		
Plymouth	20	11	Finney	Caleb				3				1		2			6		
Plymouth	17	19	Finney	Clarke				1		2		2	1				6		
Plymouth	15	9	Finney	Daniel			1			3		1					5		
Middleborough	84	31	Finney	Ebenezer				1		2			1				4		
Plymouth	17	20	Finney	Elizabeth		1	1				1	1	1				5		
Plymouth	20	2	Finney	Elkanah	1			1					1				3		
Plymouth	13	6	Finney	Ezra			1				1		1				3		
Plymouth	17	18	Finney	George				1		1			1				3		
Plimton	24	3	Finney	Ichabod					1					1			2		
Plymouth	17	24	Finney	John			1		1	1	1			1			5		
Plymouth	7	22	Finney	Josiah	1		1	1		2	1	2	1				9		
Middleborough	83	1	Finney	Lewis				1		3		1					5		
Plymouth	17	22	Finney	Lydia		1					1		1	1			4		
Plymouth	17	26	Finney	Robert				1		3			1				5		
Plymouth	13	10	Finney	Seth	1		1						1				3		
Plymouth	20	13	Finney	Solomon	1			1					1				3		
Duxbury	103	13	Fish	Adam	2	1	2		1	2	1	1	1				11		
Pembroke	35	15	Fish	Caleb				1						1			2		
Pembroke	35	16	Fish	Elnathan				1					1	1			3		
Pembroke	35	19	Fish	Hannah			1						1	2			4		
Pembroke	35	17	Fish	Isaac		2		1		2			1				6		
Kingston	30	18	Fish	Jacob	2	2	2			1	1	1					11		
Kingston	30	19	Fish	Nathaniel	2	1		1				3	1				8		
Marshfield	93	13	Fish	Thomas		1		1					2	2			6		
Pembroke	35	18	Fish	Thos	1		1	1		1	2		1				7		
Pembroke	35	14	Fish	Zacheus			1							2			4		
Scituate	135	22	Fish	Ziba							1			1			2		
Plymouth	9	15	Fitzgerald	John	1			1					1				3		
Bridgewater	57	34	Flinn	Thomas				1	1					1			3		
Bridgewater	59	4	Fobes	Alpheus	3	1	2	1		1	1		1	2			12		
Bridgewater	50	5	Fobes	Avery		1		1						1			3		
Bridgewater	59	7	Fobes	Caleb			1			1		1					3		
Bridgewater	50	4	Fobes	Daniel	1		1		1		1	1		1			6		
Bridgewater	59	5	Fobes	Ephraim				1						1			2		
Bridgewater	59	6	Fobes	Ephraim Junr			1	1						2			4		

TOWN	PG#	LN#	LAST NAME	FIRST NAME	FWM under 10	FWM 10 to 16	FWM 16 to 26	FWM 26 to 45	FWM 45 and over	FWF under 10	FWF 10 to 16	FWF 16 to 26	FWF 26 to 45	FWF 45 and over	TOTAL ALL OTHER	TOTAL SLAVES	TOTALS	DISTRICT/TOWNSHIP	NOTES
Bridgewater	59	3	Fobes	Ezra		2		1		3	1	3	1				12		
Bridgewater	59	2	Fobes	Jason		1	1	1		1	1			1			6		
Bridgewater	50	2	Fobes	Joshua				1		1				1			3		
Bridgewater	50	3	Fobes	Robert		1	2	1		1				1			6		
Bridgewater	50	1	Fobes	Solomon	2			1		1			1	1			6		
Bridgewater	49	11	Fobes	Timothy			1		1				1	1			4		
Bridgewater	49	12	Fobes	William				1		1	1	1		1			5		
Duxbury	101	13	Foord	Joseph	1		1			1			1				4		
Marshfield	103	5	Foord	Olive	1	1	1			1	1			1			6		
Marshfield	95	12	Foorde	Aruanah			2						2	1			5		
Marshfield	96	5	Foorde	Elisha Jun	3			1		2	2		1				9		
Marshfield	96	15	Foorde	John	2			1		2			1				6		
Marshfield	95	8	Foorde	Lemuel			1	1				2	1				5		
Marshfield	95	9	Foorde	Malboro	2			1					1				4		
Marshfield	96	6	Foorde	Samuel	1		1					1	1				5		
Marshfield	95	6	Foorde	Seth				1					1				2		
Marshfield	95	7	Foorde	Waterman		1		1					1				3		
Pembroke	35	3	Ford	Adam			1		1			1	2	1			6		
Abington	39	15	Ford	David	1		1			2			1				5		
Pembroke	35	11	Ford	Henry	2		1					1					4		
Abington	39	12	Ford	Jacob		3		1			1	3		1			9		
Pembroke	35	10	Ford	James	1		1			1		2	1				6		
Pembroke	35	13	Ford	John		1	1	1			1		1				5		
Abington	39	13	Ford	Jonathan			1					1					2		
Pembroke	35	21	Ford	Lot				1			1	1					3		
Abington	39	14	Ford	Lydia			1			1			1				3		
Bridgewater	57	33	Ford	Mark			1	1		1		1		1			5		
Scituate	122	9	Ford	Micah		2		1				3	1				7		
Abington	39	16	Ford	Noah	1		1	1		2	1	1					7		
Bridgewater	49	10	Ford	Prince	2	1			2	1			2	1			9		
Pembroke	35	7	Ford	Thos				1					2				3		
Pembroke	35	20	Ford	Wait			1	1			2	1	1				6		
Pembroke	35	4	Ford	Willm	1	2	1			3		2	1				10		
Marshfield	104	9	Forde	Asa	1		1				1						3		
Marshfield	96	14	Forde	Elisha	1	1		1					2				5		
Duxbury	103	26	Forde	Joshua	2	2		1		2			1				8		
Marshfield	104	11	Forde	Levi		1	1	1			1		1				5		
Halifax	15	5	Forrest	Asaph	1		1	1		2		1		2			8		
Kingston	29	23	Foster	Charles	1			1				1	1				4		
Plymouth	19	20	Foster	Daniel	2		1			3			1				6		
Pembroke	35	9	Foster	David				1				1	1				3		
Kingston	30	20	Foster	Elizabeth		1							1				2		
Scituate	122	21	Foster	Freeman	1		1					1					3		
Middleborough	84	27	Foster	Gershom	1	1	1	1		3	2		1				10		
Rochester	111	15	Foster	James	2		1	1		1	1		1	1			8		
Rochester	111	14	Foster	James Junr	1	1	1	1					1		1		6		
Scituate	127	19	Foster	John		1	1	1				2					5		
Pembroke	35	12	Foster	Lemuel			1					1	1				3		
Pembroke	35	6	Foster	Micah		3		1		1		1	1	1			8		
Pembroke	35	5	Foster	Micah Jun	2	3				1			1	1			8		
Kingston	28	23	Foster	Nathaniel	1		1						1				3		
Middleborough	84	30	Foster	Peter	1		1			2			1		1		6		
Bridgewater	67	33	Foster	Samuel	1		1	1		2			1				6		
Scituate	123	23	Foster	Samuel	3			1		1		1	1				7		
Middleborough	84	29	Foster	Thomas				1				1	1				3		
Middleborough	83	2	Foster	William			1			1		1					3		
Scituate	125	21	Frane	Bethiah									1				1		
Duxbury	93	18	Frazer	Samuel	2		2	1		2	1		1				9		
Hanover	128	6	Freeman	Asher Negro											4		4		
Middleborough	84	38	Freeman	Benjan	3	1		1		1	1		1				8		
Duxbury	100	13	Freeman	Benjm		1	3		1			2		1			8		
Middleborough	84	34	Freeman	Elisha			1				1	1	1				5		
Middleborough	84	35	Freeman	Elisha 2d			1						1				2		
Duxbury	95	10	Freeman	Enoch			2	1				2		1			6		
Duxbury	104	23	Freeman	Joseph	1	1	1					1	2	1			8		
Scituate	126	22	Freeman	Lemuel Negro											5		5		
Middleborough	84	36	Freeman	Martin	1		1			2			1				5		
Middleborough	84	37	Freeman	Nathan	3		1	1					1				6		
Scituate	130	3	Freeman	Prince Negro											4		4		
Plymouth	14	6	Freeman	Samuel				1					1				2		
Duxbury	95	20	Freeman	Wm	2		2	1		1				1			7		
Duxbury	99	5	Freman	Edmond		1	1	1	1			2		1			7		
Bridgewater	59	9	French	Asa	1		1			1			1				4		
Abington	39	10	French	Barnabas	1		1			3	2		1	1			9		
Bridgewater	67	32	French	Daniel	1		1			1			1				4		
Bridgewater	67	30	French	David	1	2				1		1					5		
Bridgewater	57	32	French	Dependence	2		1			1		1	1				6		
Bridgewater	57	31	French	Levi	1		1						1				3		
Bridgewater	67	31	French	Silas		1	1				1		1				4		
Bridgewater	57	26	French	William			1	1			1	1		1			5		
Duxbury	102	12	Frost	Isaac	1			1		1			1				4		
Abington	39	17	Fulerton	John	1			1	1			1	2	1			7		
Bridgewater	67	28	Fullarton	Asa		2	1	1					1				5		
Kingston	30	22	Fuller	Consider	1			1		3			1				6		
Halifax	16	19	Fuller	Ephraim		2		1					3				6		
Middleborough	84	28	Fuller	Gamalel	1			1		3	1		1	1			8		
Bridgewater	49	26	Fuller	Isaiah											2		2		

96

			HEADS OF HOUSEHOLD		FREE WHITE MALES					FREE WHITE FEMALES					TOTAL ALL OTHER	TOTAL SLAVES	TOTALS	DISTRICT/ TOWNSHIP	NOTES
TOWN	PG#	LN#	LAST NAME	FIRST NAME	under 10	10 to 16	16 to 26	26 to 45	45 and over	under 10	10 to 16	16 to 26	26 to 45	45 and over					
Carver	7	11	Fuller	Isechar		1			1	2	2			1			7		
Rochester	111	13	Fuller	Israel	1	1	1		1	2	1	1		1			9		
Kingston	30	23	Fuller	Jabez		1			1	2	2	1	1				8		
Bridgewater	57	36	Fuller	Jacob		1					1	1					3		
Kingston	27	7	Fuller	James				1		1		1					3		
Kingston	27	8	Fuller	John		1		1		1			1				4		
Middleborough	84	25	Fuller	John	3				1	1	1	2	1				9		
Middleborough	84	33	Fuller	Jonatha Dr	1	2			1	1				1			6		
Kingston	27	10	Fuller	Josiah		1			1					1			3		
Middleborough	84	26	Fuller	Noah					1	3	2			2			8		
Plimton	19	16	Fuller	Philamon	3	3	1	1					1	1			10		
Halifax	13	18	Fuller	Samuel	2	1			1	2	1		1				8		
Rochester	111	28	Fuller	Seth	1			1		4	1		1				8		
Pembroke	35	8	Fuller	Seth				1			1		1				3		
Halifax	17	8	Fuller	Thomas		1	3		1	1	1	1					8		
Rochester	111	12	Fuller	Zeba	2			1		3	1		1				8		
Kingston	27	3	Fuller	Zepheniah	1	1		1					1				4		
Bridgewater	57	41	Gage	Thomas	1	1		1			1	1					5		
Plymouth	10	11	Gale	Noah	4	3		1					2				10		
Scituate	125	19	Gammett	Seth	3			1		2			1				7		
Plymouth	24	2	Gammons	Benjamin			1		1	1	1			1			5		
Middleborough	83	7	Gammons	John		1	1		1		1	1		1			6		
Middleborough	83	8	Gammons	John Jr		1		1			1	1		1			5		
Rochester	111	20	Gammons	Leml	3		1			1			1				6		
Middleborough	83	5	Gammons	Southworth	2			1		1			1				5		
Bridgewater	67	35	Gannett	Joseph	2	1		2		2	1		1				9		
Scituate	131	12	Gannett	Samuel	1			1					1				3		
Bridgewater	67	34	Gannett	Simeon		1	1		1	1	2	1	1	1			9		
Plimton	26	21	Gannett	Thomas				1					1				2		
Abington	40	16	Gardner	Benjm				1				1	1				3		
Abington	40	14	Gardner	Caleb	3			1		3			1				8		
Scituate	128	20	Gardner	David				1					1				2		
Scituate	128	16	Gardner	Elizabeth						1	1		1				3		
Bridgewater	67	37	Gardner	John	1			1		1	1		1				5		
Abington	40	18	Gardner	Noah	1			1		5			1				8		
Pembroke	38	4	Gardner	Ruth			1			1	1		1				4		
Hanover	127	19	Gardner	Seth	1			1					1				3		
Pembroke	38	5	Gardner	Thos				1			1	1	1				4		
Pembroke	38	3	Gardner	Thos Jun	1	1		1		3			1				7		
Wareham	111	7	Gibbs	Abrm	1		1	1		1			1				5		
Wareham	111	10	Gibbs	Chloe	2	1				1	2	1					7		
Middleborough	83	6	Gibbs	Elisha		1		1		3			1				6		
Wareham	111	8	Gibbs	John		1		1	1	1			1				5		
Wareham	111	9	Gibbs	John Jr	2	1	2		1	1	1		2				10		
Wareham	111	11	Gibbs	Jonan	3		1		1	1	2	2		1			11		
Wareham	111	12	Gibbs	Joseph	1	1		1		2	1		1				7		
Wareham	111	6	Gibbs	Joshua	3	3		1		1	1		1				10		
Rochester	111	22	Gibbs	Thankful			1			2	1						4		
Middleborough	83	4	Gisban	Deborah Wo									1				1		
Duxbury	98	14	Glass	Ezekiel	2			1	1				1				5		
Duxbury	96	3	Glass	James	1		2		1	1			1				6		
Duxbury	95	7	Glass	Nathl	1			1				1					3		
Duxbury	95	6	Glass	Suraiah	1	2	1		1	1	1	2		1			10		
Duxbury	101	1	Glover	James	2			1					1				4		
Pembroke	38	7	Glover	James	1	1		1				1		1			5		
Abington	40	15	Gloyd	Cloe									2				2		
Abington	40	12	Gloyd	David	2		2	2		2			1				9		
Plymouth	8	11	Goddard	Benjamin			1			3			1				5		
Plymouth	16	19	Goddard	Daniel	2		1						1				4		
Pembroke	38	6	Gooden	Ameziah	3			1		1		2	1	1			9		
Duxbury	104	22	Goodwin	Job	1			1				1	1				4		
Plymouth	9	3	Goodwin	Nathaniel		1			1		2	1		2	1		8		
Plymouth	8	7	Goodwin	Thomas	1	1	1		1	2		2		1			9		
Plymouth	6	8	Goodwin	Timothy		1	1		1	1	1	1	1				7		
Halifax	15	10	Goodwin	William	1	1		1					1				4		
Plymouth	6	7	Goodwin	William	1	2	1	1		2			1		1		9		
Abington	41	20	Goold	B*i											5		5		
Rochester	111	21	Gorham	Jabez	2		1	1		3	1		1				9		
Pembroke	38	2	Gould	Willm	1			1		1		2	1				6		
Scituate	133	9	Grandison	Cuff Negro											3		3		
Marshfield	103	1	Gray	Frances				1				1	2				4		
Hanover	128	7	Gray	James	2			1		2	1		1				7		
Kingston	27	2	Gray	John		1			1		1		1	1			5		
Halifax	13	21	Gray	Samuel				1			1			1			3		
Hanover	127	22	Gray	Sarah										2			2		
Carver	12	4	Gready	Martin				1					1				2		
Abington	40	13	Green	Rachel									1				1		
Bridgewater	55	13	Green	Robert											2		2		
Rochester	111	23	Greene	Bars	3			1		1		1	1				7		
Plymouth	16	21	Greene	John	1			1					1				3		
Rochester	111	24	Greene	Richard	1			1		1		1	1				5		
Bridgewater	50	6	Greene	Robert	1	2		1						1			5		
Carver	8	3	Griffith	Ephraim	1					1		1					4		
Carver	8	4	Griffith	Obia	1		1			2		1					5		
Scituate	128	23	Gross	Elijah			1					1					2		

97

TOWN	PG#	LN#	LAST NAME	FIRST NAME	M<10	M 10-16	M 16-26	M 26-45	M 45+	F<10	F 10-16	F 16-26	F 26-45	F 45+	TOTAL ALL OTHER	TOTAL SLAVES	TOTALS	DISTRICT/ TOWNSHIP	NOTES
Hanover	123	2	Gross	Peakes	1			1					1				3		
Hanover	130	11	Gross	Zilpha										2			2		
Bridgewater	57	38	Groves	Ephraim	1							1	1	1			4		
Duxbury	102	9	Gulver	Peleg		1	1		1	2	1	1	1				8		
Pembroke	44	21	Gundery	Richard											6		6		
Abington	39	20	Gurney	Asa			1	1		1	1		1				5		
Rochester	111	17	Gurney	Benjm		1	1	1		2	1	1	1				8		
Abington	40	2	Gurney	Daniel	1			1		1			1				4		
Bridgewater	49	14	Gurney	David	3			1		2		1	1				8		
Middleborough	83	9	Gurney	David Revd		1		1			1	1	1				5		
Pembroke	38	1	Gurney	Elijah				1					1				2		
Wareham	111	13	Gurney	George	1	1		1		2	1		1				7		
Abington	40	8	Gurney	Gideon				1					1				2		
Abington	40	11	Gurney	Jacob			1	1	1	2	1	2		1			9		
Abington	39	21	Gurney	Jeremiah	1			1		1			1				4		
Abington	39	19	Gurney	John	1	2		1		2	1	3		1			11		
Abington	40	6	Gurney	Joseph				1					1				2		
Abington	40	4	Gurney	Joseph Junr		1		1		1	1		1				5		
Rochester	111	18	Gurney	Leml			1		1		1			1			4		
Rochester	111	19	Gurney	Leml Jr			1			1		1					3		
Rochester	111	16	Gurney	Levi			1			1		1		1			4		
Bridgewater	57	37	Gurney	Mehitabel	2							1		1			4		
Abington	40	3	Gurney	Nathan		1		1					1				3		
Abington	40	17	Gurney	Nathan Jr		2	2			2			1		1		8		
Abington	40	10	Gurney	Noah				1			1		1				3		
Abington	40	1	Gurney	Noah Junr	3			1		2			1				7		
Abington	39	22	Gurney	P. Joseph	2			1			1		1	1			6		
Abington	40	9	Gurney	Saml	1		1	1	1	2			1				8		
Bridgewater	67	36	Gurney	Seth	3	1		1		1	1		1	1			9		
Abington	40	5	Gurney	Thos Jrn	1	1		1		3			1				7		
Abington	40	7	Gurney	Zachary				1		2			1				4		
Bridgewater	57	39	Gurney	Zechariah				1					1				2		
Bridgewater	57	40	Gurney	Zechariah Junr	3	2		1		2	2		1				11		
Kingston	27	6	Hacher	Betsey	1						1			1			3		
Plymouth	18	1	Hackel	Zadoch	1			1		2			1				5		
Middleborough	85	16	Hackett	Elijah	1			1	1			1	1				5		
Middleborough	85	17	Hackett	George	1	1		1		1			1				5		
Middleborough	85	11	Hackett	Peleg	1			1		1	1	1					5		
Middleborough	88	27	Haksins	Job	1			1		1			1				4		
Kingston	27	41	Half	Elisha	2	2	1		1	1	1	2	1				11		
Duxbury	91	2	Hall	*	1			1	1	1	1		1	1			6		Tape Mark
Plimton	26	1	Hall	Abner	2			1		1			1				5		
Duxbury	91	15	Hall	Adam			1	1					3	1			6		
Plymouth	9	9	Hall	Asa	2			1		1		1					5		
Pembroke	37	14	Hall	Bailey			4	1		2	1		1				9		
Marshfield	97	20	Hall	Danforth	2			1		1			1				5		
Duxbury	100	9	Hall	Daniel	1	1		1				1					4		
Rochester	108	1	Hall	George	3			1		1			1				6		
Halifax	17	4	Hall	Jabez		1		1			1		1				4		
Middleborough	88	22	Hall	James		1	1		1	2			1				7		
Marshfield	102	3	Hall	Jane									1				1		
Pembroke	37	13	Hall	Jeremiah				1					1	1			3		
Pembroke	37	4	Hall	Job	1			1		1			1				4		
Middleborough	88	21	Hall	John			1	1		2			1				5		
Rochester	110	25	Hall	John			1		1	1			1				4		
Middleborough	85	13	Hall	Jonathan	3	1		1		1			1				7		
Duxbury	100	11	Hall	Joshua	2		1	1		1			1				6		
Marshfield	104	6	Hall	Lemuel			1			1			2				4		
Duxbury	100	12	Hall	Lot			1			1			1				3		
Duxbury	91	21	Hall	Luke	3			1						1			5		
Plymouth	4	16	Hall	Luke	2	1		1		2	1		1				8		
Rochester	109	27	Hall	Luther	1	1			1	1		3		1			8		
Marshfield	98	13	Hall	Samuel		1	1	1		1			1				5		
Middleborough	85	18	Hall	Seth	2	1		1		4	1	2	1				12		
Bridgewater	62	25	Hall	Silvanus	2	2		1		2			1				8		
Rochester	110	14	Hall	Solomon	1	1	2		1	1		1	2	2	1		12		
Marshfield	102	10	Hall	Timothy				1					1				2		
Plymouth	3	7	Hall	William	1			1		4			1				7		
Plymouth	9	10	Hammall	Lucy							2		1	1			4		
Plymouth	6	14	Hammatt	Priscilla	2		2			2	1	1					8		
Rochester	109	4	Hammit	John	2			1							1		4		
Rochester	109	6	Hammit	John Jr			1					1					2		
Rochester	107	27	Hammit	Shubael		1	1			1			1				4		
Rochester	109	5	Hammit	Shubael	1			1					1				3		
Rochester	110	16	Hammlin	Phebe	1	1				1			1				4		
Rochester	110	22	Hammond	Aaron				1		1		1					3		
Rochester	109	11	Hammond	Benjn		2	1		1		2	1		1			8		
Rochester	109	16	Hammond	Benjn	3			1					1				5		
Middleborough	88	38	Hammond	Christopher	1	2			1	4	1			1			10		
Rochester	109	8	Hammond	David				1					1				2		
Rochester	109	23	Hammond	Ebr		1	1		1		2	1		1			7		
Rochester	110	17	Hammond	Ebr	2		1						1				4		
Rochester	111	25	Hammond	Edward	1		3	1		1	1		1	1			9		
Scituate	133	24	Hammond	Experience	1	2		1		2		1	1				8		
Rochester	109	15	Hammond	Gidn	1	1		1		1			1	1			6		
Rochester	109	17	Hammond	Huldah										2			2		
Rochester	109	12	Hammond	Hursnewel			1		1				1				3		
Rochester	109	13	Hammond	James	2			1		1	1		1				6		

TOWN	PG#	LN#	LAST NAME	FIRST NAME	FREE WHITE MALES under 10	10 to 16	16 to 26	26 to 45	45 and over	FREE WHITE FEMALES under 10	10 to 16	16 to 26	26 to 45	45 and over	TOTAL ALL OTHER	TOTAL SLAVES	TOTALS	DISTRICT/ TOWNSHIP	NOTES
Rochester	109	25	Hammond	Jesse		1		1		4		1					7		
Rochester	109	20	Hammond	John			1	1			1		1				4		
Rochester	109	14	Hammond	Josiah					1					1			2		
Rochester	109	7	Hammond	Nathl			1		1		1		1	1			5		
Rochester	109	22	Hammond	Nathl 2	1			1		1	1		1				5		Name scratched out
Rochester	111	27	Hammond	Nathl 3	2			1				1					4		
Rochester	109	19	Hammond	Nathl Jr	2			1		1		1					5		
Rochester	109	9	Hammond	Noah	2			1				1		2			6		
Rochester	110	19	Hammond	Pollypus	1	1		1			2		1				6		
Carver	9	12	Hammond	Rowland			2		1	1	2						6		
Rochester	110	18	Hammond	Seth	2			1				1					4		
Middleborough	88	20	Hammond	Shubael		1	1		1	2	1	1		1			8		
Rochester	109	10	Hammond	Stafford			1			1			1				3		
Rochester	111	26	Hammond	Stephen	1			1				1					3		
Rochester	110	20	Hammond	Suylvanus	1	2		1		1			1				6		
Rochester	109	18	Hammond	Timo	2			1		2		1	1	1			8		
Rochester	110	1	Handy	Edward	3			1		1	2		1				8		
Rochester	109	2	Handy	Freeman				1		2	1	1					5		
Rochester	111	30	Handy	Jonn	1	1			1	2			1				6		
Rochester	111	29	Handy	Silas	2			1		1			1				5		
Duxbury	104	11	Hanks	John	1			1				1	2				5		
Abington	40	22	Harden	Jacob	1		1	1		1	2	1					7		
Bridgewater	62	26	Harden	John				1				1	1		2		5		
Bridgewater	68	5	Harden	John 2d	2	1	1		1	2			1				8		
Bridgewater	62	27	Harden	John Junr	3			1		1			1	3			9		
Bridgewater	62	28	Harden	Nathan				1					1				2		
Pembroke	38	10	Harden	Perry				1		1			1				3		
Bridgewater	68	4	Harden	Phebe		1					2		1				4		
Bridgewater	68	6	Harden	Relief						1		1					2		
Pembroke	38	23	Harden	Rheuben	1	1			1	3	1	3	1	1			12		
Pembroke	37	2	Harden	Saml		1		1		1	1		2				6		
Bridgewater	62	29	Harden	Samuel	2		1	1		1			1	1			7		
Abington	40	21	Harden	Seth		1		1				1	1				4		
Plymouth	3	23	Harlow	Amaziah		1	1			1	1						4		
Plymouth	19	24	Harlow	Anselm				1					1				2		
Middleborough	88	35	Harlow	Ellie			1			1		1					3		
Plymouth	16	29	Harlow	Ephraim	2			1		1		1					5		
Plymouth	15	20	Harlow	Ezra	1			1		2		1					5		
Plymouth	20	17	Harlow	Ezra			1	1					1				3		
Middleborough	85	15	Harlow	Ezra Capt	1	1	3		1	2			1				9		
Duxbury	103	17	Harlow	Gedion		1	1	2				1	2				7		
Plymouth	16	25	Harlow	Hannah		1				1		1					3		
Bridgewater	62	30	Harlow	Isaac		2	2	1				1	2				8		
Plymouth	21	12	Harlow	Isaac			3	1					1				5		
Bridgewater	62	31	Harlow	Isaac 2d	1			1		1	1	1					5		
Plimton	26	5	Harlow	James			2	1					1				4		
Plymouth	19	23	Harlow	James	1			1						1			3		
Plymouth	21	6	Harlow	James	1	1		1		1	1	1	1				7		
Plymouth	16	11	Harlow	Jesse			1	1	1					1			4		
Plymouth	16	28	Harlow	Jesse Jr	2	1		1		2	2		1				9		
Middleborough	85	5	Harlow	John				1					1				2		
Middleborough	85	6	Harlow	Jonathan	1	1	1		1	1		1	1				7		
Plymouth	24	5	Harlow	Joseph	2		2	1					1				6		
Plymouth	16	10	Harlow	Lazarus				1		1	1	1					4		
Plimton	19	8	Harlow	Levi	3	2		1		1			1				8		
Plymouth	16	2	Harlow	Lewis	1		1	1		1		1					5		
Plymouth	16	9	Harlow	Lothrop			2							1			3		
Plimton	26	24	Harlow	Mary		1				2	1		1				5		
Middleborough	85	4	Harlow	Mary Wo						1	1						2		
Plimton	19	5	Harlow	Nathaniel			1					1					2		
Plymouth	15	13	Harlow	Nathaniel		1	1			1		1					4		
Plymouth	22	10	Harlow	Reuben	1		1		1	3		1					7		
Plimton	19	7	Harlow	Sarah							1	2	1				4		
Plymouth	15	15	Harlow	Seth		1		1		1	1	1					5		
Plymouth	15	17	Harlow	Seth B.	1			1		1		1					4		
Plymouth	24	6	Harlow	Thomas			1			1		1					3		
Plymouth	12	26	Harlow	Zacheus	3			1		1	2	1	1				9		
Middleborough	88	34	Harlow	Zenas			1			1		1					3		
Abington	37	4	Harris	Abial	2	1		1		1	1	2	1				9		
Bridgewater	67	39	Harris	Arthur	1	1		1		1	1	1		1			7		
Bridgewater	67	38	Harris	Benjamin				1					1				2		
Abington	37	3	Harris	John	2	1		1		3			1				8		
Bridgewater	67	41	Harris	John	1			1		1			1				4		
Abington	37	1	Harris	Oliver	1	1		1		3			1				7		
Abington	37	2	Harris	Susanah		1					1		1				3		
Bridgewater	67	40	Harris	William	1			1		2			1				5		
Carver	5	7	Hart	Swansey											5		5		
Duxbury	91	14	Harte	Benjamin	1			1						1			3		
Rochester	110	27	Harte	Dory		1				1		1	1	1			5		
Bridgewater	52	31	Hartwell	Daniel	1	2		1		3	1	2	1				11		
Bridgewater	52	32	Hartwell	Isaac	2		2	1			1		1				7		
Kingston	27	11	Hartwell	Nathan	2			1		1			1				5		
Bridgewater	62	32	Harvey	Betty				1						1			2		
Bridgewater	62	34	Harvey	Bezer	2			1		1			1				5		
Bridgewater	52	33	Harvey	David				1					1	1			3		
Carver	11	14	Harvey	Frederick	2			1		2			1				6		
Plymouth	13	1	Harvey	Jonathan	1		1			1		1					4		
Bridgewater	62	33	Harvey	Mehitabel	1					2		1					4		

TOWN	PG#	LN#	LAST NAME	FIRST NAME	FREE WHITE MALES					FREE WHITE FEMALES					TOTAL ALL OTHER	TOTAL SLAVES	TOTALS	DISTRICT/TOWNSHIP	NOTES
					under 10	10 to 16	16 to 26	26 to 45	45 and over	under 10	10 to 16	16 to 26	26 to 45	45 and over					
Bridgewater	52	34	Harvey	Nathan	2	1		1		2			1				7		
Bridgewater	52	35	Harvey	Oliver	2			1					1				4		
Rochester	109	1	Haskell	Abigail	*	*	*	*	*	*	*	*	*	*	*		*		
Rochester	110	11	Haskell	David		1	1		1			2		1			6		
Middleborough	86	29	Haskell	Eli	1		1						1				3		
Middleborough	86	27	Haskell	Elisha		1			1			1		1			4		
Rochester	110	28	Haskell	Jesse	1			2				1		1	1		6		
Rochester	110	29	Haskell	Lot	1			1		4			1		1		8		
Middleborough	86	31	Haskell	Mark	1	1		1		1		1					5		
Rochester	109	3	Haskell	Nathl	2		2		1	2	3		1				12		
Middleborough	85	14	Haskell	Sarah Wo	1					1		2					4		
Middleborough	86	28	Haskell	Silas	1		1	1		1		2		1			7		
Rochester	110	12	Haskell	Timo			2		1		1	2		1			7		
Rochester	110	21	Haskell	Zebr	1		2		1	2			1	1			8		
Middleborough	86	32	Haskell	Zebulon	1		1			1		2		1			6		
Middleborough	88	31	Haskin	Susanna Wo	2								1				3		
Middleborough	86	38	Haskins	Abner	3		1			2			1				7		
Middleborough	85	12	Haskins	Benjn				1				2		1			4		
Middleborough	88	28	Haskins	Hannah Wo								2					2		
Middleborough	88	26	Haskins	James	5					1			1				8		
Middleborough	83	12	Haskins	John				1						2			3		
Middleborough	85	3	Haskins	Joshua	2	2	1		1			1	1				8		
Rochester	110	15	Haskins	Thomas	1			1						2			4		
Scituate	119	11	Haskins	William	1			1	1			1					4		
Marshfield	102	12	Hatch	Amos			1	1				1	1	1			5		
Marshfield	102	15	Hatch	Anthony	2	2			1	2	1	1	1				10		
Marshfield	101	16	Hatch	Benjm				1			1						2		
Rochester	109	24	Hatch	Benjn	2		1	1	1		2		1	1			9		
Pembroke	37	17	Hatch	Briggs	2			1		2			1	1			7		
Marshfield	103	6	Hatch	Charles	2			1		2		1					6		
Marshfield	101	15	Hatch	David		1				1		1					3		
Pembroke	37	20	Hatch	Harris	2			1		2	3	1	1				10		
Marshfield	102	16	Hatch	Ichobud	1			1					1				3		
Pembroke	37	12	Hatch	Isaac	2	1		1		2			2	1			10		
Marshfield	102	13	Hatch	Israel					1			1		1			3		
Marshfield	102	14	Hatch	Joel	1			1		1		1					4		
Bridgewater	67	43	Hatch	John		1			1	1			1	1			5		
Hanover	128	8	Hatch	John	1			1	1	1			1	1			6		
Marshfield	103	4	Hatch	John				1					1				2		
Pembroke	37	18	Hatch	John	2	2			1	1	1	1					8		
Scituate	123	22	Hatch	John	1	1		1	1				1				5		
Marshfield	102	5	Hatch	Jonathan	1	2	2		1			1		1			8		
Scituate	130	9	Hatch	Jonathan				1			1	1	1				4		
Scituate	133	7	Hatch	Jonathan Junr	3			1		2			2				8		
Duxbury	103	20	Hatch	Josiah	2	1	1		1	2	1	1					9		
Pembroke	37	15	Hatch	Josiah		1			1			1	2				5		
Rochester	110	24	Hatch	Lucy						1			2				3		
Bridgewater	67	44	Hatch	Luther	2	1		1		2			1				7		
Marshfield	102	4	Hatch	Naomi									1				1		
Marshfield	97	3	Hatch	Noah		1	1	1	1			1		1			6		
Hanover	130	12	Hatch	Orpha		1	1						2	1			5		
Marshfield	95	13	Hatch	Prince	2	1			1	1	1	1	1				8		
Scituate	134	10	Hatch	Samuel				1					1	3	1		6		
Pembroke	37	16	Hatch	Seth		1		1		1	1	1	1				6		
Hanover	127	18	Hatch	Thomas	1		1		1			1	1				5		
Pembroke	38	16	Hatch	Zephaniah				1				1	1				3		
Duxbury	93	9	Hatch	Zephemiah	1			1		1			1				4		
Wareham	111	19	Hathaway	Arthur		1		1		1	1			3			7		
Middleborough	86	41	Hathaway	Benjan	2	1		1		3	1		1				9		
Wareham	111	16	Hathaway	David	2		1		1	1	1		1				7		
Bridgewater	68	11	Hathaway	Ebenezer	1	1		1		4			1				8		
Rochester	110	10	Hathaway	Eunice	2	2				1	2		1	2			10		
Middleborough	85	20	Hathaway	Joseph		1	2		1				1				5		
Middleborough	85	19	Hathaway	Lazarus		1		1	1	3	1	3		1			10		
Middleborough	85	1	Hathaway	Levi		1			1	1	1		1				5		
Middleborough	83	10	Hathaway	Merick	1		1	1					1				4		
Rochester	110	13	Hathaway	Peleg	2			1		1			1				5		
Duxbury	93	3	Hathaway	Rufus Doct	1			1		2		1					5		
Wareham	111	18	Hathaway	Salathiel	3	1		1		1	2		1				9		
Wareham	111	17	Hathaway	Savoy	1	2		1					1	2			7		
Plymouth	18	17	Hathaway	Silas	2		2	1		1		1	1				8		
Middleborough	86	30	Hathaway	Isaac Jun	2			1		2	1		1				7		
Middleborough	88	30	Hathawway	Gilbert	1		1			1		1					4		
Pembroke	37	3	Hathway	Josiah	2			1		3	1		1				8		
Scituate	134	19	Hawland	Consider	1		1	1					1				4		
Scituate	131	22	Hayden	Daniel	2	1		1		1	1	1	1				8		
Scituate	135	25	Hayden	Luther						1	1	1					3		
Scituate	133	19	Hayden	Peleg	1	1			1	1	1		1				6		
Pembroke	37	10	Hayford	Daniel		1		1			1		1				4		
Bridgewater	50	7	Hayward	Amos			1	1					2				4		
Bridgewater	58	15	Hayward	Asaph	1		1	1		3		1	1				8		
Bridgewater	59	17	Hayward	Azariah	1		1		1			2		1			6		
Bridgewater	59	19	Hayward	Azariah Junr		1		1		2	2		1				7		
Bridgewater	59	16	Hayward	Benjamin				1				1		1			3		
Bridgewater	59	10	Hayward	Beza	1			1						3			5		
Bridgewater	52	24	Hayward	Charles	3			1					1				5		
Bridgewater	52	25	Hayward	Cornelius	1									2			4		

			HEADS OF HOUSEHOLD		FREE WHITE MALES					FREE WHITE FEMALES					TOTAL ALL OTHER	TOTAL SLAVES	TOTALS	DISTRICT/ TOWNSHIP	NOTES
TOWN	PG#	LN#	LAST NAME	FIRST NAME	under 10	10 to 16	16 to 26	26 to 45	45 and over	under 10	10 to 16	16 to 26	26 to 45	45 and over					
Bridgewater	49	19	Hayward	Daniel	1	1			1		1	2		1			7		
Bridgewater	49	16	Hayward	Edward	2		1		1			1	2				7		
Bridgewater	59	14	Hayward	Edward		1	1		1				1				4		
Bridgewater	59	20	Hayward	Eliab		1		1	1				2	1			6		
Bridgewater	59	12	Hayward	Elijah	2	2			1				2				7		
Bridgewater	52	26	Hayward	Elijah 2d		1			1					3			5		
Bridgewater	52	27	Hayward	Elijah 3d	1	1		1		3			1				7		
Duxbury	100	19	Hayward	Ester				2						1			3		
Bridgewater	52	30	Hayward	Ezra					1					1			2		
Bridgewater	59	11	Hayward	Hezekiah		1	1		1	1				1			5		
Bridgewater	62	24	Hayward	Independence	2		1						1		1		6		
Bridgewater	49	18	Hayward	John			1		1	1	2		1				6		
Bridgewater	49	15	Hayward	Jonathan		1	2		1	1		1		1			7		
Bridgewater	58	14	Hayward	Joseph		1	1		1	1		1		1			6		
Bridgewater	62	23	Hayward	Joseph					1					1			2		
Bridgewater	52	28	Hayward	Luther		2		1		1			2	1			7		
Plymouth	1	2	Hayward	Nathan			1	1	1		1	1	1	1	1		7		
Bridgewater	67	45	Hayward	Oliver	1		1	1		1			3				7		
Bridgewater	50	9	Hayward	Robert			2	1	1			1	1	1			7		
Bridgewater	67	42	Hayward	Sarah	1					1	1	1					4		
Bridgewater	59	18	Hayward	Solomon	3	4		1		2			2				12		
Bridgewater	52	29	Hayward	Solomon 2d				1		1	2		1				5		
Bridgewater	49	17	Hayward	Thomas	1		1	1		2	1		1	1			8		
Bridgewater	59	21	Hayward	Thomas	2			1		2			1				6		
Bridgewater	59	15	Hayward	Timothy	1			1		3		2					7		
Bridgewater	58	13	Hayward	Waldo	2	1	1	1		1			1				7		
Bridgewater	50	8	Hayward	Walter	1			1					1				3		
Bridgewater	59	13	Hayward	Ziba			1	1		1	1			1			6		
Abington	37	15	Hearsey	Daniel	1			1		3			1				6		
Abington	37	10	Hearsey	David		2		1				1	1	1			6		
Abington	37	13	Hearsey	Isaac	1			1					1	1			5		
Abington	37	21	Hearsey	Jane								1	1	1			3		
Abington	37	16	Hearsey	Joseph				1					1				2		
Bridgewater	68	10	Hearsey	Joseph		1							1				2		
Abington	40	20	Hearsey	Luther	1		1			2		1					5		
Abington	40	19	Hearsey	Obediah	1	2		1		1	1	1			1		8		
Abington	40	23	Hearsey	Seth	1		1	1		2			1				6		
Bridgewater	68	8	Hearsey	Solomon		1	1		1	1				1			5		
Bridgewater	68	9	Hearsey	Stephen	2	1			1	5		1	1				11		
Abington	37	14	Hearsey	Thos	3			1		1			1				6		
Bridgewater	68	7	Hearsey	William				1					1				2		
Bridgewater	68	18	Hearsey	William Junr	1		1		1		1	2		1			7		
Plymouth	7	1	Hedge	Barnabas					1				1		2		4		
Plymouth	7	2	Hedge	Barnabas Jr	2		1	1		1			1	1			7		
Halifax	15	8	Hefferds	John	1	1		1		2	1		1				7		
Middleborough	83	13	Hefford	Ebenezer	3	1			1	1	1	4	1				12		
Middleborough	88	23	Hefford	John	2			1					1				4		
Rochester	110	3	Heller	Benjn			1						1				2		
Rochester	110	5	Heller	David		1		1		1		1	1	1			6		
Rochester	110	9	Heller	Isaac	2			1					1				4		
Rochester	110	2	Heller	John				1						1			2		
Rochester	110	6	Heller	Jonn	4			1		1			1	1			8		
Rochester	110	8	Heller	Moses				2						1			3		
Rochester	110	4	Heller	Timoy		1	1	1		2	1		1	1			8		
Duxbury	94	20	Hemet	Asa	1		1						1				3		
Plymouth	15	11	Hempton	Oliver				1		1			1				3		
Abington	40	24	Her*t	Ebenz K.		1	1		1	1	2	2	1				9		
Plymouth	14	3	Herring	Wyatt	2		1						1	1			5		
Duxbury	103	19	Hewet	Joseph			1			2			1				4		
Marshfield	93	15	Hewet	Joseph	1		1	1				2	1	1			7		
Pembroke	37	1	Hicks	John	2			1		2			1				6		
Bridgewater	68	2	Hide	Ephraim			3	1		2	1		1				8		
Rochester	109	26	Higgins	Heman	2		1	1		1	1		1				7		
Scituate	129	8	Hiland	Mary										1			1		
Scituate	136	38	Hiland	Rebecca								1		1			2		
Scituate	129	25	Hiland	Samuel	1	1	2	1		3			1				9		
Scituate	129	5	Hiland	William					1					1			2		
Wareham	111	15	Hilchborn	Salisbury					1					1			2		
Hanover	130	19	Hill	Abner					1								1		
Bridgewater	62	42	Hill	David				1	1					2			4		
Bridgewater	67	46	Hill	Jacob	1	2	2	1	1		1		1				9		
Abington	37	5	Hill	Jonathan	1				1	1	1			1			5		
Abington	37	8	Hill	Joseph		2			1		1	2		1			7		
Bridgewater	68	1	Hill	Josiah Junr					1		1	1		1			4		
Pembroke	37	7	Hill	Leonard	1				1				1				3		
Pembroke	38	18	Hill	Saml			1		1				1	1			4		
Pembroke	38	19	Hill	Saml Junr	1			1		2	1		1				6		
Pembroke	38	17	Hill	Thos	1	1			1				1	2			6		
Middleborough	86	40	Hinds	Abinoum Capt	1			1		1							4		
Middleborough	88	29	Hinds	Ebenzr Revd					1					1			2		
Middleborough	86	24	Hinds	John	2	2	1	1		2	2		1				11		
Middleborough	86	26	Hinds	Leonard		1		1		2		1	1				6		
Pembroke	37	6	Hitchcock	Gad	1	2	1		2	3	1	3	1		2		16		
Plymouth	1	20	Hitchill	Ebenezer	1			1		1			1				4		
Middleborough	88	24	Hoar	Bradock	3				1	1							6		
Middleborough	85	2	Hoar	Peter Majr	1	1			1			2	1				7		
Middleborough	88	25	Hoar	Seth	1		1		1				1				4		

TOWN	PG#	LN#	LAST NAME	FIRST NAME	FREE WHITE MALES under 10	10 to 16	16 to 26	26 to 45	45 and over	FREE WHITE FEMALES under 10	10 to 16	16 to 26	26 to 45	45 and over	TOTAL ALL OTHER	TOTAL SLAVES	TOTALS	DISTRICT/ TOWNSHIP	NOTES
Middleborough	86	36	Hoar	William	1			1		3	1		1				7		
Abington	37	18	Hobart	Aaron		1	1		1	1	1	2		1	1		9		
Abington	37	17	Hobart	Aaron Jr		2			1	3	1		1				8		
Abington	37	20	Hobart	Elijah	1			1	1	4	2	1	1				11		
Pembroke	38	21	Hobart	Isaac		2	1		1	1			1				6		
Hanover	128	18	Hobart	Mary		1							1	1			3		
Bridgewater	58	18	Hobart	Nathaniel Junr	1		1			1	2		1				7		
Abington	37	12	Hobart	Noah	2	1		1				1	1				6		
Bridgewater	68	12	Hobart	Seth	1	2		1		2	1	1	1				9		
Pembroke	38	22	Hobart	Thos		1		1			1	1	1				5		
Duxbury	100	17	Hodges	Nathl Jr	2	1		1			1		1				6		
Plymouth	13	13	Holbrook	Eliphalet		1	2		1	1		1		1			7		
Plymouth	19	27	Holbrook	Gideon			1	1		1	3		1				7		
Plymouth	17	23	Holbrook	Hannah			1						1				2		
Abington	37	11	Holbrook	Willm	1	3		1	1	1		1	1				9		
Rochester	110	26	Holland	Richard		1		1					1				3		
Kingston	27	39	Hollis	Samuel	1			1		2		2		1	2		9		
Plymouth	26	9	Hollis	Samuel	1		1			1			1				4		
Middleborough	86	34	Holloway	Asa			1			2		1					4		
Middleborough	86	35	Holloway	Isaac			1			3		1	1				6		
Middleborough	86	33	Holloway	Josiah				1									1		
Middleborough	88	37	Holloway	Zephanh				1					1				2		
Kingston	27	31	Holmes	Abner	1	1	1		1	1	2	2		1			10		
Plymouth	12	19	Holmes	Abner		1						1					2		
Marshfield	98	6	Holmes	Abraham	1		1			2			1				5		
Plymouth	19	3	Holmes	Andrew	2		1			1			1				5		
Kingston	29	13	Holmes	Anselm		2							1				3		
Plymouth	12	14	Holmes	Anselm			1			1			1				3		
Plymouth	17	4	Holmes	Barnabas	2	1	2		1	2	1	1		1			11		
Plymouth	21	9	Holmes	Barnabas			1			2		1					4		
Plymouth	21	15	Holmes	Barnabas	2	3	1	1		2		1					10		
Duxbury	97	19	Holmes	Bartlett	2		1	2					1				6		
Plymouth	19	22	Holmes	Bartlett		1		1				1		2			5		
Rochester	109	28	Holmes	Bethia	1		1						2	1			5		
Plymouth	15	22	Holmes	Chandler	1			1		1			1				4		
Kingston	27	40	Holmes	Charles		1		1		1	1		1				5		
Rochester	108	2	Holmes	Church	2		1			1	1			1			6		
Bridgewater	62	36	Holmes	Cornelius	3	1	2		1	1			1	1			10		
Plymouth	15	30	Holmes	Corrthial	2	1	1		1			1	2	1			9		
Plymouth	15	24	Holmes	David		1		1		1		1		1			5		
Plimton	20	3	Holmes	Ebenezer	1		1			1			1				4		
Plymouth	3	16	Holmes	Ebenezer	1			1				1		1			4		
Rochester	110	7	Holmes	Ebr	1		2	2		2			1				8		
Plymouth	18	5	Holmes	Eleazer		1	1	1		2	1	1		3			10		
Plymouth	22	8	Holmes	Elkanah				1						2			3		
Bridgewater	62	35	Holmes	Ellis			1	1		2		1		1			6		
Plymouth	18	4	Holmes	Ellis	1		1			3		1					6		
Plymouth	11	15	Holmes	Elnathan		1		1				1		1			4		
Plymouth	11	20	Holmes	Elnathan Jr	1	2	1			1	2		1	1			9		
Kingston	27	26	Holmes	Ephraim		1	1						1				3		
Kingston	29	33	Holmes	Ephraim		1	1						1				3		
Plymouth	11	27	Holmes	Ephraim		1						1					2		
Middleborough	85	7	Holmes	Ezra	1			1		1		1					4		
Middleborough	88	36	Holmes	Fear Wo							1		1				2		
Plimton	24	12	Holmes	Francis		1	1		1		1	2		1			7		
Plymouth	8	1	Holmes	George				1					1				2		
Plymouth	19	7	Holmes	Gilbert			1	1		2			1				5		
Kingston	28	25	Holmes	Heman	2		1						1				4		
Plymouth	11	16	Holmes	Ichabod		1	3	1			1		1	1			8		
Plymouth	18	6	Holmes	Ichabod	1							1	1				3		
Plymouth	21	19	Holmes	James		1		1				3					6		
Kingston	27	30	Holmes	Jedediah	2	2	3	1				1		1			10		
Kingston	27	35	Holmes	Jedediah		1	1	1		2			1				6		
Plymouth	19	4	Holmes	Jeremiah			1	1				1		1			4		
Plymouth	22	25	Holmes	Jeremiah	2		1	1		1			1	1			7		
Bridgewater	52	37	Holmes	John		1				1		1					3		
Middleborough	85	10	Holmes	John				1					1				2		
Kingston	27	36	Holmes	Jonathan		1		1		1			1	1	1		7		
Kingston	27	38	Holmes	Jonathan		1		2			1	1					5		
Plymouth	23	24	Holmes	Jonathan				1					1				2		
Kingston	27	32	Holmes	Joseph				1				3	1				5		
Plymouth	6	15	Holmes	Joseph			1			1	1	4	1				8		
Plymouth	16	16	Holmes	Joseph			1			4		1	1				7		
Kingston	27	29	Holmes	Joshua		1		1						2			4		
Scituate	133	37	Holmes	Kezia										2			2		
Plymouth	3	1	Holmes	Martha	1		1						1				3		
Plymouth	11	3	Holmes	Mary		1	2			2		2		3			10		
Kingston	27	34	Holmes	Melatiah		1	1	1				3		1			7		
Halifax	17	7	Holmes	Nathaniel	4		1						1				6		
Kingston	27	27	Holmes	Nathaniel		1	1						1				3		
Kingston	29	34	Holmes	Nathaniel	1		1							1			3		
Plymouth	4	19	Holmes	Nathaniel		1		1		1		1		1			5		
Plymouth	8	22	Holmes	Nathaniel	1		1			1		1					4		
Plymouth	12	8	Holmes	Nathaniel	1		1			1		1		1			5		
Plymouth	19	6	Holmes	Nathaniel		1		1				2		1			5		

102

TOWN	PG#	LN#	LAST NAME	FIRST NAME	FREE WHITE MALES					FREE WHITE FEMALES					TOTAL ALL OTHER	TOTAL SLAVES	TOTALS	DISTRICT/ TOWNSHIP	NOTES
					under 10	10 to 16	16 to 26	26 to 45	45 and over	under 10	10 to 16	16 to 26	26 to 45	45 and over					
Duxbury	95	1	Holmes	Nathl				1		2			1				4		
Duxbury	97	24	Holmes	Nathl	2			1					1				4		
Halifax	15	12	Holmes	Oliver		1	1		1	1	1	1		1			7		
Plimton	24	13	Holmes	Peleg	1		1			1		1					4		
Kingston	28	26	Holmes	Pelham	1			1				1					3		
Plymouth	5	23	Holmes	Richard	1	1	1		1	2	1	4		1			12		
Plymouth	10	10	Holmes	Richard			1	1	1	2	1	1	1	1			9		
Kingston	30	25	Holmes	Robert		1	1		1			2		1			6		
Plymouth	24	21	Holmes	Robert				1					1				2		
Plymouth	3	8	Holmes	Rowland	1			1		1			1				4		
Rochester	110	23	Holmes	Saml	3			1		1	1	1	1				8		
Plymouth	3	17	Holmes	Samuel				1		2		1		1			5		
Plymouth	16	27	Holmes	Samuel	3	2		1			1		1				8		
Plymouth	22	5	Holmes	Seth		1	3		1			1		2	1		9		
Plymouth	22	6	Holmes	Seth	1			1		1	1	1					5		
Plymouth	15	12	Holmes	Silvanus					1					1			2		
Kingston	27	37	Holmes	Silvester		1		1		2		1	1				6		
Carver	9	6	Holmes	Simeon				1						3			4		
Halifax	17	6	Holmes	Solomon				1			2		1				4		
Plymouth	22	7	Holmes	Stephen			1		1			1					3		
Kingston	27	33	Holmes	Thomas	2			1	1				1				5		
Plymouth	13	22	Holmes	Thomas	2		2	1				1					6		
Kingston	27	28	Holmes	Tilden	1			1		2		1					5		
Plymouth	10	9	Holmes	William	4		1	1		1	1	2	1				11		
Plimton	23	17	Holmes	Zacheus				1			1	1	1				4		
Plymouth	9	23	Holmes	Zepheniah	1			1				1	1				4		
Pembroke	37	19	Homes	John		1			1			2	1	1			6		
Pembroke	38	15	Homes	Sarah							1	2	1				4		
Plimton	21	10	Hooker	Asaph		1		1		2			1				5		
Bridgewater	47	44	Hooper	Apollos		1	1					1					3		
Scituate	127	3	Hooper	Betty									2				2		
Bridgewater	47	43	Hooper	David			2		1	2	1		1				7		
Bridgewater	62	37	Hooper	Hezekiah				1					1				2		
Bridgewater	62	41	Hooper	James	1			1			1	1	1	1	1		7		
Bridgewater	68	3	Hooper	John				1					1		1		3		
Bridgewater	62	39	Hooper	Joseph	1	1		1		2			1				6		
Bridgewater	47	41	Hooper	Luther		1		1		1	1	2	1				7		
Bridgewater	47	42	Hooper	Nathaniel				1						1			2		
Scituate	129	3	Hooper	Sarah										1			1		
Bridgewater	62	40	Hooper	William	2	1		1					1				5		
Bridgewater	62	38	Hooper	Winslow	1		1	2		2			1				7		
Bridgewater	62	43	Horton	Barnabas	1	1		1		1	1		1	1			7		
Bridgewater	58	19	Horton	Isaac				1		1	1		1				4		
Abington	37	23	Houpe	Deborough								2					2		
Middleborough	86	25	Hour	Job	1	1		1		3		2	1				9		
Bridgewater	52	36	House	Abel				1					1				2		
Scituate	124	12	House	Coomes	1			1		1			1				4		
Hanover	126	18	House	David				1					1	1			3		
Pembroke	37	11	House	Saml			1		1		1	1	1				5		
Rochester	109	21	Hovey	Danl			1	1			1	1					4		
Plymouth	22	29	Hovey	Ivory Revd				1					3				4		
Bridgewater	51	18	Howard	Abiel				1		1		1					3		
Bridgewater	51	17	Howard	Alfred				1				1					2		
Bridgewater	58	2	Howard	Alfred	2			1		2			1	2			8		
Bridgewater	58	5	Howard	Barnabas		1		1					1	1			4		
Bridgewater	58	9	Howard	Caleb	1	2		1		4	2	1	1				12		
Bridgewater	68	14	Howard	Caleb		1						1	2	1			5		
Bridgewater	52	39	Howard	Daniel	1		1	2	1	2		2	4	1			14		
Bridgewater	57	42	Howard	Daniel 2d	1	2	1	1	1	1		2	1				10		
Plymouth	5	9	Howard	Ebenezer	1		2		1	2			1				7		
Bridgewater	52	38	Howard	Edward	1	1		1		1			1	1	1		8		
Bridgewater	52	40	Howard	Eliakim		1	3	1		1		2	1	2			11		
Wareham	111	14	Howard	Enos		1	2		2	1		1	1				8		
Bridgewater	52	43	Howard	Gamaliel	1			1		2			1				5		
Bridgewater	51	11	Howard	George		1		1					1				3		
Bridgewater	51	15	Howard	George Junr	1	2	1	1		1	2	1	1				10		
Bridgewater	57	43	Howard	Gideon	1	1		1		3		1	1				8		
Bridgewater	58	6	Howard	Ichabod	1	1			1	2	1		1				7		
Bridgewater	51	13	Howard	James				1					1				2		
Bridgewater	51	14	Howard	James Junr	3	1	2	1		2	1	2	1				13		
Bridgewater	68	13	Howard	Jennet									1				1		
Bridgewater	51	7	Howard	Jesse				1						1	1		3		
Duxbury	98	2	Howard	Jesse	2			1		1			1				5		
Bridgewater	51	8	Howard	Jesse Junr			1						1				2		
Bridgewater	58	1	Howard	John	1	1		1		1	1		1				6		
Bridgewater	58	10	Howard	Jonas	1	1		1		2	2		1				8		
Bridgewater	52	41	Howard	Jonathan		1	2		1		1			2			7		
Bridgewater	51	6	Howard	Jonathan 2d	2		2					2	1	1			8		
Bridgewater	52	42	Howard	Jonathan 2d		1	3		1			2	2	1			10		
Bridgewater	51	5	Howard	Jonathan 3d	1			1					1				3		
Bridgewater	62	44	Howard	Jonathan 3d	1			1		1			1				4		
Bridgewater	58	12	Howard	Joshua	2		1						1				4		
Bridgewater	51	9	Howard	Lloyd		1				2			1				4		
Bridgewater	52	44	Howard	Martin	2		1	1	1			1	1				7		

TOWN	PG#	LN#	LAST NAME	FIRST NAME	FREE WHITE MALES under 10	10 to 16	16 to 26	26 to 45	45 and over	FREE WHITE FEMALES under 10	10 to 16	16 to 26	26 to 45	45 and over	TOTAL ALL OTHER	TOTAL SLAVES	TOTALS	DISTRICT/ TOWNSHIP	NOTES
Bridgewater	58	3	Howard	Mary										4			4		
Bridgewater	51	2	Howard	Nathan			1	1					1	1			4		
Bridgewater	51	4	Howard	Nathan 3d	1			1				1					3		
Bridgewater	51	3	Howard	Nathan Junr		2		1		1	1	2		1			8		
Bridgewater	51	12	Howard	Nehemiah	2			1	2			1					6		
Bridgewater	58	4	Howard	Oliver	1	1	1	1		4	2	1	1				12		
Scituate	123	17	Howard	Perez	3			1						2			6		
Bridgewater	58	7	Howard	Robert		1		1					1	1			4		
Bridgewater	58	8	Howard	Robert Junr	1			1		2	1		1				6		
Bridgewater	51	10	Howard	Seth	1	3		1		2			2				9		
Bridgewater	58	11	Howard	Silence								2	1				3		
Bridgewater	51	1	Howard	Simeon	1			1		1			1				4		
Bridgewater	51	16	Howard	Thaddeus		1		1		2	1		1				6		
Bridgewater	65	10	Howe	Azor	2	1		1		4			1				9		
Abington	37	9	Howe	Nathl 2d	1			1	1		2		2				7		
Carver	8	5	Howes	Jacob	4			1					1				6		
Plymouth	17	10	Howes	Silvanus				1				1		1			3		
Plymouth	20	15	Howland	Abraham	1			1		1			1				4		
Pembroke	38	11	Howland	Allen	1		1	1				1					4		
Marshfield	94	1	Howland	Arthur	1			1			1		1				4		
Carver	7	13	Howland	Calvin	1			1			2		1				5		
Middleborough	83	14	Howland	Consider	3	2			1	2			1				9		
Pembroke	37	8	Howland	Daniel	1			1					1				3		
Pembroke	38	14	Howland	Daniel	1	1	1	1					1				5		
Middleborough	86	39	Howland	Ebenezer	1	2		1		4			1				9		
Middleborough	83	11	Howland	Isaac				1					1				2		
Pembroke	38	20	Howland	Isaac		1		1				1	1				4		
Plymouth	20	4	Howland	Isaac	4	2	1	1					1				9		
Plymouth	20	16	Howland	Jacob		1				1		1					3		
Marshfield	93	7	Howland	Jarusha								1		2			3		
Carver	7	12	Howland	John Revd				1									1		
Pembroke	37	5	Howland	Joseph		1		1				2		2			6		
Plymouth	6	12	Howland	Joseph				1					1				2		
Pembroke	38	13	Howland	Luther	1		1					1					3		
Middleborough	88	32	Howland	Malica	1	1	1	1	1	1	2	2	2				12		
Pembroke	37	9	Howland	Mary						1	2		1				4		
Duxbury	104	15	Howland	Perez	2	1		1					2				6		
Pembroke	38	9	Howland	Prince	1	1	1	1			2	1	1				8		
Pembroke	38	12	Howland	Robart	1			1			1		2				5		
Middleborough	86	37	Howland	Rufus			1	1		2			1				5		
Plymouth	17	12	Howland	Sarah	1						1	1	1				4		
Pembroke	38	8	Howland	Thos		1		1					1				3		
Middleborough	88	33	Howland	William	1			1		2		1					5		
Plymouth	26	8	Hoyt	Israel	1	1		1			1		1				5		
Bridgewater	68	16	Hudson	John		2	1	1		1	1	1		1			8		
Bridgewater	68	15	Hudson	Nathan		1		1						1			3		
Bridgewater	68	17	Hudson	William				1						1			2		
Abington	37	19	Humble	Majn	1		1	1		1	1	1		1			7		
Bridgewater	58	20	Humphrey	James	2			1		2		1					6		
Scituate	124	17	Humphris	Edward				1					1				2		
Abington	37	7	Hunt	Ephraim		1		3				1	1	1			7		
Middleborough	85	9	Hunt	Ephraim		1	1					1					3		
Bridgewater	58	16	Hunt	John		1		1		1			1				4		
Marshfield	96	7	Hunt	Joseph		1		2		1			1				5		
Duxbury	98	9	Hunt	Judah			1		1			2	1	1			7		
Bridgewater	58	17	Hunt	Mathew	1	2		1		2			1				7		
Middleborough	85	8	Hunt	Rebecca Wo									1		1		2		
Duxbury	95	21	Hunt	Thomas Jun	2	1	1	1	1	2	1	1	1				11		
Abington	37	22	Hunt	Thos	2	2	2	1					1	1			9		
Abington	37	6	Hunt	Thos Junr	1			1		1			1	1			5		
Plymouth	13	8	Hurtins	William	1		1	1	1	4	1	1	1				11		
Marshfield	99	15	Hyland	John				1					1				2		
Bridgewater	51	19	Inglee	James			1			1			1				3		
Kingston	30	32	Inglee	Lemuel			1			1		2					4		
Halifax	16	6	Inglee	Moses		1		1		1	1		1				5		
Kingston	30	33	Inglee	Moses	2			1		2		1	1				8		
Middleborough	87	1	Inglee	Rebecca Wo											2		2		
Plymouth	14	24	Inglee	Solomon	2	2	1	2		1	1		1				10		
Plymouth	10	1	Jackson	Charles		1	1	1		1			1				5		
Plymouth	7	28	Jackson	Daniel	5	1		1			1		1				9		
Bridgewater	55	20	Jackson	Ephraim		1		1	1	1	2		1	1			8		
Plymouth	1	15	Jackson	Henry	1		1						1				3		
Plymouth	19	14	Jackson	Isaac	1			1			2	2		1			7		
Bridgewater	55	15	Jackson	John											6		6		
Scituate	133	33	Jackson	Jonathan		1	1	1					2	1			6		
Plymouth	1	14	Jackson	Nathaniel		1	1	1		1	1						5		
Plymouth	19	15	Jackson	Ransome			1			1		1					3		
Middleborough	87	2	Jackson	Rebecca Wo	1								1				2		
Plymouth	7	26	Jackson	Samuel	3	1	1			1	1	1					9		
Plymouth	7	27	Jackson	Samuel		1	1	1					1				5		
Plymouth	10	3	Jackson	Sarah							1	2	1	1			5		
Plymouth	9	11	Jackson	Thomas			1						1				2		
Plymouth	10	2	Jackson	Thomas	3	1		1		1	1		1				8		
Plymouth	9	12	Jackson	William	2			1		1	1	2	1				9		
Plymouth	9	13	Jackson	William H.		1	1	1				1		1	2		7		
Plymouth	14	4	Jackson	Woodward		1					1	1					3		

TOWN	PG#	LN#	HEADS OF HOUSEHOLD		FREE WHITE MALES					FREE WHITE FEMALES					TOTAL ALL OTHER	TOTAL SLAVES	TOTALS	DISTRICT/ TOWNSHIP	NOTES
			LAST NAME	FIRST NAME	under 10	10 to 16	16 to 26	26 to 45	45 and over	under 10	10 to 16	16 to 26	26 to 45	45 and over					
Hanover	123	5	Jacobs	David	1	1			1		1	1		1			6		
Scituate	128	5	Jacobs	Deborah									1		1		2		
Scituate	125	22	Jacobs	James			1	1	1		1	1		1	2		8		
Scituate	119	19	Jacobs	John					1			1		1			3		
Abington	37	30	Jacobs	Joseph	1	1	1		1	1	1		1				7		
Scituate	127	4	Jacobs	Joshu Junr		1		1		2	1		1				6		
Scituate	128	2	Jacobs	Joshua					1		1	1					3		
Scituate	119	18	Jacobs	Lemuel		2		1		1	1		1				6		
Scituate	128	1	Jacobs	Mary									1				1		
Hanover	123	7	Jacobs	Nathaniel		2	1		1				1				5		
Hanover	123	6	Jacobs	Perez			1			3	1		1				6		
Pembroke	40	19	Jacobs	Saml		2		1						1			4		
Scituate	127	12	Jacobs	Susanna			1							1			2		
Scituate	126	19	Jacobs	Walter			1	1		1		1					4		
Scituate	135	21	James	Benja			1	1				1					3		
Scituate	119	20	James	Elisha		1		1	1	1		1					5		
Scituate	127	21	James	Hannah									1				1		
Scituate	127	22	James	John	3	1		1		2			1				8		
Scituate	119	16	James	William	1	1			1	1	2	1					7		
Bridgewater	58	21	Jameson	William		1	1	1		1	1			1			6		
Scituate	136	16	Jenkins	Abigail			1				1			1			3		
Scituate	135	1	Jenkins	Caleb	2			1		2			1				6		
Scituate	133	21	Jenkins	Calvin	2	1		1		3	1	1	1	1			11		
Scituate	135	3	Jenkins	Charles	4	1		1			1		1				8		
Scituate	136	17	Jenkins	Daniel	2		1	1					1				6		
Abington	37	24	Jenkins	David		2	2		1	3		1	1	1			11		
Scituate	136	28	Jenkins	Eli	1			1					1				3		
Scituate	136	49	Jenkins	Elijah	1			1		2		1	1				6		
Scituate	135	20	Jenkins	Gera		1		1				2		1			5		
Scituate	135	13	Jenkins	Gideon	3	1	2		1	1	1	1	1				11		
Abington	37	27	Jenkins	Isaiah		2	1		1	2	1	1					9		
Abington	37	26	Jenkins	Isaiah Jun	1			1		3		1					6		
Scituate	133	20	Jenkins	James		1	1		1	1	1	1					7		
Abington	37	29	Jenkins	Joseph	3			1		3			1	1			9		
Abington	37	25	Jenkins	Malichi	1			1		1		1	1				5		
Abington	37	28	Jenkins	Merit		2							1				3		
Scituate	136	41	Jenkins	Oliver				1		2	1		1				5		
Scituate	135	2	Jenkins	Samuel				1			1	1	1				4		
Scituate	136	7	Jenkins	Samuel Junr				1		1			1				3		
Scituate	133	6	Jenkins	Thomas		1		1						1			3		
Rochester	108	3	Jenne	Joseph			2			3			1				6		
Rochester	108	5	Jenne	Lettes	2	1		1		1			1				6		
Rochester	108	4	Jenne	Nathan		1		1		1			1				4		
Plymouth	4	2	Jennings	Joseph	1		1		1	1			1				5		
Pembroke	40	18	Jennings	Nathl	1		1		1	2	2	1		2			10		
Bridgewater	61	43	Jess	Lucy											6		6		
Bridgewater	54	25	Johnson	Bethiah		3	1			1		2	1				8		
Plymouth	22	9	Johnson	Hannah		1	1					1	1	1			5		
Bridgewater	54	24	Johnson	Isaac	3			1		1	1		1	1			8		
Pembroke	40	17	Johnson	Isaac	2		1			2			1	1			7		
Bridgewater	51	22	Johnson	Isaiah				1					1				2		
Plymouth	22	11	Johnson	Jacob			1			1							2		
Bridgewater	51	21	Johnson	James		1	3			1		1					6		
Kingston	27	42	Johnson	John		2			1	3	1	1	1				9		
Plymouth	21	5	Johnson	Joseph	1			1		1	1		1				5		
Bridgewater	68	19	Johnson	Josiah				1						1			2		
Bridgewater	68	20	Johnson	Nathan	2		1			1	1		1				6		
Kingston	27	43	Johnson	Richard	1		1			2			1				5		
Bridgewater	51	20	Johnson	Thomas			2		2	1		1	1				7		
Bridgewater	49	27	Jonah	Thomas											4		4		
Marshfield	102	2	Jones	Amos			1		1	1	2	2	2	1			10		
Bridgewater	58	22	Jones	Asa	2		1	1		1		2					7		
Pembroke	40	20	Jones	Charls	1			1		1			1				4		
Middleborough	87	4	Jones	Consider				1			1	1					3		
Middleborough	87	3	Jones	Ebenezer		1		1		2	1		1				6		
Bridgewater	65	12	Jones	John				1		2			1	1			5		
Marshfield	101	8	Jones	John				1				1					2		
Scituate	123	12	Jones	John	1	1	1		1	1	1	1					8		
Scituate	133	25	Jones	Samuel P	4	1		1		2	1	1					10		
Pembroke	40	16	Jones	Simeon	2			1		1			1				5		
Scituate	126	2	Jordan	David	1	2	2		1	1	2	2		1			12		
Scituate	124	9	Jordan	Nathl		1	2		1					1			5		
Pembroke	40	10	Joselyn	B Joseph			1	1						1			3		
Pembroke	40	7	Joselyn	Charles Jun	2		1	1		2		1	1				8		
Pembroke	40	1	Joselyn	Eleazer	4	2		1		2	1		1				11		
Pembroke	40	6	Joselyn	Elisha				1		1	1						3		
Pembroke	40	2	Joselyn	Francis	1	2		1		3			1				8		
Pembroke	40	12	Joselyn	Henry							1	1	1	1			5		
Pembroke	40	13	Joselyn	Henry Jun			1			4			1				6		
Pembroke	40	9	Joselyn	Isaiah				1						2	2		5		
Pembroke	40	15	Joselyn	Jabez	1			1		1		1					4		
Pembroke	40	5	Joselyn	Jacob	2		1			1		1					5		
Pembroke	40	11	Joselyn	Joseph				1						1			2		
Pembroke	40	14	Joselyn	Josiah	1		1		1				1	1			5		
Pembroke	40	3	Joselyn	Sarah									1	1			2		
Pembroke	40	4	Joselyn	W. Saml	1		1					1					3		

TOWN	PG#	LN#	LAST NAME	FIRST NAME	FWM under 10	FWM 10 to 16	FWM 16 to 26	FWM 26 to 45	FWM 45 and over	FWF under 10	FWF 10 to 16	FWF 16 to 26	FWF 26 to 45	FWF 45 and over	TOTAL ALL OTHER	TOTAL SLAVES	TOTALS	DISTRICT/ TOWNSHIP	NOTES
Hanover	132	22	Josleyn	Isaac	2	1	2		1		1	1		1			9		
Hanover	132	11	Josleyn	Jonathan	2			1		2			1				6		
Hanover	132	18	Josleyn	Olive								1		1			2		
Hanover	132	19	Josleyn	Seth	1			1		1			1				4		
Hanover	125	4	Josliyn	Christiana	1					1			1				3		
Bridgewater	68	21	Josselyn	Joseph	4	4		1		1			1				11		
Bridgewater	68	22	Josselyn	Mary									1				1		
Bridgewater	49	22	Jotham	Calvin											4		4		
Bridgewater	49	21	Jotham	Luther											5		5		
Duxbury	94	8	Joyce	Asa	3		1			1			1				6		
Marshfield	99	20	Joyce	David	3		1			2			1				7		
Marshfield	98	2	Joyce	John		1		1		1			2	1			6		
Marshfield	99	21	Joyce	Jonathan				1				1	1	1			4		
Duxbury	98	7	Joyce	Lucy						2			1				3		
Marshfield	99	18	Joyce	Nathl				1					1				2		
Marshfield	99	19	Joyce	Samuel	2		1			2			1				6		
Pembroke	40	8	Joyce	Seth	1		1			1			1				4		
Marshfield	99	17	Joyce	Thomas		1	1					1	1	1			5		
Rochester	108	6	Jucket	Peter				1					1				2		
Duxbury	91	22	Kea*	*				1		1			1				3		Tape Mark
Plymouth	5	5	Kean	William	2	1	1		1	1		1	1				8		
Pembroke	39	4	Keen	Asa				1				2					3		
Pembroke	39	3	Keen	Asa Jun	2		1			2			1				6		
Marshfield	98	11	Keen	Benjm	1		2			1			1				5		
Pembroke	39	2	Keen	Desiah									1				1		
Abington	37	32	Keen	Ebenezer				1					1				2		
Pembroke	40	23	Keen	Galen		1				4		1					6		
Duxbury	103	27	Keen	Isaac			1	1			3		1				6		
Pembroke	40	22	Keen	Isaac		1	1	1				1	1				6		
Pembroke	39	8	Keen	James			1						1				2		
Rochester	108	7	Keen	John			2	1	1	1		1	1	1			8		
Pembroke	39	6	Keen	Joseph				1				2	1				4		
Pembroke	39	7	Keen	Joseph Jun	1		1			1			1				4		
Pembroke	40	21	Keen	Josiah		1	1			4	3	1	1				11		
Pembroke	39	1	Keen	Lemuel				1		2		1		1			5		
Duxbury	103	25	Keen	Lot		1	1			1			1				5		
Pembroke	39	5	Keen	Nathll				1					1				2		
Duxbury	91	11	Keen	Simeon	1		1						1				3		
Middleborough	87	5	Keene	Seth	1	2		1		2	1		1				8		
Bridgewater	55	31	Keith	Ambrose	1		1						1				3		
Bridgewater	50	16	Keith	Amos		1		1			1	1	2				6		
Bridgewater	61	4	Keith	Benjamin				1					1				2		
Bridgewater	55	22	Keith	Benjamin 2d	3	1		1		1			1		1		8		
Bridgewater	61	5	Keith	Benjamin Junr	2	1	1	1		2		1	1				9		
Bridgewater	65	28	Keith	Calvin	3	1							1				5		
Middleborough	87	10	Keith	Cyrus	1	1	1			1		1					6		
Bridgewater	50	12	Keith	Daniel				1					1				2		
Bridgewater	50	13	Keith	Daniel Junr				1			1		1				3		
Bridgewater	65	25	Keith	David		1		1		1		1		1			5		
Bridgewater	50	19	Keith	Edward	1			1		1		1	1				6		
Bridgewater	65	29	Keith	Eleazer		2	1			1			1	1			6		
Bridgewater	65	30	Keith	Eleazer Junr			1			1		1					3		
Duxbury	91	29	Keith	George	2	2		1		4			1				10		
Marshfield	94	8	Keith	George			2				2						4		
Bridgewater	61	9	Keith	Hartwell	4	1		1			2		1				9		
Bridgewater	65	23	Keith	Holman	1	1		1		3	1		1				8		
Bridgewater	61	2	Keith	Howe	3	1		1					1				6		
Bridgewater	61	3	Keith	Isaac				1		2			1				4		
Bridgewater	65	22	Keith	Isaac	1	3		1		2			1				8		
Bridgewater	65	20	Keith	James				1			1		1	1			4		
Bridgewater	65	21	Keith	James Junr	3	2			1	1		1	2	1			11		
Bridgewater	50	11	Keith	Jeremiah			1			1	1	1	1				6		
Bridgewater	65	31	Keith	John		2	1	1					1				5		
Bridgewater	65	32	Keith	John Junr			1					1					2		
Bridgewater	55	23	Keith	Jonathan	1	1	1	1		3	3	1	1				13		
Bridgewater	61	8	Keith	Jonathan	2	1		1		1	1		1				7		
Middleborough	87	8	Keith	Joseph Capt		1		1		1				1			4		
Bridgewater	55	21	Keith	Levi		1		1		1	1		1				5		
Bridgewater	65	26	Keith	Levi	1	1		1					1				5		
Bridgewater	55	24	Keith	Levi 3d	1		1						1				3		
Bridgewater	61	6	Keith	Marshal	2		1						1				4		
Middleborough	87	9	Keith	Martin	3		1			1			1				6		
Bridgewater	55	29	Keith	Nathan	1	1	1				1	1	1				6		
Bridgewater	61	7	Keith	Robert		1		1				1		1			3		
Bridgewater	50	15	Keith	Salmon	1	2	2	1	1	1	1		1				10		
Bridgewater	50	18	Keith	Samuel			4	1	1				2	1			9		
Bridgewater	50	10	Keith	Seth	2	2	1			3			1	1			11		
Bridgewater	55	28	Keith	Shepherd			1			4			1				6		
Bridgewater	54	31	Keith	Simeon		1	2	1		2	2		1				9		
Bridgewater	50	17	Keith	Solomon	1	2	1			1		1					7		
Bridgewater	65	33	Keith	Thankful			2					1		1			4		
Bridgewater	50	14	Keith	William		2		1		2		1					7		
Bridgewater	65	24	Keith	William	3	1		1			1		1				7		
Bridgewater	65	27	Keith	Zenas	2	1		1		1	1		1				7		
Plymouth	11	22	Kempton	John			1	1					2	1			5		
Plymouth	8	15	Kempton	Zacheus	3	1		1		1	2	1	1				10		
Plymouth	7	3	Kendall	James Revd		2		1			1	2					6		

TOWN	PG#	LN#	LAST NAME	FIRST NAME	M under 10	M 10 to 16	M 16 to 26	M 26 to 45	M 45 and over	F under 10	F 10 to 16	F 16 to 26	F 26 to 45	F 45 and over	TOTAL ALL OTHER	TOTAL SLAVES	TOTALS	DISTRICT/ TOWNSHIP	NOTES
Wareham	111	20	Kendricks	Huldah			1	1		1		1		1			5		
Scituate	124	21	Kent	David					1		2		1				4		
Duxbury	93	16	Kent	Ichabod			1	1			3		1				6		
Marshfield	94	14	Kent	Nathaniel			1	1		3	1		2	1			9		
Marshfield	94	16	Kent	Peleg		1		1				1		1			4		
Scituate	124	22	Kent	Samuel		2	1			1			1				5		
Duxbury	91	3	Kent	William		1	2		1	1	1	1		1			8		
Bridgewater	61	10	Keyes	Walter				1		2			1				4		
Rochester	108	13	Killy	Amos				1		1			3	1	1		7		
Carver	11	15	King	Amaziah			2		1	2	2			1			8		
Rochester	108	12	King	Ebr	4	2		1		1			1	1			10		
Rochester	108	10	King	Geo				1					1	1			3		
Abington	37	31	King	John	1		2	1		2	1	1					8		
Rochester	108	9	King	John	1	2	1		1	1		1	1				8		
Rochester	108	8	King	Molly	2								2	2			6		
Rochester	108	11	King	Nathl		1		1	1	1	1	1					6		
Bridgewater	55	26	Kingman	Abel	2	1		1		2		1	1				8		
Bridgewater	54	30	Kingman	Abiah									1				1		
Middleborough	87	6	Kingman	Abner		1		1					1				3		
Bridgewater	65	19	Kingman	Barza	1			1		4			1	1			8		
Bridgewater	54	29	Kingman	Caleb				1					1	1	1		3		
Bridgewater	65	17	Kingman	David				1				1	1				3		
Hanover	132	14	Kingman	David			1			3	2	2					8		
Bridgewater	65	18	Kingman	Ezra		1	1	1		2	2	1					8		
Bridgewater	55	27	Kingman	Henry				1					1				2		
Middleborough	87	7	Kingman	John		1		1				1		1			4		
Bridgewater	54	26	Kingman	Jonathan		1		1					1				3		
Bridgewater	54	28	Kingman	Jonathan Junr	2	1		1		1	1		1				7		
Bridgewater	54	27	Kingman	Joseph	1			1		1	1			1			5		
Bridgewater	55	25	Kingman	Matthew		1	1	1		1		1	1				6		
Bridgewater	55	30	Kingman	Seth	4	1		1		1		1	1	1			10		
Middleborough	87	11	Kingsley	Zilpah Wo	1					1			1				3		
Bridgewater	65	34	Kinsley	Daniel	1			1			2		1				6		
Bridgewater	61	1	Kinsley	Nymphas				1					2				3		
Bridgewater	65	35	Kinsley	Rodulphus	1			1		2			1				5		
Bridgewater	54	32	Knapp	Phebe						2	1	2		1			6		
Bridgewater	55	32	Knolton	Thomas	2	1	1	1		1	1		1				8		
Duxbury	94	1	Konder	William	1			1		5			1				8		
Plymouth	10	8	Kyes	Oliver	1			1		1			1				4		
Scituate	123	1	Lambert	Zaccheus					1		1	1		1			4		
Plimton	19	13	Lamson	Deborah		1						1		1			3		
Plymouth	11	5	Lamson	George			1			2			1				5		
Plimton	19	15	Lamson	Gideon	1	1		1		2	2	2	1				10		
Plymouth	5	10	Landman	Peter	4			1		1	2		1				9		
Plymouth	5	14	Landman	Sarah	1	1						1	1				4		
Abington	37	37	Lane	Andrew			1					1					2		
Scituate	121	22	Lane	Benjm	1		1	1		4			1				8		
Abington	37	35	Lane	Charles	3			1	1	1		1	1				8		
Abington	37	36	Lane	Daniel Jun		2	3		1	3		1	1	1			12		
Scituate	122	2	Lapham	Abigail									1				1		
Marshfield	101	17	Lapham	Adam		1		1					1				3		
Pembroke	39	20	Lapham	Caleb		1								1			2		
Scituate	123	15	Lapham	Charles	1			1		1		1					4		
Marshfield	101	1	Lapham	Daniel					1					1			2		
Marshfield	104	7	Lapham	Isaac		1		1		1			1				4		
Marshfield	95	11	Lapham	Jabez				1		1		1					3		
Marshfield	96	13	Lapham	Jesse			2		1			1	1	1			5		
Marshfield	95	10	Lapham	Joseph		1					1	1		1			5		
Pembroke	39	13	Lapham	Lemuel				1					1				2		
Scituate	124	20	Lapham	Michael				1		2			1				4		
Marshfield	101	10	Lapham	Roger	1			1		1		1					4		
Marshfield	104	2	Lapham	Stephen					1			1	1	2			5		
Marshfield	101	2	Lapham	Sylvanus	1			1		1			1				4		
Scituate	124	14	Lapham	Thomas				2						3			5		
Scituate	124	23	Lapham	Thos Junr		1		1		3	1		1	1			8		
Bridgewater	61	11	Latham	Chilton			1							1			2		
Bridgewater	66	1	Latham	Seth				1					2				3		
Bridgewater	65	40	Latham	Woodward			2	1				1	1				5		
Bridgewater	61	14	Lathrop	Jacob	1	1	1	1		3			1	1			9		
Plymouth	22	21	Laurence	Daniel	1	1		1		4	1	1	1	1	2		13		
Plymouth	3	14	Lavery	Betsy	1						1	1					3		
Plymouth	4	13	Lavery	Nehemiah	2			1		2		1					6		
Kingston	27	4	Lavery	Thomas	1			1		3			1				6		
Abington	37	33	Lazel	Luther		1		1				1	1				4		
Bridgewater	65	39	Lazell	Byrum	1			1	1	2		1					6		
Bridgewater	61	12	Lazell	Isaac			1	2		3	3	1	1		4		15		
Bridgewater	65	37	Lazell	John				1				1	1				3		
Bridgewater	65	38	Lazell	John Junr	2			1		1	1		1				6		
Bridgewater	61	13	Lazell	Nathan	1	1	1	2		3	4	1	1	1			15		
Bridgewater	65	36	Lazell	Silvanus				1				2	2	1	1		8		
Bridgewater	47	25	Leach	Abraham	1	1	1	1		1		1		1			7		
Bridgewater	61	15	Leach	Apollos	1		2	1		1			1				6		
Bridgewater	61	20	Leach	Benjamin		1			1	3			1				6		
Bridgewater	50	24	Leach	Bernice				1		1		1					3		
Bridgewater	47	26	Leach	Bethiah								3	1	1			5		
Bridgewater	47	23	Leach	Bezer	1			2		2			1				6		

TOWN	PG#	LN#	LAST NAME	FIRST NAME	FREE WHITE MALES					FREE WHITE FEMALES					TOTAL ALL OTHER	TOTAL SLAVES	TOTALS	DISTRICT/ TOWNSHIP	NOTES
					under 10	10 to 16	16 to 26	26 to 45	45 and over	under 10	10 to 16	16 to 26	26 to 45	45 and over					
Bridgewater	50	22	Leach	Ebenezer	1			1					1				3		
Bridgewater	61	17	Leach	Hassadiah		2						1	1	1			5		
Bridgewater	47	22	Leach	Ichabod			2		1		1			1			5		
Bridgewater	50	23	Leach	Jedediah	1		2		1				1	1			6		
Halifax	18	16	Leach	John			1	1				2					4		
Middleborough	89	3	Leach	John			1	1						1			3		
Middleborough	89	4	Leach	John Jur	1			1		1			1				4		
Bridgewater	50	20	Leach	Joseph				1		1			1	1			4		
Plymouth	17	25	Leach	Lemuel			1		1	1	1			1			5		
Plymouth	20	14	Leach	Lemuel	2			1		1			1	1			6		
Bridgewater	61	18	Leach	Levi			2			1		1					4		
Bridgewater	61	19	Leach	Libeus	2			1		3			1				7		
Bridgewater	50	21	Leach	Luke	2			1		2	2		1				8		
Bridgewater	47	27	Leach	Mehitabel	1	1	1			3	2		1				9		
Bridgewater	55	34	Leach	Nathan	1	1	2		1	2				1			8		
Bridgewater	61	16	Leach	Nehemiah				1		2				1			4		
Halifax	18	22	Leach	Silvanus				1		1	1		1				4		
Bridgewater	47	24	Leach	Thomas	1	1			1	1		1	1				6		
Halifax	18	23	Leach	Thomson				1	1	1			1				4		
Rochester	108	22	Leavit	Joseph			1		1	1			1				4		
Rochester	108	21	Leavit	Joseph Jr	1			1		1			1				4		
Scituate	122	12	Leavitt	Gad	4			1		1			1				7		
Plymouth	8	16	LeBaron	Bartlett				1		1	2		1				5		
Plymouth	7	7	LeBaron	Isaac			1		1		1			2			5		
Plymouth	4	8	LeBaron	James			1						2				3		
Middleborough	90	39	LeBaron	Japeth			1	1	1	1	1	1		1			7		
Middleborough	89	5	LeBaron	Lazarus				1		1			1				3		
Middleborough	90	27	LeBaron	Levi	1	2		1		2	1		1				8		
Plymouth	7	6	LeBaron	William				1			1	4					6		
Middleborough	89	13	Leonard	Abigail Wo										1			1		
Wareham	111	21	Leonard	Archippus	1	1				2	1	1	1				8		
Bridgewater	64	31	Leonard	Barney	1							1	1				4		
Middleborough	90	33	Leonard	Benjan Capt	1	1	3	1	1		1			2	1		11		
Middleborough	90	41	Leonard	Daniel			1			2			1				4		
Bridgewater	64	32	Leonard	David	2	2	1		1	2	1		1				10		
Marshfield	97	13	Leonard	Elijah Revd	1			1				1	1				4		
Plimton	19	11	Leonard	Eliphalet			1					1					2		
Middleborough	87	13	Leonard	Elkanah	1	1	1	1	1	1		1		1			8		
Middleborough	90	35	Leonard	Ephraim	2		1			1		1	1				6		
Middleborough	90	40	Leonard	Ephraim 2d	1		1					1					3		
Middleborough	90	32	Leonard	George 2d	3	2	1		1	2		2	1				12		
Middleborough	87	12	Leonard	George Dr			1	1					1	1			4		
Middleborough	90	21	Leonard	Gideon	1	1			1	1	2		1				7		
Middleborough	89	7	Leonard	henry				1					1				2		
Plimton	19	12	Leonard	Henry	1			1					1				3		
Bridgewater	65	11	Leonard	Jacob	2	1		1				1	1				6		
Bridgewater	64	30	Leonard	Jonas		2	1	2					1	1			7		
Bridgewater	64	28	Leonard	Jonathan			1	1					1		1		4		
Middleborough	90	31	Leonard	Jonathan		1		1		4	2		2	1			11		
Middleborough	87	14	Leonard	Joseph				1			1						2		
Middleborough	87	15	Leonard	Joseph 2d			2		1	2		1	1				7		
Middleborough	90	28	Leonard	Josiah	1		1					1					3		
Middleborough	89	8	Leonard	Josiah 2d	1		1		3		1		1				7		
Middleborough	89	14	Leonard	Micah	2	2		1		1			1				7		
Middleborough	89	11	Leonard	Moses	1		1		1	1			1	1			6		
Middleborough	90	22	Leonard	Nathan Dr	1	3		1		3	1		1				10		
Middleborough	90	29	Leonard	Nathl	3	1				2			1				8		
Middleborough	90	30	Leonard	Nathl 2d	2		1				1	1					5		
Bridgewater	64	29	Leonard	Nehemiah	1		1	1		2	1		1				7		
Middleborough	90	38	Leonard	Perez		1						1		1			4		
Plymouth	20	22	Leonard	Phillip			1	1			1			1			4		
Bridgewater	61	21	Leonard	Samuel	1	2	2		1		1	2		1			10		
Middleborough	89	1	Leonard	Samuel			1				1	1					3		
Bridgewater	64	26	Leonard	Silvanus	3		1			1			2	1			9		
Bridgewater	64	27	Leonard	Solomon			1				1		1				3		
Plymouth	16	20	Leonard	Thomas			1			3			1	2			7		
Plymouth	20	23	Leonard	Warren	1		1			1			1				4		
Plymouth	12	1	Leonard	William	1		1			3			1				6		
Middleborough	90	37	Leonard	Zadoch	2		1						1				4		
Pembroke	39	19	Levit	Kindsman	3	1		1		1	1	1	1				9		
Pembroke	39	11	Levitt	John			1		1					1			3		
Marshfield	95	15	Lewis	Bela	1	1		1		2	1		1				7		
Duxbury	91	10	Lewis	Calvin	1	1			1	1	1		1				6		
Marshfield	98	1	Lewis	Daniel		1			1				1	2			5		
Bridgewater	64	33	Lewis	Eleazer		1			1				1				3		
Middleborough	90	23	Lewis	Lathrop	1	1		1		2		1	1				7		
Duxbury	91	4	Lewis	Luther			2				1		1				4		
Plymouth	8	24	Lewis	Nathaniel	2			1		2			2				7		
Bridgewater	55	19	Lewis	Peter											3		3		
Scituate	133	42	Lincoln	Hannah										2			2		
Scituate	123	21	Lincoln	James		1	1		1	1		1		1			6		
Rochester	108	26	Lincoln	John			1						1				2		
Abington	37	34	Lincoln	Joseph				1		2	2	2	1	1			9		
Pembroke	39	9	Lincoln	Levi			1		1			1		1			3		
Pembroke	39	14	Lincoln	Lydia									2				2		
Bridgewater	55	33	Lincoln	Nehemiah	2	1	1		1	2		1	1	1			10		
Bridgewater	54	43	Lincoln	Oliver			2		1			1		1			5		

TOWN	PG#	LN#	LAST NAME	FIRST NAME	FREE WHITE MALES					FREE WHITE FEMALES					TOTAL ALL OTHER	TOTAL SLAVES	TOTALS	DISTRICT/TOWNSHIP	NOTES
					under 10	10 to 16	16 to 26	26 to 45	45 and over	under 10	10 to 16	16 to 26	26 to 45	45 and over					
Wareham	111	22	Lincoln	Rufus	3	2			1		1		1				8		
Rochester	108	24	Lincoln	Sherman	2			1	1	1			2				7		
Scituate	123	19	Lincoln	Solomon	2			1	1	1	1	1		1			7		
Middleborough	90	36	Ling	Silvanus	3			1				1					5		
Pembroke	39	12	Linsey	James	1			1		2	1		1				6		
Scituate	129	13	Litchfield	Abner				1		2			1				4		
Scituate	134	31	Litchfield	Abner H.	4	1	1	1		1	1	1	1				11		
Scituate	130	11	Litchfield	Amos			2	1					1				4		
Scituate	129	15	Litchfield	Daniel		2		1	1		1	1	1				7		
Scituate	135	47	Litchfield	Eleazer	2	1	1	1		1	2		1				9		
Scituate	134	38	Litchfield	Elisha		1			1				1				3		
Scituate	129	16	Litchfield	Francis				1		2			1				4		
Scituate	129	12	Litchfield	Frany									1				1		
Scituate	129	18	Litchfield	James					1				1				2		
Scituate	135	42	Litchfield	Job				1	1				1				3		
Scituate	129	20	Litchfield	John	1			1	3				1				6		
Scituate	134	32	Litchfield	Lawrence	2	3	1		1	2		1	1				11		
Scituate	133	13	Litchfield	Lucinda	1						1						2		
Scituate	134	39	Litchfield	Nathaniel	1			1		1			1				4		
Scituate	134	33	Litchfield	Priscilla								1	1				2		
Scituate	134	35	Litchfield	Rhoda								1	1				2		
Scituate	135	36	Litchfield	Rowland	1	1	1	1		2	2		1				9		
Scituate	129	19	Litchfield	Silas	1			1		1			1				4		
Scituate	135	49	Litchfield	Simeon	4			1		2			1				8		
Scituate	135	38	Litchfield	Stephen	1			1	1	1		2					6		
Scituate	135	46	Litchfield	Thomas				1	1			2	2	1			7		
Scituate	136	2	Litchfield	Ward	3	2	1	1		1			1				9		
Pembroke	39	15	Little	Charles			2	1		2	1	1	1				8		
Marshfield	97	1	Little	Ephraim			1	1					1				3		
Marshfield	97	22	Little	George Esq	2		1		1	2	2	1	1				10		
Pembroke	39	16	Little	Isaac	1		2		1	2	1		1				8		
Scituate	136	30	Little	James		1		1		1		1	1				5		
Marshfield	98	19	Little	Jedediah	1			1		2			1				5		
Marshfield	97	2	Little	John		1	1	1			2		1				7		
Marshfield	98	17	Little	Luther		1		1		2		1	1				6		
Marshfield	98	18	Little	Penelope							1		1				2		
Marshfield	98	14	Little	Thomas				1					1				2		
Marshfield	98	15	Little	Thomas Jun	2			1		2	1		1				7		
Middleborough	89	6	Littlejohn	James	1			1	1			1	1				5		
Middleborough	89	12	Littlejohn	William	2			1		1			1				5		
Plimton	26	19	Lobdall	Ebenezer	1	3			1	1		3	1				10		
Hanover	130	5	Long	Stephen Negro											6		6		
Middleborough	89	2	Long	Thomas	1		1			1		1		1			5		
Rochester	108	17	Look	Allice									2				2		
Rochester	108	19	Look	Henry	2			1		1			1				5		
Rochester	108	18	Look	John	3	1		1		1			1				7		
Middleborough	89	9	Look	Joseph	1			1			1						3		
Rochester	108	20	Look	Savory				1			2		1				4		
Hanover	126	17	Loper	Joseph	1			1	1				1	1			5		
Duxbury	100	8	Loreing	Freeman	2	1	1	1		2			1				8		
Duxbury	95	16	Loreing	George			2						1				3		
Duxbury	99	15	Loreing	Jotham		1			1			1	1	1			5		
Duxbury	102	22	Loreing	Levi					1		1		1				3		
Duxbury	102	23	Loreing	Perez		1	2		1		1	1	1				7		
Duxbury	102	19	Loreing	Samuel	1	1			2	1	1	1	1	2			10		
Duxbury	104	24	Loreing	William		1	1		1		1	1	1				6		
Duxbury	104	25	Loreing	Wm Jun	1			1			1		1				4		
Plimton	26	22	Loring	Caleb		1		1	1				1				4		
Plimton	26	16	Loring	Ezekiel	1	3	1		1	3		2	1	1	1		14		
Plimton	21	25	Loring	Hannah								2			1		3		
Plimton	24	18	Loring	Jacob		2		1		2			1				6		
Plimton	21	15	Loring	Melzer	2	1	2		1		1		1				8		
Pembroke	39	17	Loring	Nathll		2		1	2			2		1			8		
Plimton	21	17	Loring	Simeon	1			1		1			1				4		
Bridgewater	54	41	Lothrop	Daniel					1				1				2		
Bridgewater	54	39	Lothrop	David			1		1	1	1		1	1			6		
Plymouth	14	11	Lothrop	David					1		1			1			3		
Plymouth	6	10	Lothrop	Isaac			1		2			1	1				5		
Bridgewater	54	40	Lothrop	Jonathan				1	1					1			3		
Bridgewater	54	37	Lothrop	Josiah					1				1				2		
Bridgewater	54	38	Lothrop	Josiah Junr		1		1		2	1		1				6		
Bridgewater	54	33	Lothrop	Lemuel			1		1				1				3		
Bridgewater	54	34	Lothrop	Mark		1	3		1	1	1		1				8		
Bridgewater	54	36	Lothrop	Seth		2			1	1			1				5		
Bridgewater	54	35	Lothrop	Zephaniah	2	1	1		1	1			2	1			9		
Duxbury	101	2	Louden	Micah Jun	1			1					1				3		
Duxbury	101	3	Loudon	Micah					1			2	1	1			5		
Duxbury	101	4	Loudon	Sylvanus			1			4			1				6		
Abington	37	39	Lovel	Caleb	1			1		2	3		1				8		
Abington	37	38	Lovel	Obediah		1		1		1			1				4		
Middleborough	90	24	Lovell	Joseph	2	1		1		2	1	1	1				9		
Middleborough	90	26	Lovell	Lucy Wo	2				1	2			1				6		
Middleborough	90	25	Lovell	Patience Wo									1				1		
Pembroke	39	18	Lowden	John					1				1				2		
Bridgewater	66	2	Lowden	Nathaniel					1			1	1				3		
Pembroke	39	10	Lowden	Richard			1		1				1				3		

TOWN	PG#	LN#	HEADS OF HOUSEHOLD		FREE WHITE MALES					FREE WHITE FEMALES					TOTAL ALL OTHER	TOTAL SLAVES	TOTALS	DISTRICT/ TOWNSHIP	NOTES
			LAST NAME	FIRST NAME	under 10	10 to 16	16 to 26	26 to 45	45 and over	under 10	10 to 16	16 to 26	26 to 45	45 and over					
Marshfield	96	3	Lowe	Jeremiah	1			1	1	1		1					5		
Marshfield	95	19	Lowe	Wm	1	1	2		1	1		2	1	1			10		
Marshfield	96	1	Lowe	Thomas	1			1		1			1				4		
Carver	9	3	Lucas	Abijah	3	1			1	2	1			1			9		
Carver	12	15	Lucas	Anselm			1			3			1				5		
Plymouth	19	12	Lucas	Anselm			1	1		3			1				6		
Carver	10	16	Lucas	Barnabas	2	2		1		2			1				8		
Plymouth	19	13	Lucas	Bela	1	1		1	1	1	1			2			8		
Carver	9	2	Lucas	Beza	3			1					2	1			6		
Middleborough	89	10	Lucas	Caleb	2		1					1					4		
Carver	12	17	Lucas	Ephraim	1			1		4			1				7		
Carver	7	21	Lucas	Isaac L.	1	2		1		1	2		1				8		
Carver	10	15	Lucas	Joanna		1								1			2		
Carver	9	1	Lucas	John			1	1	1			1	1	1			6		
Carver	12	24	Lucas	Joseph			1		1			2		1			5		
Bridgewater	54	42	Lucas	Lazares			1	1	1	2			1				6		
Plymouth	12	2	Lucas	Levi	2			1					1				4		
Kingston	27	44	Lucas	Nathan		1				1	1	1		1			6		
Carver	10	17	Lucas	Nehemiah	2			1		1			1				5		
Carver	9	21	Lucas	Samuel	3	1	2		1		1	1		1			10		
Plymouth	22	1	Lucas	Wiliam	4	2		1		1	1			1			10		
Rochester	108	16	Luce	Bars		1		1						1			3		
Plymouth	18	8	Luce	Crosby	1	2			1	2	1	1		1			9		
Plymouth	10	22	Luce	Ebenezer			1					1	1				3		
Rochester	108	25	Luce	Lucy		1				1			1				3		
Rochester	108	14	Luce	Rowland	3	1	2	1		1	1	1	1	1			12		
Plymouth	16	4	Luce	Seth				1						1			2		
Rochester	108	15	Luce	Stephen			1						1				2		
Rochester	108	23	Lumbard	Mary	2					1	1		1				5		
Middleborough	90	34	Lyon	Jedediah		1		1					2				4		
Halifax	15	1	Lyon	Obediah	2	1	1		1		1	2		1			9		
Duxbury	101	19	MaCathla	Daniel	1	1	1		1	2	2			1			9		
Duxbury	95	22	Macfarlin	Sarah										1			1		
Middleborough	89	39	Macomber	Aletha Wo	2					1			1				4		
Middleborough	89	46	Macomber	Elijah			2		1		1	1		1			6		
Middleborough	89	47	Macomber	Enoch	2			1		1		1					5		
Bridgewater	54	44	Macomber	Jacob				1		1		2		1			5		
Middleborough	89	31	Macomber	John	3	2		1		2		2	1				11		
Middleborough	90	3	Macomber	Joshua			1			3			1				5		
Middleborough	89	45	Macomber	Lemuel	1		1	1		2	1	2	1				9		
Middleborough	89	27	Macomber	Luther	1	1		1		1			1	1			6		
Middleborough	89	26	Macomber	Nathl Lt		1		1	1	1	2	2	1				10		
Middleborough	89	20	Macomber	Simeon		1	1	1		2		1	1				7		
Bridgewater	52	17	Macomber	Thomas		1	1	1			1	1	1				6		
Hanover	129	5	Macomber	Thomas			1						1				2		
Plymouth	3	20	Macumber	Elijah	1		1						1				3		
Marshfield	97	8	Macumber	William		1		1		1			1				5		
Marshfield	97	9	Macumber	Wm Jun	3		1			2			1				7		
Pembroke	42	9	Magoon	Aaron		1	2		1	2	1	2		1			10		
Pembroke	42	7	Magoon	Abner		1		2				5		2			10		
Pembroke	42	6	Magoon	Abner Junr	1		1			1			1				4		
Pembroke	42	14	Magoon	Isaac		1		1						1			3		
Pembroke	42	11	Magoon	John			2	2	1			3		1			9		
Pembroke	42	10	Magoon	Joseph		1	2		1				1				5		
Duxbury	103	28	Magoon	Joshua	2	1		1		2	1	1	1				9		
Pembroke	42	16	Magoon	Seth	1	1		1	1	2			1	1			8		
Pembroke	42	8	Magoon	Thos	1			1				2	1	1			6		
Plimton	23	6	Magoun	James	1	1		1				1	1				5		
Pembroke	42	3	Mahuren	Isaac	1	1		1		3		1	1	1			9		
Hanover	125	5	Mallin	John Revd	1			1					1	1			4		
Pembroke	42	13	Man	David	2	3	1		1	1		1	1	1			11		
Pembroke	42	12	Man	Ebenezer	1	1		1		1	1			2			7		
Rochester	107	14	Manhal	Allen	1	1		1				1	2		2		8		
Bridgewater	52	19	Manly	Daniel				1		1		1		1			4		
Bridgewater	52	20	Manly	Daniel Junr	3	1	1		1	1		1	1				9		
Bridgewater	52	16	Manly	Lewis	4		1						1				6		
Bridgewater	52	18	Manly	Nathaniel		1			1	4	2	2		1			11		
Hanover	127	12	Mann	Benja Junr	1			1					1	1			4		
Hanover	127	11	Mann	Benjamin		1		1		1		2		1			6		
Hanover	127	14	Mann	Charles			1			1		1	1				4		
Scituate	135	41	Mann	David				1						1			2		
Scituate	135	39	Mann	Deborah				1					1	2			4		
Scituate	136	45	Mann	Deborah		1							1	1			3		
Scituate	136	11	Mann	John	2		1	1		2	1						7		
Scituate	134	14	Mann	Jonathan		1	1		1			2		1			6		
Hanover	128	1	Mann	Joseph			1	1						1			3		
Rochester	107	26	Mann	Joseph	2			1		1			1				6		
Hanover	127	8	Mann	Joshua	2		1	1		1			1				6		
Scituate	133	8	Mann	Josiah		1		1			1	1	1				5		
Hanover	127	13	Mann	Levi	2	1		1		3			1				8		
Scituate	135	40	Mann	Susanna									1				1		
Plymouth	23	9	Mantor	Prince	1			1		1			1				4		
Bridgewater	66	10	Marshall	Allen		1		1					1	1			4		
Plymouth	10	25	Marshall	Barsheba						1	1		1				3		
Bridgewater	52	21	Marshall	Hayward	2			1		1			1				5		

TOWN	PG#	LN#	LAST NAME	FIRST NAME	FREE WHITE MALES					FREE WHITE FEMALES					TOTAL ALL OTHER	TOTAL SLAVES	TOTALS	DISTRICT/ TOWNSHIP	NOTES
					under 10	10 to 16	16 to 26	26 to 45	45 and over	under 10	10 to 16	16 to 26	26 to 45	45 and over					
Rochester	107	23	Martin	Abigail		1						1		1			3		
Plymouth	7	20	Massey	Stephen	4	2			1	2	1	1	1				12		
Rochester	107	17	Mathews	Nathan		1	1		1	2	1	1	1				8		
Plymouth	5	3	Mathews	Thomas	1			1	1				1	1			5		
Wareham	112	4	Maxham	David		1			1	1	1			1			5		
Wareham	112	3	Maxham	Reubin	3		3		1		1	2		1			11		
Rochester	108	28	Maxham	Thomas	1			1	1	1			1				5		
Wareham	112	1	Maxhie	Andrew	1	2	1		1	2		1		1			9		
Middleborough	89	44	McConeley	John	4				1	1			1	1			8		
Middleborough	90	17	McDale	John	1		2			1			1				5		
Pembroke	42	1	McFarland	Deborah										2			2		
Pembroke	39	21	McFarland	Foster	3	1		1	1	1			1				8		
Middleborough	90	20	McFarland	James			1			1				1			3		
Pembroke	42	15	McFarland	Rebeckah	2								1	1			4		
Pembroke	42	2	McFarland	Simeon					2				1	1	1		4		
Carver	12	10	McFarling	Huit	2		1	1		2			1				7		
Kingston	27	47	McGlocklin	Elisha	2			1		2			1				6		
Kingston	27	46	McGlocklin	John			1							1			2		
Kingston	27	45	McGlocklin	Robert			1	1				2	1	1			6		
Pembroke	39	22	McLathland	Joseph	2	2		1		2			1				8		
Rochester	107	20	Mead	Zacheus	2	1		1	1	3	3	1	1	1			14		
Bridgewater	54	45	Mehurin	Jonathan	2				1	1		1	1				6		
Bridgewater	64	42	Mehurin	Josiah				1		1	1	2		1			6		
Bridgewater	64	43	Mehurin	Josiah Junr	1			1					1				3		
Bridgewater	62	2	Melen	Samuel Junr				1					1				2		
Rochester	107	8	Mendal	Abner	2			1					1				4		
Rochester	107	6	Mendal	Caleb	1		1	1	1				1	1			6		
Rochester	107	1	Mendal	Moses	*	*	*	1	*	*	*	*	*	*	*	*	1		Tape mark
Rochester	107	13	Mendal	Timo	2			1		2			1	1			7		
Rochester	107	24	Mendel	Barse	1			1					1	1			4		
Rochester	107	4	Mendel	Danl	3				1	1			1				6		
Rochester	107	18	Mendel	David			1			3	1	1		1			7		
Rochester	107	11	Mendel	Ebr	1			1		1				1			4		
Rochester	107	19	Mendel	Jonn		1		1		2			1				5		
Scituate	135	31	Merritt	Amos	4	1		1			1	1	1				9		
Scituate	135	27	Merritt	Asahel	2			1					1				4		
Scituate	134	36	Merritt	Caleb				1					1	1			3		
Scituate	129	10	Merritt	Consider	2	2	1		1	1		1	2	1			11		
Scituate	134	15	Merritt	Daniel	3	2		1					1				7		
Scituate	135	28	Merritt	Elizabeth									1	1			2		
Scituate	136	25	Merritt	Ensign			1			1				2			4		
Scituate	133	23	Merritt	Gamaliel	2	1		1		1	2	1	1				9		
Scituate	136	15	Merritt	Israel				1		3			1				5		
Scituate	133	16	Merritt	John					2			1		2			5		
Scituate	136	26	Merritt	Malichi	1			1		4				1			7		
Scituate	133	22	Merritt	Nehemiah	1			1	1	1	1		1	1			6		
Scituate	136	27	Merritt	Noah	2			1		1	1		1				6		
Scituate	131	1	Merritt	Seth	3	2		1		1	1		1				9		
Rochester	107	15	Merry	Wm	1		1			1			2				5		
Rochester	107	9	Millard	John			1	1					1	1			4		
Middleborough	90	11	Miller	Anram		1		1				1	2				5		
Middleborough	90	10	Miller	Elias		1		1						2			4		
Middleborough	89	30	Miller	Isaac				1									1		
Middleborough	89	16	Miller	Jacob		2		1		1		4		1			9		
Middleborough	89	34	Miller	Jedediah			2	1				1		1			5		
Middleborough	89	21	Miller	John		1		1		1	1		1				5		
Middleborough	89	22	Miller	John 2d Cap				1				1	1				3		
Middleborough	89	23	Miller	John 3d	1			1		2			1				5		
Middleborough	89	35	Miller	Joseph			1					1					2		
Middleborough	89	37	Miller	Lucy										1			1		
Middleborough	89	36	Miller	Mary										1			1		
Middleborough	89	38	Miller	Peter		3	1		1	3			1	1			10		
Middleborough	89	25	Miller	Samuel		1		1		1	1		1				5		
Middleborough	89	32	Miller	Seth	1		1	1					1				5		
Bridgewater	55	16	Mingo	Cloe											5		5		
Rochester	107	16	Mitchel	Calvin		1	2	1					1				5		
Marshfield	102	19	Mitchel	James			1							1			2		
Marshfield	101	13	Mitchel	Rispah		2	1				1	1		1			6		
Marshfield	101	7	Mitchel	Sarah		1							1	1			3		
Kingston	27	17	Mitchell	Benjamin			2							1			4		
Bridgewater	66	4	Mitchell	Bradford		1	2	2		1		1					7		
Bridgewater	64	40	Mitchell	Cary			1							1			2		
Bridgewater	66	3	Mitchell	Cushing		3		1					1	1			6		
Bridgewater	64	39	Mitchell	Daniel	1		1	1				1	1	1	1		7		
Bridgewater	64	35	Mitchell	Edward 3d			2	1		3		1	1				8		
Bridgewater	64	34	Mitchell	Edward Junr			2	1						2			5		
Bridgewater	66	6	Mitchell	Jacob				1						1			2		
Bridgewater	64	41	Mitchell	John	1	1	1		1			2	1				7		
Kingston	27	48	Mitchell	John	1			2		1			1				5		
Bridgewater	66	5	Mitchell	Nahum	1		1	1		1			2		1		7		
Bridgewater	64	38	Mitchell	Nathan	1			1		1	1	1		1	2		8		
Bridgewater	66	7	Mitchell	Seth					2				1	1			4		
Bridgewater	66	8	Mitchell	Seth Junr	3				1	1			1				6		
Bridgewater	64	36	Mitchell	Theodore		1	1			1		2					5		
Bridgewater	64	37	Mitchell	William	1			1		2			2	1			7		
Bridgewater	66	9	Mitchell	Zenas	1			1					1				3		
Rochester	107	10	Mondal	Seth	1		3		1	1	3	1	1	1			12		

111

TOWN	PG#	LN#	HEADS OF HOUSEHOLD LAST NAME	FIRST NAME	FREE WHITE MALES under 10	10 to 16	16 to 26	26 to 45	45 and over	FREE WHITE FEMALES under 10	10 to 16	16 to 26	26 to 45	45 and over	TOTAL ALL OTHER	TOTAL SLAVES	TOTALS	DISTRICT/ TOWNSHIP	NOTES
Scituate	136	35	Monson	Nehemiah	2		1			1			1				5		
Middleborough	89	15	Monson	Robert	1		1						1				3		
Middleborough	90	1	Montgomery	Hugh	1		1	1		3	2	2					10		
Rochester	107	12	Moore	Jonn	2			1			2		1				6		
Middleborough	89	33	Moranville	Lewis				1					1				2		
Middleborough	90	18	Moranville	Lewis Jr			1			1		1					3		
Rochester	107	25	Morell	John		1	1			1		1					4		
Wareham	112	2	Morey	Benjm		2		1					1				4		
Plymouth	21	21	Morey	Cornelius	2	2		1		1	1		1				8		
Middleborough	89	17	Morey	Mary Wo			1						1	1			3		
Plymouth	17	29	Morey	Silas	3	1		1		2	1		1				9		
Plymouth	21	20	Morey	Silvanus	2			1		2			1				6		
Middleborough	89	42	Morison	William	1		1		1	1	1	2		1			8		
Carver	12	8	Morrisey	John	1		1						1				3		
Rochester	108	27	Morse	*		1		1		2	2						6		Tape mark
Bridgewater	64	44	Morse	Ephraim	1		1	1					3	1			7		
Middleborough	90	5	Morse	Isaac		2		1					1				4		
Middleborough	90	6	Morse	Isaac Junr		1				2			1				4		
Rochester	107	7	Morse	John			2		1	1	2		1				7		
Middleborough	90	4	Morse	Joseph	2			1					1				4		
Rochester	107	5	Morse	Joshua		1	1	1				2		1			6		
Middleborough	90	7	Morse	Levi		1		1		1			1				4		
Rochester	107	3	Morse	Melatiah	1			1				1					3		
Middleborough	90	16	Morse	William	1			1		1				1			4		
Rochester	107	2	Morton	Bartlett	*	*	*	1	*	3							4		
Plymouth	11	1	Morton	Benjamin	2			1		2	2		1				8		
Middleborough	89	28	Morton	Caleb	1			1		2			1				5		
Plymouth	20	10	Morton	Caleb			1						1				2		
Plymouth	11	14	Morton	Cary			1		1					1			3		
Plymouth	4	1	Morton	Edward		1	1	1		1	1		1	1			7		
Plymouth	18	9	Morton	Eleazer	2	1	2		1	2			1				9		
Carver	11	17	Morton	Elisha			1	1						1			3		
Plymouth	20	9	Morton	Ezekiel		1		1		1	1	1					5		
Kingston	29	12	Morton	Ezra			1			1			1				3		
Middleborough	90	13	Morton	George	1		1	1		1			1	1			6		
Plymouth	12	10	Morton	george	1	1		1		2		1		2			9		
Plymouth	17	7	Morton	Ichabod			1	1		1		1		2			6		
Middleborough	89	18	Morton	Ichabod Dr	1		1	1		4	1		1				9		
Plymouth	17	6	Morton	Ichabod Jr		1		1		3	1		1				8		
Middleborough	89	29	Morton	Isaac	3			1					1				6		
Carver	9	22	Morton	Job		1		1		3	1		1	1			8		
Scituate	136	37	Morton	John			1							1			2		
Middleborough	90	14	Morton	John 2d			2			1	1		1				5		
Middleborough	89	24	Morton	John Capt	2	1		1		1		1	1				7		
Plymouth	20	3	Morton	Josiah	1	2		1		2			2				8		
Halifax	18	14	Morton	Nathaniel	2	1		1		1			1				6		
Plymouth	4	4	Morton	Osborne	1		1			1		1	1	1			7		
Plymouth	20	8	Morton	Rebecca	1	1				2			1				5		
Plymouth	17	17	Morton	Samuel	1			1		2			1				5		
Plymouth	1	4	Morton	Seth	1		1			1			1	1			5		
Middleborough	90	2	Morton	Seth Junr		3			1	1			1	1			10		
Hanover	132	12	Morton	Silas	2			1		2			1				6		
Plymouth	18	27	Morton	Thomas	1	1	1	1	1	3	1		2				11		
Plymouth	20	18	Morton	Thomas			2		1		2	3	1				9		
Plymouth	19	5	Morton	William Jr		1		1		2			1				5		
Middleborough	89	19	Morton	Zephaniah		1	1		1	1	1	1		1			7		
Scituate	134	27	Mott	Atwood				1				1		2			4		
Scituate	131	13	Mott	Stephen	1	1		1		2	1	1		1			8		
Rochester	107	21	Muggs	Caleb	1			1					1				3		
Rochester	107	22	Muggs	Ebr	1			1	1	3			1				7		
Carver	12	13	Munham	John				1		2	1		1				5		
Pembroke	42	4	Munro	Henry			1		1	2	1			2			8		
Bridgewater	66	11	Munro	Henry			1						1				2		
Halifax	16	13	Munroe	Bennel	1			1		1			1				4		
Hanover	125	10	Munroe	Mary									1	2			3		
Hanover	125	2	Munroe	Shubael	2			1		2			1	1			7		
Halifax	17	11	Munroe	William	1			1		2	1			1			6		
Middleborough	90	15	Munson	Thomas				1				2		1			4		
Carver	12	2	Murdock	Elisha		1		1		4	1		1				8		
Carver	12	9	Murdock	John	2		2	1		1	1	1	1	1			10		
Middleborough	90	8	Murdock	John			2		1			1		1			5		
Middleborough	90	9	Murdock	John Jr	3	1		1		1			1				7		
Middleborough	90	12	Murdock	Levi		1		1		1			1				4		
Middleborough	90	19	Murdock	Luther	1			1					1				3		
Carver	12	1	Murdock	William	3			1		1		1		1			6		
Pembroke	42	5	Muro	Joseph	1		1						1				3		
Middleborough	89	43	Muxsom	Abigail Wo							1	1		1			3		
Middleborough	89	40	Muxsom	Caleb		1	3		1			1	1				8		
Middleborough	89	41	Muxsom	Samuel	2	2	1		1	2				1			9		
Abington	37	46	Nash	Asa	1			1		1			1				4		
Abington	35	5	Nash	Daniel	1			1	1	2		2		2			9		
Abington	37	43	Nash	James	1	2		1		2			1				7		
Scituate	134	6	Nash	James	1		1		1			2	2		2		6		
Abington	37	44	Nash	John		1			1				1				3		
Scituate	121	20	Nash	John	1			1		1			1				4		
Abington	37	41	Nash	Jonathan				1					1				2		
Scituate	133	17	Nash	Joseph		1		1				2		1	1		6		

TOWN	PG#	LN#	HEADS OF HOUSEHOLD		FREE WHITE MALES					FREE WHITE FEMALES					TOTAL ALL OTHER	TOTAL SLAVES	TOTALS	DISTRICT/ TOWNSHIP	NOTES
			LAST NAME	FIRST NAME	under 10	10 to 16	16 to 26	26 to 45	45 and over	under 10	10 to 16	16 to 26	26 to 45	45 and over					
Scituate	135	4	Nash	Joseph Junr	1			1					2				4		
Abington	35	4	Nash	Luke	2	1	1	1	1	3	2	1	1				13		
Abington	37	45	Nash	Lydia			1						1				2		
Abington	35	3	Nash	Matthew		1		1				1		1			5		
Abington	37	42	Nash	Nathl				1		4			1				6		
Abington	35	1	Nash	Peter			2		1			1					4		
Scituate	133	18	Nash	Solon	2			1		1			1				5		
Scituate	128	19	Neal	Joseph	2			1		1			1				5		
Kingston	30	5	Negro	Cuff											6		6		
Kingston	30	21	Negro	Quash											3		3		
Rochester	106	6	Negro	Thos											3		3		
Plymouth	3	2	Nelson	Ebenezer	1	1		1		2			1	1			7		
Plymouth	3	3	Nelson	Ebenezer		1			1		1		1	1			5		
Middleborough	87	21	Nelson	Ebenzr Mr	1	1	1	1		1	1	2	1	1			10		
Plymouth	4	9	Nelson	Hezekiah	1			1	1	2	1	1	1	1			9		
Middleborough	87	17	Nelson	Hiram	1			1					1				3		
Middleborough	87	22	Nelson	Isaac		1		1			1	2					5		
Middleborough	87	18	Nelson	John Col	1		2	1		1			3	1			9		
Plymouth	3	5	Nelson	Joseph W.		1		1				1	1	1			5		
Plymouth	3	11	Nelson	Lemuel				1				1	1	1			4		
Middleborough	87	27	Nelson	Saml Revd	1		1		1	1			4	1			9		
Middleborough	87	19	Nelson	Thomas		1	1		1	1	1			2			7		
Plymouth	5	16	Nelson	Thomas				1		1			1	1			4		
Middleborough	87	20	Nelson	Thos Jr Dr	1			1		2			2				6		
Plymouth	14	12	Nelson	William	1		1	1		2			1				6		
Middleborough	87	16	Nelson	William Mr		1	1	1		1			1				5		
Bridgewater	53	1	Newberry	Lemuel	1		1	1			1						4		
Rochester	106	2	Nichols	Asa	3		1					1					5		
Scituate	133	12	Nichols	Meriam	1		1	1		1				1			5		
Scituate	130	1	Nichols	Noah					1	2	2		2				7		
Plymouth	6	23	Nicholson	Hannah	2	1	2			2		3	1				11		
Plymouth	12	18	Nicholson	Seth	3			1		3			1	1			9		
Hanover	128	19	Nickerson	Joseph Negro											3		3		
Plymouth	18	23	Nicols	Moses	3	1		1		1	1	1	1				9		
Middleborough	87	23	Niles	David	1			1	1				1				4		
Middleborough	87	26	Niles	Samuel				1	1					1			3		
Abington	35	2	Noles	Saml	1			1		1		2		1	1		7		
Middleborough	87	31	Norcut	Elijah			1					1					2		
Middleborough	87	29	Norcut	Elizabeth Wo										1			1		
Middleborough	87	28	Norcut	Ephraim	2			1		1			1				5		
Middleborough	87	24	Norcut	John					1				1	1			3		
Middleborough	87	25	Norcut	John Junr	4		1	1		2	1	1					10		
Middleborough	87	30	Norcut	William				1				1	1				3		
Wareham	112	7	Norris	Oliver	1			1					1				3		
Plymouth	24	13	Norris	Samuel	1			1		1			1				4		
Scituate	134	12	Northey	Bettey	1		1			1	2			1			6		
Scituate	134	18	Northey	Elizabeth							1			1			2		
Scituate	127	9	Northey	Mary									1	1			2		
Scituate	127	10	Northey	Robert	1			1		2			1				5		
Abington	37	47	Norton	Benjm	1			1					1				3		
Abington	37	48	Norton	Saml	1		1	1		3	2	1	1	1			11		
Abington	35	7	Noyes	Benjm	3			1					1				5		
Abington	35	10	Noyes	Daniel	1			1	1	1			1	1			6		
Bridgewater	66	12	Noyes	Ebenezer					1				1	1			3		
Abington	35	6	Noyes	Eliab	1		2						1	2			7		
Abington	35	8	Noyes	Ephraim	3	1	1	1				1	1	1			9		
Abington	35	9	Noyes	Ichabod			1							2			3		
Bridgewater	52	22	Noyes	John	1	1	1		1	1	1			2			8		
Abington	37	40	Noyes	Matthew	1	1		1				1	1	1			6		
Bridgewater	52	23	Noyes	Simeon			1			4		1					6		
Rochester	106	5	Nye	Bars	2	1		1					1				5		
Wareham	112	6	Nye	David			1		2				1	1	1		6		
Plimton	23	15	Nye	Elias	3			1		2			1				7		
Rochester	106	7	Nye	Geo	2	2		1			1	1	1	1			9		
Wareham	112	5	Nye	Jabez		1			1			1	1	1			5		
Rochester	106	4	Nye	John					1				1	1			3		
Plimton	22	10	Nye	Jonathan		1	1		1			1	1	1			6		
Rochester	106	3	Nye	Nathan	1			1	1	2	2	1	1				9		
Rochester	106	8	Nye	Stephen		1		1					1				3		
Rochester	106	1	Nye	Wm Jr	3	2		1		1		1	1				9		
Pembroke	42	23	Oakham	Allis									1	1			2		
Marshfield	97	5	Oakman	Amos	2			1		1	1		1	1			7		
Marshfield	102	7	Oakman	Constant F.		3		1		3			1				8		
Marshfield	104	3	Oakman	Louisa							1			1			2		
Marshfield	102	6	Oakman	Tobias					1				1	1			3		
Plymouth	6	19	Obrien	James		2	1		1				1				5		
Plymouth	12	28	Obrien	Joseph	1								1				3		
Plymouth	6	5	O'Larrie	Edmund	4			1					1	1			7		
Pembroke	42	21	Oldham	David		1			1	2				2			6		
Pembroke	42	22	Oldham	David Junr	1		1			1			1				4		
Duxbury	103	1	Oldham	John	1	2			1	2		1	2				9		
Pembroke	42	20	Oldham	John					1		1			1			3		
Scituate	124	11	Oldham	Jonathan		1		1						1			3		
Middleborough	88	2	Oliver	Nathan	2			1		2		1					6		
Middleborough	88	1	Oliver	Phebe Wo							1			1			2		
Rochester	106	9	Oliver	Susanna									1				1		

TOWN	PG#	LN#	LAST NAME	FIRST NAME	FREE WHITE MALES					FREE WHITE FEMALES					TOTAL ALL OTHER	TOTAL SLAVES	TOTALS	DISTRICT/ TOWNSHIP	NOTES
					under 10	10 to 16	16 to 26	26 to 45	45 and over	under 10	10 to 16	16 to 26	26 to 45	45 and over					
Wareham	112	8	Olliver	Peter											6		6		
Middleborough	88	3	Omen	Job			1			1			1				3		
Abington	35	11	Orcut	Elijah		1	1		1	1	1		1				6		
Bridgewater	64	45	Orcutt	Deborah									1				1		
Bridgewater	53	2	Orcutt	Ephraim	3	1			1	2	1		3				11		
Bridgewater	55	36	Orcutt	Leonard			1			1			1		1		4		
Bridgewater	53	3	Orcutt	Nathan	1	2	1			1			1				6		
Bridgewater	55	35	Orcutt	Nathaniel			1	1		1			1				4		
Bridgewater	66	15	Orr	Hector	1			1		2		1			1		6		
Bridgewater	66	14	Orr	Hugh	2	1				3			2				10		
Bridgewater	66	16	Orr	Mary								1	1	1			3		
Scituate	126	11	Osborn	Ebenz			1						1				2		
Bridgewater	66	17	Osborne	Thomas	1	2		1		3	1		1				9		
Pembroke	42	19	Osbourn	George		1		1						1			3		
Pembroke	42	17	Osbourn	George Junr			1				1			1			3		
Pembroke	42	24	Osbourn	John	2		1							1			4		
Pembroke	42	18	Osbourn	Levi			1			1				1			3		
Scituate	133	29	Otis	Abijah	2			1		2			1				6		
Plymouth	14	10	Otis	Barnabas		2	1			1			1				5		
Scituate	133	28	Otis	David	2	1		1	1	2	2	3		1			13		
Scituate	136	18	Otis	Ensign			1		1	3				1			6		
Scituate	123	14	Otis	Ephraim		2			1	1		1		1	1		7		
Scituate	130	18	Otis	Ignatius			1		1				4	1			7		
Scituate	127	20	Otis	James	1	1		1	1				3	1			8		
Scituate	134	29	Otis	John	2	1			1	3		1	2	1			11		
Scituate	136	47	Otis	John Junr	1			1					1				3		
Scituate	136	4	Otis	Joshua				1					1	1			3		
Scituate	136	5	Otis	Joshua Junr			2	1				2		1			6		
Bridgewater	66	13	Otis	Josiah	1	1	2		1	1	1		2				9		
Scituate	133	34	Otis	Mary								1		1			2		
Scituate	131	21	Otis	Paul	2									1	1		6		
Scituate	136	46	Otis	Phebe							1	1	1				3		
Scituate	136	50	Otis	Prince		1	1		1				1				4		
Scituate	133	30	Otis	Prince									1				1		
Bridgewater	56	13	Packard	Abiah				1			1		1				3		
Bridgewater	53	23	Packard	Abiah Junr			1			3			1				5		
Bridgewater	53	34	Packard	Adin		1	1		1	1	1	1		2			8		
Bridgewater	56	2	Packard	Ames	1	1		1		1			1	1			6		
Bridgewater	53	33	Packard	Benjamin				1					1				2		
Bridgewater	53	37	Packard	Content		1	1			2			1				7		
Bridgewater	53	27	Packard	Cyrus	1	1		1		2			1				6		
Bridgewater	53	30	Packard	Daniel	1		1			2		2					6		
Bridgewater	56	6	Packard	Ebenezer				1					1				2		
Bridgewater	53	9	Packard	Elijah	3	1		1		2			1				8		
Bridgewater	53	26	Packard	Elijah	2			1		2			1				6		
Bridgewater	56	9	Packard	Eliphalet	3	1	1	1					1	2			9		
Bridgewater	53	24	Packard	Howard		1		1		1			1				4		
Bridgewater	56	21	Packard	Isaiah	3			1		1	1	1	1				8		
Bridgewater	56	1	Packard	Jonah	1	1		1		1	1		1	1			7		
Bridgewater	53	31	Packard	Jonas	2	1			1	1	3	1		1			10		
Bridgewater	53	8	Packard	Jonathan			1	2		1				2	1		7		
Bridgewater	54	1	Packard	Jonathan 2d	3			1	1	1			1				6		
Bridgewater	56	11	Packard	Joseph	2		1			2			1				6		
Bridgewater	56	15	Packard	Kezia	2	1					1		1				5		
Bridgewater	53	28	Packard	Lemuel	2	2	1	1					1	1			8		
Bridgewater	56	3	Packard	Levi	2			1		1			1				6		
Bridgewater	56	8	Packard	Lot			1			3			1				5		
Bridgewater	53	32	Packard	Nathan			1			1				1			3		
Bridgewater	56	10	Packard	Noah	2		1			3	1		1				8		
Bridgewater	54	2	Packard	Oliver			1					1					2		
Bridgewater	53	29	Packard	Parmenas	3	1	2	1		1	1		1				10		
Bridgewater	53	35	Packard	Ransom	1		1						1				3		
Bridgewater	56	7	Packard	Robert	2		1			3	1	1					8		
Bridgewater	56	4	Packard	Silas	2		1	2			1	1	1				8		
Bridgewater	53	10	Packard	Simeon	1		1			1		1	1				5		
Bridgewater	56	20	Packard	Simeon				1					1				2		
Bridgewater	53	25	Packard	Thomas				1					1				2		
Bridgewater	56	16	Packard	Thomas Junr	3	1	1	1					1	2			9		
Bridgewater	55	38	Packard	William				1					1				2		
Plymouth	14	25	Packard	Zadock	2			1		1	1		1				6		
Bridgewater	56	22	Packard	Zenas	2			1		2	1		1				7		
Bridgewater	54	4	Packard	Zion	2			1		1		1	1	1			7		
Middleborough	88	13	Paddock	Benjan	1			1			1		1				4		
Middleborough	86	23	Paddock	John				1		4	1		1				7		
Middleborough	83	28	Paddock	Zachariah				1									1		
Abington	35	30	Pain	Zebulon		1	2		1	1			1	1			7		
Abington	35	31	Pain	Zebulon Junr	5	2	2	1		1	2		1				14		
Rochester	106	25	Paine	Epm	1		1						1				3		
Scituate	122	20	Palmer	Benjamin				1				1	1				3		
Scituate	122	15	Palmer	Jane										2			2		
Halifax	17	15	Palmer	Joshua	4	2		1		1			1				9		
Scituate	122	11	Palmer	Lydia										2			2		
Scituate	121	11	Palmer	Nehemiah			1					1	1				3		
Halifax	15	14	Paris	Daniel	2			1		2			1				6		
Kingston	28	1	Paris	Martin	2			1					1				4		

TOWN	PG#	LN#	HEADS OF HOUSEHOLD		FREE WHITE MALES					FREE WHITE FEMALES					TOTAL ALL OTHER	TOTAL SLAVES	TOTALS	DISTRICT/ TOWNSHIP	NOTES
			LAST NAME	FIRST NAME	under 10	10 to 16	16 to 26	26 to 45	45 and over	under 10	10 to 16	16 to 26	26 to 45	45 and over					
Plimton	24	1	Parker	Betsey					1				1	3			5		
Rochester	106	13	Parker	Ebr			2	1		1			1	1			6		
Scituate	135	35	Parker	Eleazer			1	1			2			2			6		
Plimton	23	24	Parker	Jonathan		1		1	1				1				4		
Middleborough	83	20	Parker	Micah		1	1	1					1				4		
Plimton	22	1	Parker	Oliver	1		2	1		1		1					6		
Plimton	23	25	Parker	Polacarpus				1		1			1				3		
Rochester	106	12	Parker	Polly	1								1				2		
Abington	35	34	Parkman	Daniel				1			1	1	1	1			5		
Rochester	106	17	Parlow	David	1			1			1		1				4		
Rochester	106	14	Parlow	Jesse	4			1	1	2			1	1			10		
Rochester	106	15	Parlow	Thomas	3		1	1			2		2				9		
Rochester	106	16	Parlow	Wm				1									1		
Pembroke	41	4	Parris	Benjamen	1	2		1					1	1			6		
Bridgewater	63	30	Parris	Benjamin	2			1		1		1	1				6		
Middleborough	86	1	Parris	Isaac	3	1	1	1			1	1	1				9		
Middleborough	86	3	Parris	Moses	1	1	1	1					1				5		
Middleborough	86	2	Parris	Samuel		1		1		1				1			4		
Plymouth	23	22	Parsons	William	1			1		3	2		1				8		
Duxbury	96	8	Partridge	Calvin	1		2	1	1	2		1	1				9		
Duxbury	97	16	Partridge	George Esquire				1			1	1	1				4		
Duxbury	101	7	Partridge	Lucresia									1				1		
Duxbury	96	6	Patengal	Daniel	2	1	1										4		
Plymouth	15	19	Paty	John	1	2	1	1		1	1		1				8		
Plymouth	18	25	Paty	Silvanus	1	1		1		2			1				6		
Plymouth	15	28	Paty	Thomas	2		1					1					4		
Plymouth	23	18	Pearce	Jesse	2	2		1			1		1				7		
Plymouth	23	10	Pearce	Richard			2		1		1			1			5		
Plymouth	23	11	Pearce	Richard Jr	1			1		1			1				4		
Rochester	106	24	Pease	Asa				1					3		1		5		
Wareham	112	10	Pease	Cors	2	1	2		1	1			1	1			9		
Rochester	106	23	Pease	Theos				1				3		1			5		
Rochester	106	22	Pease	Theos Jr				1					1				2		
Rochester	106	20	Peckham	David		1	1	1	1	1		1	3		1		10		
Middleborough	88	6	Peirce	Abiel Capt				1			2		1				4		
Middleborough	88	7	Peirce	Abiel Jur	2	1		1			1		1				6		
Middleborough	86	11	Peirce	Abner			1						1				2		
Middleborough	86	4	Peirce	Abrm			1		1	4	2		1				9		
Middleborough	85	39	Peirce	Arodia	2	1	1		1				1				7		
Rochester	105	2	Peirce	Asa	1			1		2	1		1	1			7		
Middleborough	86	10	Peirce	Betsey Wo	1	2		1				1	1				6		
Middleborough	83	26	Peirce	Edmund	1		1							1			3		
Middleborough	85	34	Peirce	Eleazer	2			1		1			1				5		
Middleborough	88	17	Peirce	Eliphalet	1		1	1		3	1		1				8		
Middleborough	86	8	Peirce	Elisha			1			2			1				4		
Middleborough	83	24	Peirce	Elkanah		1				1	1						3		
Middleborough	86	16	Peirce	Ephraim	1			1		1		2					5		
Middleborough	83	25	Peirce	Freeman		1				1		1					3		
Middleborough	85	38	Peirce	George			1		1	1			1	1			6		
Scituate	135	33	Peirce	Hayward Esqr	2	3		1		1	1	1	1				10		
Middleborough	85	37	Peirce	Hermon	1		1			2	1		1	1			7		
Middleborough	86	9	Peirce	James Capt	2	1	1	1		1	1	2		1			10		
Middleborough	83	18	Peirce	Job 2d		2		2					2	1			7		
Duxbury	104	12	Peirce	Joseph		1	1	1					1	1			5		
Rochester	105	3	Peirce	Joshua		1		1		3			1				6		
Middleborough	85	35	Peirce	Levi			1	1		1		1					4		
Middleborough	85	36	Peirce	Levi 2d	1			1		1			1				4		
Middleborough	83	23	Peirce	Richard	5	2	1		1				1	1			11		
Middleborough	85	25	Peirce	Richard Junr	2				1	4				1			8		
Rochester	106	18	Peirce	Saml	1	1	1	1					1	1			6		
Middleborough	85	30	Peirce	Silas	1	1	1	1	1	1	2	2		1			11		
Middleborough	85	33	Peirce	Silas	1			1		1			1				4		
Middleborough	86	5	Peirce	Simeon	2	2		1		2	2		1				10		
Middleborough	88	9	Peirce	William	3		1	1		1		1	2				9		
Rochester	106	11	Peirce	Wm	3			1					1				5		
Scituate	133	15	Pencin	Simeon		2	1	1				2		1			7		
Abington	35	33	Penniman	Bethuel		1	1	1		1				1			5		
Bridgewater	56	19	Perkins	Abigail									1	1			2		
Bridgewater	63	4	Perkins	Abraham				1						1			2		
Middleborough	83	30	Perkins	Azel	1	1		1		1			1				5		
Middleborough	86	18	Perkins	Barnabas			1			1		1					3		
Rochester	106	19	Perkins	Benjn	3	2	2	1		1	1	1	1				12		
Plimton	21	8	Perkins	Bezimel				1		1			1	1			4		
Duxbury	96	13	Perkins	Calvin	1		1			1			1				4		
Kingston	29	7	Perkins	Daniel			1			1		1					3		
Bridgewater	63	1	Perkins	Ebenezer	3			1		1			1				6		
Bridgewater	64	47	Perkins	Enoch	3	1		1		2			1	1			9		
Plymouth	16	7	Perkins	George			1						1				2		
Carver	7	20	Perkins	Gideon	2	1		1		1	2		1				8		
Middleborough	88	15	Perkins	Isaac				1						1			2		
Middleborough	86	17	Perkins	Isaac 2d			4	1			1	2		1			9		
Bridgewater	64	46	Perkins	Jacob		2							1	1			4		
Middleborough	86	14	Perkins	Jacob	1			1		1			1	1			5		
Bridgewater	63	2	Perkins	James	1		1	1	1				2	3			9		
Bridgewater	55	39	Perkins	Jesse	1		1	1			1		1	1			6		
Plimton	26	23	Perkins	John	3	1	1	1			2		2				10		
Bridgewater	56	17	Perkins	Jonah	2		1	1		1		1	1				7		
Plimton	21	7	Perkins	Jonah	2		1		1		1		1				6		

115

TOWN	PG#	LN#	HEADS OF HOUSEHOLD LAST NAME	FIRST NAME	FREE WHITE MALES under 10	10 to 16	16 to 26	26 to 45	45 and over	FREE WHITE FEMALES under 10	10 to 16	16 to 26	26 to 45	45 and over	TOTAL ALL OTHER	TOTAL SLAVES	TOTALS	DISTRICT/TOWNSHIP	NOTES
Bridgewater	53	38	Perkins	Jonathan					1			1		1			3		
Bridgewater	56	5	Perkins	Jonathan Junr		1		1					1				3		
Middleborough	88	18	Perkins	Joshua	4	2			1	1			1				9		
Bridgewater	56	14	Perkins	Luke	1	1	2						1				6		
Carver	7	22	Perkins	Luke	1			1			1		1				4		
Plimton	19	6	Perkins	Luke	1			1		1		1					4		
Plimton	23	14	Perkins	Luke				1			1		1				3		
Bridgewater	53	36	Perkins	Mark		1		1			4		1				7		
Middleborough	83	22	Perkins	Nathan	1			1		1		1					4		
Bridgewater	53	6	Perkins	Nathaniel		1	1		1		1	3		1			8		
Bridgewater	53	7	Perkins	Nathaniel Junr	1		2				2		1				6		
Bridgewater	63	31	Perkins	Priscilla								1	1				2		
Bridgewater	53	4	Perkins	Richard				1				2	1				4		
Bridgewater	63	3	Perkins	Rufus			3			1	1	1					6		
Carver	7	23	Perkins	Samson			1					1					2		
Plimton	24	2	Perkins	Seth	2		1	1		2			1				7		
Bridgewater	56	18	Perkins	Shepard	1	1		1				1					4		
Middleborough	86	6	Perkins	Thomas				1		2			1				4		
Bridgewater	53	5	Perkins	William			1					1					2		
Bridgewater	55	40	Perkins	Zadoc	2		1					1					4		
Plimton	23	12	Perkins	Zepheniah	1		1	1			1		1				5		
Hanover	130	15	Perrey	Adam	1	2	1		1	2			1				8		
Pembroke	41	5	Perrey	Henry			1	1					1				3		
Hanover	128	17	Perrey	Israel		1	2		1	1	1		1				7		
Pembroke	41	8	Perrey	Seth		1	1	1		1		1					5		
Pembroke	41	11	Perrey	Smal	1		1	1	1	1		2	1				9		
Middleborough	88	4	Perry	Andrew		1		1		1			1				4		
Pembroke	41	10	Perry	Barnabas	2		1			2			1				6		
Wareham	112	9	Perry	David	1		1	1		1		1	1				6		
Middleborough	88	16	Perry	Elijah Dr		1	1		1			1		1			5		
Hanover	126	7	Perry	Isaac				1				1		2			4		
Pembroke	41	6	Perry	James	1			1		2			1				5		
Middleborough	88	12	Perry	John	2			1		1			2	1			7		
Plymouth	19	9	Perry	John	2			1		2			1				6		
Carver	11	2	Perry	Jonathan	1			1		3	1		1				7		
Middleborough	88	11	Perry	Joshua				1				1	2				4		
Carver	11	5	Perry	Judah	2			1		1			1				5		
Hanover	129	14	Perry	Samuel B.	4	1		1		2	1		1				10		
Duxbury	104	5	Peterson	Elijah			4	1				1		1			7		
Duxbury	103	21	Peterson	Jebez	1			1				1					3		
Duxbury	99	19	Peterson	Joshua	2	2		1				1	1				7		
Duxbury	104	7	Peterson	Judah		1	1					1					3		
Duxbury	104	6	Peterson	Luther	2		1	1		3			1				8		
Duxbury	91	30	Peterson	Lydia									2		5		7		
Hanover	125	14	Peterson	Mary								1	3				4		
Duxbury	102	8	Peterson	Nehemiah		2		1			1	1	1				6		
Middleborough	83	19	Peterson	Perez	2			1		2		1	1				7		
Duxbury	94	6	Peterson	Reuben	2	2	1		1	2	1	1		1			11		
Marshfield	94	17	Peterson	Samuel		1	1		1	1		1	1				6		
Duxbury	96	11	Peterson	Thadeus			2		1	2	1		1				7		
Duxbury	104	3	Peterson	Thomas				1					1				2		
Duxbury	104	4	Peterson	William	1			1				1					3		
Bridgewater	53	41	Pettingill	Akerman			2						1				3		
Bridgewater	53	40	Pettingill	Daniel	1			1	1	2			1	1			7		
Bridgewater	53	42	Pettingill	Hugh	2	2		1		3		1	1				10		
Rochester	106	21	Phelps	Edward												3	3		
Pembroke	41	2	Philips	Blany				1				1	1				3		
Pembroke	41	3	Philips	Christopher	1	1	3			1			1				8		
Pembroke	41	1	Philips	Lot	1		2		1	2	2	1	2				11		
Bridgewater	54	6	Phillips	Abiel	2			1		2	1		1				7		
Duxbury	102	14	Phillips	Benjm	1			1				1	1				4		
Duxbury	91	17	Phillips	Daniel	3	1			2			1	1				8		
Bridgewater	56	12	Phillips	Ebenezer				1					1				2		
Duxbury	91	13	Phillips	Elisha Esq		1	1			1		1	1				5		
Bridgewater	54	5	Phillips	Isaac	1			1		1			1				4		
Bridgewater	66	24	Phillips	John	1			2		2			1				6		
Bridgewater	54	7	Phillips	Lewis	1			1		2			1				5		
Bridgewater	66	21	Phillips	Mark				1				2					4		
Bridgewater	66	22	Phillips	Mark Junr	2	1		1		2		1	1				8		
Bridgewater	66	23	Phillips	Thomas	1			1		1	1		1				5		
Duxbury	101	11	Phillips	Thomas		1			1	2	2		1				7		
Bridgewater	66	25	Phillips	Turner		2		1		1			1				5		
Middleborough	86	13	Phinney	Jonathan		1	1		2	1		1		1			7		
Bridgewater	54	3	Phinney	Pelitiah				1					1				2		
Middleborough	83	27	Pickens	Esther Wo								2	2	1			5		
Middleborough	85	28	Pickens	George	1			1		2			1				5		
Middleborough	86	12	Pickens	Isaac	1			1		3		1					6		
Middleborough	85	29	Pickens	John	4			1		1	1		2				9		
Middleborough	85	32	Pickens	Samuel		1	1		1	1			1				5		
Middleborough	85	26	Pickens	Silas	1			1		3			1				6		
Middleborough	85	27	Pickens	Zatto	2			1		2			1				6		
Pembroke	41	14	Pierce	Abram				1				1		1			3		
Bridgewater	65	15	Pierce	America											7		7		
Scituate	131	23	Pierce	Calvin		1	1		1		1	1	1				6		
Pembroke	41	13	Pierce	Christopher	1		1	1		1	2		2				8		
Pembroke	41	12	Pierce	Elizabeth	1						1		1				3		

TOWN	PG#	LN#	LAST NAME	FIRST NAME	FREE WHITE MALES under 10	10 to 16	16 to 26	26 to 45	45 and over	FREE WHITE FEMALES under 10	10 to 16	16 to 26	26 to 45	45 and over	TOTAL ALL OTHER	TOTAL SLAVES	TOTALS	DISTRICT/ TOWNSHIP	NOTES
Bridgewater	63	5	Pierce	Jacob	2			1					1				4		
Scituate	134	41	Pierce	Martha									1				1		
Scituate	131	15	Pierce	Mathew		1	2		1		1		1				6		
Bridgewater	55	14	Pierce	Peter											5		5		
Scituate	131	2	Pierce	Seth			1	1	1			1	1				5		
Middleborough	85	23	Pierre	Job Capt	1	1			1			2		1	1		7		
Bridgewater	63	27	Pincin	Benjamin				1		1	1		1	1			5		
Bridgewater	63	28	Pincin	Benjamin Junr	1		1			1		1					4		
Bridgewater	63	26	Pincin	William		1		1		1	1		1	1			6		
Wareham	112	11	Pine	Wm					1					1			2		
Rochester	106	10	Pitcher	Thos	2	2		1		1			2				8		
Plymouth	11	10	Polden	Jonas	2			1		2			1				6		
Plymouth	13	2	Polden	Jonathan		1		1					1	1	1		4		
Plymouth	4	17	Polden	Thomas	2			1				1					4		
Plymouth	8	17	Polder	George			1					1		1			3		
Bridgewater	63	32	Pool	Asa	2			1					1				5		
Abington	35	16	Pool	Aseph		1						1					2		
Abington	35	15	Pool	Benjm	1	1		1		2	1		1				7		
Abington	35	18	Pool	Jacob	1		1		1	1	1	1		2			8		
Abington	35	19	Pool	James	1	3		1					1				6		
Halifax	18	15	Pool	John	3	1	2		1	1	1	1		1			11		
Abington	35	26	Pool	Joseph			2		1			1	2	2			8		
Abington	35	28	Pool	Joseph Junr					1					2			3		
Abington	35	17	Pool	Joshua	1				1					1			3		
Abington	35	24	Pool	Micah	2	1	2	1			1	2	1	1			11		
Bridgewater	63	29	Pool	William	2		1			1		1					5		
Bridgewater	63	7	Pope	Benjamin	1	1		1					1				4		
Rochester	105	1	Pope	Seth	2	2	2		1	1	1			1			10		
Rochester	106	26	Pope	Seth Jr				1					1				2		
Plymouth	1	11	Pope	Thomas	2			1				1		1			5		
Bridgewater	53	22	Porter	Isaac	4			1		2	1		1				9		
Bridgewater	56	23	Porter	James		1			1	1		1	1				5		
Abington	35	12	Porter	John			1	1				1		1			4		
Bridgewater	55	37	Porter	John					1			1		2			4		
Bridgewater	63	25	Porter	John	1			1		1			1				4		
Marshfield	101	4	Porter	John	2	1			1	3	1		1				9		
Abington	35	14	Porter	John M. Jun			2	1		2			1				6		
Halifax	16	7	Porter	Jonathan				1		4	1		1				7		
Marshfield	104	13	Porter	Oliver	2	1			1		1			1			6		
Middleborough	83	29	Porter	Oliver	1		1			1		1					4		
Abington	35	13	Porter	Seth		1	1	1					1	1			5		
Middleborough	85	21	Porter	William Capt	2	1		1		2			1	1			8		
Abington	35	29	Porter	Willm			1	1						1			3		
Middleborough	85	22	Porter	Zachariah	1			2		2		1					6		
Middleborough	83	31	Potter	Prince											2		2		
Middleborough	85	31	Pratt	Aberdean	1	1		1		1			1				5		
Middleborough	88	8	Pratt	Abiel Wo									2	1			3		
Middleborough	86	15	Pratt	Abner		1	3		1				1	1			7		
Bridgewater	63	11	Pratt	Asa				1					1				2		
Middleborough	88	19	Pratt	Benjamin	1			1			1		2	1			6		
Middleborough	86	7	Pratt	calvin	1			1					1				3		
Halifax	13	19	Pratt	Consider		2	1		1	1	2		1				8		
Bridgewater	63	12	Pratt	Cornelius	3	1			1		1		1				7		
Bridgewater	66	18	Pratt	David		2			1	1				1			5		
Middleborough	86	21	Pratt	Ebenezer	3	1		1		1	1	1	1				9		
Bridgewater	53	43	Pratt	Enoch	2	1		1		1			1				6		
Carver	9	19	Pratt	Ephraim	3	1	1	1		1	1		1				9		
Carver	10	3	Pratt	Hannah		1				2			1				4		
Middleborough	88	5	Pratt	Holmon				1									1		
Carver	10	2	Pratt	Isaiah	1			1		2			1				5		
Abington	35	25	Pratt	Jane			1				1		1				3		
Middleborough	88	10	Pratt	Job	4			1		2	1		1				9		
Pembroke	41	9	Pratt	John			1			1		1					3		
Bridgewater	47	28	Pratt	Jonah	1			1		1			1				4		
Hanover	126	8	Pratt	Jonathan	2				1		1	1	1	1			7		
Middleborough	86	22	Pratt	Joseph	2	1		1		2			1				7		
Bridgewater	66	19	Pratt	Joshua	1	1			1	1	2		1				7		
Pembroke	41	7	Pratt	Joshua	1		1		1			1		1			5		
Plimton	22	8	Pratt	Joshua		1		1					1	1			4		
Middleborough	83	17	Pratt	Kimball				1				1					2		
Middleborough	83	16	Pratt	Ludia Wo										1			1		
Middleborough	83	21	Pratt	Nathan	2			1		1			1				5		
Bridgewater	63	8	Pratt	Nathaniel	1	2			1	1	1	1		1			8		
Bridgewater	63	24	Pratt	Nathaniel					1			1		1			3		
Abington	35	23	Pratt	Nathl			1			1			1				3		
Abington	35	22	Pratt	Noah	3			1				1	1				6		
Carver	10	1	Pratt	Noah					1					1			2		
Bridgewater	66	20	Pratt	Oliver	1			1		1			1				4		
Abington	35	21	Pratt	Philip Junr	1		1						1				3		
Abington	35	27	Pratt	Philip Junr	1			1		3	3		1	1			10		
Middleborough	86	19	Pratt	Phineas	1			1		4	1		1				8		
Middleborough	86	20	Pratt	Phineas 2d	1			1		3			1				6		
Bridgewater	63	10	Pratt	Silvanus	1			1				2		1			5		
Bridgewater	63	9	Pratt	Simeon	3		1	1			1		1				7		
Bridgewater	53	39	Pratt	Thomas	2			1		3	2		1				9		
Middleborough	85	24	Pratt	Thomas	1	1		1					1				4		
Abington	35	32	Pratt	Thos	1				1			1		1			4		

TOWN	PG#	LN#	HEADS OF HOUSEHOLD		FREE WHITE MALES					FREE WHITE FEMALES					TOTAL ALL OTHER	TOTAL SLAVES	TOTALS	DISTRICT/ TOWNSHIP	NOTES
			LAST NAME	FIRST NAME	under 10	10 to 16	16 to 26	26 to 45	45 and over	under 10	10 to 16	16 to 26	26 to 45	45 and over					
Middleborough	83	15	Pratt	Wm Capt		3	2		1				1	1			8		
Bridgewater	63	6	Price	Benjamin	1				2				1	2			6		
Scituate	134	42	Prince	Noah	1	1			2				1	1			6		
Plymouth	4	3	Prince	Eunice		1		1		1	1		2		2		8		
Kingston	27	50	Prince	John	3			1		3		1	1				9		
Kingston	27	49	Prince	Kimball					1					1			2		
Hanover	125	25	Prince	Melvin Negro											4		4		
Duxbury	100	3	Prior	Benjm			1		1				1	1			4		
Duxbury	100	6	Prior	Eliphaz					1				1				2		
Duxbury	100	4	Prior	Jabez	1			1		1			1				4		
Duxbury	97	18	Prior	Joseph	2			1					1				4		
Duxbury	99	16	Prior	Joseph			2	1	1	1	1	1	1				8		
Duxbury	100	5	Prior	Mathew	1			1					1				3		
Duxbury	100	7	Prior	Sylvanus	2			1		2			1				6		
Scituate	136	23	Prouty	Caleb	2		2		1		1			1			7		
Scituate	128	12	Prouty	David		1	1	1		1		1		1			6		
Scituate	128	10	Prouty	William			3	1	1			2	1	1			9		
Abington	35	20	Puffer	John	2			1		1				1			5		
Middleborough	88	14	Purington	Patience Wo		1	2					2	1	1			7		
Duxbury	94	13	Putnam	Jonathan	1	1	1	1	1		1	3		1			10		
Bridgewater	65	16	Quawko	James											5		5		
Pembroke	44	26	Ramsdal	Anna							1		2				3		
Pembroke	41	23	Ramsdal	Charles				1	1	1	1						4		
Pembroke	41	17	Ramsdal	Garsham	4			2		2			1	1			10		
Pembroke	41	22	Ramsdal	Lazerus				1		1			2				4		
Pembroke	41	15	Ramsdal	Saml	2	1	1		1				1				6		
Pembroke	44	24	Ramsdal	Simeon				1			2		1				4		
Abington	33	9	Ramsdel	Edmond				2						2			4		
Abington	35	37	Ramsdel	Noah	2			1		2			1	1			7		
Bridgewater	63	39	Ramsdell	Joseph		1		1		3			1	2			8		
Hanover	130	14	Ramsdell	Joseph			1		1			1	1	1			5		
Hanover	125	3	Ramsdell	Mary										1			1		
Middleborough	81	32	Ramsdell	Seth	3	2		1		2	1		1				10		
Middleborough	82	1	Ramsdell	William			1			1			1				3		
Pembroke	44	23	Ramsford	John	2	2		1		2	1		1				9		
Duxbury	102	21	Ran	William	4			1		1			1				7		
Pembroke	41	21	Randal	Charles	1		1	1	1	1			1	1			7		
Rochester	105	22	Randal	David			2	1				1		1			5		
Rochester	105	4	Randal	Ebr	2			1		1			1				5		
Rochester	105	12	Randal	Jethro	1	1		1		3		1		1			8		
Rochester	105	7	Randal	Job	2	1		1		2	1		1				8		
Pembroke	44	28	Randal	John	1			1		1		1					4		
Rochester	105	17	Randal	John			2					2	1				5		
Rochester	105	18	Randal	Leml		2	1	1			1	3		2			10		
Rochester	105	8	Randal	Lewis		1	1	1	1	1	1		1				7		
Pembroke	44	25	Randal	Mercy	2			1		2			1				6		
Rochester	105	13	Randal	Saml	3			1					1				5		
Rochester	105	14	Randal	Seth	1	1	1	1				2		1			7		
Duxbury	103	24	Randal	Thomas	2	1		1		2			1				7		
Rochester	105	6	Randal	Thomas	1			1		2			1	1			8		
Hanover	126	5	Randall	Elijah	1	1			1	1				1			5		
Scituate	124	3	Randall	Hannah										3			3		
Hanover	126	6	Randall	Lott	1		1		1			2		1			6		
Plimton	24	27	Randall	Onisamus		1		1		1	1	1	1				6		
Scituate	125	18	Randall	Samuel		1		1		1		4		1			8		
Scituate	121	6	Randall	Sarah										1			1		
Hanover	128	12	Randall	Stephen				1					1				2		
Scituate	124	7	Randall	Zipporah										1			1		
Plymouth	8	9	Randell	Ruth	2	1				1			1				5		
Carver	10	4	Randsome	Benjamin	1			1		1	1	1	2	1			8		
Carver	10	11	Randsome	David				1						2			3		
Carver	10	12	Randsome	Joseph		1	1	1			1	1	1				3		
Carver	7	1	Ranhorne	Rebecca									1	1			2		
Middleborough	81	30	Ransom	Lemuel		1		1					1	1			4		
Bridgewater	56	24	Rathbun	Volentine W	1			1		1			1				4		
Scituate	136	36	Ray	Caleb	2			1				1		1			5		
Bridgewater	53	21	Ray	Jeremiah	2			1					1				4		
Middleborough	84	20	Raymond	Amos		1	1						1	1			4		
Plymouth	24	12	Raymond	Asa			1			3			1				5		
Plymouth	23	8	Raymond	Caleb	2			1					1				4		
Plymouth	4	18	Raymond	Clarke		1		1					1	1			4		
Middleborough	81	25	Raymond	Edward		4	2	1	1				1				9		
Plymouth	26	6	Raymond	Ezekiel	2		2	1	1			1	1	1			9		
Middleborough	81	34	Raymond	Joseph	2			1					1	1			5		
Middleborough	84	14	Raymond	Joshua				1		2			1				4		
Plymouth	23	20	Raymond	Lemuel	2			1		1			1				5		
Plymouth	20	26	Raymond	Nathaniel	2		1		1	1	1	1	1				8		
Plymouth	20	27	Raymond	Nathaniel Jr		1							1				2		
Middleborough	84	16	Raymond	Samuel		1		1					1	1			4		
Middleborough	84	17	Raymond	Samuel 2d				1		2			1				4		
Rochester	105	5	Raymond	Stephen			1						1				2		
Plymouth	8	13	Reap	John M	2			1		1			1				5		
Middleborough	84	7	Redding	Luther			1		1		2	4		2			10		
Middleborough	82	2	Redding	Thankfull									1				1		
Middleborough	82	4	Reding	Joseph	1	1		1				1	1				5		
Middleborough	84	18	Reed	Anna Wo									1				1		
Middleborough	81	33	Reed	Bailey	3			1		3	1		1				9		

TOWN	PG#	LN#	HEADS OF HOUSEHOLD LAST NAME	FIRST NAME	FREE WHITE MALES under 10	10 to 16	16 to 26	26 to 45	45 and over	FREE WHITE FEMALES under 10	10 to 16	16 to 26	26 to 45	45 and over	TOTAL ALL OTHER	TOTAL SLAVES	TOTALS	DISTRICT/ TOWNSHIP	NOTES
Abington	35	35	Reed	Bela				1	1	1		1		1			5		
Pembroke	41	19	Reed	Bela	1			1		1			1				4		
Abington	35	42	Reed	Bezer			1					1		1			3		
Middleborough	81	37	Reed	Charles					1	1		2	1	1			6		
Abington	33	3	Reed	Daniel		1		1	1			1	1				5		
Abington	35	46	Reed	Daniel Jun	2	3	1	1		2			1				10		
Bridgewater	63	41	Reed	Deborah		1	3				1			1			6		
Middleborough	81	26	Reed	Elijah		2		1		1	2	1	1				8		
Bridgewater	53	16	Reed	Ezekiel	1			1		2			1				5		
Rochester	105	24	Reed	Ichabod	1	1	1	1		2	1	3	1				11		
Abington	33	2	Reed	Isaac	1	1		1		2			2				7		
Middleborough	84	15	Reed	Jacob				1				1	1				3		
Abington	33	8	Reed	Jacob Jun	1			1		2	2	1					7		
Abington	33	4	Reed	James				1		1			1	2			5		
Abington	35	36	Reed	James	4	1		2	1	1	1	1	1	1			13		
Plymouth	18	16	Reed	James	2			1		2			1				6		
Middleborough	82	6	Reed	Joanna Wo									1				1		
Abington	35	40	Reed	Joel	2			1		2			1				6		
Abington	35	38	Reed	John	2		1	1		1		1	2	1			9		
Bridgewater	53	14	Reed	John	2		2		1	1			1	1	1		9		
Bridgewater	63	40	Reed	Jonathan	3			1		2	1		1				8		
Middleborough	81	38	Reed	Joshua	2			1		2			1				6		
Pembroke	41	20	Reed	Levi	1			1				1					3		
Middleborough	84	13	Reed	Luke		1		1		1	1	1					6		
Middleborough	84	19	Reed	Lydia									2	1			3		
Rochester	105	15	Reed	Mary									1	1			2		
Abington	35	45	Reed	Micah		2		1		1	1		1				6		
Middleborough	81	21	Reed	Nathan	4		1						1				6		
Plymouth	9	19	Reed	Nathan		1		1		1			1				4		
Abington	35	39	Reed	Obediah		1		1						1			3		
Abington	35	41	Reed	Obediah Jun	3	1		1		1			1				7		
Abington	33	7	Reed	Paul	1			1					1	2			5		
Pembroke	41	16	Reed	Philip			1					1					2		
Abington	35	47	Reed	Saml	3			1		3	1	1	1				10		
Middleborough	81	27	Reed	Samuel	3	1		2		1	1	2		1			11		
Abington	33	5	Reed	Stephen	1			1					2				4		
Abington	33	1	Reed	Tho			1	1				1	1	1			5		
Abington	35	48	Reed	Thos Junr	1	3		1		2			1	1			9		
Bridgewater	53	15	Reed	Timothy	1			1					1				3		
Pembroke	44	27	Reed	Willm				1				1		1			3		
Rochester	105	10	Reed	Wm			1				2	1	1				5		
Pembroke	41	18	Reed	Zadock	1		2			2	1	1		1			9		
Abington	35	43	Remington	Thos				1					1				2		
Abington	35	44	Remington	Thos Jun		1					1						2		
Bridgewater	54	9	Reynolds	Elizabeth							1		2				3		
Rochester	105	25	Reynolds	Isaac	2			1		1		1					5		
Bridgewater	54	8	Reynolds	Jonas	1		1	1				2					5		
Bridgewater	54	10	Reynolds	Joseph	1	1		1		1	1	1	1				7		
Bridgewater	54	11	Reynolds	Joseph Junr		1	1			2			1				5		
Bridgewater	54	13	Reynolds	Polly	1		1			2			1				5		
Bridgewater	53	18	Richard	John				1			1	1	1				4		
Bridgewater	53	17	Richard	Josiah		2	1	1		1		1	1				7		
Bridgewater	53	19	Richard	Seth	2	1		1				1	1				6		
Bridgewater	63	35	Richards	Benjamin		2		1		1		1	2				7		
Bridgewater	63	13	Richards	James			1			1		1	1				4		
Bridgewater	61	42	Richards	Prince											4		4		
Bridgewater	63	16	Richards	Salmon	3	2		1				1	1				8		
Bridgewater	63	15	Richards	Seth				1					1				2		
Abington	33	6	Richmond	Andrew	1			1		3			1				6		
Middleborough	81	29	Richmond	Apollus				1		1			1				3		
Middleborough	81	36	Richmond	Edward			1	1	1			1	1	1			6		
Middleborough	84	21	Richmond	Eleazer	1		1	1	1	1	1		1				7		
Middleborough	84	9	Richmond	Elijah	1	1				1			1				4		
Bridgewater	53	20	Richmond	Isaac	1	1	1	1		2			1				7		
Middleborough	82	3	Richmond	Israel	3		3		1	1	2			1			11		
Middleborough	81	28	Richmond	Job				1					1				2		
Middleborough	81	20	Richmond	John		1		1	1				2	2			7		
Middleborough	81	22	Richmond	Joseph Capt	2		2	1			1	1	1				8		
Middleborough	84	6	Richmond	Micah			1	1		1		1					4		
Middleborough	81	23	Richmond	Rufus				1					1				2		
Plymouth	8	14	Richmond	Salome		1	1			1		2		1			6		
Middleborough	81	24	Richmond	Seth	1			1		1			1				4		
Middleborough	81	31	Richmond	Stephen				1				1	1	1			4		
Bridgewater	54	12	Rickard	Jacob				1				1	1				3		
Plymouth	5	8	Ricket	Anselm	1			1				1					3		
Plymouth	20	29	Ricket	Eleazer				1					1				2		
Plimton	19	24	Ricket	Isaac	3	1		1		1	3		1				10		
Plimton	19	23	Ricket	Samuel		1		1				1	1				4		
Plymouth	18	19	Ricket	Samuel	2	1		1		2			2				8		
Plimton	20	1	Ricket	Simeon	1	1		1		2			1				6		
Middleborough	84	10	Rider	Benjan			1	1						1			3		
Middleborough	81	39	Rider	Chapman	1							1	1				4		
Rochester	105	11	Rider	David	3	1	2	1		1	1	1	1				12		
Middleborough	84	1	Rider	Elisha	1	1	2		1	2	1	1		1			10		
Carver	10	20	Rider	Giles				1		1			1				3		
Middleborough	84	12	Rider	Isaac	2	1		2		3	2		2	1			13		
Plymouth	3	4	Rider	Job	2	1			1				1	2			7		

TOWN	PG#	LN#	LAST NAME	FIRST NAME	FREE WHITE MALES under 10	10 to 16	16 to 26	26 to 45	45 and over	FREE WHITE FEMALES under 10	10 to 16	16 to 26	26 to 45	45 and over	TOTAL ALL OTHER	TOTAL SLAVES	TOTALS	DISTRICT/ TOWNSHIP	NOTES
Plymouth	20	21	Rider	Joshua		1							1				2		
Middleborough	84	4	Rider	Robert		3		1						1			5		
Rochester	105	19	Rider	Saml	3		1	1			1	2		1			9		
Middleborough	84	8	Rider	Samuel			4	1		2	2	2		1			12		
Plymouth	20	19	Rider	Samuel			1	1		1		1		1			5		
Plymouth	5	11	Rider	Seth				1					1	1			3		
Plymouth	15	23	Rider	Seth	1	1		1		2	1	1					7		
Plymouth	10	18	Rider	William				1			2	1	1	1			6		
Kingston	27	15	Riley	Hezekiah	2	2				1		1		1			7		
Kingston	28	19	Ring	Elizabeth	1	1				2			1				5		
Kingston	28	2	Ring	Franis	1	1		2	1	1	2	2		1			11		
Kingston	29	36	Ripley	Calvin		1	4	1		3	1	1	1				12		
Bridgewater	53	11	Ripley	Daniel	2			1		2	1	1	1				8		
Duxbury	101	21	Ripley	Daniel	2			1		2		1		1			7		
Plimton	21	21	Ripley	Ezekiel	1	1		1		3		1					7		
Middleborough	84	11	Ripley	Hezekiah				1		2		1					4		
Plimton	23	20	Ripley	Isaiah		1	2	1				2		1			7		
Plimton	21	24	Ripley	Josiah			2	1		1				1			5		
Bridgewater	53	13	Ripley	Marlbry	2	1		1		1	1		1				7		
Plymouth	11	9	Ripley	Nathaniel		1	1	1					1	2			6		
Bridgewater	53	12	Ripley	Solomon			1	1		1			1	1			5		
Plymouth	19	16	Ripley	Thadeus		1		1		4			1	1			8		
Plimton	21	20	Ripley	Timothy		1	1	1	1		1	3		1			9		
Plimton	19	14	Ripley	William				1					1				2		
Abington	33	10	Ripley	Willm		1	1	1		3	1		2	1	1		11		
Plymouth	3	15	River	Joseph				1		1		1					3		
Plymouth	12	15	Robbins	Anselm	5		1	1				1	1				9		
Plymouth	4	10	Robbins	Benjamin	1	1		1		4			1				8		
Plymouth	4	21	Robbins	Charles	3		1						1	1			6		
Carver	12	16	Robbins	Eleazer	1		1	1		2	1	1		1			8		
Plymouth	14	1	Robbins	James			2			1			1				4		
Plymouth	10	28	Robbins	Jane			3							2			5		
Carver	9	4	Robbins	Joseph	2			1			2		1				6		
Plymouth	11	13	Robbins	Mercy	1	1					1		1				4		
Plymouth	4	12	Robbins	Nathaniel				1				1					2		
Plymouth	1	21	Robbins	Samuel	2	2	1	1									6		
Plymouth	3	18	Robbins	Samuel	2		1	1			2		1				7		
Plymouth	3	9	Robbins	Seth	1			1					1				3		
Hanover	125	11	Robbins	Timothy		1	1	1				4		2			9		
Plymouth	4	11	Robbins	William	3	2		1			1		1				8		
Plymouth	9	1	Roberts	Robert				1			1		1				3		
Middleborough	84	5	Robins	Benjan	2			1		2			1				6		
Middleborough	84	3	Robins	Manasseh				1		1		1					3		
Middleborough	84	2	Robins	Moses				1						1			2		
Middleborough	81	35	Robins	Samuel	2			1		1	1		1				6		
Middleborough	82	5	Robins	Seth	1			1					1				3		
Bridgewater	63	33	Robinson	Benjamin	1	1	1		2	3		2	1	1			12		
Bridgewater	63	14	Robinson	Dyer	3		1	1				1		1			7		
Bridgewater	63	34	Robinson	William			2		1	3	1	1	1				9		
Plymouth	13	19	Rogers	Abigail		1	1							1			3		
Marshfield	100	11	Rogers	Adam			1	1					2	1			5		
Marshfield	100	9	Rogers	Amos		1		1			2	2					6		
Marshfield	100	20	Rogers	Asa	2	2		1		2	1		1				9		
Marshfield	99	3	Rogers	Aurunah	2			1		1	1		1				6		
Marshfield	99	4	Rogers	Benjm	1	1		1					1				4		
Hanover	132	23	Rogers	Caleb				1		1			1				3		
Rochester	105	23	Rogers	Ebr	1			1			1						3		
Plymouth	15	14	Rogers	George		1				1	1						3		
Marshfield	104	10	Rogers	Isaac	3			1		1			1				6		
Marshfield	99	2	Rogers	Israel				1					1	1			3		
Marshfield	100	19	Rogers	James	1	1		1		3	1		1	1			9		
Plymouth	15	16	Rogers	John				1						1			2		
Marshfield	100	17	Rogers	Joseph				1		1	1	1		1			5		
Rochester	105	21	Rogers	Moosen			1						1				2		
Marshfield	100	10	Rogers	Nathl		2		1			1	1		1			6		
Marshfield	100	1	Rogers	Nathl Jun				1			2	2		1			6		
Duxbury	91	9	Rogers	Peleg				1		2				1			4		
Marshfield	100	21	Rogers	Peleg				1				1		1			3		
Marshfield	104	5	Rogers	Prince				1						1			2		
Bridgewater	63	38	Rogers	Samuel	3		1	1		1			1				7		
Marshfield	101	20	Rogers	Samuel				1		1		1		1			4		
Plymouth	13	20	Rogers	Samuel				1		1		1					3		
Plymouth	4	6	Rogers	Silvanus				1		1		1					3		
Marshfield	97	17	Rogers	Simeon		1		1						1			3		
Marshfield	100	18	Rogers	Stephen		1		1					1	1			4		
Marshfield	99	1	Rogers	Thomas		1							2	1			5		
Plymouth	12	21	Rogers	Thomas	2			1					1				4		
Plymouth	14	20	Rogers	Thomas		1			1	1		1					4		
Marshfield	97	16	Rogers	Thomas Jun					1			1	2	1			5		
Marshfield	100	8	Rogers	Thomas Junior	1	4	2		1	1			1				10		
Marshfield	98	12	Rogers	Timothy		1		1						1			3		
Scituate	128	3	Rogers	Walter		1	1			3			1				6		
Plymouth	7	25	Rogers	William	1	1		1		1			1				5		
Marshfield	99	5	Rogers	Zackeus				1						1			2		
Marshfield	99	6	Rogers	Zackeus Jun	2	1		1		1			1				6		

TOWN	PG#	LN#	HEADS OF HOUSEHOLD		FREE WHITE MALES					FREE WHITE FEMALES					TOTAL ALL OTHER	TOTAL SLAVES	TOTALS	DISTRICT/ TOWNSHIP	NOTES
			LAST NAME	FIRST NAME	under 10	10 to 16	16 to 26	26 to 45	45 and over	under 10	10 to 16	16 to 26	26 to 45	45 and over					
Scituate	126	12	Rose	Laban	2			1		2			1				6		
Scituate	123	8	Rose	Reuben			1		1		1	2		1			6		
Hanover	128	21	Rose	Seth	1			1				1					3		
Hanover	128	20	Rose	Timothy					1					1			2		
Hanover	129	8	Rose	Timothy Junr				1		2			1				4		
Rochester	105	16	Ruggles	Elisha	4	2	1	1		1	1	2	1	1			14		
Scituate	122	5	Ruggles	John				1						1			2		
Rochester	105	20	Ruggles	Nathl	1	1	1	1	1	3	1	1		1			11		
Rochester	105	9	Ruggles	Polly						1			1	1			3		
Scituate	122	4	Ruggles	Thomas	2	1		1		1	2	1	1				9		
Duxbury	101	20	Rusel	Stephen	2			1		2	1		1	1			8		
Duxbury	102	16	Russell	Lucy								2		1			3		
Bridgewater	63	37	Russel	Abigail										1			1		
Bridgewater	63	36	Russel	Nathaniel	1		1	1				2	2				7		
Scituate	131	19	Russell	Eunice		1							1	1			3		
Kingston	28	24	Russell	George				1		1			2				4		
Plymouth	10	5	Russell	John	1	2		1		1			1				6		
Scituate	133	31	Russell	John	1			1		1	2		1	1			7		
Kingston	29	32	Russell	Melzer	1			1		1			1				4		
Rochester	105	26	Russell	Stephen	1				1			1		1			4		
Bridgewater	63	17	Ryder	Samuel			2						2				4		
Pembroke	44	43	Salmon	Peter		2			1	1			1		1		6		
Hanover	129	10	Salmon	Robert	2	3			1	2			2				10		
Scituate	124	6	Sampson	Araunah	1			1		1	2	1	1				7		
Pembroke	43	15	Sampson	Gideon		1		1						1			3		
Wareham	112	17	Sampson	Ichabod		2	1		2	1		2		1			9		
Pembroke	43	9	Sampson	Isaiah	2	1	1	1				1	1				7		
Pembroke	44	41	Sampson	Jonathan	2			1		4			1				8		
Bridgewater	56	34	Sampson	Micah		2	1	1			1		2	1			8		
Pembroke	43	10	Sampson	Miles	3			1	2	1	1		1	1			10		
Bridgewater	56	35	Sampson	Stephen	1		1			1			1				4		
Pembroke	43	5	Sampson	Stephen	1		1						1				3		
Halifax	13	15	Samson	Abiha	1	1	1	1				1	1				6		
Duxbury	98	17	Samson	Abner				1					1				2		
Duxbury	99	6	Samson	Andrew			1	1			1			1			4		
Middleborough	78	19	Samson	Anna Wo			1							1			2		
Duxbury	101	16	Samson	Anthony				1					1				2		
Marshfield	101	9	Samson	Aron			1			1			1				3		
Duxbury	98	18	Samson	Bartlett			1			1			1				3		
Duxbury	103	11	Samson	Bradford	2		1	1				1					5		
Marshfield	96	16	Samson	Chandler			2	1		2			1				6		
Duxbury	101	10	Samson	Colson	3	2	1	1	1	1	1		1				11		
Duxbury	99	10	Samson	Constant	1			1				1					3		
Kingston	29	29	Samson	Croade				1		2			1				4		
Kingston	29	3	Samson	Crocker	1	1			1	2		1	1				7		
Kingston	29	4	Samson	Desire		1						1	2	1			5		
Plymouth	15	8	Samson	Ebenezer	1			1	1	2	3		2				10		
Middleborough	80	7	Samson	Elias	2		2	1		1	1		1				8		
Duxbury	95	3	Samson	Elijah			1	1	1		2	1		1			7		
Duxbury	98	15	Samson	Elijah Jun	2			1		1	1		1				6		
Plimton	21	13	Samson	George	3	2	2		1	1				1			10		
Duxbury	101	14	Samson	Ichobud	3	1			1				1				6		
Duxbury	98	20	Samson	Isaac	1			1		2			1				5		
Middleborough	80	6	Samson	Isaac	2			1		1			1				5		
Kingston	28	3	Samson	Jeremiah	1	2	2		1	2	1	1	1				11		
Duxbury	98	3	Samson	Job	1	1		1		1	1		1				6		
Duxbury	100	14	Samson	John			2		1	2	2	3	1				11		
Middleborough	79	31	Samson	John				1				1	1				3		
Middleborough	80	4	Samson	John Dr	1		1			1	1		1				6		
Middleborough	80	12	Samson	Jonathan	1			1		1	3	2		1			9		
Plymouth	13	15	Samson	Jonathan		1		1				2	1				5		
Carver	11	3	Samson	Joseph	1			1		1			1				4		
Kingston	30	49	Samson	Joseph	1				2	1	1	1					6		
Plymouth	23	13	Samson	Joseph	1		1	2		1			1				6		
Middleborough	78	14	Samson	Lazarus			1			1		1					3		
Duxbury	104	13	Samson	Mary										2			2		
Plymouth	23	17	Samson	Mary		1	1					4	1				7		
Middleborough	78	13	Samson	Mersbah Wo			1					1		1	1		4		
Duxbury	101	9	Samson	Miles			1	1					1				3		
Duxbury	93	19	Samson	Nathan				1						4			5		
Middleborough	79	32	Samson	Nathan	1		1			1		1					4		
Duxbury	104	18	Samson	Nathl					1	3			2	1			7		
Duxbury	101	12	Samson	Noah			1	1						2			4		
Middleborough	79	35	Samson	Obadiah	1			1		1		1					4		
Kingston	28	4	Samson	Oliver	1				1	2		1					5		
Marshfield	104	17	Samson	Paul			1	1	1				1				4		
Plimton	21	1	Samson	Peleg		1			1	1	2		1				6		
Plimton	21	14	Samson	Philamon	1			1		2	2		1				7		
Kingston	29	5	Samson	Priscilla		1				1			1	1			4		
Plimton	23	23	Samson	Rebecca								1		1			2		
Middleborough	80	9	Samson	Ruth Wo					1					1			2		
Kingston	27	51	Samson	Samuel					1					1			2		
Middleborough	79	37	Samson	Samuel	3			1		2			1				7		
Marshfield	93	9	Samson	Sarah	1						1	1					3		
Plymouth	3	22	Samson	Stephen					1			1	1	1			4		
Duxbury	98	16	Samson	Studley	1	2		1		1	1		1				7		

TOWN	PG#	LN#	LAST NAME	FIRST NAME	FREE WHITE MALES					FREE WHITE FEMALES					TOTAL ALL OTHER	TOTAL SLAVES	TOTALS	DISTRICT/ TOWNSHIP	NOTES
					under 10	10 to 16	16 to 26	26 to 45	45 and over	under 10	10 to 16	16 to 26	26 to 45	45 and over					
Duxbury	100	16	Samson	Sylvanus	1			1		2	1		2				7		
Middleborough	78	11	Samson	Thankfull										1			1		
Middleborough	79	38	Samson	Thomas	1			1					1				3		
Plimton	24	25	Samson	Thomas		1		1			1			1			4		
Duxbury	96	4	Samson	Thomas	2		1	1		2	1		1				8		
Middleborough	80	5	Samson	Uriah				1		2			1				4		
Duxbury	101	15	Samson	Wm	3				2	1	3		1				10		
Bridgewater	63	18	Sanger	Zedekiah	2	5	4	1	1	3		1	2				19		
Plymouth	16	24	Sargent	William				1		2			1				4		
Plymouth	19	2	Saunders	Bella	1			1		3			1				6		
Wareham	112	25	Saunders	Joseph		1		1			1	2		1			6		
Wareham	112	24	Saunders	Nathl			1			2			1				4		
Carver	12	11	Savery	Peleg	2	1		1	1	3			1				9		
Carver	7	9	Savery	Thomas			1	1		1	1		1				5		
Wareham	113	12	Savory	Isaac	1	2	1			1	1	1	1				9		
Wareham	112	20	Savory	Saml Jr	1	1		2		1	2	3	1				11		
Wareham	112	19	Savory	Samuel	2	1		1	1	1	1		2	1			10		
Wareham	113	11	Savory	Thomas		1	1	1					1				5		
Wareham	112	13	Scott	Primus											4		4		
Abington	33	31	Seamon	Thomas				1		1		1	1				5		
Bridgewater	47	30	Sears	Abner						1			1	2			4		
Plymouth	1	17	Sears	Barthll		1							1				2		
Middleborough	80	1	Sears	Earl	1			1						1			3		
Halifax	18	10	Sears	Edward				1					1	1			3		
Halifax	18	9	Sears	Holmes	2	1		1				1		1			5		
Middleborough	79	40	Sears	Leonard	3			1					1	1			6		
Rochester	105	49	Sears	Nathan		1	1		1	1	1			1			6		
Scituate	130	13	Sears	Peter	1			1	1	2	1		2				8		
Plymouth	18	29	Sears	Thomas			1			1			1				3		
Plymouth	17	13	Sears	Willard		2	1		1	2				1			7		
Pembroke	44	47	Setetson	Susa							2	1	1				4		
Bridgewater	64	3	Sever	Christopher	1	1			1	1				1			5		
Kingston	30	31	Sever	James	2		1	1				1	2				7		
Kingston	30	36	Sever	John	5		1	1		1			2	1			11		
Kingston	30	37	Sever	William			2	1		1			1	2			7		
Middleborough	79	27	Severy	Daniel	2	1		1		1			1				6		
Middleborough	82	12	Severy	Nathan	1	2							1				4		
Plymouth	14	17	Seymour	Benjamin	2			2		2	1	1	1				9		
Middleborough	80	10	Sharp	Gibbins		1		1					1	1			4		
Middleborough	80	11	Sharp	Gibbins Jr	1			1		2			1				5		
Rochester	105	50	Shattalar	Hannah	*	*	*	*	*	*	*	*	*	*			*		Tape Mark
Middleborough	77	32	Shaw	Abraham		1		1	1			1	1	1			6		
Abington	33	37	Shaw	Abram			1		1	3				1			6		
Abington	33	36	Shaw	Abram Jun	1			1		3				1			6		
Rochester	105	65	Shaw	Ambrose	2	1	1		1	1	1	1		1			9		
Pembroke	44	29	Shaw	Amous		1			1					1			3		
Abington	33	34	Shaw	Asa	1			1		1		1		1			5		
Bridgewater	47	29	Shaw	Asahel	1		3	1	1	2				1			9		
Carver	7	19	Shaw	Benjamin	2	1		1		1	1	1		1			9		
Abington	33	30	Shaw	Brackley	1	2		1	1	2	1	1		1			11		
Abington	33	35	Shaw	Brackley Jun		1	1			2			2	2			6		
Abington	33	16	Shaw	Calvin	1		3		1	1	2		1	4			13		
Middleborough	82	9	Shaw	Chipman	1	3		1		1		1	1				8		
Carver	11	20	Shaw	Crispus		1		1		1				1			4		
Abington	33	13	Shaw	Daniel		2		1				1	1	1			6		
Carver	11	18	Shaw	David				1						1			2		
Middleborough	78	23	Shaw	David	3	2		1	1				1				8		
Abington	33	28	Shaw	Ebenezer			1		1	2			1				5		
Carver	12	7	Shaw	Elder	1			1					1				3		
Middleborough	80	20	Shaw	Eli	1			1		2			1				5		
Abington	33	27	Shaw	Elijah		1	1		1	1	1			1			6		
Middleborough	77	22	Shaw	Elijah	1			2					2				5		
Middleborough	79	29	Shaw	Elkanah			1	1					1	1			4		
Abington	33	15	Shaw	Ezra		1		1					2	1			5		
Middleborough	78	1	Shaw	Gaius			1			2	1						4		
Middleborough	82	10	Shaw	George Dr			1							1			3		
Middleborough	82	13	Shaw	George Jr Capt	1	1	1	1		2	1		1				8		
Plymouth	8	5	Shaw	Ichabod	1			1				1	1	2	1		7		
Plymouth	18	7	Shaw	Ichabod			1			1			1	1			3		
Middleborough	80	15	Shaw	Isaac				1						2			3		
Middleborough	79	25	Shaw	Isaac 2d	2			1				1	1				5		
Abington	33	33	Shaw	Jacob	1			1		1				1			4		
Middleborough	82	11	Shaw	Jacob	2	2	2	1					1	1			9		
Carver	8	12	Shaw	James	2	1		1		2	1						8		
Pembroke	43	12	Shaw	James			1							1			2		
Middleborough	78	3	Shaw	James Dr					1			1		1			4		
Middleborough	78	4	Shaw	James Jr		1	1			1		1	1	1			7		
Carver	9	10	Shaw	John					1					1	1		3		
Middleborough	79	39	Shaw	John 2d Lt	3			1		2	2	2	1				11		
Middleborough	79	34	Shaw	John 3d	1	1		1	1	3			1	1			9		
Carver	9	9	Shaw	John Jr			2		1	2			2				9		
Carver	8	13	Shaw	Jonathan	2	1		1		2			2	1			10		
Middleborough	79	20	Shaw	Jonathan				1		1			1				3		
Abington	33	24	Shaw	Joseph		1	1		1			1	1	1			6		
Carver	8	16	Shaw	Joseph	1	1	4			1			2				12		
Middleborough	78	2	Shaw	Joseph	3	1	1			1	2		1				10		

TOWN	PG#	LN#	HEADS OF HOUSEHOLD — LAST NAME	FIRST NAME	FREE WHITE MALES under 10	10 to 16	16 to 26	26 to 45	45 and over	FREE WHITE FEMALES under 10	10 to 16	16 to 26	26 to 45	45 and over	TOTAL ALL OTHER	TOTAL SLAVES	TOTALS	DISTRICT/ TOWNSHIP	NOTES
Middleborough	77	37	Shaw	Joshua Capt	1			1	1	2			1				7		
Abington	33	32	Shaw	Levi			1						1				2		
Carver	7	18	Shaw	Levi			1						1				2		
Middleborough	79	26	Shaw	Mark	1	1		1				1	1				5		
Middleborough	79	30	Shaw	Mary Wo									1	1			2		
Bridgewater	54	22	Shaw	Micah	2		1	1		2	1		1				8		
Middleborough	79	28	Shaw	Patience Wo			1				1			1			3		
Bridgewater	63	19	Shaw	Samuel	2			1				1		1	1		6		
Middleborough	79	33	Shaw	Samuel	2			1		3			1				7		
Abington	33	11	Shaw	Silas	2		1	1		1			1				6		
Carver	5	5	Shaw	Silvanus	2	2		1		2	1		1				9		
Plymouth	21	13	Shaw	Silvanus			1		1				1	1			4		
Plymouth	8	6	Shaw	Southworth			1			1			1				3		
Middleborough	79	19	Shaw	Sullivan	2		1			1			1				5		
Bridgewater	54	19	Shaw	William	1				1				1	1			4		
Middleborough	79	23	Shaw	William 2d	1		1		1	3		1	1				8		
Middleborough	79	22	Shaw	William Capt					1		1			1			3		
Bridgewater	54	20	Shaw	William Junr	1	2		1			1	2					7		
Marshfield	94	11	Shaw	William Revd	1				1	2		1	1	1			7		
Bridgewater	63	42	Shaw	Zechariah		1	1		1				1	2			6		
Middleborough	79	36	Shaw	Zephaniah	3		1		1	1	2	2	1	1			12		
Marshfield	99	14	Shearman	Abiel	3				1	2	2		1				9		
Marshfield	99	13	Shearman	Aron	1		1						1				3		
Marshfield	99	16	Shearman	Ebenezer		2	1		1	2			3	1			10		
Middleborough	82	16	Shearman	Edward					1				1	1			3		
Pembroke	44	33	Shearman	Elisha				1		2			1	1			5		
Duxbury	91	18	Shearman	Elizabeth		1				1	1		1	1			5		
Middleborough	77	38	Shearman	Henry	1	1			1	2	2	1	1				10		
Marshfield	99	12	Shearman	Ichabod	2				1	2	1		1				7		
Duxbury	91	16	Shearman	Ignatius		1		1	1	1		1	1	1			7		
Middleborough	79	18	Shearman	Job	4	1		1			2		1				9		
Marshfield	99	11	Shearman	Joseph	1		1	1			1		1	1			6		
Duxbury	91	19	Shearman	Lucy										1			1		
Middleborough	77	36	Shearman	Nehemh	3	1		1		1	2		1				10		
Scituate	134	11	Shearman	Otis	2			1						1			4		
Middleborough	82	15	Shearman	Simeon					1				1	1			3		
Rochester	105	44	Sherman	Abigail			1					1	1	1			4		
Plimton	22	23	Sherman	Asa	2	2		1		2			1				8		
Rochester	105	45	Sherman	Cornelius	1			1		2	1		1				6		
Carver	10	7	Sherman	John	2	2		1			1		1				7		
Rochester	105	69	Sherman	John		2	2	1	1	1	1	2	1	1			12		
Rochester	105	30	Sherman	Joseph	1			1		1		1		1			5		
Rochester	105	41	Sherman	Joshua		2	1	1		1	2		1				8		
Rochester	105	47	Sherman	Joshua 2d	4			1		1	1	1	1				9		
Carver	8	11	Sherman	Nathaniel		1	2		1	1	1		1				7		
Rochester	105	31	Sherman	Richard	1	1		1		1			1				5		
Carver	8	8	Sherman	Rufus		1	3		1			2	1				8		
Plymouth	11	12	Sherman	Samuel	2			1		1			1				5		
Rochester	105	46	Sherman	Thos	2			1		2		1	1				7		
Rochester	105	66	Sherman	Thos 2d	2			1		2			1				6		
Rochester	105	40	Sherman	Wm		2	1	1				1		1			6		
Plymouth	18	15	Shurlliff	Isaac			1					1	1				3		
Plymouth	11	4	Shurlliff	Lydia										2			2		
Carver	8	15	Shurtleff	Barnabas		1	1	1			1	1		1			6		
Carver	9	13	Shurtleff	Benjamin	3	1	3	1		2	1		1				12		
Carver	8	23	Shurtleff	David	2	1	2	1		1	1	3	1				12		
Carver	9	15	Shurtleff	Ebenezer	1			1	1			1	1				5		
Carver	8	1	Shurtleff	Francis		1		1			1		1				4		
Carver	9	16	Shurtleff	Gideon	4	1		1		3	2		1				12		
Carver	12	5	Shurtleff	Lothrop				1		2		1					4		
Carver	9	14	Shurtleff	William				1						1			2		
Plimton	21	11	Shurtlif	Elkanah	1			1					1	1			4		
Middleborough	82	14	Shurtliff	Timothy	1	1		1	1	1	1		1				7		
Marshfield	100	2	Silvester	Amasa	2			1		3			1				7		
Hanover	126	3	Silvester	Edmund		1		1					1				3		
Hanover	129	6	Silvester	Elijah	1			1		1			1				4		
Scituate	124	2	Silvester	Elisha			1	1				1		2			5		
Scituate	124	13	Silvester	Fruitful Negro											8		8		
Marshfield	97	11	Silvester	Hatch		1		1		1	1		1	1			6		
Scituate	127	1	Silvester	Israel		1	1	1				1	1	1			7		
Hanover	129	3	Silvester	Jacob				1						1			2		
Scituate	128	21	Silvester	Jacob	2	1		2						2			7		
Hanover	125	6	Silvester	Joel	3			1		1			1				6		
Plymouth	15	27	Silvester	John	1			1		1			1				4		
Scituate	119	10	Silvester	John	2	1		1		1	2						8		
Marshfield	102	11	Silvester	Jonathan				1		1				1			3		
Bridgewater	54	16	Silvester	Joseph			1	1					1	1			4		
Marshfield	99	7	Silvester	Joseph				1						1			2		
Bridgewater	54	17	Silvester	Joseph Junr	1	1		1		2	2						8		
Scituate	128	22	Silvester	Margarett		2	1							1			4		
Pembroke	43	1	Silvester	Mathew		2		1		1	1			3	1		9		
Hanover	126	2	Silvester	Michael		1		1					1	1			4		
Plymouth	15	26	Silvester	Nathaniel	2			1		1			1	3			8		
Hanover	126	4	Silvester	Robert				1		2	1		1				5		
Halifax	17	3	Silvester	Sally	1		2						1	1			5		

TOWN	PG#	LN#	HEADS OF HOUSEHOLD LAST NAME	FIRST NAME	FREE WHITE MALES under 10	10 to 16	16 to 26	26 to 45	45 and over	FREE WHITE FEMALES under 10	10 to 16	16 to 26	26 to 45	45 and over	TOTAL ALL OTHER	TOTAL SLAVES	TOTALS	DISTRICT/ TOWNSHIP	NOTES
Scituate	125	23	Silvester	Sarah									2				2		
Bridgewater	51	36	Silvester	Seth	3			1		1			1				6		
Scituate	126	23	Silvester	Thomas				1						1			2		
Scituate	121	16	Silvester	Thos Junr		1	1		1	2		2		2			9		
Middleborough	82	17	Simmond	Abraham	1			1		1			1				4		
Plymouth	7	13	Simmonds	Lemuel	1		1		1	1	1	2		1			8		
Plymouth	11	19	Simmons	Bennet	1			1			2		1				5		
Scituate	127	6	Simmons	Charles	3			1					1				5		
Hanover	126	24	Simmons	Elisha	3	1	1					1	1				8		
Rochester	105	36	Simmons	John		1		1		1		1	1				5		
Rochester	105	43	Simmons	John	2	1		1		1	1		1				7		
Hanover	126	25	Simmons	Joshua				1					1	1			3		
Scituate	127	5	Simmons	Leah								1	1				2		
Middleborough	77	33	Simmons	Margett						1			2				3		
Kingston	28	5	Simmons	Noah		2	3	1	1				1				8		
Middleborough	77	41	Simmons	Noah	1			1				1					3		
Scituate	125	16	Simmons	Peleg				1					1				2		
Scituate	127	8	Simmons	Samuel	3	1		1		1			2				8		
Middleborough	78	10	Simmons	Thomas		1		1					1				3		
Marshfield	93	19	Simons	Benjamin		1	2	2	1	1		2	1	1			11		
Duxbury	94	22	Simons	Charles			1			1			1				3		
Duxbury	104	8	Simons	Consider			1	1				2	1				5		
Duxbury	93	4	Simons	Cyrus				1					1				2		
Duxbury	103	3	Simons	Jesse	1			1				1	1				4		
Duxbury	104	2	Simons	Jesse		1	1	1				1	1	1			6		
Duxbury	103	6	Simons	Levi	1			1					1				3		
Duxbury	103	7	Simons	Lydia									1				1		
Duxbury	103	4	Simons	Nathl		1		1		5	1	1	1				10		
Duxbury	96	9	Simons	Noah		1	1	1			1		1				5		
Duxbury	93	7	Simons	Seth	2	1		1		1			1				6		
Marshfield	98	8	Simons	Thomas			1				1						2		
Duxbury	93	5	Simons	Wm				1					1				2		
Duxbury	93	6	Simons	Wm Jun		1		1					1				3		
Middleborough	78	17	Smith	Abiel				1		1			1				3		
Hanover	129	1	Smith	Albert Esq	3	1		1		1	1		1				8		
Duxbury	98	19	Smith	Benjm	2	1	1		1	2	2	2	1				12		
Wareham	112	23	Smith	Chloe	2	2							1				5		
Middleborough	78	5	Smith	Daniel		1		1		1			1				4		
Middleborough	78	6	Smith	Daniel Jur	1			1		2		0	1				5		
Middleborough	77	29	Smith	Ebenz Capt	2			1		2	3		1				9		
Middleborough	80	8	Smith	Elijah		1		1		1			1				4		
Rochester	105	29	Smith	Elijah	1		1			1							3		
Middleborough	78	16	Smith	Ezra	1	1							1				3		
Duxbury	103	16	Smith	Hannah									1				1		
Rochester	105	35	Smith	Henry	1			1		1			1				4		
Bridgewater	63	47	Smith	Henry T.	3			1		2			1				7		
Middleborough	79	21	Smith	Israel	1		2		1		1	2	2	1			10		
Middleborough	77	28	Smith	Jabez			1						1				2		
Abington	33	23	Smith	Jacob		1	1		1		1	2		1			7		
Abington	33	18	Smith	James	2					1			1	1			6		
Middleborough	77	25	Smith	James Jr	1			1		1		1					4		
Middleborough	77	27	Smith	James Lt		2			1		2	1	1	3			10		
Rochester	105	33	Smith	John				1					1				2		
Middleborough	80	13	Smith	John 3d	1			1		1		2					5		
Middleborough	77	34	Smith	John Capt	1		1	1		1		2	1				7		
Wareham	113	10	Smith	Jonah	2	1		1			1		1				6		
Bridgewater	63	45	Smith	Joseph					1		1		1				3		
Middleborough	77	35	Smith	Joseph	3	2		1		1	2		1	1			11		
Pembroke	44	37	Smith	Joseph	3		1		1	1	3		1				10		
Bridgewater	63	46	Smith	Joseph Junr		1				1		1					3		
Middleborough	77	42	Smith	Joshua	1	1		1		1	2	1	1	1			9		
Hanover	129	9	Smith	Josiah		1		1		4			1				7		
Pembroke	43	2	Smith	Josiah	1		3	1			1		1				7		
Middleborough	78	8	Smith	Mary Wo	1					3		1					5		
Pembroke	43	16	Smith	Nathl			1	1		1				1			4		
Abington	33	25	Smith	Nehemiah	3			1			1	2	1				8		
Wareham	112	22	Smith	Peter	1			1					1				3		
Plymouth	13	12	Smith	Sarah									2				2		
Middleborough	78	9	Smith	Thomas				1		3			1				5		
Middleborough	80	14	Smith	Thomas				1		3			1				5		
Rochester	105	32	Smith	Wm	1	1	1	1					1				5		
Middleborough	77	24	Smith	Zenas				1				1					2		
Abington	33	22	Smith	Zenus	2		2	1		2		1	1				9		
Bridgewater	51	34	Snell	Alvin	1		1						1				3		
Bridgewater	63	20	Snell	Benjamin		1			1	3			1	1			7		
Bridgewater	56	31	Snell	Caleb		1	1	1				1	2				6		
Bridgewater	56	26	Snell	Elijah		1			1		1	1	1		1		6		
Bridgewater	56	27	Snell	Elijah Jun	2	1	1						1				5		
Bridgewater	56	28	Snell	Ephraim	1	1		1		2	3		1				9		
Bridgewater	51	30	Snell	Isaachar Junr			1						1				2		
Bridgewater	51	27	Snell	Issachar	1	1			1			2	1	1			7		
Bridgewater	56	25	Snell	Jonah				1					1				2		
Bridgewater	54	21	Snell	Joseph	1	2			1	3	1		1				9		
Bridgewater	56	29	Snell	Nathan			1		1	2	2	1	1				8		
Bridgewater	56	30	Snell	Nathan Junr	1		1						1				3		
Bridgewater	51	26	Snell	Nathaniel		1			2			2		1			6		

TOWN	PG#	LN#	LAST NAME	FIRST NAME	FREE WHITE MALES					FREE WHITE FEMALES					TOTAL ALL OTHER	TOTAL SLAVES	TOTALS	DISTRICT/ TOWNSHIP	NOTES
					under 10	10 to 16	16 to 26	26 to 45	45 and over	under 10	10 to 16	16 to 26	26 to 45	45 and over					
Bridgewater	51	24	Snell	Oliver	2			1		1			1				5		
Bridgewater	64	1	Snell	Pilycarpus			1		1	1	1		1				5		
Bridgewater	54	18	Snell	Shepherd	1			1		1			1				4		
Bridgewater	64	2	Snell	Stephen	2			1					1				4		
Bridgewater	63	21	Snell	William		1			1	2		2	1	1			8		
Bridgewater	51	23	Snell	Zebedee		1	1		2	1	2		1				8		
Bridgewater	51	25	Snell	Zechariah	3			1		1		1					6		
Rochester	105	55	Snow	*			1			1		1					3		Tape Mark
Middleborough	80	16	Snow	Aaron		1	2				1		1				5		
Rochester	105	57	Snow	Bowman				1					1				2		
Bridgewater	56	32	Snow	Daniel		1	1		1		2	1	1				7		
Rochester	105	64	Snow	Ebr				1		3	1	1	1				8		
Rochester	105	37	Snow	Hannah		1		1		1	3			1			7		
Rochester	105	58	Snow	James	2			1	1				1				5		
Bridgewater	56	33	Snow	John	2	2		1		2		1	1				9		
Bridgewater	51	28	Snow	Jonathan	1	2		1		2	1	1	1				9		
Rochester	105	34	Snow	Jonn	3	1		1	1	1	1	1	1	1			11		
Rochester	105	59	Snow	Joseph				1					1				2		
Rochester	105	56	Snow	Joshua	3			1		1			1				6		
Rochester	105	60	Snow	Prince	3			1		2			1				7		
Rochester	105	61	Snow	Rebecca	1					1			1	1			4		
Rochester	105	70	Snow	Saml	1		1	1				1					4		
Bridgewater	54	23	Snow	Seth		1	1			2			1				5		
Bridgewater	51	29	Snow	Silas		2	1				1	1	1				6		
Rochester	105	38	Snow	Susanna		1	1						1				3		
Rochester	105	27	Snow	Thomas	2	2	1			2	1		1				9		
Rochester	105	42	Soper	Alexr	2	1	1		1	2	1	2		2			12		
Scituate	119	7	Soper	Anna										1			1		
Pembroke	44	32	Soper	Elexander	1				1			1	1				4		
Pembroke	44	31	Soper	Isaac	2			1		2			3	1			9		
Pembroke	44	30	Soper	Nathl		1		1				1	1				4		
Plimton	24	26	Soule	Aaron	1			1					1				3		
Duxbury	99	12	Soule	Abigal		2	1	1				1		2			7		
Plimton	19	2	Soule	Asaph	1	1			1		2			1			7		
Halifax	13	17	Soule	Benjamin		2		1				1	1				5		
Plimton	22	16	Soule	Daniel	2			1		1	2		1				7		
Plimton	19	1	Soule	Ebenezer				1		2	1	2		1			7		
Plimton	24	20	Soule	Ephraim				1					1				2		
Duxbury	97	2	Soule	Ezekiel		2	3	1		1							8		
Middleborough	77	26	Soule	Isaac			3		1		1	2	1				8		
Halifax	18	1	Soule	Jabez		1	2		1	1	1		1				7		
Halifax	16	9	Soule	Jacob				1			1						2		
Middleborough	77	30	Soule	Jacob			1	1	1	3		1					7		
Middleborough	77	23	Soule	James 2d	2	1		1			1		2				7		
Middleborough	80	17	Soule	Joh Cap	2	2		1	1		1	1	1				9		
Duxbury	102	11	Soule	Joseph	1			1			1						3		
Duxbury	96	5	Soule	Josiah		2	1	1	1	3		1					9		
Duxbury	97	12	Soule	Mercy				1		1				1			2		
Duxbury	96	1	Soule	Nathl	1			1		2			1				5		
Duxbury	104	10	Soule	Nathl			1		1	1				1			4		
Duxbury	94	5	Soule	Simeon	1	1	2		1	1	2		1				9		
Duxbury	97	3	Soule	Wm	3	2		1			1		1				8		
Plimton	24	19	Soule	Zacheus	1			1		1			1				4		
Scituate	124	10	Souther	Laban		1		1					1				3		
Duxbury	97	6	Southworth	Edward	1	2	2		1			1		1			8		
Duxbury	97	7	Southworth	Edward Jun	1		1	1		1		1					5		
Middleborough	80	3	Southworth	Gideon		1	2		1	1		2	1				8		
Duxbury	93	12	Southworth	James			1	2	1	1	2		1				8		
Duxbury	97	8	Southworth	James Jun	1		1	1		1	1	1					6		
Bridgewater	51	32	Southworth	Lemuel				1		1		1		1			4		
Bridgewater	51	35	Southworth	Mary										2			2		
Middleborough	80	2	Southworth	Nath	2			1		2	1	1		2			9		
Duxbury	100	15	Southworth	Nathl	1	1	1	1	1	1	1		1				8		
Bridgewater	54	14	Southworth	Perez	2	3			1	4	2		1				13		
Middleborough	78	7	Southworth	Seth	1		1	1					1				4		
Scituate	119	21	Southworth	Thos	1			1					1				3		
Scituate	127	15	Sparrell	James	3	1	1	1				2		1			9		
Middleborough	82	7	Sparrow	Edward Col	1	1	1				1	1		2			8		
Middleborough	82	8	Sparrow	Edward Junr			1	1					1				3		
Pembroke	44	42	Spear	Chrisehina		1						1		1			3		
Middleborough	78	15	Spooner	Benjamin		1			1	4	1			1			8		
Plymouth	1	8	Spooner	Ephraim			1	1	1	1		1	1				6		
Plymouth	11	7	Spooner	Nathaniel	3	2		1				2	1	1	1		12		
Middleborough	78	18	Spooner	Samuel	2			1		1	1		1				6		
Scituate	121	4	Sprague	Asher			1		1	1			1	1			5		
Bridgewater	66	26	Sprague	Ephraim		1	2	1		1	2		1				8		
Duxbury	103	12	Sprague	Huldah	1								1				2		
Marshfield	95	3	Sprague	James				1						1			2		
Marshfield	98	5	Sprague	James Jun	1		2		1					1			5		
Marshfield	102	18	Sprague	Jonathan		1	1		1	1	1	1		1			7		
Marshfield	95	4	Sprague	Luther	2			1					1				4		
Marshfield	95	5	Sprague	Melzer	1			1		2			1				5		
Hanover	126	23	Sprague	Priscilla									1	1			2		
Duxbury	95	4	Sprague	Seth	2	1	2		1	4	1	3	2	1			17		
Duxbury	98	11	Sprague	Uriah		1			1	1	3			2			8		
Abington	33	14	Sprague	Willm		1	1		1		1			1			5		

TOWN	PG#	LN#	LAST NAME	FIRST NAME	FREE WHITE MALES					FREE WHITE FEMALES					TOTAL ALL OTHER	TOTAL SLAVES	TOTALS	DISTRICT/ TOWNSHIP	NOTES
					under 10	10 to 16	16 to 26	26 to 45	45 and over	under 10	10 to 16	16 to 26	26 to 45	45 and over					
Middleborough	80	18	Sprout	Thomas Lt	2				2	2	1		2		1		10		
Pembroke	44	35	Standish	Amos		2			1			1	1				5		
Plimton	24	23	Standish	Ebenezer	1	1		1					1				4		
Hanover	132	17	Standish	Hannah								1	2				3		
Rochester	105	67	Standish	Isaiah	1	1		1				1		1			5		
Middleborough	77	31	Standish	Jonathan	2		1						1				4		
Middleborough	78	12	Standish	Joshua	4			1					1				6		
Pembroke	43	11	Standish	Miles	2		1	1		3			1				8		
Middleborough	80	19	Standish	Moses	1			1		3	1		1				7		
Carver	12	3	Standish	Nathaniel	1		1	1		3	2		1				9		
Plimton	24	14	Standish	Sadrich					1		1	2		1			5		
Plimton	24	15	Standish	Sadrich	1		1						1				3		
Pembroke	43	8	Standish	Willm			1		1		1	1	1	1			6		
Pembroke	44	46	Standish	Willm			1		1				1		1		4		
Pembroke	43	7	Standish	Willm Jun	1		1	1		1			1				5		
Scituate	130	2	Standley	Mary								2		2			4		
Bridgewater	66	31	Starr	James		1			1		1			1			4		
Bridgewater	66	32	Starr	James Junr		1				1		1					3		
Carver	10	13	Stephens	Edward					1		1						2		
Pembroke	43	4	Stephens	Edwards	1		1		1			1	1				5		
Plymouth	15	3	Stephens	John	2	1		1		2			1				7		
Pembroke	44	36	Stephens	Nathan			1		1			1	1	1			5		
Plymouth	15	4	Stephens	William		2			1	1			1	2			7		
Pembroke	44	34	Stetson	Abel	1				1				3	1			6		
Bridgewater	63	44	Stetson	Abisha		1	1	1		2			1				6		
Pembroke	43	13	Stetson	Abner	4					1	1	1	1				8		
Scituate	122	8	Stetson	Abner			1	2	1				1				5		
Hanover	130	3	Stetson	Benja Junr			1						1				2		
Hanover	132	24	Stetson	Benjamin					1			1		1			3		
Scituate	121	18	Stetson	Benjamin	1			1	1	3		1					7		
Scituate	133	43	Stetson	Benjn Junr	1			1		1			1				4		
Plimton	23	2	Stetson	Caleb		1			1	1	3			2			8		
Hanover	132	25	Stetson	Edward	1			1				1					3		
Kingston	30	35	Stetson	Elisha	1			1	1	1			1	1			6		
Scituate	119	14	Stetson	Elizabeth								1	2				3		
Abington	33	20	Stetson	Ephraim		1		1		2			1				5		
Scituate	119	8	Stetson	Ephraim	1		1		1	2	3	1	1				10		
Scituate	125	6	Stetson	Gideon					1								1		
Scituate	125	2	Stetson	Isaac					1			1	1				3		
Abington	33	17	Stetson	Jacob	1		1			1			1				4		
Scituate	133	5	Stetson	James	3	1		1		1	1		1				8		
Pembroke	44	39	Stetson	Jeremiah		1			1				2	1			5		
Pembroke	44	38	Stetson	Jeremiah Jr	1	1		1		1	1		1				6		
Bridgewater	63	23	Stetson	John		2		1		2			1				6		
Hanover	128	14	Stetson	John			2		1				1	1			5		
Pembroke	43	3	Stetson	John			1	1		3			2	1			8		
Carver	11	1	Stetson	Jonathan	1			1		1			1				4		
Abington	88	88	Stetson	Levi	1	1	1	1	1	1	1	1	0				0		
Pembroke	43	6	Stetson	Lot	1	1		1		1	1		1				6		
Scituate	119	25	Stetson	Lydia									2		1		3		
Hanover	132	21	Stetson	Martha		1					1	2		1			5		
Scituate	122	10	Stetson	Mathew				1	1				1				3		
Scituate	119	13	Stetson	Micah	3	1	1		1	3	2		1				12		
Hanover	125	22	Stetson	Nathaniel	3			1					1				5		
Hanover	130	18	Stetson	Nathl					1								1		
Abington	33	26	Stetson	Oliver	3	1				1			1				6		
Abington	33	21	Stetson	Peleg							2	1	1				4		
Bridgewater	63	43	Stetson	Ruth	1		1			2	2	2		1			9		
Hanover	125	15	Stetson	Saml			2	1		1			1	1			6		
Pembroke	43	14	Stetson	Saml					1			1		1			3		
Kingston	29	2	Stetson	Samuel	2	1	3		1	3	2	1		1			14		
Hanover	125	12	Stetson	Seth		1		1					1	1	1		5		
Scituate	119	12	Stetson	Silas	4			1		1		1	1				8		
Scituate	121	3	Stetson	Snow	1			1		2	1		1				6		
Scituate	122	7	Stetson	Stephen			3	1				1	2	1			8		
Pembroke	44	44	Stetson	Thos	2		1	1				2		1			7		
Hanover	128	23	Stetson	Turner	1		1	1		2			1	1			7		
Abington	33	12	Stetson	Whitcom	2		1						1				4		
Marshfield	95	18	Stevens	John	2			1		2			1				6		
Wareham	112	14	Stevens	Mary	2		1			1		1	1				6		
Marshfield	95	17	Stevens	Nathaniel	2			1					1				4		
Rochester	105	62	Stevens	Noah	1	1		1		1	1			1			6		
Marshfield	95	16	Stevens	William				1					3	1			5		
Hanover	125	19	Stirling	Ruth									1				1		
Bridgewater	51	33	Stock	John				1			1		1				3		
Scituate	134	7	Stockbridge	Charles	1			1		1	3						7		
Hanover	132	6	Stockbridge	David	1	2	3	1	1	2			1	2	1		14		
Scituate	130	24	Stockbridge	James			3	1	1		1		1	1			8		
Scituate	129	2	Stockbridge	Saml Junr		1		1					1				3		
Scituate	129	1	Stockbridge	Samuel		1	1		1			1	1	1			6		
Scituate	122	17	Stockbridge	Stephen				1					1	1			3		
Hanover	128	16	Stockbridge	William	1	1	1			1		1		2			9		
Abington	33	19	Stoddard	Nathan				1			2		1				4		
Scituate	134	9	Stodder	Canturbury			1						1				2		

TOWN	PG#	LN#	LAST NAME	FIRST NAME	FREE WHITE MALES					FREE WHITE FEMALES					TOTAL ALL OTHER	TOTAL SLAVES	TOTALS	DISTRICT/ TOWNSHIP	NOTES
					under 10	10 to 16	16 to 26	26 to 45	45 and over	under 10	10 to 16	16 to 26	26 to 45	45 and over					
Scituate	123	18	Stodder	Edward		1							1				2		
Scituate	128	11	Stodder	Hezekiah	1		1		1	1	1		1				6		
Scituate	128	7	Stodder	Hezekiah Junr	2	1	1		1	2	2	1	1				11		
Scituate	119	9	Stodder	Melzar			1				2	1					4		
Scituate	128	17	Stodder	Obadiah	3	1	1							1			6		
Scituate	130	25	Stodder	Seth	1		1	1	1	1				2			7		
Bridgewater	63	22	Storre	Elijah		1	1		1		1	1		1			6		
Plymouth	9	14	Straffens	William	2		1						1	1			5		
Plymouth	10	24	Strattens	George	2		1					1					4		
Middleborough	78	20	Strobridge	Henry	1	1		1		2	1		1				7		
Middleborough	77	43	Strobridge	Jane Wo									1				1		
Middleborough	77	40	Strobridge	Sarah Wo									1				1		
Middleborough	77	39	Strobridge	William	1	1		1		2			1				6		
Rochester	105	39	Stuart	Thankful									1				1		
Scituate	134	20	Studley	Amasa				1									1		
Pembroke	44	40	Studley	Benjn	2		1	1		2	1		2				9		
Hanover	130	20	Studley	Elihab	2		2		1	1	1	1	1				9		
Hanover	125	23	Studley	Gideon		1	1		1			2	2	1			8		
Hanover	126	15	Studley	Jabez			1		1			1	1				4		
Hanover	130	21	Studley	Japheth	2	2		1		1	1	1		1			9		
Scituate	134	44	Studley	John	1	2		1		3	1		1	1			10		
Scituate	131	24	Studley	Lewis	3			1		1		1		1			7		
Scituate	130	6	Studley	Olive										2			2		
Scituate	125	1	Studley	William		1		1						1			3		
Halifax	17	1	Sturtevant	Amasa				1		1			2	1			5		
Halifax	17	22	Sturtevant	Barzillai	3		2	1		1							8		
Rochester	105	48	Sturtevant	Charles	2	1	1		3	2	1	1	1	1			13		
Wareham	113	4	Sturtevant	David	1		1			2		1					5		
Halifax	17	17	Sturtevant	Dependent		2	1		1	2	2		1				9		
Kingston	27	1	Sturtevant	Elijah					1	1	1	1	1				6		
Bridgewater	51	31	Sturtevant	Ephraim			1			1	1		1				4		
Wareham	113	9	Sturtevant	Heman			1				1		1				3		
Wareham	113	1	Sturtevant	Jonan	3			1						1			5		
Wareham	113	8	Sturtevant	Joseph		1	1		1				2	1			6		
Wareham	112	15	Sturtevant	Leml	2	1		1		2	1		1				8		
Plimton	24	17	Sturtevant	Nehemiah		1		1		1		2		1			6		
Halifax	17	21	Sturtevant	Paul			1			2			1				4		
Middleborough	78	21	Sturtevant	Robert		1	1		1					1			4		
Middleborough	78	22	Sturtevant	Robert Jr	1	1		1						1			4		
Wareham	112	16	Sturtevant	Rowland				2						3			5		
Bridgewater	54	15	Sturtevant	Silas			1		1				1	1			4		
Plymouth	14	21	Sturtevant	Silvanus	1			1		2			1				5		
Halifax	16	22	Sturtevant	Simion	3			1					1				5		
Halifax	17	2	Sturtevant	Simion	1		1		1		1		1				5		
Halifax	17	5	Sturtevant	Stafford		2		1		2	2		1				8		
Middleborough	79	24	Sturtevant	Thomas Dr	3	1	1		1	2	1	2		2			13		
Plymouth	8	21	Sturtevant	William				2		3			1				6		
Halifax	18	3	Sturtevant	Winslow	1			1		2			1				5		
Halifax	16	4	Sturtevant	Zaba			1						1	2			4		
Carver	7	2	Sturtevants	William			2	1					3				6		
Pembroke	44	45	Sturtivant	Levi	2		1	1		1			1				6		
Scituate	134	37	Sutton	Abner		1	2		1		1	2		1			8		
Scituate	131	6	Sutton	Hannah									1				1		
Scituate	131	5	Sutton	Ray			1						1				2		
Wareham	112	18	Swift	Asa		3	3		1			1	1				9		
Wareham	113	6	Swift	Elisha	1		2		1	2				1			7		
Wareham	112	21	Swift	Enoch	1			1	1			1	1	1			6		
Bridgewater	66	27	Swift	Isaac		1		1									2		
Bridgewater	66	30	Swift	Isaac Junr		1		1	1		1						4		
Plymouth	24	22	Swift	Jacob		1		1			2			1			5		
Rochester	105	68	Swift	James	1	4	1	1		1	1	1	1	2			13		
Wareham	113	7	Swift	Jesse			1	2	1			3		1			8		
Bridgewater	66	28	Swift	Jireh	2	2	1		1	1		1	1	1			10		
Plymouth	20	24	Swift	John	1		2		1	1	2	1		3			11		
Plymouth	20	25	Swift	John Jr	1		1			1		1					4		
Wareham	113	5	Swift	Jonah			1	1		1	1		1	1			6		
Wareham	112	12	Swift	Lemuel		1	2	1		1	1	1		1			8		
Wareham	113	2	Swift	Micah				1		1				1			3		
Plymouth	24	23	Swift	Phineas	1	1		1				2	1	1			7		
Rochester	105	63	Swift	Saml	1			1		1			1				4		
Bridgewater	66	29	Swift	William				1				1	1				3		
Wareham	113	3	Swift	Wm			1						1				2		
Plymouth	7	10	Symmes	Isaac	1								1				3		
Plymouth	8	8	Symmes	Joanna		1						1		3			5		
Wareham	113	13	Taber	Admiral	3		1	1		3	2			1			11		
Pembroke	43	44	Tailer	Archelous	1		2		1			1		1			6		
Pembroke	43	43	Tailer	Caleb	1	1	1		1			1		1			6		
Pembroke	43	42	Tailer	Joseph		1		1	1			1	2				6		
Pembroke	43	27	Tailer	Joshua	1		1			1			1				4		
Scituate	119	23	Talman	Joseph		1			1	1		2	1	1			7		
Bridgewater	49	24	Tarbut	Jacob											5		5		
Bridgewater	49	23	Tarbut	Tobey											3		3		
Marshfield	93	17	Taylor	Jehtro	1			2	1			1	1	1			7		

TOWN	PG#	LN#	HEADS OF HOUSEHOLD		FREE WHITE MALES					FREE WHITE FEMALES					TOTAL ALL OTHER	TOTAL SLAVES	TOTALS	DISTRICT/ TOWNSHIP	NOTES
			LAST NAME	FIRST NAME	under 10	10 to 16	16 to 26	26 to 45	45 and over	under 10	10 to 16	16 to 26	26 to 45	45 and over					
Duxbury	94	19	Taylor	John				1		1			1				3		
Plymouth	1	9	Taylor	Mary	3					2			3				8		
Scituate	122	1	Taylor	Richard			1			2			1				4		
Rochester	105	76	Temple	Saml	1			1					1				3		
Pembroke	43	18	Terry	Joseph		2	1	1		4	1		1				10		
Plymouth	1	1	Thacher	James		1		1		1	2		2				7		
Rochester	107	30	Thacher	Lot	3	3	2	1		2		2	1				14		
Abington	33	49	Thaxter	Gridley	1	2		1		4		1	1				10		
Bridgewater	56	36	Thayer	Abijah	1			1				1	1				4		
Bridgewater	56	39	Thayer	Abijah 2d			2					1		1			4		
Bridgewater	52	5	Thayer	Enoch					1			1	1				4		
Bridgewater	51	44	Thayer	Enos		1		1					1				3		
Bridgewater	51	43	Thayer	Hannah									2				2		
Bridgewater	52	4	Thayer	Jeremiah	2	3		1				1	1				8		
Bridgewater	64	4	Thayer	John	1			1		3			1				6		
Bridgewater	56	37	Thayer	Leavitt	1	1	3	1				2	1				9		
Bridgewater	56	38	Thayer	Richard	1	1		1		1	2		2				8		
Abington	33	42	Thayer	Saml		1	1	1		3	1		1				8		
Bridgewater	51	42	Thayer	Seth	4	2		1		1			1				9		
Marshfield	96	4	Thomas	Abijah				1		1			2				4		
Middleborough	73	23	Thomas	Abner	1			1		1			1				4		
Middleborough	75	22	Thomas	Abraham	2			1		1		1					5		
Marshfield	98	16	Thomas	Asa	1			1					1	1			4		
Middleborough	73	6	Thomas	August	1			1				2					4		
Middleborough	75	25	Thomas	Barzilla				1					1				2		
Middleborough	75	40	Thomas	Benjan		1		1		1			1				4		
Marshfield	103	3	Thomas	Briggs		1		1		1	2		2				7		
Middleborough	73	17	Thomas	Calvin			1						1				2		
Duxbury	96	18	Thomas	Charles	3			1					1				5		
Marshfield	94	15	Thomas	Charles			1			1		1					3		
Middleborough	75	33	Thomas	Churchill	1	1		1		2			1				6		
Middleborough	73	7	Thomas	Daniel	3			1		1			1				6		
Middleborough	74	10	Thomas	David			2	1					1				4		
Middleborough	76	20	Thomas	Ebenezer		1		1					1				3		
Middleborough	74	9	Thomas	Edward			1	1		1			1	1			5		
Middleborough	75	36	Thomas	Eleazer				1					1				2		
Middleborough	75	37	Thomas	Eleazer Jr		2		1		2	1	1	1				8		
Carver	5	6	Thomas	Eli	1	1		1		2	1		1				7		
Middleborough	75	32	Thomas	Elijah		1	1	1	1	1			1	1			7		
Middleborough	74	6	Thomas	Elisha	3	3		1		3	1		1				12		
Middleborough	76	7	Thomas	Elizabeth Wo								1	1				2		
Middleborough	76	19	Thomas	Elkanah	1			1					1				3		
Middleborough	75	26	Thomas	Enoch	1			1			2	4	1				9		
Middleborough	74	13	Thomas	Enoch 2d	1			1		2	1		1				6		
Middleborough	76	16	Thomas	Ephraim				1					1				2		
Middleborough	76	1	Thomas	Ezra	1	1		1		1	3		1				8		
Middleborough	74	3	Thomas	Fear									1				1		
Kingston	30	26	Thomas	Hannah				1					1	1			3		
Middleborough	75	30	Thomas	Henry	2			1		3	1		1				8		
Middleborough	74	14	Thomas	Hushar		1		1					1				3		
Middleborough	74	11	Thomas	Hushar Capt 2d	2			1				1	1				5		
Pembroke	43	29	Thomas	Ichabod		1		1		2			1	3			8		
Marshfield	94	5	Thomas	Isaac				1		3			1				5		
Middleborough	73	27	Thomas	Isaac				1					1				2		
Pembroke	43	22	Thomas	Isaac	1		1	1		2	1	1					7		
Plymouth	13	21	Thomas	Isaac	1			1		2		1	1				6		
Middleborough	73	28	Thomas	Isaac 2d	1			1		1			1				4		
Middleborough	73	29	Thomas	Isaac 3d				1				1					2		
Pembroke	43	19	Thomas	Isaac Jun	4			1		1			1				7		
Kingston	28	6	Thomas	Isaiah	1	2	1	1				2	2	1			10		
Middleborough	74	8	Thomas	Israel		1	1	1				1	1	1			6		
Plimton	24	21	Thomas	Jabez		1				1			1				3		
Middleborough	75	29	Thomas	Jacob			1			1		1					3		
Bridgewater	64	5	Thomas	James				1					1				2		
Middleborough	75	41	Thomas	James	2	2		1		2	2	1	1				12		
Middleborough	75	34	Thomas	Jedediah				1				1					2		
Middleborough	74	1	Thomas	Jedediah 2d	1			1		2			1				5		
Middleborough	76	6	Thomas	Jeremiah	2	1		1		2	1		1				8		
Kingston	27	25	Thomas	John	3			1		1		1	2				8		
Marshfield	94	12	Thomas	John	1		1	1		2	2		1				8		
Pembroke	43	23	Thomas	John		2	1		2			1	1	1	1		9		
Middleborough	74	20	Thomas	Jonathan	1			1				1	1				4		
Middleborough	73	26	Thomas	Joseph		1	2	1		2	1	2	1	1			11		
Plymouth	6	9	Thomas	Joshua	1	2		1		1	1	1		2			9		
Duxbury	97	9	Thomas	Josiah			1			1		1					3		
Duxbury	99	18	Thomas	Josiah			1			1		1					3		
Middleborough	76	4	Thomas	Josiah				1		2			1				4		
Marshfield	93	16	Thomas	Judah		1	1	1	1	1		1	1	1			8		
Middleborough	76	2	Thomas	Lemuel				1		2	1		1				5		
Middleborough	75	38	Thomas	Levi		1	1		1	2			1				6		
Marshfield	94	10	Thomas	Luther		1		1		1				2			5		
Middleborough	75	27	Thomas	Moses										2			2		
Middleborough	75	28	Thomas	Moses Jur			1			1		1					3		

TOWN	PG#	LN#	LAST NAME	FIRST NAME	FREE WHITE MALES under 10	10 to 16	16 to 26	26 to 45	45 and over	FREE WHITE FEMALES under 10	10 to 16	16 to 26	26 to 45	45 and over	TOTAL ALL OTHER	TOTAL SLAVES	TOTALS	DISTRICT/ TOWNSHIP	NOTES
Marshfield	94	9	Thomas	Nathaniel					1					1			2		
Plymouth	6	13	Thomas	Nathaniel			1			1	1		1				4		
Pembroke	43	21	Thomas	Nathl	2		3		1	1	2	1		1			11		
Scituate	136	14	Thomas	Nehemiah Revd	1			1		2	1		1				6		
Middleborough	73	22	Thomas	Nelson Capt	1		1		1	1			1				5		
Plimton	22	12	Thomas	Noah		1			1	1	2			1			6		
Duxbury	99	17	Thomas	Peleg	1	1			1				1	1			5		
Marshfield	93	20	Thomas	Peleg		1		1		1			1	1			5		
Middleborough	76	21	Thomas	Peleg				1		3			1				5		
Middleborough	75	39	Thomas	Perez	2	1	2		1	2	1	1					11		
Middleborough	76	5	Thomas	Samuel	1			1		1	1		1				5		
Middleborough	75	23	Thomas	Seth	2		1		1	2	1		1	1			9		
Middleborough	76	9	Thomas	Silas	3			1					1	1			6		
Middleborough	75	31	Thomas	Silvanus Lt			1	1	1			2	1	1			7		
Middleborough	75	24	Thomas	Simeon	2			1		1	1	1	2	1			9		
Middleborough	73	5	Thomas	Solomon	2			1		1	2		1				7		
Middleborough	76	3	Thomas	Solomon	1			1		2	2		1				7		
Marshfield	96	12	Thomas	William					1	2			2				5		
Plymouth	6	11	Thomas	William		1			2					1			4		
Bridgewater	64	6	Thomas	Winslow	1			1		1		1	1				5		
Duxbury	93	20	Thomas	Winslow	4			1		2	1		1				9		
Pembroke	43	24	Thomas	Zadoch			2		1			1		1			5		
Middleborough	75	35	Thomas	Zebedee	1			1		1			1				4		
Middleborough	73	20	Thomas	Zenas		1		1		2	2		1				7		
Marshfield	94	4	Thomas	Zenus				1				3		1			5		
Middleborough	73	24	Thomas	Zephannah			1	1				3		1			6		
Scituate	122	18	Thompson	Hesther										4			4		
Bridgewater	52	6	Thompson	Jacob	1			1		2		1					5		
Bridgewater	51	40	Thompson	James			1			1	1	1					4		
Bridgewater	51	38	Thompson	Thomas		1		1					2	1			5		
Bridgewater	51	39	Thompson	Thomas Junr	1			1		1	1		1				5		
Halifax	18	21	Thomson	Abel	1			1			1		1				4		
Halifax	16	14	Thomson	Adam		2	2		1			1		1			7		
Halifax	16	21	Thomson	Amasa					1					1			2		
Halifax	16	23	Thomson	Asa			3		1			1		1			6		
Middleborough	74	21	Thomson	Benjn	1			1		2	1		1				6		
Middleborough	73	18	Thomson	Caleb	3	1	3		1	2	1	2		2			15		
Bridgewater	56	42	Thomson	Daniel				1						1			2		
Halifax	13	5	Thomson	Ebenezer				1						2			3		
Halifax	13	10	Thomson	Ebenezer		1		1						2			4		
Halifax	13	22	Thomson	Ebenezer		1		1					1				3		
Halifax	13	8	Thomson	Eliab	1			1		2			1				5		
Middleborough	73	31	Thomson	Ephraim	1			1		1		1					4		
Halifax	13	7	Thomson	Ezekiel	2			1		1	1		1				6		
Halifax	13	13	Thomson	Ezra	2	1	1	1		3		1	1				10		
Halifax	16	15	Thomson	Ichabod		1		1			1	1		2			6		
Halifax	16	12	Thomson	Isaac		2					2						4		
Middleborough	73	1	Thomson	Isaac Esqr Hon	1	2	1		1	1	2	1	1	1			11		
Halifax	13	9	Thomson	Jacob	1	1		1	1	3			1	1			9		
Middleborough	73	12	Thomson	Jacob Cap		1						2		1			5		
Middleborough	73	30	Thomson	John				1		0			1				2		
Halifax	18	13	Thomson	Jonah		1		1									2		
Abington	33	50	Thomson	Joseph	1			1			2		1				5		
Abington	41	21	Thomson	Joseph											9		9		
Halifax	18	19	Thomson	Joseph				1		1			1	1			4		
Halifax	13	12	Thomson	Levi				1			1		1				3		
Middleborough	73	2	Thomson	Molly Wd			1					1		1			3		
Halifax	13	2	Thomson	Moses	1			1		1	1		1				5		
Middleborough	73	35	Thomson	Nathan					1			1		1			3		
Halifax	16	10	Thomson	Nathan				1					1				2		
Halifax	13	11	Thomson	Nathaniel	3			1		2	2		1				9		
Middleborough	76	10	Thomson	Nathl			2		1			3		1			7		
Middleborough	74	18	Thomson	Nathl 2d		1			1		1	3		1			7		
Halifax	16	24	Thomson	Nehemiah	1			1		1			1				4		
Halifax	15	17	Thomson	Reuben	4			1		1			1	1			8		
Middleborough	74	19	Thomson	Ruth Wo									1				1		
Halifax	13	3	Thomson	Thomas				1				1		2			4		
Middleborough	73	15	Thomson	Thomas	3			1		2			1				7		
Kingston	28	21	Thomson	Timothy	1			1					1				3		
Middleborough	74	17	Thomson	William Capt			2		1	1	1	2		1			8		
Halifax	16	11	Thomson	Zacheus				1		3			1				5		
Halifax	13	1	Thomson	Zebediah			1	1					1				3		
Middleborough	74	7	Thrasher	Daniel	1	2	1		1	2			1	1			9		
Plymouth	23	21	Thrasher	George	3			1		4	2		1				11		
Middleborough	74	5	Thrasher	Job	1			1				1		1			4		
Middleborough	73	38	Thrasher	John	1			1		1		1	1				5		
Plymouth	24	20	Thrasher	Jonathan	1	3		1		2	1		1				9		
Middleborough	73	39	Thrasher	Samuel				1									1		
Bridgewater	56	43	Thresher	Seth	2			1					1				4		
Plymouth	6	1	Tibble	Joseph		2	1		1			1	1	1			7		
Bridgewater	52	2	Tibou	Amasa	3	1	1	1		2	3						12		

TOWN	PG#	LN#	LAST NAME	FIRST NAME	FWM <10	FWM 10-16	FWM 16-26	FWM 26-45	FWM 45+	FWF <10	FWF 10-16	FWF 16-26	FWF 26-45	FWF 45+	TOTAL ALL OTHER	TOTAL SLAVES	TOTALS	DISTRICT/ TOWNSHIP	NOTES
Bridgewater	56	40	Tibou	William	4	2			1					1			8		
Scituate	136	9	Tilden	Abigail			1					2		1			4		
Scituate	136	10	Tilden	Amos	1			1		2			1				5		
Marshfield	104	1	Tilden	Elisha	1	1		1		1			1				5		
Hanover	129	20	Tilden	Job				3						1			4		
Hanover	129	19	Tilden	Job Junr		1		1		3	1	1	1				8		
Bridgewater	52	3	Tilden	John	1		1		1	1				1			5		
Scituate	136	3	Tilden	John	3		1	1		1		1	1				8		
Marshfield	97	10	Tilden	Joseph	2	2	2		1	2			1	3			13		
Marshfield	97	12	Tilden	Joshua		1	1	1		1							4		
Marshfield	101	21	Tilden	Jotham	2			1		1			1	1			6		
Marshfield	97	4	Tilden	Mary		1							1	2			4		
Marshfield	102	8	Tilden	Samuel		1	1		1	1				1			5		
Marshfield	102	9	Tilden	Samuel Jun	1			1		3			1	1			7		
Scituate	131	18	Tilden	Sarah										2			2		
Marshfield	101	6	Tilden	Wales		1			1	1	1			1			5		
Scituate	127	17	Tildon	Thatcher	3			1		1			1				6		
Carver	10	22	Tilsn	Isaiah			1	1		1				1			4		
Middleborough	76	22	Tilson	Culverson			1			1			1				3		
Bridgewater	52	7	Tilson	Elisha	1			1					1	1			4		
Halifax	15	2	Tilson	Ephraim	2	1		1		2		2	1				9		
Halifax	18	11	Tilson	Ephraim				1				2	1	1			5		
Bridgewater	52	1	Tilson	Holmes	1			1		1			1	1			5		
Halifax	15	7	Tilson	John	2			1		3	1		1	1			9		
Carver	11	4	Tilson	Jonathan	1			1		1			1				4		
Halifax	18	2	Tilson	Joseph			1			3	1		1				6		
Middleborough	76	13	Tilson	Silas Lt		1		1				1	1				4		
Plymouth	4	20	Tincolm	Hezekiah				1					1	1			3		
Middleborough	73	16	Tinkham	Abigail									1	1			2		
Middleborough	73	21	Tinkham	Abishaw Capt		1		1					1	1			4		
Rochester	105	73	Tinkham	Abrm			1						1				2		
Rochester	105	71	Tinkham	Charles			2		1	1	1		1	1			7		
Middleborough	76	14	Tinkham	Cornelius		1	1		2				1	1			6		
Middleborough	73	37	Tinkham	Deborah Wo		1	1						1	1			4		
Middleborough	73	3	Tinkham	Ebenezer				1					1				2		
Middleborough	73	11	Tinkham	Ebenz 2d	3			1		2			1				7		
Middleborough	76	8	Tinkham	Elisha	2		3		1	2	1		1				10		
Rochester	105	74	Tinkham	Eliza		1				1	1		1	1			5		
Halifax	15	4	Tinkham	Ephraim				1					1				2		
Middleborough	73	14	Tinkham	Hazuel	2	1		1					1				5		
Middleborough	73	25	Tinkham	Isaac			2		1	1	1		1				6		
Middleborough	73	19	Tinkham	James	4		2		1	1		2	1				11		
Middleborough	73	10	Tinkham	Jesse	1	2		1		1		1	1				9		
Middleborough	73	34	Tinkham	Joanna									1				1		
Middleborough	76	15	Tinkham	John Lt	1	2	1		1		1	1	1				8		
Halifax	16	17	Tinkham	Joseph	1			1					2	1			5		
Middleborough	76	17	Tinkham	Levi	2		1			1			2				6		
Middleborough	73	9	Tinkham	Parience Wo									1				1		
Middleborough	74	12	Tinkham	Peter	1	1			2				1				5		
Rochester	105	72	Tinkham	Peter				1					1				2		
Middleborough	73	13	Tinkham	Seth				1					1				2		
Middleborough	73	8	Tinkham	Silas			1		1			2	1	1			6		
Middleborough	76	18	Tinkham	Squire	2		1						1				4		
Middleborough	73	4	Tinkham	Zebedee		1	1	1					1	1			5		
Bridgewater	64	9	Tirrel	John				1					1				2		
Bridgewater	64	10	Tirrel	John Junr			1			2			1				4		
Bridgewater	51	41	Tirrel	Lemuel	2		1			3	1		1				8		
Abington	33	44	Tirrel	Thos	1			1		3	2			1			8		
Abington	33	39	Tirril	Isaac	1	1	2	1	1	1		2	1	1			11		
Abington	33	38	Tirril	John				1						1			2		
Abington	33	52	Tirril	Lemuel	1		1	1					3	1			7		
Abington	33	51	Tirril	Nathl			1			1			1				3		
Middleborough	74	4	Tisdael	Isaac			1	1					1				3		
Bridgewater	47	31	Tisdell	Abraham				1				1	1	1			4		
Rochester	107	29	Tobey	Thos		2		1		1	1		1				6		
Marshfield	98	7	Toleman	Benjamin			2	1	1				1	1			6		
Pembroke	43	28	Tolman	Benjn			1		1				1				3		
Scituate	121	7	Tolman	Chas		2		1		1	1	1	1				7		
Bridgewater	66	35	Tolman	Daniel	1	2		1		2	1		1				8		
Abington	33	46	Tolman	John		1		1						1			3		
Scituate	122	24	Tolman	John	2	2		1				1	1	1			8		
Scituate	121	9	Tolman	Samuel	2	1		1				1	2	1			8		
Pembroke	43	17	Tolman	Stephen	1							2	2	1			6		
Plymouth	7	12	Torence	Thomas				1		2	1		1				5		
Rochester	105	78	Torey	Joseph	1			1					1				3		
Scituate	121	21	Torrey	Caleb			1		1	1		1		2			5		
Abington	33	43	Torrey	David		1	2	2	1				1	1			8		
Scituate	124	5	Torrey	George	2	2		1		1	1	1	1				9		
Scituate	121	23	Torrey	Isaac			1	1					1	1			4		
Scituate	130	10	Torrey	James	1	2		1		3	1		1	1	1		11		
Plymouth	14	9	Torrey	John	2	1	1		1			1	2				8		
Plymouth	6	21	Torrey	Joshua			1			1			1				3		
Abington	33	40	Torrey	Josiah				1		2		3	1	1	1		9		

TOWN	PG#	LN#	LAST NAME	FIRST NAME	FREE WHITE MALES					FREE WHITE FEMALES					TOTAL ALL OTHER	TOTAL SLAVES	TOTALS	DISTRICT/ TOWNSHIP	NOTES
					under 10	10 to 16	16 to 26	26 to 45	45 and over	under 10	10 to 16	16 to 26	26 to 45	45 and over					
Hanover	129	21	Torrey	Meriam									1	1			2		
Bridgewater	64	8	Torrey	Philip	2			1					1				4		
Bridgewater	64	7	Torrey	Thomas			1	1						2			4		
Plymouth	6	18	Torrey	Thomas	3	1		1			1		1				7		
Abington	33	48	Torrey	Willm	3			1					1				5		
Pembroke	43	40	Torrey	Willm	1	1		1	1	1	2	1		2			10		
Scituate	125	8	Totman	Sarah									1				1		
Scituate	127	11	Totman	Stephen	3	1		1		2	1	1		1			10		
Scituate	121	2	Tower	Mathew	1		1	1		1	2		1				7		
Abington	33	41	Townsend	Eunice		2	2			1	1			1			7		
Abington	33	45	Townsend	Ezekiel				1			1	1	1				4		
Abington	33	47	Townsend	Ezekiel Junr		1	1						1				3		
Middleborough	76	12	Townsend	Job				1		3	1		1	1			7		
Middleborough	73	33	Townsend	Silas		1		1		1		1					4		
Middleborough	74	2	Towsend	Abner	1	1		1		1			1				5		
Middleborough	76	11	Towsend	John		1			2				2	1			6		
Pembroke	43	38	Tracy	Jacob	2			1		1			1				5		
Bridgewater	56	44	Trask	William				1		1				1	1		4		
Plymouth	11	23	Traske	Joseph				1					1	1			3		
Bridgewater	55	18	Travellar	Henry											3		3		
Plymouth	10	21	Tribble	Joseph			1						1				2		
Middleborough	73	32	Tribon	Metzer	1		1						1				3		
Rochester	105	75	Trip	Jesse				1					1	1			3		
Rochester	105	77	Trip	Jesse Jr	3		1			1			1				6		
Rochester	107	28	Trip	Peleg		1	1			1			1				4		
Marshfield	97	7	Truant	John			1	1					1				3		
Marshfield	97	6	Truant	Samuel		1	1	1					1	1			5		
Hanover	129	18	Tubbs	Joseph			1			1		1					3		
Pembroke	43	46	Tubbs	Joseph			1	1		1	1						4		
Pembroke	43	45	Tubbs	Morris	1	2	2	1		1			1				8		
Pembroke	43	20	Tubbs	Nehemiah	1		1				1						3		
Bridgewater	66	33	Tucker	Benjamin	1		1										2		
Middleborough	74	16	Tucker	Daniel	4	3		1		3	1		1				13		
Bridgewater	66	34	Tucker	Jedidah							1			1			2		
Middleborough	74	15	Tucker	Samuel		1		1					1				4		
Plymouth	9	24	Tufts	Jonathan	2			1		2		1	1				7		
Kingston	28	16	Tupper	Peleg	2			1		2	1		1				7		
Scituate	121	1	Turner	Abner				1					1	1			3		
Hanover	130	8	Turner	Amos		1	2	1					2	3			9		
Pembroke	43	30	Turner	Caleb			1			1			1				3		
Middleborough	73	36	Turner	Caleb Revd		1	1	1					1	2			6		
Pembroke	43	33	Turner	Calven	1	1	3	1		1	1			2			10		
Pembroke	43	34	Turner	Charles	1	1		1					1				4		
Scituate	119	1	Turner	Charles Jun	4			1		2			1	1	1		10		
Plymouth	1	6	Turner	David				1		1			1				3		
Scituate	123	16	Turner	Elijah Esq	1	1	1		1	1	1	2	2	1			11		
Pembroke	43	35	Turner	Elisha	2	2		1		1				1			7		
Scituate	127	18	Turner	Elisha		1		1		1			1				4		
Pembroke	43	31	Turner	George				1					1	2			4		
Scituate	126	6	Turner	Harris	1			1		1		1					4		
Hanover	127	24	Turner	Isaac	1		1	1					1	1			5		
Scituate	121	13	Turner	Israel		2		1		1	2		1				7		
Scituate	135	19	Turner	James		2		2				1	1	1			7		
Pembroke	43	39	Turner	Japhet	1		3						1	1			6		
Pembroke	43	37	Turner	Job	2	2		1		2	1	2		2			12		
Pembroke	43	47	Turner	John		1	1	1		1	1		1	1			7		
Scituate	126	21	Turner	John	1			1		1			1	1			5		
Scituate	129	4	Turner	Jonathan			1	1					2				4		
Scituate	119	2	Turner	Joseph				1									1		
Pembroke	43	32	Turner	Joshua				1		1	1	1		1			5		
Pembroke	43	25	Turner	Joshua 2d			1	1					1	1	1		5		
Pembroke	43	26	Turner	Joshua 3d			1						1				2		
Hanover	128	2	Turner	Leah									1	1			2		
Plymouth	10	14	Turner	Lothrop	2			1		3	1	1	1				9		
Hanover	128	10	Turner	Marlbry				1					1				2		
Scituate	124	15	Turner	Nathaniel	1		1	1		3			1				7		
Scituate	135	17	Turner	Nathl Junr		1		1		3		1	1				7		
Scituate	130	8	Turner	Rowland	2	2		1				2	1				8		
Bridgewater	51	37	Turner	Samuel	1	1		1		2			1				6		
Bridgewater	56	41	Turner	Samuel	1			1		2			1	1			6		
Scituate	124	4	Turner	Seth	1	2		1		1		2		1			8		
Pembroke	43	36	Turner	Thomas		1	1	1					1	1			6		
Scituate	125	12	Turner	William Esq				1		1			1	1			4		
Pembroke	43	41	Turner	Willm	1			1						2			4		
Carver	9	20	Vale	Jacob	2			1		1			1				5		
Middleborough	73	45	Valentine	John				1						1			2		
Plymouth	21	18	Vallier	Simeon		2	1	1		4			1				9		
Middleborough	73	44	Vaughan	Daniel 2d	1			1		1			1				4		
Rochester	107	31	Vaughan	Danl	2	2	1		1	1	1	1		1			10		
Middleborough	73	51	Vaughan	David Capt		2		1						2			5		
Middleborough	73	54	Vaughan	David Jr	2	2		1		1	1	1					8		
Middleborough	73	46	Vaughan	Ebenezer		1	1	1					1	1			5		
Middleborough	73	48	Vaughan	Elkanah	3			1					1				5		
Middleborough	73	50	Vaughan	Ephraim W			1			1			1				3		

TOWN	PG#	LN#	LAST NAME	FIRST NAME	FREE WHITE MALES					FREE WHITE FEMALES					TOTAL ALL OTHER	TOTAL SLAVES	TOTALS	DISTRICT/ TOWNSHIP	NOTES
					under 10	10 to 16	16 to 26	26 to 45	45 and over	under 10	10 to 16	16 to 26	26 to 45	45 and over					
Middleborough	73	42	Vaughan	George Capt	1		2		1		1	1		2			8		
Middleborough	73	47	Vaughan	Jabez				2				1					3		
Carver	10	21	Vaughan	James		1		1		2	1		1				6		
Middleborough	73	53	Vaughan	Jesse	1			1		2				1			5		
Middleborough	73	55	Vaughan	Joanna Wo									1				1		
Carver	9	17	Vaughan	John	3		2		1	2	1			1			10		
Middleborough	73	40	Vaughan	Joseph	1			1					1				3		
Middleborough	73	41	Vaughan	Nathan			1						1	1			3		
Carver	7	4	Vaughan	Nathaniel	1			1		1	1			1			5		
Middleborough	73	43	Vaughan	Peter	3			1		1			1	1			7		
Carver	9	18	Vaughan	Samuel		1	3		1			2		1			8		
Middleborough	73	52	Vaughan	Silvanus		1		1		1			1				4		
Middleborough	73	49	Vaughan	Zebulon				1				1		1			3		
Scituate	136	22	Vinal	Asa	1	1				3			1				7		
Scituate	135	44	Vinal	Ignatius				1		1			1				3		
Scituate	131	11	Vinal	Israel				1			2						3		
Scituate	135	45	Vinal	Job	3	2				1	2		1				10		
Scituate	135	29	Vinal	Jonathan	1			1					1	1			4		
Scituate	135	9	Vinal	Judith			1						2	1			4		
Scituate	136	24	Vinal	Lemuel		1				1	1	1		1			5		
Scituate	135	43	Vinal	Levi	3	1		1		1	1		1	1			9		
Marshfield	97	18	Vinal	Lucy	1						1		1	2			5		
Scituate	131	4	Vinal	Lydia			1						1				2		
Scituate	131	9	Vinal	Mary									1				1		
Scituate	131	7	Vinal	Nathl	1	2		1		3	1	1		1			10		
Scituate	134	34	Vinal	Nathl Junr	1			1		1	1			1			5		
Marshfield	102	17	Vinal	Seth				1					1	1			3		
Scituate	135	7	Vinal	Stephen	2			1		1				1			5		
Scituate	135	8	Vinal	William	2	1		1				1	1	1			7		
Scituate	136	48	Vinal	William Junr	1	1		2				1	1	1			7		
Abington	41	1	Vining	Asa	2			1						1			4		
Abington	41	6	Vining	Benjm		1		1	1		1		2				6		
Abington	41	3	Vining	David	1			1				1					3		
Abington	41	5	Vining	Ebid	2	1		1		1	1		4	1			11		
Abington	41	4	Vining	Elisha					1	1		1	1	1			5		
Abington	41	2	Vining	Richard	2			1		2			1	1			7		
Bridgewater	64	11	Vinton	William			2							1			3		
Plymouth	9	26	Virgin	John	2		1	1					1				5		
Bridgewater	61	31	Wade	Betty								1		1			2		
Scituate	134	30	Wade	Charlotte	1		1			1	2		1				6		
Pembroke	44	1	Wade	Isaac		1	2		1	2		2		1			9		
Bridgewater	61	29	Wade	James					1	1			1	1			4		
Scituate	131	17	Wade	Jotham			1			4			1				6		
Pembroke	44	3	Wade	Levi		1		1						1			3		
Scituate	131	3	Wade	Mary										3			3		
Scituate	133	45	Wade	Mercy		1	1			1		2		1			6		
Bridgewater	61	32	Wade	Molly	2							1		1			4		
Scituate	133	47	Wade	Nathl				1					1				2		
Scituate	133	46	Wade	Nathl Junr	2	1		1		2	2		1				9		
Bridgewater	61	30	Wade	Robert	1						1	2	2	2			9		
Duxbury	98	12	Wadsworth	Ahira Jun			1					1					2		
Kingston	30	30	Wadsworth	Cephas		1		1				1		1			4		
Plymouth	24	15	Wadsworth	Christopher		1		1						1			3		
Duxbury	99	13	Wadsworth	Dura	2	2		1		3			1				9		
Duxbury	97	10	Wadsworth	Eden	2			1			2		1				6		
Duxbury	99	14	Wadsworth	Ira	1	1		1			1		1				5		
Duxbury	97	4	Wadsworth	Joseph	1	2			1	1	2	1		1			9		
Duxbury	97	11	Wadsworth	Joseph Jun	1			1					1				3		
Marshfield	104	16	Wadsworth	Luke		1	2	1						2			6		
Duxbury	98	23	Wadsworth	Robert			1			1			1	1			4		
Duxbury	100	10	Wadsworth	Senaca		2		1	1	1	2	1					8		
Duxbury	98	6	Wadsworth	Zenoth	1			1		1				1			4		
Duxbury	95	2	Wadworth	Wait	2		1		1	1	2		1				8		
Bridgewater	65	2	Waite	James						1					1		2		
Bridgewater	65	3	Waite	James Junr	3	4	1	1				1	1				11		
Bridgewater	47	32	Waldon	Benjamin			1			1			1				3		
Hanover	132	10	Wales	Atherton		1		1					1	1			4		
Bridgewater	52	12	Wales	John	1			1		3			1				7		
Bridgewater	61	33	Wales	Samuel				1		3			1				5		
Bridgewater	52	8	Wales	Thomas	1	1		1		1		1	1				6		
Abington	41	9	Wales	Willm	1	2	1	1		3	1		1	1			11		
Marshfield	96	9	Walker	Asa		1		1		2			1				5		
Marshfield	94	2	Walker	Benjamin	3		1		1	2		1	1	1			10		
Marshfield	94	3	Walker	Betty										2			2		
Marshfield	96	8	Walker	Daniel	2	1		1				2		1			7		
Pembroke	44	11	Walker	Isaac			2	2		2		1		1			8		
Marshfield	96	17	Walker	Joel			1						1				2		
Pembroke	44	12	Walker	John				1				1					2		
Pembroke	44	13	Walker	John Jr	4			1					1				6		
Marshfield	93	5	Walker	Levi			1			3	1		1				6		
Duxbury	97	1	Walker	Samuel	2	1		1		2			1				7		
Carver	9	5	Ward	Benjamin	1	1	1		1	1		1		1			7		
Carver	9	8	Ward	Drusilla	1					2		2	2	1			6		
Plymouth	16	15	Warner	Benjamin	3		1			1			1				6		
Middleborough	69	32	Warner	Joseph					1				1				2		
Plymouth	11	21	Warren	Benjamin				2				1		1			4		

TOWN	PG#	LN#	LAST NAME	FIRST NAME	FREE WHITE MALES					FREE WHITE FEMALES					TOTAL ALL OTHER	TOTAL SLAVES	TOTALS	DISTRICT/ TOWNSHIP	NOTES
					under 10	10 to 16	16 to 26	26 to 45	45 and over	under 10	10 to 16	16 to 26	26 to 45	45 and over					
Plymouth	8	4	Warren	David	1			1		1		1		1			5		
Bridgewater	52	9	Warren	Ebenezer	4	1		1		1	1	2		1			11		
Plymouth	1	13	Warren	Henry	3	1		1		1	1		2				9		
Plymouth	1	5	Warren	James			1	1				1		2			5		
Bridgewater	52	10	Warren	Nathan	3			1		2	2		1				9		
Middleborough	72	17	Warren	Nathan	3	2		1					1				7		
Middleborough	72	19	Warren	Silvanus Lt		3			1				1				5		
Middleborough	71	42	Washburn	Abiel 2d				1		1			1				3		
Middleborough	72	13	Washburn	Abiel Col	3			1		3			2				10		
Bridgewater	66	40	Washburn	Benjamin				1				1	1				3		
Middleborough	71	39	Washburn	Benjan	3	1	2		1		1	1		1			10		
Kingston	28	10	Washburn	Bildao	2	1		1	1	3	1	1	1				11		
Bridgewater	66	38	Washburn	Calvin			2		1			1		1			5		
Bridgewater	66	36	Washburn	Daniel		1			1				2	1			5		
Bridgewater	66	43	Washburn	Desire			1					1		1			3		
Kingston	28	7	Washburn	Ebenezer			1		1		1	2	1				6		
Bridgewater	64	25	Washburn	Eleazer	1	2	2		1		1	1	1				9		
Kingston	30	39	Washburn	Elisha		2		1		2		1	1				7		
Kingston	28	15	Washburn	Elkanah	1			1		1	3		1				7		
Kingston	28	13	Washburn	Ezekiel				1				1	1				3		
Bridgewater	61	23	Washburn	Jacob	1			1		2		1					5		
Middleborough	72	11	Washburn	James			3	1			2	2	1		1		10		
Kingston	28	18	Washburn	Jehial		1		1					1				3		
Bridgewater	66	42	Washburn	Jeremiah		1			1			1		1			4		
Kingston	28	11	Washburn	John	2			1		1	1		1				6		
Middleborough	72	8	Washburn	Jonathan			2		1	2	2		1				7		
Bridgewater	66	41	Washburn	Joshua	3	1		1			1		1				7		
Kingston	28	9	Washburn	Judah			1		1		1	1	1		1		6		
Middleborough	71	40	Washburn	Judith Wo								1	1				2		
Bridgewater	64	24	Washburn	Levi	1	1		1		2	1	3	1				11		
Bridgewater	66	45	Washburn	Lois									1				1		
Plymouth	12	6	Washburn	Nathaniel				1		1			1				3		
Bridgewater	66	37	Washburn	Oliver	3	1	1	1		1		1	1				9		
Middleborough	73	61	Washburn	Perez	1			1		1		1					4		
Kingston	29	19	Washburn	Phillip	2			1					1	1			5		
Plymouth	12	4	Washburn	Prince	1	1		1		1			1				5		
Bridgewater	66	44	Washburn	Rebecca								1		1			2		
Kingston	29	16	Washburn	Rufus	2		1	1				1	1				6		
Bridgewater	65	1	Washburn	Salmon			1			1		1					3		
Kingston	29	20	Washburn	Seth			1			3		1					5		
Plymouth	20	28	Washburn	Seth	1				1				1				3		
Kingston	29	17	Washburn	Silva	2					1			1				4		
Kingston	28	12	Washburn	Simeon	1								1		1		4		
Bridgewater	61	22	Washburn	Solomon	3	1	1		1				1				7		
Middleborough	71	29	Washburn	Solomon		1		1		3	1		1				7		
Bridgewater	66	39	Washburn	Thomas				1				1		2			4		
Middleborough	71	22	Washburn	Thomas	2	2			1	1	1		1				8		
Plymouth	14	13	Washburn	Thomas	1			1			1		1				4		
Carver	5	2	Washburn	William		1		1			1		1				4		
Bridgewater	61	24	Washburn	Zenas	1		1					1			1		4		
Marshfield	103	2	Waterman	Asa Esq	1	2			1	2			1				7		
Kingston	28	14	Waterman	Benjamin	1			1		1	1		1				5		
Marshfield	104	14	Waterman	Deborah			1						2				3		
Scituate	122	22	Waterman	Deborah								1		1			2		
Halifax	17	18	Waterman	Eleazer				1			2		1				4		
Duxbury	95	11	Waterman	Eliphalet	1			1		1			1				4		
Halifax	17	16	Waterman	Elisha		2	3		1		1	2		1			10		
Duxbury	104	17	Waterman	Ephraim				1			1	3	1				6		
Halifax	18	5	Waterman	Isaac	1		1	1		3		1	1				8		
Halifax	17	20	Waterman	Jabez		1	2		1			1		1			6		
Halifax	18	12	Waterman	John		1		1	1	2	1	1		1			8		
Kingston	29	37	Waterman	Jonah		1		1				1		1			4		
Middleborough	69	28	Waterman	Joshua		1		1				1		1			4		
Halifax	16	3	Waterman	Moses	2			1		1			1				6		
Marshfield	104	4	Waterman	Nathl	2			1		2	1		1				7		
Scituate	122	23	Waterman	Samuel		1		1		1	1	1					5		
Plimton	21	19	Waterman	Thomas		1			1				1	1			4		
Halifax	16	5	Waterman	William					1					1			2		
Plymouth	1	7	Watson	George		1		1	1	1			1	1			6		
Duxbury	100	20	Watson	John			1			3		1					5		
Plymouth	26	7	Watson	John	1	1	2		1	1	1	1	2				10		
Plymouth	9	16	Watson	William		1		1				1	1				4		
Scituate	133	48	Webb	Barnabas	1	2		1		3	1	1	1				10		
Scituate	133	44	Webb	Paul			1						1				2		
Pembroke	44	8	Webb	Saml		1		1		1	1	1					5		
Scituate	136	8	Webb	Seth	1			1					1				3		
Duxbury	104	9	Wells	Robert	1	1		1			2		1				6		
Kingston	28	8	West	Jonah			1	1					1				3		
Plymouth	3	6	Westcoat	Benjamin	2	1		1		2	1		1	1			9		
Plymouth	26	3	Westcoat	Joseph	2			1		1			1				5		
Middleborough	69	25	Westgard	Jonathan	5	1		1		1	1	1					10		
Duxbury	102	2	Weston	Abigal									3				3		
Duxbury	93	10	Weston	Asa	2	1	2		1			1	1				8		

133

TOWN	PG#	LN#	LAST NAME	FIRST NAME	M under 10	M 10 to 16	M 16 to 26	M 26 to 45	M 45 and over	F under 10	F 10 to 16	F 16 to 26	F 26 to 45	F 45 and over	TOTAL ALL OTHER	TOTAL SLAVES	TOTALS	DISTRICT/TOWNSHIP	NOTES
Duxbury	94	9	Weston	Azra	2		6		1				1	1			11		
Duxbury	94	10	Weston	Azra Jun	2			1		1	1		1				6		
Duxbury	103	15	Weston	Chandler	1			1		2			1	1			6		
Middleborough	73	57	Weston	Daniel	2	1		1		1		1					6		
Middleborough	73	58	Weston	Daniel 2d				1		2		1	1				5		
Middleborough	72	5	Weston	David				1					1				2		
Middleborough	72	6	Weston	David Jr	2			1			2	1	1				7		
Middleborough	72	18	Weston	Edmund				1					1	1			3		
Marshfield	93	11	Weston	Eleaner	1							1		1			3		
Duxbury	103	22	Weston	Ichobud		1		1				1		1			4		
Plimton	26	17	Weston	Jabez	2	2		1		1		1	1				8		
Duxbury	93	11	Weston	Jacob	1	2		1		1	1		1	1			8		
Duxbury	104	19	Weston	James	2			1						1			4		
Middleborough	69	30	Weston	John Lt				1		1	2	1		1			6		
Duxbury	93	1	Weston	Joseph	2	2	2		1	2	1	1	1				12		
Duxbury	103	2	Weston	Levi	2			1	1	1	4		1	2			12		
Plymouth	7	16	Weston	Lewis	1		1					1					3		
Duxbury	95	5	Weston	Michel				1				1	2	1			5		
Plimton	22	3	Weston	Noah				1				1	3	1			6		
Duxbury	93	2	Weston	Peleg				1						1			2		
Middleborough	71	41	Weston	Rufus			2		1		1			2			6		
Bridgewater	47	33	Weston	Seth	1			1		1			1				4		
Middleborough	72	7	Weston	Seth	2	1		1		2	1		1				8		
Middleborough	72	12	Weston	Thomas			1	1				1	1				4		
Marshfield	93	10	Weston	William	1	1		1			1		1				5		
Plymouth	7	11	Weston	William	1	1		1		1	1	1	1				7		
Plymouth	7	23	Weston	William	1			2		2	2		1	2			10		
Plimton	22	4	Weston	Zadock			1		1	1	2		1				6		
Duxbury	97	13	Weston	Zebdiel		1	1	1					1				4		
Middleborough	71	25	Weston	Zecharh				2		2	1	1	1	1			8		
Bridgewater	65	9	Wetherell	Prince			1						1	2			4		
Duxbury	91	26	Wetherly	Charles			1			2			1				4		
Scituate	127	2	Wethrell	Josiah			1						1				2		
Plymouth	9	5	Wethrell	Thomas			1		1	1		1	1	1			6		
Plymouth	9	21	Wethrell	Thomas	1			1					1				3		
Scituate	122	19	Wheeler	Willm W.		1		1					1				3		
Scituate	129	22	Whitcomb	John			1	3	1			1		1			7		
Hanover	130	22	Whitcomb	Saml	3			1					1				5		
Scituate	129	21	Whitcomb	Sarah				1						1	1		3		
Bridgewater	61	35	White	Benjamin				1					1				2		
Carver	11	21	White	Benjamin		1		1					1				3		
Marshfield	93	4	White	Benjamin				1			1		1				3		
Middleborough	72	24	White	Bethnael	1		1					1					3		
Hanover	125	9	White	Cornelius		1		1					1				3		
Duxbury	91	8	White	Daniel	3	2		1		2	1		1				10		
Middleborough	72	3	White	Daniel	2	1	1	1		2	1		1				9		
Wareham	113	15	White	Ebz	1		1	1		1	1						5		
Wareham	113	14	White	Edward	1		1	1	1	1	1	1	1				8		
Duxbury	91	20	White	Elizabeth				1	1			1	2	2			7		
Pembroke	44	2	White	Jacob	3			1		1			1				6		
Marshfield	102	20	White	James				1		2		1	1				5		
Marshfield	102	21	White	Joanna										1			1		
Plymouth	1	3	White	Joanna									2				2		
Halifax	18	17	White	Joel	1	2		1		2		3		1			10		
Abington	41	16	White	John	3	3		2		1	1	1	1	1			13		
Duxbury	102	5	White	Joseph	3		1	1		1			1	1			8		
Middleborough	72	2	White	Joshua Esqr				1					1				2		
Rochester	107	34	White	Justes	1	1		1		3	1		1				8		
Bridgewater	61	34	White	Lucy		1				1	2	1		1			6		
Marshfield	93	3	White	Luther		1		1					1	1			4		
Abington	41	17	White	Micah	2	1		1		1	1	1					7		
Bridgewater	55	1	White	Micah				1					1				2		
Wareham	113	16	White	Nathl	1	1		1					2				5		
Marshfield	101	19	White	Orphen									1				1		
Pembroke	44	9	White	S. Gideon	2			1		2	3	1	1				11		
Middleborough	72	1	White	Samuel				1		2			1				4		
Scituate	136	13	White	Sarah	1			1					1	1			4		
Middleborough	71	37	White	Silas		1	1		1		2	1		1			7		
Scituate	136	12	White	Timothy	2			1		1			1		1		6		
Duxbury	103	5	White	Tobias				1		1		1	1	1			5		
Pembroke	44	5	White	Willm	1	3		1			1	1		1			8		
Hanover	129	17	White	Benjamin	1		2		1		2			1			7		
Hanover	127	1	Whiting	Abel		1			1		1		1				4		
Plymouth	3	10	Whiting	Abraham	1			1		1			1	1			5		
Scituate	128	15	Whiting	Archelaus			1						1				2		
Hanover	127	7	Whiting	Asa	2			1		1			1				5		
Abington	41	14	Whiting	Barzilla		1	1	1	1	2			1	1			8		
Scituate	128	13	Whiting	Benja	2			1					1				4		
Plymouth	20	12	Whiting	Benjamin	1			1		1			1				4		
Hanover	127	6	Whiting	Caleb	2	1		1		2	1		1				8		
Plymouth	17	16	Whiting	Ephraim	3			1			1	1	1				7		
Scituate	128	14	Whiting	Ezekiel				1				3		1			5		
Scituate	128	18	Whiting	Galen	2		1						1				4		
Plymouth	17	15	Whiting	Joseph	2			1			1	1					5		

TOWN	PG#	LN#	LAST NAME	FIRST NAME	M under 10	M 10 to 16	M 16 to 26	M 26 to 45	M 45 and over	F under 10	F 10 to 16	F 16 to 26	F 26 to 45	F 45 and over	TOTAL ALL OTHER	TOTAL SLAVES	TOTALS	DISTRICT/ TOWNSHIP	NOTES
Abington	41	15	Whiting	Jotham	1				1	1	1	1	1	1			7		
Plymouth	17	21	Whiting	Levi			1	1		1			1				4		
Hanover	127	5	Whiting	Lydia								1	1	3			5		
Plymouth	20	20	Whiting	Nathan	1			1		1			1				4		
Pembroke	44	4	Whiting	Oliver				1	2	1			3	1			8		
Hanover	127	4	Whiting	Ozias				1			1	1					3		
Bridgewater	52	15	Whiting	Philip	1	2		1					1				5		
Middleborough	69	26	Whiting	Ruth Wo									2	1			3		
Hanover	127	2	Whiting	Thomas			1		1		1	1		1			5		
Hanover	130	25	Whiting	Thomas Junr	1		1	1		1	1	1					6		
Abington	41	13	Whiting	Thos		2		1		1			1	1			6		
Hanover	127	3	Whiting	William		1		1		1			1	1			5		
Bridgewater	64	15	Whitman	Benjamin				1		1			1	1			4		
Hanover	132	1	Whitman	Benjamin Esq	1	2		2		3	1		1				10		
Bridgewater	64	22	Whitman	Benjamin Junr	1			1					1				3		
Bridgewater	64	18	Whitman	Eleazer		1	2	1				2	2	1			9		
Pembroke	44	6	Whitman	Elijah	2			1		2	2		1				8		
Abington	41	7	Whitman	Ephraim		1	3	1	1	1	2	1	1	1			12		
Bridgewater	64	16	Whitman	Ezra	1				1	1	1	2	1	1			8		
Bridgewater	64	23	Whitman	Isaac	1				1		2		1				5		
Bridgewater	64	12	Whitman	John	2	3	1		1	1			1	1			10		
Bridgewater	64	19	Whitman	Joseph	2	2		1					1				6		
Pembroke	44	10	Whitman	Kilborn	2	1		1		1			1		1		7		
Bridgewater	64	21	Whitman	Nathan	2	1		1				1		1			6		
Bridgewater	64	17	Whitman	Nicholas					1			1		1			3		
Bridgewater	65	5	Whitman	Noah		2	1	2		1		2	1				9		
Bridgewater	64	14	Whitman	Peter			1	1			1	3		1			7		
Rochester	107	48	Whitman	Richard	1			1					1				3		
Bridgewater	64	20	Whitman	Seth A.		1		1		1			1				4		
Bridgewater	64	13	Whitman	Simeon	1				1					1			3		
Bridgewater	65	4	Whitman	Zechariah			1		1			2		1			5		
Bridgewater	61	27	Whitmarsh	Hannah									1	1			2		
Bridgewater	61	25	Whitmarsh	Jacob				1						1			2		
Bridgewater	61	26	Whitmarsh	Lot	1	2	2	1		2			2				10		
Abington	41	8	Whitmash	Levi	2	1		1		1			1	1			7		
Hanover	130	24	Whitney	James	1			1		1	1		1				5		
Rochester	107	45	Whitridge	Joseph			1					1					2		
Rochester	107	43	Whitridge	Peleg	1			1					1				3		
Rochester	107	46	Whitridge	Thos		1		1						1			3		
Rochester	107	47	Whitridge	Wm		1	1						1				3		
Bridgewater	52	11	Whitten	Joseph		2		1		1			1	1			6		
Bridgewater	61	28	Whitten	Marlborough	3			1		1		1					6		
Halifax	15	3	Whitting	Abraham				1					1	2			4		
Bridgewater	47	36	Wilber	Baruch		1	1						1				3		
Middleborough	72	23	Wilber	Benjamin	1			1	1	1			1				5		
Bridgewater	47	34	Wilber	George		1		1					1	1			4		
Bridgewater	47	35	Wilber	Gideon	1	1	2	2				1	1	1			9		
Bridgewater	47	37	Wilber	Isaac	1		1		1	2	3		1				9		
Bridgewater	47	38	Wilber	Lemuel	1		1		1				1	1			5		
Bridgewater	47	39	Wilber	Lemuel Junr	1			1					1				3		
Rochester	107	49	Wilber	Owen		1		1		5			1				8		
Middleborough	71	44	Wilder	Benariah			1			1			1				3		
Middleborough	71	43	Wilder	Ebenezer				1					1				2		
Scituate	124	19	Wilder	Joanna										2			2		
Middleborough	72	22	Wilder	Nath Cap	1	3	2		1		1	2		1			11		
Middleborough	69	24	Wilder	Nathl Junr				1		2		1	1				5		
Plymouth	14	22	Wilkens	Samuel	1		1	2		2			1				7		
Wareham	109	21	Wilkins	Mabel				1					1				2		
Abington	41	12	Wilks	John		1	1	1		2	1	1	2	2			11		
Abington	41	11	Willet	John		1				1							3		
Abington	41	10	Willett	Anna									1	1			2		
Bridgewater	55	3	Williams	George				2		1		2	1				6		
Middleborough	72	10	Williams	George				1		3			1				5		
Bridgewater	55	4	Williams	George Junr	1	1	1			1	1	2					7		
Scituate	135	32	Williams	John				2						1			3		
Middleborough	69	29	Williams	Joshua	3			1	1	1			1				7		
Bridgewater	55	5	Williams	Perez	2	1		1					1	1			8		
Marshfield	96	2	Williamson	Abner				1		1			1				3		
Marshfield	103	7	Williamson	Nathaniel	4			1		1			1				7		
Marshfield	101	14	Williamson	Samuel	1			1		1		1					4		
Marshfield	94	6	Williamson	Timothy					1				2	1			5		
Marshfield	94	7	Williamson	Timothy Jr	1		1			1		1		1			5		
Bridgewater	65	6	Willis	Benjamin		1		1	1					1			4		
Bridgewater	65	8	Willis	Daniel	3				1	1	3		1				9		
Bridgewater	52	13	Willis	Ephraim	2	3		1	1	1		1	1				10		
Bridgewater	55	7	Willis	Isaac				1					1				2		
Bridgewater	55	8	Willis	Isaac Junr	1	1		1		3	1		1				8		
Bridgewater	55	12	Willis	Jedediah	2		2		1			2	2	1			10		
Bridgewater	65	7	Willis	Joab				2	1			1	1	1			6		
Bridgewater	52	14	Willis	John	1		1	1		3		1		3			11		
Bridgewater	55	10	Willis	John		2	1	1	1	1		1		2			9		
Bridgewater	55	11	Willis	Jonah	2		1	1		2		1					7		
Bridgewater	55	2	Willis	Zebulon	1			1		2			1	1			6		
Kingston	29	8	Willis	Zepheniah	1			1		2			1	1	1		8		
Scituate	122	6	Wilson	Abigail									2				2		

TOWN	PG#	LN#	LAST NAME	FIRST NAME	under 10	10 to 16	16 to 26	26 to 45	45 and over	under 10	10 to 16	16 to 26	26 to 45	45 and over	TOTAL ALL OTHER	TOTAL SLAVES	TOTALS	DISTRICT/ TOWNSHIP	NOTES
			HEADS OF HOUSEHOLD		FREE WHITE MALES					FREE WHITE FEMALES									
Hanover	129	23	Wing	Batchelor		1	3	1	1		2			1			9		
Rochester	107	41	Wing	Buffer	2		1	1		1	1		1				7		
Rochester	107	33	Wing	Elisha			1			1			1				3		
Hanover	129	24	Wing	Hannah										3			3		
Hanover	130	2	Wing	Isaiah				1					1				2		
Rochester	107	36	Wing	John Jr	1	1		1	1	2			1				7		
Plymouth	23	6	Wing	Jonathan		2			1	1	1			1			6		
Rochester	107	32	Wing	Joseph			1		1				3	1			6		
Rochester	107	35	Wing	Philip	3	1		1		1	2		1				9		
Wareham	109	22	Wing	Stephen		2	1	1					2	1			7		
Rochester	107	42	Wingate	Wanton	1	1	1		1	3			1	1			9		
Duxbury	91	1	Winslow	*				1	1			1	2	1			6		Tape Mark
Middleborough	72	9	Winslow	Asa	1				1	4	2		1				9		
Middleborough	69	33	Winslow	Benjamin				1					1	1			3		
Rochester	107	44	Winslow	Benjn	2	1	1			1			1	1			8		
Rochester	107	38	Winslow	Dorcas				1	1	1				1	1		5		
Duxbury	93	22	Winslow	Edward															Enumeration left blank
Duxbury	94	21	Winslow	Edward				1					2				3		
Bridgewater	55	6	Winslow	Jonah			1			1			1				3		
Pembroke	44	14	Winslow	Joseph	1		1			1			1				4		
Rochester	107	39	Winslow	Leml	1		1					1	1				4		
Rochester	107	40	Winslow	Micah			1						1				2		
Rochester	107	37	Winslow	Nathan	1	1		1					1				4		
Scituate	121	10	Winslow	Nathaniel		2		1		1	2		2				8		
Scituate	121	5	Winslow	Nathl Junr			1			2	1						4		
Hanover	126	9	Winslow	Oliver	1		1						1				3		
Marshfield	94	19	Winslow	Snow				1					1				2		
Hanover	130	9	Winslow	Thomas		1		1		1		1					4		
Marshfield	98	10	Winslow	Thomas		1		1		1			1				4		
Duxbury	99	9	Winson	Nathl		1	2		1	1	3	1		1			10		
Duxbury	96	20	Winsor	Edward Junr	1		2	1		1			1				6		
Duxbury	98	4	Winsor	James	3			1		2		1	1				8		
Duxbury	96	19	Winsor	Jerusha			1			2			1				5		
Duxbury	95	13	Winsor	John	1	2		1		2		2		1			9		
Duxbury	95	12	Winsor	Joseph	1	2	2	1	1				1	1	1		10		
Kingston	27	5	Winsor	Peter		1		1		1			1				4		
Duxbury	98	1	Winsor	Samuel	2	1	3		1	1			1				10		
Duxbury	96	16	Winsor	Wm		1	1	1		2	1	1	1				8		
Pembroke	44	16	Witherel	Amos		2			1			1	1	1			6		
Pembroke	44	18	Witherel	Amos Jun			1			1			1				3		
Pembroke	44	17	Witherel	Joshua		1	1	1				1	1				5		
Pembroke	44	7	Witherly	Joseph				1					1	1			3		
Pembroke	44	15	Witherly	Josiah	2			1		1	1	3		1			9		
Bridgewater	55	9	Withington	Ebenezer			1			2			1				4		
Scituate	128	4	Withington	John		1	1						1	1			4		
Scituate	134	16	Withrell	Simeon		1	1		1	2	1	3	1				10		
Middleborough	73	60	Wood	Abner Junr		1				3		1					5		
Middleborough	73	59	Wood	Abner Lt				1			2		1	1	1		5		
Middleborough	71	26	Wood	Amos				1				1	1				3		
Middleborough	71	28	Wood	Anul Lt	3			1		1			1				6		
Middleborough	71	33	Wood	Daniel			1						1				2		
Carver	12	22	Wood	David	1	1		1	1	1	1	1					7		
Middleborough	72	14	Wood	Ebenezer		1			1		2		1				5		
Middleborough	71	36	Wood	Elnathan		1			1			1	1				4		
Middleborough	69	35	Wood	Ephraim				1	1	1			1				3		
Middleborough	69	36	Wood	Ezra	1			1		1			1				4		
Middleborough	69	27	Wood	Freeman			1	1		5	2		1	1			11		
Middleborough	72	16	Wood	Gorham			1						1				2		
Middleborough	72	20	Wood	Ichabod Lt	2		2		1	1	1		2				9		
Middleborough	69	34	Wood	Isaac	2				1	1			1				5		
Middleborough	71	31	Wood	Israel	1	1	2		1	1			1				7		
Middleborough	71	32	Wood	Jacob	3	1		1		1			1				7		
Middleborough	72	21	Wood	Joshua		2	1			1		1					5		
Halifax	16	18	Wood	Judah	3	1								1			6		
Middleborough	69	31	Wood	Nelson Lt		1	1						1				3		
Middleborough	72	4	Wood	Nichols	1	2		1		2	1	1					8		
Middleborough	71	27	Wood	Peter Cap	3	2			2	2			1				10		
Middleborough	71	38	Wood	Sarah Wo									1				1		
Middleborough	71	34	Wood	Silas			1	2					1				4		
Middleborough	71	30	Wood	Silvanus	2			1		2			1	1			7		
Bridgewater	47	40	Wood	Simeon	2	1	2		1	1	2		1				10		
Middleborough	71	23	Wood	Thomas	1			1		1			1				4		
Middleborough	71	24	Wood	Thomas 2d Cap	2	1		1		1	2		1				8		
Middleborough	71	35	Wood	Timothy	1		1	1		1		1					5		
Middleborough	72	15	Wood	Wilkes			1			1		1					3		
Middleborough	73	56	Wood	Zenas Capt	3	1		1		3			1				9		
Halifax	16	16	Wood	Timothy		2		2	1	2	1		2	1			11		
Halifax	13	16	Woods	Ebenezer			1			2			1				4		
Halifax	13	4	Woods	Francis	1		1			1			1				4		
Halifax	13	14	Woods	Joshua			1			3	1		1				6		
Halifax	16	8	Woods	William			1						1				2		
Scituate	136	39	Woodworth	Benjn		1	1		1			2		1			6		
Hanover	125	20	Woodworth	John			1							1			2		

TOWN	PG#	LN#	LAST NAME	FIRST NAME	FREE WHITE MALES					FREE WHITE FEMALES					TOTAL ALL OTHER	TOTAL SLAVES	TOTALS	DISTRICT/ TOWNSHIP	NOTES
					under 10	10 to 16	16 to 26	26 to 45	45 and over	under 10	10 to 16	16 to 26	26 to 45	45 and over					
Scituate	126	1	Woodworth	John	1				1	2	1		1				6		
Plimton	19	21	Wright	Billa	2	1		1		2	1		1				8		
Carver	11	19	Wright	Caleb	2			1		1			1				5		
Plimton	19	20	Wright	Chandler	1			1		2			1				5		
Marshfield	94	13	Wright	Daniel			1		1		1	1		1			5		
Plimton	21	18	Wright	Ebenezer		1			1			3		1			6		
Plimton	26	20	Wright	Ebenezer	2	1		1					1	1			6		
Plimton	22	24	Wright	Isaac	2	1		1		2	1		1				8		
Marshfield	95	14	Wright	Jabez	1	1		1	1	1			1				6		
Plimton	22	21	Wright	Jacob				1						1			2		
Plymouth	26	2	Wright	James	1		1			1		1					4		
Scituate	130	20	Wright	James				1	1	3			1				6		
Scituate	121	8	Wright	Jesse	1		1	1				1	1				5		
Plimton	26	7	Wright	John			1			1			1				3		
Plimton	19	9	Wright	Joseph	2	2		1		1			1				7		
Plymouth	23	16	Wright	Joshua	1	1	1		2	1	1	2	1	1			11		
Plimton	21	9	Wright	Levi	1				1		2			1			5		
Hanover	126	16	Wright	Lydia										1			1		
Carver	11	6	Wright	Moses	1	1		1		3			1				7		
Plimton	22	20	Wright	Peleg			1						1				2		
Plimton	22	19	Wright	Samuel				1			1	1	2				5		
Plymouth	23	23	Wright	Samuel		3	1			1	1		1				7		
Plimton	21	12	Wright	Sarah										2			2		
Carver	11	8	Wrightington	Thomas	1	2	2	1		1				1			8		
Duxbury	98	10	Yendal	Samuel		1		1		4			1				7		
Scituate	135	16	Young	Ezekiel				1				1		1			3		
Scituate	135	14	Young	Gideon	1			1		2			1				5		
Wareham	113	19	Young	Henry	1	1	1	1	2	1		1					8		
Hanover	123	8	Young	Job	4			1		1	1		1				8		
Wareham	113	20	Young	John	3			1					1				5		
Scituate	136	34	Young	Joseph		2	1		1	2	1		1				8		
Scituate	135	15	Young	Joshua	1	2	1	1	1	2		2		1			11		
Bridgewater	61	36	Young	Robert	1	1	2		1		1			1			7		
Wareham	113	18	Young	Solomon	1			1		1			1	1			5		
Scituate	136	20	Young	Stephen	1			1		1			1				4		
Bridgewater	61	37	Young	Thomas	3	1		1		2			2	1			10		
Wareham	113	17	Young	Zacheus	1			1					1	1			4		
Plymouth	26	13		Cato Negro											2		2		
Abington	41	22		Charles											6		6		Last name left blank
Pembroke	44	22		Dick											4		4		No last name listed
Plymouth	26	14		Dolphin Negro											8		8		
Plymouth	26	11		Plato Negro											6		6		
Plymouth	26	12		Prince Negro											7		7		

NOTES

www.ingramcontent.com/pod-product-compliance
Lightning Source LLC
Chambersburg PA
CBHW080255290526
45790CB00005B/1821